GOD'S GIFT
OF THE UNIVERSE

PAUL O'CALLAGHAN

GOD'S GIFT OF THE UNIVERSE

AN INTRODUCTION TO CREATION THEOLOGY

THE CATHOLIC UNIVERSITY
OF AMERICA PRESS

Washington, D.C.

The paper used in this publication meets the minimum requirements of American National Standards for Information Science—Permanence of Paper for Printed Library Materials, ANSI Z39.48-1984.
∞

Cataloging-in-Publication Data available
from the Library of Congress
ISBN 978-0-8132-3449-6

CONTENTS

PREFACE

This book on creation theology is the last of a trilogy, all published by the Catholic University of America Press. The first, which came out in 2011, on Christian eschatology, points to the future, and is centered especially on the Christian virtue of *hope*, which in turn is determined—content- and meaning-wise—by Jesus Christ, our Lord and Savior and eschatological judge. Thus the title of the work, *Christ Our Hope*.[1] The second volume, published in 2016, refers to the present moment and deals with theological anthropology, the life of Christ in the justified believer. It considers the reality and outworkings of Christian grace, which reveals our existence and life as a gift of God, and thus sheds a powerful light on the human person who is made by love and made to love. Perhaps the key virtue involved here is the infused virtue of *charity*, the true motor of Christian existence, what gives meaning and expression to corporeity, freedom, sociality. The book is entitled *Children of God in the World*.[2] The present volume will attempt to consider the act by which God created the world, both material and spiritual. Obviously, it refers to the past. Besides, it is based on Christian *faith* in the triune God, and is entitled *God's Gift of the Universe.*

The reader may notice that the chronological presentation of these texts seems to be moving in the wrong direction. By right we should *start* with creation, then pass on to anthropology, and finish off with eschatology. This is the classical system. But doing so would involve neglecting central elements of both creation theology and theological anthropology. True, we know little about *what* will take place in the next life and at the end of the world; we should apply our eschatological imagination with care. But we know, through faith and hope, *that* the world and human

1. See P. O'Callaghan, *Christ Our Hope: An Introduction to Eschatology* (Washington, D.C.: The Catholic University of America Press, 2011).

2. See P. O'Callaghan, *Children of God in the World: An Introduction to Theological Anthropology* (Washington, D.C.: The Catholic University of America Press, 2016).

persons will have a definitive future. We have but an approximative and imaginary understanding of what eternal life, judgment, and final resurrection will involve, but the future of the believer is guaranteed by God's power and promise. Christian believers will not just wander aimlessly into an unknown future and walk around forever in sterile circles. Rather they are sure, in the depth of their hearts, that God is preparing for them "a new heavens and a new earth in which justice dwells" (2 Pt 3:13), that Christ has gone "to prepare a place for us" (Jn 14:2), that "the Spirit and the Bride say 'Come'" (Rv 22:17). Our hope is certain, although its exact profile is as yet unknown: "What no eye has seen, nor ear heard, nor the heart of man conceived, what God has prepared for those who love him" (1 Cor 2:9).

And of course the knowledge of our future destiny makes all the difference for a proper understanding of anthropology and creation. We would perceive neither the meaning nor the underlying dignity of human life without an appreciation of its eternal destiny. Indeed without the promise of immortality human existence would be senseless; true personhood, a pipe dream.[3] But at a deeper level the same may be said of creation. For Christians not only ask *what* the world is or *how* it works, but *why* it was created in the first place, what it is meant to achieve, what is its destiny. It is said that the final cause (the reason why things are made or actions are carried out) is first in intention but last in execution.[4] Without an ultimate purpose or aim for the world the best explanation we could give for its existence would probably be that of the eternal return: the world and all it contains would just keep going around in circles, endlessly, forever, with no ultimate purpose.[5] That the universe has an ultimate purpose is attributed by Christians to an omnipotent deity, Father, Son, and Holy Spirit, who dreams up a universe, lovingly places it in existence, blesses it abundantly with life, and draws it along powerfully and skillfully so that it can achieve its ultimate end. This idea—that the world made by God will go back to God—will arise time and again throughout the text, as will the following four elements.

First, the radical quality of God's creation of the world is emphasized by the fact that the world was made *ex nihilo*, without external presupposi-

3. See ibid., 5–6 and 37–38.

4. See Thomas Aquinas, *Summa Theologiae* [hereafter *ST*] I-II, q. 1, a. 1, ad 1.

5. See, e.g., M. Eliade, *Cosmos and History: The Myth of the Eternal Return* (New York: Harper and Row, 1959).

tions of any kind. Christians of all stripes have accepted this doctrine from as early as the second century A.D. As a result, of course, the entire meaning and purpose of the created world is to be found in God and God alone.

Second, the created world, such as it is, is more accessible to reasoned human reflection than are important elements of Christian eschatology, or anthropology for that matter. For the latter we stand in need of divine revelation. However, we come to know many aspects of the created world through our own thought processes, *through reason*. This means that creation as a theological discipline must dialogue in depth with both philosophy and science. It should become clear throughout the text that the different aspects of the mystery of creation are the fruit of a rich confluence between faith by which we accept divine revelation, on the one hand, and reason/experience with which we live in contact with the world around us and read it in the light of faith. Certain aspects of the theology of creation, of course, are more directly dependent on faith, for example, the trinitarian heart of creation, the meaning of the glory of God, the existence and life of the angels and the reality of original sin. But the study of creation may be considered as a typically *transversal* discipline expressing the inter- and trans-disciplinary bond between theology, philosophy, and science.

Third, a particularly important aspect of the mystery of creation is its *Christological underpinning*. This might seem strange at first sight, for the reality of the incarnation of the Word was not at issue when the world was created. Besides it is clear from scripture that Christ is our Savior. But in God's mind, as we shall see, the incarnation is the high-point of creation. For God created the world not only *through* the Word/Son, but also *for* him. In effect, the Christological aspect of creation is what clarifies its eschatological dimension, and sets the scene for topics such as the trinitarian origin of creation, the glory of God, and workings of providence.

Fourth, the fact that creation took place with a clearly defined purpose and develops throughout time is contextualized by two further elements. First, that God created the world with time, in such a way that the *temporality* of creation is a constituent part of the created condition and is what makes it possible for the world to evolve and for beings to become what God wanted them to be from the beginning; second, the reality of *evil*, that things are not now what they should be, that they stand in need of divine saving power in order to reach their ultimate end.

The theology of creation may be considered a "bridge-subject" between philosophy and systematic theology. Many issues dealt with in philosophy—being, existence, matter, spirit, teleology, evil—are dealt with in the study of creation. Besides, the doctrine of creation serves as a basis for many other Christian doctrines. Virtually every element of systematic theological reflection and praxis involves or implies the doctrine of creation in some way. As a result the Christian view of creation may be said to challenge and enrich every aspect of Christian life and thought. In the words of Sokolowski, "The Christian understanding of God and the world is not an inert background for more controversial issues; it enters into their formulation and helps determine how they must be decided."[6] For the moment we may cite the following words of Joseph Ratzinger from a 1983 conference on catechesis, centered on

> belief in God the Creator and in his creation within the Church's profession of faith. Again and again one hears misgivings, as though too strong an emphasis on this aspect of the faith could endanger the central importance of Christology. There may well be reasons for such misgivings, in the light of earlier stages of theological development. But today it seems to me that the opposite concern is much more appropriate: the marginalization of the doctrine of creation is having a reductive effect on the concept of God and, therefore, on Christology as well. Anything having to do with religion is classified nowadays as psychology or sociology; the material world is relegated to the departments of physics and engineering. Yet only if being itself, including matter, comes from God's hands and remains in God's hands can God really be our savior and grant us life—real life. Today there is a fatal tendency, wherever matter comes into play in the beliefs that we proclaim, to balk and retreat into the symbolic; this happens starting with creation, through the Virgin Birth of Jesus and his Resurrection, to the Real Presence of Christ in the transubstantiation of bread and wine, and on to our resurrection and the Lord's Second Coming. It is hardly an indifferent theological debate when the resurrection of the individual is relocated in death, which is not only to deny the soul, but also to dispute the genuine corporeality of salvation. A decisive renewal of faith in creation is thus the prerequisite also for the credibility and depth of Christology and eschatology.[7]

6. R. S. Sokolowski, *The God of Faith and Reason: Foundations of Christian Theology* (Washington, D.C.: The Catholic University of America Press, 1995), 34.

7. J. Ratzinger, "Handing on the Faith and the Sources of the Faith," 13–40, in his *Handing on the Faith in an Age of Disbelief* (San Francisco, Calif.: Ignatius Press, 2006), 35.

And in a 1993 interview, Ratzinger repeats many of these points.

> I believe that faith in creation and its proper understanding is a problem of fundamental importance, because if God has no real relationship with the world, if the latter is not involved in God's design, then faith loses its foundations and is dissolved in the vague sphere of sentiment. In this context it will be necessary to focus the dialog between science and faith differently. . . . This is connected with the foundations of moral theology: is everything just evolution and history, or is there such a thing as a created human identity? This means we have to consider in a decisive way the dialog between faith and philosophy. Besides, dialog with world religions is ever more urgent, and in that context the proper understanding of the figure of Christ. Also the question of God, which is fundamental for the faith, must be reformulated. This implies an important role given to the body between the Old and New Testament, as well as the relationship between the Church and Israel. The question of faith and culture is closely bound up with the idea of God, and here emerges again the problem of relativism and the knowability of truth: are all religions mere symbols? It is possible to associate "God" and the "gods" more closely? Or, where are the confines? In my view it is necessary in this context to deal more closely with the essence of the liturgy, with the question of the rules and limits of inculturation. Lastly, our understanding of the human being always provides a serious challenge; the issue of feminism is an example of this.[8]

The text is made up of a preliminary chapter, three parts, and a conclusion, divided into fourteen chapters. The preliminary first chapter deals with our access to the origins of the universe: through different religions, through modern science, and especially through the dialogue between faith and reason. The first part (chapters 2–5) attempts to unveil the mystery of creation throughout history: in the Old Testament (especially its teaching on the relationship with salvation and wisdom and the Book of Genesis), in the New Testament (especially the relationship with Christ), in the early centuries when the doctrine of creation *ex nihilo* and creation in and through the Word consolidated. This took place in an attempt to clarify the contribution of Platonic spiritualism, of Gnosticism, and of pantheism. The second part (chapters 6–11) attempts to provide a systematic explanation of the doctrine of creation: the role of the Word incarnate in creation and the meaning of God's transcendence and immanence; the

8. J. Ratzinger, "Keeper of the Straight and Narrow," *Time Magazine*, December 6, 1993.

purpose of creation in the context of the mystery of evil and the trinitarian love of God; the finalization of creation in the "glory of God"; the issues involving conservation, *concursus,* temporality, and providence in the created world; the reality of the material world and the ecological challenge; and lastly the existence of the spiritual world: angels and demons, their existence and role. The third part (chapters 12–13) deals with the history and systematic reflection on the roots of moral and physical evil, and especially with what is called original sin. The conclusion provides a synthetic summing up of the whole text, in an order that does not always correspond to the book chapters. Direct references are made throughout this chapter to the location in the text where the topics in question are explained in detail. If readers not enticed to read the whole text, I would recommend them at least to read this final chapter first, and follow through on whatever issues interest them especially.

Biblical texts are taken from the Revised Standard Version translation. Texts from modern authors are cited directly from the works in question. Other texts, from church documents, the Church Fathers, and medieval and modern authors, are for the most part my own translations.

I began teaching creation theology over thirty years ago to first-year undergraduate theology students as well as in postgraduate courses. I have always seen it as a prologue to the whole of systematic theology. I am convinced that without it the other treatises—especially Christology, anthropology, eschatology, sacraments, ecclesiology—would not be properly founded. I am very grateful to my students who over the years have listened patiently through my lectures, and for the questions they asked and inquiries they made that over time helped me clarify my own explanations. I am particularly grateful to my colleagues at the School of Theology at the Pontifical University of the Holy Cross in Rome, especially Giuseppe Tanzella-Nitti, astrophysicist and professor of fundamental theology, who helped me to clarify important issues of a scientific kind; Santiago Sanz Sánchez, with whom I dialogued extensively and who has published important material in this area in the theology of Joseph Ratzinger; José Ángel Lombo and Juan J. Sanguineti from the Santa Croce School of Philosophy; José Morales from the University of Navarre, who opened up many theological and cultural horizons for me; Antonio Ducay for his help in the area of Christology; Giulio Maspero, given his expertise in patristics and trinitarian theology; Vito Reale for his help in understanding Augustine; and to Robert Wielockx for help in the area of medieval philosophy and theology. I am especially grateful, and not for the first time, to the Catholic University of America Press, for the efficiency and professionalism put into preparing, correcting, and publishing the manuscript—especially by John Martino, Theresa Walker, and Paul Higgins.

ABBREVIATIONS

BDAG	*Greek-English Lexicon of the New Testament* (ed. Bauer et al.)
CCC	*Catechism of the Catholic Church*
DH	*Enchiridion symbolorum* (ed. Denzinger et al.)
GS	*Gaudium et Spes* (Vatican Council II)
LS	*Laudato Si'* (Pope Francis)
NIDNTTE	*New International Dictionary of New Testament Theology and Exegesis* (ed. Silva)
PL	Patrologiae cursus completus, series latina (ed. Migne)
SCG	*Summa contra Gentiles* (Thomas Aquinas)
ST	*Summa Theologiae* (Thomas Aquinas)
WA	*Martin Luthers Werke* (Martin Luther)

GOD'S GIFT
OF THE UNIVERSE

1

Situating the Doctrine of Creation

ACCESSING THE MYSTERY OF CREATION EX NIHILO

AS WE SAW IN THE INTRODUCTION, the church teaches that the universe was created by God with complete freedom, *ex nihilo*, without presuppositions of any kind. The doctrine of creation *ex nihilo* is central to Christianity. It is a fundamental doctrine of faith. In the words of the Eastern Orthodox theologian John Zizioulas, "to distinguish the teaching of the Church from that of the [second century] Gnostics, it is not enough simply to say that the world is the creation of God. We must go on to say that it is created *ex nihilo*, from nothing."[1] And on a positive note, in the words of K. L. Schmitz: "creation is not as such a remedy for some lack, but is rather an unexpected surplus that comes without prior conditions set by the recipient. . . . Creation is to be understood as the reception of a good not due in any way, so that there cannot be even a subject of that reception. It is absolute reception; there is not something which receives, but sheer receiving."[2]

Gerhard May in his influential work on creation *ex nihilo* says that the latter

> has the odd distinction of being a biblically compelled piece of metaphysical theology. Once it had been clearly formulated in the second century A.D., the doctrine became pivotal for reflection on a number of other teachings in the Abrahamic faiths—concerning divine action, grace, theodicy, religious lan-

1. J. D. Zizioulas, "Creation and Salvation," in his *Lectures in Christian Dogmatics,* ed. D. H. Knight (London: T and T Clark, 2008), 83–119, at 87.

2. K. L. Schmitz, *The Gift: Creation* (Milwaukee, Wis.: Marquette University Press, 1982), 33.

guage, intercessory prayer and questions of divine temporality. . . . The driving motive which underlies the Christian doctrine of *creatio ex nihilo* is the attempt to do justice to the absolute sovereignty and unlimited freedom of the Biblical God.[3]

And in the words of David Fergusson, "one implication of the sharp ontological distinction between creator and creation is that it belongs not to theology but to natural science to discover how the world works. This is a corollary of the Christian refusal to divinize the world."[4] There is something deeply programmatic in the following words of Janet Soskice: "*creatio ex nihilo* is not a teaching about the cosmos but about God."[5] All religions hold to the presence or influence of the divine in the world we live in, but by no means do they hold that God created the world *ex nihilo*.

Many consequences may be drawn from the doctrine of *creatio ex nihilo*. In this first chapter, I intend to set the stage for the *genesis* of the doctrine of creation, that is, the way Christian believers became conscious and convinced of it in the first place. I shall attempt to undertake this at an elementary level, as further epistemological issues will arise in later chapters.

Firstly I shall situate the concept of the origin of the world in a religious context outside Christianity, in four stages: in oriental religions such as *Hinduism*, and then in *Jewish* and *Muslim* theology, and also in the passage from what might be called ancient religion to *modernity*. Secondly, I shall briefly consider the relationship between creation and modern/contemporary scientific explanations of *inertia and matter*, on the development and *evolution* of the cosmos, and in its physical *origin*. The sciences, especially biology, physics, astronomy, and cosmology, offer a wide variety of explanations in respect of the origin, development, and purpose of the universe. But as we shall see, theology and philosophy are anything but indifferent in the development of science. Science, philosophy, and theology challenge one another positively, although their methodologies and

3. G. May, *Creatio ex nihilo: The Doctrine of "creation out of nothing" in Early Christian Thought* (Edinburgh: T and T Clark, 1994), viii.

4. D. Fergusson, "Creation," in *The Oxford Handbook of Systematic Theology*, ed. J. Webster, K. Tanner, and I. R. Torrance (Oxford: Oxford University Press, 2007), 72–90, at 80.

5. J. M. Soskice, "Why *Creatio ex nihilo* for Theology Today?," in *Creation ex nihilo: Origins, Development, Contemporary Challenges*, ed. G. A. Anderson and M. Bockmuehl (Notre Dame, Ind.: University of Notre Dame Press, 2018), 37–54, at 38.

conclusions are clearly distinct in each case.[6] The purpose of the latter presentation is merely to *situate* the doctrine of creation in a scientific context. Lastly, I shall consider the role of *faith and reason* in the genesis of the Christian doctrine of creation. This involves a wholly relevant dialogue between philosophy and theology. The application of the dynamic and living bond between faith and reason will be central in several chapters of this text.

Creation and Religions

ORIENTAL RELIGIONS

The basic difference as regards the origin of the world between Hinduism and Abrahamic religions such as Judaism, Christianity, and Islam, lies in the fact that Hinduism—not unlike Buddhism and Jainism—views the world as eternal, passing through many phases of creation and destruction.[7] The term "beginning" refers for Hindu philosophy to the beginning of a phase, or better, a passage from one phase to another, but not to the absolute beginning of the world as such. Whereas with Abrahamic religions there is a start and a finish, a clearly-bound segment, with a definitive beginning, called creation, and an absolute end, called the *eschaton*. In Hinduism, there is simply an infinite line, eternal and even repetitive. The term "creation" for Hinduism refers in fact to different things: the birth of matter, the birth of consciousness, the birth of living creatures, or the birth of culture. Besides, creation stories are many and varied. Brahma is considered the first god in the Hindu trinity, or *trimurti*. The triumvirate consists of three gods who are responsible respectively for the creation, upkeep, and destruction of the world. The other two are called Vishnu and Shiva: Vishnu is the preserver of the universe, while Shiva's role is to destroy it in order to recreate it anew. The notion of creation *ex nihilo* is definitely absent.

6. See the ample study of G. Tanzella-Nitti, *Teologia fondamentale in contesto scientifico* (Rome: Città nuova, 2015–18), in three volumes, especially the first: *Teologia della credibilità in contesto scientifico*.

7. For a comparative study of the doctrine of creation in Hinduism, Buddhism, and Christianity, some useful chapters may be found in the work *Buddhism, Christianity and the Question of Creation: Karmic or Divine?*, ed. P. Schmidt-Leukel (Aldershot: Ashgate, 2006).

CREATION IN JUDAISM

The doctrine of creation is fundamental to Judaism as it is found in the Hebrew scriptures.[8] However, Rabbinic Judaism, contemporary with Jesus, did not openly teach creation *ex nihilo*.[9] Later on, in the medieval period, it did become common doctrine for the Jews. The twelfth-century Jewish philosopher Moses Maimonides helped definitively to establish creation *ex nihilo* as proper to the Jewish tradition. He had the following to say:

> Those who follow the Law of Moses, our Teacher, hold that the whole Universe, that is, everything except God, has been brought by Him into existence out of non-existence. In the beginning God alone existed, and nothing else; neither angels, nor spheres, nor the things that are contained within the spheres existed. He then produced from nothing all existing things such as they are, by His will and desire. Even time itself is among the things he created.[10]

CREATION IN ISLAM

The conviction that God created all things without presuppositions of any kind is present in Islam as a whole. In the *Qur'ān* itself, however, God is certainly considered as the creator, but the notion of creation *ex nihilo* is not clearly elucidated.[11] That comes later on at a philosophical and theological level with tenth-century philosophers such as Avicenna.[12] He says: "This is what it means that a thing is created, that is, receiving its existence from another. . . . As a result everything, in relation to the first cause, is cre-

8. See chapter 2 below. See also H. Jonas, "Jewish and Christian Elements in the Western Philosophical Tradition," in *Creation: The Impact of an Idea*, ed. D. O'Connor and F. Oakley (New York: Charles Scribner's Sons, 1969), 241–58; J. M. Soskice, "Why *Creatio ex nihilo*," 45–47; D. Davies, "Reason, Will, and Purpose. What is at Stake for Maimonides and his Followers in the Doctrine of Creation?," in ibid., 213–31.

9. See J. Neusner, *Confronting Creation: How Judaism Reads Genesis: An Anthology of Genesis Rabbah* (Columbia: University of South Carolina Press, 1991), and *Judaism's Story of Creation: Scripture, Halakhah, Aggadah* (Leiden: Brill, 2000).

10. M. Maimonides, *Guide for the Perplexed*, ed. M. Friedländer, 2nd ed. (Skokie, Ill.: Varda Books, 2002), 2:13.

11. See D. C. Peterson, "Creation," in *Encyclopaedia of Qur'ān*, ed. J. D. McAuliffe (Leiden: Brill, 2001), 1:472–80.

12. See R. Acar, *Talking about God and Talking about Creation: Avicenna's and Thomas Aquinas' Positions* (Leiden: Brill, 2005); I. Kalin, "Will, Necessity and Creation as Monistic Theophany in the Islamic Philosophical Tradition," in *Creation and the God of Abraham*, ed. D. B. Burrell, C. Cogliati, J. M. Soskice, and W. R. Stoeger, 2nd ed. (Cambridge: Cambridge University Press, 2013), 107–32.

ated. . . . Therefore, every single thing, except the primal One, exists after not having existed with respect to itself."[13] And he describes creation as "the bringing into existence of something after absolute non-existence."[14]

David Fergusson is of the opinion that Christian theology typified by Aquinas and Scotus

> did not experience the tension with philosophy that was present in Islamic thought in the Middle Ages. Al-Ghazālī . . . famously argued that the universe had a beginning in time through the use of the so-called *kalam* [Islamic scholastic theology] cosmological argument. This was rehearsed at a time when Islamic philosophers such as Avicenna had argued for the eternity of the world on the basis of their reading of the classical philosophers [especially Aristotle]. Convinced that the *Qur'ān* taught that the creation had a beginning, Al-Ghazālī argued vigorously against the conclusions of his philosophical predecessors [in particular Avicenna]. Yet this friction between philosophical and theological trends was generally not present in the Christian tradition, where the compatibility of reason and revelation was widely accepted.[15]

In the words of Daniel Peterson:

> While the *Qur'ān* forcefully asserts God's role as peerless creator of the universe and summons humanity to serve and to worship him on that account, it does not appear that a theory of *creatio ex nihilo* can be constructed on the basis of *qur'ānic* material alone. Rather, it is only with the development of the Islamic sciences, such as *ḥadīth* (reports of the sayings and the deeds of Muḥammad and his early followers), *qur'ānic* commentary (*tafsīr*), theology (*'ilm al-kalām*), and philosophy (*fal-safa*) that one finds extensive discussion about the divine act of creation from absolute nothingness.[16]

So it may be seen that in both Jewish and Islamic thought the notion of creation *ex nihilo* arose and was consolidated in the context of medieval philosophical reflection on God's action in the world.

13. Avicenna, *al-Shifā': al-Ilāhiyyāt*, 8:3.
14. Ibid., 6:2.
15. Fergusson, "Creation," 84.
16. Peterson, *Creation*, 479.

THE PASSAGE FROM ANCIENT NEAR EASTERN RELIGIONS TO MODERNITY

Peoples from ancient times have attempted in a wide variety of ways to understand and describe the origin of the universe, the way in which the gods brought the world into existence and continue influencing its life. Ancient religions, situated mainly in the Near East, look upon the origins of the universe in a wide variety of ways, which change quite radically with modernity. Three such elements have been suggested by Richard Clifford.[17]

First, ancient Near Eastern peoples considered creation as a process within nature that involved the clashing of wills, a conflict between spiritual centers, whereas for moderns, creation is usually perceived as an "impersonal interaction of physical forces extending over eons."[18] *Second,* for the former, the product of creation is principally human society in cities and countries organized for the service of the gods. For moderns, creation involves primarily the physical world, the planets, the sun, and the stars; human civilization and culture is considered an add-on, albeit an important one, with its own rules and dynamic. In the *third* place, ancient religions tell stories to describe the process of creation, providing humans with a variety of myths. These stories were devised to explain the situation they were in, and because they "saw creation as involving wills, story was a natural way of reporting."[19] For moderns, however, what is of interest is precise scientific reporting on the impersonal dynamics and evolution of the physical universe. In effect, moderns collect vast amounts of data, and expect it ultimately to explain all things without exception. For ancient peoples, on the other hand, the "criterion for truth was compatibility with tradition and dramatic plausibility."[20] Both aspects—the ancient and the modern—are present in the Jewish and Christian understandings of creation. How this takes place we shall see presently.

But we may still ask: how did this passage from the mythical to the scientific, from the ancient to the modern, take place? Joseph Ratzinger

17. See R. J. Clifford, "*Creatio ex nihilo* in the Old Testament/Hebrew Bible," in *Creation ex nihilo* (ed. Anderson and Bockmuehl), 55–76, at 56.

18. Ibid., 56.

19. Ibid., 57.

20. Ibid.

explains the change-about in reference to four names.[21] First of all, the Dominican philosopher *Giordano Bruno*, who insisted in a pantheistic context on the divinity of the cosmos; his reinstatement of pure pagan Greek cosmology occasioned a recession for faith in creation. According to Bruno, if the world *depends* on something or someone, it would no longer depend on itself. From this follows that the world has to be self-grounding, and if so, divine. Individual things are undeniably contingent, but the world as a whole is not.[22] Ratzinger observes that for Bruno "the dependence implied by faith in creation is unacceptable. It is seen as the real barrier to human freedom, the basis of all other restrictions, the first thing needing to be eliminated if mankind is to be liberated."[23] His position was not accepted by the church.

The second name is the astronomer and physicist *Galileo Galilei* who urged philosophers to revert to Greece, not as an aesthetic horizon (which was typical of the Renaissance), but in terms of "a reversion to the mathematical side of Platonic thought," for "God does geometry."[24] In this way the knowledge of God is replaced by the knowledge of the mathematical structures of nature, and the concept of nature, understood scientifically, takes the place of creation.[25] Besides, he holds, natural science deals only with objectivity, of which the rational God is the guarantor, whereas subjectivity, "the life of the soul," is arbitrary and private. The personal is excluded from the real, the subjective from the objective. Ratzinger concludes that for Galileo "the existence of human beings is an obstacle and irritation for 'science,' because they are not something science can exactly 'objectify.'"[26]

In the third place, in contrast with Greek-loving Bruno and Galileo, Ratzinger mentions a resolute de-hellenizer, *Martin Luther*, who posits a

21. See J. Ratzinger, *"In the Beginning." A Catholic Understanding of Creation and the Fall* (Grand Rapids, Mich.: Eerdmans, 1990), 82–92. On the dynamics of modernity, see my study "Cultural Challenges to Faith. A Reflection on the Dynamics of Modernity," *Church, Communication and Culture* 2, no. 1 (2017): 25–40.

22. See R. Buttiglione and A. Scola, "Von Abraham zu Prometheus: Zur Problematik der Schöpfung innerhalb des modern Denkens," *Communio (Deutsche Ausg.)* 15 (1976): 30–41.

23. Ratzinger, *"In the Beginning,"* 84.

24. Ibid.

25. See H. Staudinger and W. Behler, *Chance und Risiko der Gegenwart: eine kritische Analyse der wissenschaftlich-technischen Welt* (Paderborn: F. Schöningh, 1976), 56.

26. Ratzinger, *"In the Beginning,"* 86.

clear opposition between grace (the heart of the Christian gospel) and creation (all the rest). He insists that all Greek influence must be removed from Christian thought and praxis in order to return to the purity of the origins. For Luther the cosmos "is an expression of everything that is proper to human beings," including their past, their sin, their damnation, and the law.[27] Man can only *be* when he is saved, and this takes place through faith. Creation is a simple presupposition to God's saving work.[28] Science and philosophy (especially Aristotle's) are irrelevant for the believer.

Fourth and last, Ratzinger mentions *G. W. F. Hegel.* The latter made a considerable effort to overcome the opposition between nature and history, between science and the drama of evil and redemption (I shall consider Hegel's position on creation in chapter 4). When given a practical expression in the writings of Karl Marx, Hegel's notion of creation is simply eliminated. For Marx, the world need no longer be contemplated, but only changed.[29] Not unlike Giordano Bruno, "the decisive option underlying all the thought of Karl Marx is ultimately a protest against the dependence that creation signifies: the hatred of life as we encounter it."[30]

This process gives rise, Ratzinger says, to three forms of what he calls the "concealment" of the doctrine of creation.[31] First, it is concealed by a scientific concept of nature. Second, resentment in respect of technology is turned against humans, seen as a disease of nature, thus rendering creation irrelevant. Thirdly, Ratzinger says, a theological concealment of the concept of creation appears, as created nature is undermined and weakened for the sake of grace and salvation. Summing up this argument he says: "This undermining of creation can never become a vehicle of grace, but only an *odium generis humani* [a hate for humankind], a Gnostic disenchantment with creation."[32]

Though I shall consider some aspects of Gnosticism in chapter 4, I will cite Ratzinger's words here:

27. Ibid., 87.

28. On Luther's understanding of creation, see P. O'Callaghan, *God and Mediation: A Retrospective Appraisal of Luther the Reformer* (Minneapolis, Minn.: Fortress Press, 2017), 33–35.

29. See F. Engels and K. Marx, *Ludwig Feuerbach and the End of Classical German Philosophy* (London: Union Books, 2009).

30. Ratzinger, *"In the Beginning,"* 91.

31. See ibid., 92.

32. Ibid., 95.

> The common core of Gnosticism … is the repudiation of creation … the mystery of suffering, of love, of substitutionary redemption, is rejected in favor of a control of the world and of life through knowledge.… But love becomes an unbearable feeling of dependence, of subjection.… The Gnostic option aims at knowledge and at power through knowledge.… Gnosticism will not entrust itself to a world already created, but only to a world still to be created. There is no need for trust, only skill.[33]

For the Christian believer, on the contrary,

> the doctrine of redemption is based on the doctrine of creation, on an irrevocable Yes to creation. The fundamental opposition set up by modernity between loving and making turns out to be identical with the opposition between trusting being and doubting being.… The latter manifests itself as the belief in progress, the principle of hope, the principle of class struggle.… We can win the future only if we do not lose creation.[34]

Ratzinger concludes: "the obscuring of faith in creation, which eventually led to its almost complete disappearance, is closely connected with the 'spirit of modernity.' It is a fundamental part of what constitutes modernity. To go straight to the point: the foundations of modernity are the reason for the disappearance of 'creation' from the horizons of historically influential thought."[35]

Creation and Science

The doctrine of creation attempts to provide answers to the many of the same questions asked by the sciences: where the world came from, how it developed, how it works, where it is going. This has brought about over the centuries an ample debate between the findings of science and the conclusions of faith, as well as their complex interaction.

Two fundamental styles emerged from this dialogue.[36] One might be called the concordist model, which attempts to place the findings of faith on the same epistemological plane as those of science, comparing them and

33. Ibid., 96.
34. Ibid., 100.
35. Ibid., 82.
36. I have drawn this from my study of Pannenberg: P. O'Callaghan, "Whose Future? Pannenberg's Eschatological Verification of Theological Truth," *Irish Theological Quarterly* 66 (2001): 19–49.

seeking agreement between the two. This model is based on the notion of a single universe, created by the one God, uniformly accessible to the human mind, with a single though complex truth structure. By way of example scientists might attempt to seek confirmation for the big bang in the doctrine of creation, or of biological evolution in that of eschatological process and consummation. Theologians might do the same thing in reverse. In practice, however, theology has for the most part turned out to be the loser in many of these discussions. The concordist method often fails, firstly because the concrete findings of theology and science may simply not be commensurate with one another, as they develop on the basis of different methodologies. Besides, as we saw above, theology attempts to reflect on the nature and action of God one and three, and God is not a being that may be compared with created beings. Thirdly, the method easily fails because science speaks frequently of a multiverse, not a (single) universe, in which there are to be found a variety of different worlds, many of which are still to be discovered, each one with its own laws and origins and time scale.[37]

The other style might be designated as the significance model, which works on the basis that whereas theology deals with God and his action, science attempts to describe the universe and its dynamics. Science tells us about nature, of how things work, of what their essence is; theology tells us where they came from, why they exist, what they are for, what are their meaning and significance. One would provide the facts, the other the spin. Science should be real, theology relevant; science objective, theology subjective. One and the other would refer ultimately to the same reality, but from mutually exclusive points of view. However, this approach is not entirely satisfactory either, for both science and theology attempt to speak about truth, about the way things are. In other words, science has its intentionality and is therefore also subjective, attempting to explain the why and the wherefore of the universe; theology is rooted in the real and thus has an objective side to it.

An enormous number of issues could be discussed in the dialogue between faith and science in the context of creation. But it is beyond the

37. See J. Leslie, *Universes* (London: Routledge, 1989); B. Carr (ed.), *Universe or Multiverse?* (Cambridge: Cambridge University Press, 2007); D. N. Page, "Does God Love the Multiverse?," *The Blackwell Companion to Science and Christianity*, ed. A. G. Padgett and J. B. Stump (Malden, Mass.: Wiley-Blackwell, 2012), 198–206.

bounds of this work to deal with them fully. I shall very succinctly deal with three issues: the question of inertia, that of evolution, and the beginning of the universe.

INERTIA AND DIVINE INTERVENTION

One of the reasons why theology and science became alienated from one another in modern times may be situated in the rise of a mechanistic view of physics and in particular the introduction of the principle of inertia.[38] The latter was developed by Galileo and Descartes, and formalized by Newton; it led to the removal of natural processes from their dependence on God, although none of the three thinkers excluded the existence of the supreme divinity.

Descartes held that each element of the natural world tends to preserve its status and continue acting as long as external factors do not intervene to change it. In the words of Pannenberg, "this made the idea of the tireless activity of the first cause of all events no longer necessary to explain the continuance of history or existence in general."[39] Thus, interventions on the material world may only derive from other material bodies. Inertia according to Descartes is not simply a manifestation of what Isaac Newton called the *vis insita,* a force of continuance within the body itself. For Descartes it was, rather, a sign of the divine immutability which preserves the creature just as it was created. This means that all changes and movements are the result of the action of some bodies on others, as bodies are always in some form of movement which they transmit to one another continuously. Movement, says Descartes, is "the action by which any body passes from one place to another . . . the transference of one part of matter or of one body from the vicinity of those bodies which are in immediate contact with it, and which we regard as being in repose, into the vicinity of other."[40] When the principle of inertia is combined with that of the movement of bodies, then there is no further need for God to act as the first cause within natural processes.

38. See W. Pannenberg, "The Doctrine of Creation and Modern Science," *Zygon* 23 (1988): 3–22, at 4; F. C. Copleston, *A History of Philosophy*, vol. 4 (New York: Image Books, 1994), 124–31.

39. W. Pannenberg, *Theology and the Philosophy of Science* (Philadelphia: Westminster Press, 1976), 308. See also H. Blumenberg, *The Legitimacy of the Modern Age* (Cambridge, Mass.: MIT Press, 1985), 78–80.

40. Descartes, *Principia philosophica* 2:24 (author's translation).

The philosopher Frederick Copleston sums up this position as follows: "God, we may say, created the world with a certain amount of energy, and the total quantity of energy in the world remains the same, though it is constantly being transferred from one body to the other."[41] This according to Descartes is seen as a reflection of the immutability of God. "From the fact that God is in no way subject to change and that He acts always in the same manner, we can arrive at the knowledge of certain rules which I call the laws of nature," says Descartes.[42] The first law of inertia is that "each thing, so far as it depends on itself, continues always in the same state of rest or motion and never changes except through the agency of some other thing." The second is that "every moving body tends to continue its movement in a straight line." And Copleston speculates: "All this suggests a deistic conception of the world. The picture which naturally occurs to the mind is that of God creating the world as a system of bodies in motion and then leaving it to carry on by itself."[43]

Blaise Pascal said: "I cannot forgive Descartes," who was his contemporary. "He would have liked, in the whole of his philosophy, to be able to by-pass God. But he could not help making Him give a shove to set the world in motion; after that he has nothing further to do with God."[44] Other authors do not agree with this diagnosis, and argue that Descartes's insistence on the infinite number of independent moments of existence that go to make up the life of creatures means that God has to constantly recreate the world.[45] Copleston observes that "God supplies the continuity by his never-ceasing creative activity. . . . The universe is seen to depend in every positive aspect and at every moment on God."[46]

However, the possible danger of Descartes's position gradually became obvious to theologians.[47] The revealed doctrine regarding the action and presence of God in the created world, in Pannenberg's words, came "to be interpreted as an expression of a primitive understanding of the natural or-

41. Copleston, *A History of Philosophy*, 4:132.

42. Descartes, *Principia philosophica* 2:37.

43. See Copleston, *A History of Philosophy*, 4:133.

44. B. Pascal, *Pensées*, ed. and trans. W. F. Trotter, no. 77.

45. See Descartes, *Principia philosophica* 1:21.

46. Copleston, *A History of Philosophy*, 4:135.

47. Especially J. F. Buddeus; see W. Pannenberg, "The Doctrine of Creation and Modern Science," 5.

der, as an expression of some archaic, mythical conception of the world,"[48] in that God is naively said to intervene in the world.

Something of a kind may be found in the more mechanistic view of physics proposed by Isaac Newton, some years after Descartes. Movement is no longer attributed to contact between bodies, as Descartes had suggested, but to the notion of force, the *vis impressa,* that moves bodies even over great distances in space. Though some eighteenth-century Christian apologists thought that the existence of the force of gravity provided an argument for the existence of God, who actively intervenes to keep the machine going, at a metaphysical level his interventions in the natural world seem to be superfluous. At best, Copleston says, God "constitutes absolute space and time through His omnipresence and eternity; and He is said to know things in infinite space as it were in His sensorium, because through His omnipresence everything is immediately present to Him."[49] However, "the concepts of absolute space and time provide weak foundations for a proof of God's existence" as "a self-sustaining mechanism."[50]

The fact is that Newton wrote more about theology than he did about science.[51] Interestingly, in works which were not published in his lifetime, he denied the fundamental Christian doctrines of incarnation and Trinity.[52] In fact his position is clearly Arian (we shall see the implications of this in chapter 5). "Newton became convinced that the earliest Christian Church held an authentic and uncorrupted non-Trinitarian faith which understood Christ as an exalted and yet created mediator between God and the universe."[53] The God of Newton seems to be voluntarist, remote, and completely transcendent, supremely free, and therefore arbitrary and inscrutable,[54] closer to Greek than to Christian categories, to the spiritual than to the incarnational.

48. Ibid., 6.

49. F. C. Copleston, *A History of Philosophy,* vol. 5 (New York: Image Books, 1994), 155.

50. Ibid., 5:156.

51. See S. Oliver, "Trinity, Motion and Creation *ex nihilo,*" in *Creation and the God of Abraham* (ed. Burrell et al.), 133–51, esp. 147–50. For a historical perspective, see R. Iliffe, *Priest of Nature: The Religious Worlds of Isaac Newton* (Oxford: Oxford University Press, 2017).

52. See M. J. Buckley, *At the Origins of Modern Atheism,* 2nd ed. (New Haven, Conn.: Yale University Press, 1990), 99–144.

53. S. Oliver, "Trinity, Motion and Creation *ex nihilo,*" 147.

54. See ibid. and I. Newton, *Principia mathematica,* gen. scholium (2nd and 3rd eds.), ed. Koyré and Cohen (Cambridge, Mass.: Harvard University Press, 1972), 46–53.

CREATION AND BIOLOGICAL EVOLUTION

Life has existed on our planet for at least three billion years. Human life arose in one form or another about three million years ago. And scientists, especially biologists, have attempted to explain two things: the origin of the enormous variety of life forms inhabiting the planet and the singularity of human life. In the absence of further data of scientific provenance, most philosophers and theologians have traditionally held that God (or the supreme being) created all the different species at one and the same time, and that these species have been handed on from one generation to the next, substantially unchanged from the beginning. This position is normally called creationism.

The natural historian Charles Darwin published his famous work *The Origin of the Species by Means of Natural Selection* in 1859, following up on the insights of J.-B. Lamarck some fifty years earlier. In it Darwin challenged the classical creationist position. He explained that life forms developed from simple original elements to more complex ones over very long periods of time, on the basis of interactions with other living beings, a process he called natural selection. This vast yet simple process involved life of all kinds: plant, animal, and human. "All living things were joined up in one single evolutionary tree of life. In the struggle for life those organisms better adapted to their environments would be more likely to pass on their adaptations to their offspring, so leaving more progeny to subsequent generations, the process of 'natural selection.'"[55] This is what we nowadays call evolution. Interestingly, we may note, the terms *creation* and *Creator* occur more than one hundred times in *The Origin of the Species,* whereas the term *evolution* is simply absent.[56]

In any case the theory provided for biologists something like what the general theory of relativity provided for physicists: a global explanation of everything living. The geneticist and biologist Theodosius Dobzhansky,

55. D. R. Alexander, "Creation and Evolution," in *The Blackwell Companion to Science and Christianity,* ed. A. G. Padgett and J. B. Stump (Malden, Mass.: Wiley-Blackwell, 2012), 233–45, at 233.

56. D. R. Alexander, *Creation or Evolution: Do We Have to Choose?* (Oxford: Monarch Books, 2008), 169.

exaggerating somewhat, sums this up as follows: "nothing in biology makes sense except in the light of evolution."[57]

DIFFERENT EXPLANATIONS OF THE MECHANISM OF EVOLUTION

Nowadays few people reasonably doubt the *fact* of evolution. But the devil is in the details. In fact the mechanisms of the evolutionary process are not always clear, and have been extensively discussed and diversely explained by evolutionary biologists.[58] Though many explanations have been given, three principal ones may be mentioned, that refer respectively to the present, to the past (or beginning), and to the end (or purpose): theistic Darwinism, intelligent design, and teleological evolution.

First, some speak of random mutations and survival of the fittest and accept Darwin's position as correct at a scientific level, though not as a philosophy capable of explaining the origin of life in its different forms in ultimate terms. It is said that God uses the natural process of evolution as part of his creative plan, foreseeing its development and various products. This is usually called theistic Darwinism. The position includes what Fred Hoyle and others call the anthropic principle, which means that creation was fine-tuned from the very first moment to allow for the emergence of human life. "The universe could not have produced stars, planets, and carbon-based life forms had the temperature, the rate of expansion, and the formation of the forces of nature not been precise."[59] This position is also developed by Francis S. Collins,[60] who supervised the Human Genome Project. Knowledge of the beauty and symmetry of human genes and genomes convinced him that the world was created ultimately by a wise and loving creator. But this did not mean that God had to keep on

57. See T. Dobzhansky, "Nothing in Biology Makes Sense Except in the Light of Evolution," *The American Biology Teacher* (1973): 125–29.

58. On evolution in general, see M. Artigas, *Las fronteras del evolucionismo* (Pamplona: Eunsa, 2004); C. Chagas (ed.), *Ricerche recenti su l'evoluzione dei primati* (Milan: Jaca Book, 1987); A. R. Dulles, "God and Evolution," *First Things* 176 (2007): 19–24; L. Galleni, "Evolution" (2002), available at https://doi.org/10.17421/2037-2329-2002-LG-1 and inters.org/evolution.

59. Fergusson, "Creation," 88; see also J. Polkinghorne, *Science and Creation: The Search for Understanding* (London: Templeton Foundation Press, 2006).

60. See F. S. Collins, *The Language of God: A Scientist Presents Evidence for Belief* (New York: Free Press, 2007).

intervening in the world, thus giving new shape to the process. So we can see that this account does not explain how and why the world came into being in the first place. Perhaps it just describes the way it evolved.

Darwinism has the advantage of explaining evolution in philosophically simple terms with the categories of matter and motion. It postulates continuity between the different life forms in the evolution process. However if it accepts that everything is composed of matter, biology will sooner or later be reduced to chemistry, and chemistry in turn to physics. Everything then will end up being explained in terms of laws, forces, particles, and properties described by physics, in materialistic terms. What we call "life" would be a kind of epiphenomenon, not a reality in its own right.

The fact is that Darwinism does tend toward a naturalistic rather than a theological explanation of the world. In fact the paleontologist Stephen Gould "has sometimes been forthright about acknowledging the weakness of the claim that profound evolutionary innovation occurs through the accumulation of micromutations by natural selection."[61] And he adds that

> before Darwin, we thought that a benevolent God had created us . . . [since Darwin we have learned that] no intervening spirit watches lovingly over the affairs of nature (though Newton's clock-winding god might have set up the machinery at the beginning of time and then let it run). No vital forces propel evolutionary change. And whatever we think of God, his existence is not manifest in the products of nature.[62]

Darwinian evolutionism in other words should simply avoid the God-hypothesis, according to Gould.

Second, given the enormous complexity of life structures that exist in the present moment, some authors are convinced that primitive, elementary life forms were simply unable to serve as a basis for such advanced forms of evolution as have been postulated by scientists, terminating in the evolution of human life. Certain life organisms could not come to exist and survive purely on the basis of random mutations, they would say. It would make no sense for example for the eye to evolve should there be no elementary retina already present. A suitable explanation would need to be given for the phenomenon of macroevolution. Thus some authors

61. Ibid., 192.

62. S. J. Gould, cited in Johnson, *Darwin on Trial*, 193.

have concluded that evolution should be explained in terms of what they call intelligent design.[63] The theologian Ian McFarland observes: "the overwhelming dominance of bacteria in the terrestrial biosphere ... suggests that evolution has no inherent bias toward the complex. Instead, the appearance of increasingly complex entities over time appears to be epiphenomenal ... complex life forms may be expected to emerge over time even if the evolutionary process itself is essentially isotropic, lacking any inherent directionality."[64]

The position however finds little support among scientists and seems to be inspired by a philosophical-religious view to ensure that God "fits in" to the picture, a kind of concordist understanding of the relationship between faith and science which I critiqued earlier in this chapter. It would seem as if God's intervention is applied in those stages of evolving reality that we do not (yet) know. To be fair, the authors who defend intelligent design are cautious about explaining the evolution of the world in terms of a "God of the gaps" figure.[65]

Third, another school holds that the evolution in biological organisms cannot be understood purely in terms of the laws of mechanics, physics, and chemistry. This is the position for example of Michael Polanyi.[66] The behavior of living organisms needs to take into account the fact that living beings strive for life and growth, what philosophers usually term teleology, or goal-orientation. The evolutionary process is "driven" as it were from the future; it manifests direction and purpose. We can observe that the

63. See, e.g., M. J. Behe, *Darwin's Black Box: The Biochemical Challenge to Evolution* (New York: Free Press, 2006), and *The Edge of Evolution: The Search for the Limits of Darwinism* (New York: Free Press, 2007); M. Ruse and W. A. Dembski (eds.), *Debating Design: from Darwin to DNA*, 2nd ed. (Cambridge: Cambridge University Press, 2007); S. C. Meyer, *Signature in the Cell: DNA Evidence for Intelligent Design* (New York: HarperCollins, 2009), and *Darwin's Doubt: The Explosive Origin of Animal Life and the Case for Intelligent Design* (New York: HarperOne, 2013).

64. I. A. McFarland, *From Nothing: A Theology of Creation* (Louisville, Ky.: Westminster John Knox Press, 2014), 154.

65. See *Debating Design* (ed. Ruse and Dembski).

66. "Scientific obscurantism has pervaded our culture and now distorts even science itself by imposing on it false ideals of exactitude. Whenever they speak of organs and their functions in the organism, biologists are haunted by the ghost of 'teleology.' They try to exorcise such conceptions by affirming that eventually all of them will be reduced to physics and chemistry. The fact that such a suggestion is meaningless does not worry them.... The shadow of these absurdities lies deep on the current theory of evolution by natural selection." M. Polanyi, *Knowing and Being* (Chicago: University of Chicago Press, 1969), 42. See also his essay "Life's Irreducible Structure," in ibid., 225–39. Polanyi follows Teilhard de Chardin and Bergson in this position.

internal finality of living beings brings them to act in ways that are simply absent in mere stones and minerals. In other words purely mechanical principles cannot account for the emergence of life in all its complexity. Darwinism is incapable of explaining why single cell organisms end up evolving into complex multicellular plants and animals when the former cope with the environment quite effectively within their own terms.[67] So what is it then that makes evolution happen?

The atheistic philosopher Thomas Nagel points out three things that we encounter around us that are not easy to account for in a materialist Darwinian framework: consciousness, reason or mind, and moral values.[68] Consciousness involves a firing of synapses in the brain, but it is not limited to that. Though present in forms of life inferior to the human, it is a true subjective experience that cannot be explained materially without emptying the associated experiences. The same may be said of reason and truth. So how can the mind itself, that explains to us the process of life, be a product of evolution? A theory of evolution that takes place simply through natural selection would undermine the reliability, indeed the viability, of reason. The same may be said of the moral order: the materialist-reductionist view of evolution provides no basis for moral values and laws. Nagel recognizes among other things the need to introduce teleology into our conception of nature so that the emergence of the human mind, of reason and of a value system may not be considered just a chance event. Doubtless, science obtains exact results by restricting itself to reliable measurable phenomena, that is by filtering out subjectivity, striving, feeling. But of course this filtering out might well amount to a reduction of reality itself.[69]

The philosopher Etienne Gilson in a 1971 work on evolution[70] pointed out that Francis Bacon and other modern authors initiated and perpetrated a significant philosophical error by eliminating two of Aristotle's four causes from science, the formal and the final. In effect if everything is explained in a mechanical way, only the material and efficient causes are

67. See Polkinghorne, *Science and Creation.*

68. See T. Nagel, *Mind and Cosmos: Why the Materialist Neo-Darwinian Conception of Nature Is Almost Certainly False* (Oxford: Oxford University Press, 2012).

69. This position is defended by J. F. Haught, *God after Darwin: A Theology of Evolution* (Boulder, Colo.: Westview Press, 1999).

70. See É. Gilson, *From Aristotle to Darwin and Back Again: A Journey in Final Causality, Species, and Evolution* (Notre Dame, Ind.: University of Notre Dame Press, 1984).

applicable, whereas the formal and final causes are rendered superfluous. Without a form it would be impossible to account for the identity of any substance, attributed in the case of humans to a soul considered as the *forma corporis*, the form of the body.[71] And without a final cause there is no purpose or striving or goal within nature, unless it is imposed by an extrinsic agent, perhaps even a violent one. The brain would not develop were it not carrying out the function of thinking, nor the eye the function of seeing; if there was nothing to think about and project into the future, the function would simply not develop.

God's intervention—or better, his role in the evolution process—is possible, though different, in each of the three cases. With *theistic Darwinism* God is said to initiate the process by creating matter and energies that will develop into vegetative, animal, and human life. This position is present to some degree in Deist authors. For *intelligent design*, development may be accompanied by divine intervention at certain stages with a view to producing otherwise inexplicably complex living organisms. In the *teleological* view, lastly, the thrust or striving of creation may be explained in terms of a partaking in the dynamic presence of God to his creation. Many Christians however resist the notion of divine interventionism in the evolutionary process, seeing in it a sign of divine imperfection in the original work of creation. Philip Johnson asks if this reluctance might not indicate a tacit return to Deism, in which God is exiled "to the shadowy realm before the Big Bang."[72] In chapter 9, on conservation, concursus, and providence, I shall examine the question of the intervention of God more closely from a theological standpoint.

CHURCH TEACHING ON EVOLUTION AND ITS THEOLOGICAL SIGNIFICANCE

The Catholic Church has consistently held that the human soul is not produced by any biological cause but is created immediately by God.[73] Thus

71. See O'Callaghan, *Children of God in the World*, 417–35.

72. P. E. Johnson and H. Van Till, "God and Evolution: An Exchange," *First Things* 34 (1993): 32–41, at 41.

73. See H. Denzinger, P. Hünermann and A. E. Nash (eds.), *Enchiridion symbolorum, definitionum et declarationum de rebus fidei et morum*, 43rd ed. (San Francisco, Calif.: Ignatius Press, 2012) [hereafter DH], 190, 360, 3896.

God is clearly involved in the life process. Besides, divine providence is a central Christian teaching, as we shall see in chapter 9. John Paul II in a message on evolution at the Pontifical Academy of Sciences in 1996 said that though there are many theories of evolution, the idea of the evolution of the human body from lower forms of life is "more than a hypothesis."[74] Still, he insisted that human life is situated above biological life by an "ontological difference," attributable to the spiritual soul, which does not simply emerge spontaneously from evolving matter.

The Pope's affirmations were taken by some to indicate full acceptance of the neo-Darwinian view that evolution is sufficiently explained by random mutations and mutual selection (or survival of the fittest) without the presence of any governing finality. Christoph Schönborn, however, says this is not the case.[75] In an earlier audience John Paul II had the following to say: "The evolution of human beings, of which science seeks to determine the stages and discern the mechanism, presents an internal finality which arouses admiration. This finality, which guides beings in a direction for which they are not responsible, obliges one to suppose a Mind which is its inventor, its creator."[76] Likewise Benedict XVI has said: "We are not some causal and meaningless product of evolution. Each of us is the thought of God. Each of us is willed, each of us is loved, each of us is necessary."[77] And so Schönborn rejects the mechanistic or materialistic version of neo-Darwinianism as "an unguided, unplanned process of random variation and natural selection."[78]

The Orthodox theologian John Zizioulas holds that Darwin certainly challenged us by claiming that the difference between man and the other animals is simply one of degree. Whether this is true or not, he adds:

> The difference between man and all other animals is freedom.... An animal cannot be an artist. To reject the existing world and create a world of its own, which will bear its personal stamp, is a characteristic only of man.... Art is not about copying the given world.... Art bears a restlessness that is directed towards

74. John Paul II, *Message to the Pontifical Academy of Sciences*, October 22, 1996, par. 4. All papal texts can be found at www.vatican.va.

75. C. Schönborn, "Finding Design in Nature," *The New York Times*, July 7, 2005.

76. John Paul II, "The Proofs for God's Existence," Papal Audience, July 10, 1985, par. 5.

77. Benedict XVI, *Inauguration Homily to the Pontificate*, April 24, 2005.

78. Schönborn, "Finding Design."

finding a greater freedom by breaking up forms to find the new thing the artist desires, something so deeply personal that no one else can recognize it.[79]

The problem that arises here of course, Zizioulas adds, is that "if man's freedom is exercised and respected, then creation is in danger. And we may ask ourselves: 'Why have we been entrusted with this dangerous freedom?' . . . The answer is that freedom is the one means by which creation can be in communion with God and live on."[80]

Joseph Ratzinger observes that living organisms of all kinds are superior to simple human artifacts, in three ways. First,

an organism is incomparably smarter and more daring than the most sophisticated machines. They are duly planned and constructed in comparison with an organism. A second difference goes deeper: an organism moves itself from within, unlike a machine, which must be operated by someone from without. And finally there is a third difference: an organism has the power to reproduce itself; it can renew and continue the project that it itself is. . . . Every organism is, as [the French biochemist Jacques] Monod asserts, conservatively designed. . . . For modern biology evolution is not the specific property of living beings; their specific property is, rather, precisely that they are unchanging: they reproduce themselves; their project endures.[81]

Of course Darwin did not think that his theory of evolution obviated the need to believe in God who creates and guides the universe.[82] However as Christian authors opposed different aspects of his theory as contrary to faith, it became more and more common among atheistic or agnostic authors to perceive God as an unnecessary element in the process of evolution and to espouse Darwin's cause as their own. In fact strenuous defenders of Darwin have tended to become more and more atheistic in

79. Zizioulas, "Creation and Salvation," 96.

80. Ibid., 97.

81. Ratzinger, *"In the Beginning,"* 54. See J. Monod, *Chance and Necessity: An Essay on the Natural Philosophy of Modern Biology* (New York: Alfred A. Knopf, 1971), 116: "For modern theory evolution is not a property of living beings, since it stems from the very imperfections of the conservative mechanism which indeed constitutes their unique privilege."

82. See Darwin's earlier work, *The Foundations of the Origin of Species: A Sketch Written in 1842*. Darwin concludes the second edition of *On the Origin of Species* as follows: "There is grandeur in this view of life, with its several powers, having been originally breathed by the Creator into a few forms or into one; and that, whilst this planet has gone cycling on according to the fixed law of gravity, from so simple a beginning endless forms most beautiful and most wonderful have been, and are being, evolved." It may well be that the phrase was included in the second edition to ensure its publication.

bent, and evolution to be seen as a strict alternative to creation.[83] Either we are created by God, it said, down to the last detail, or we evolve entirely from the most elementary forms of life.

The former position has often been referred to as creationism, according to which God created all existing species, exactly as they are now, at the beginning of the world. Thus our scientific study of reality reveals to us, no more and no less, just what God intended to create from the beginning. Evolution, as the spontaneous growth through natural selection of an extraordinary variety of lifeforms, provided a popular alternative in which God's position and power seemed to be of little or no relevance. We have already seen some of the ways it might be held that God was involved in the evolutionary process.

But whatever explanation is given for the inner workings of evolution, it should be clear that a God who can *create a living world*, without presuppositions of any kind, a world that is capable of developing, of growing, of diversifying and of embellishing itself,[84] is much greater than a God who applies a set of fixed rules to living and nonliving beings from the beginning. A precisely programmed world, however sophisticated, is a mechanical, material world which lives and acts within time, and to which the passage of time makes no substantial difference (as the Greeks held). An evolving world, however, by definition is a *living world* in which time is an intrinsic qualifier. And the God of the Bible, we are told time and again, is "the God of the living," the God who gives life, who is totally different from the god or gods who regulate and control the universe from without. In chapter 9 we shall consider the question of the profound theological relevance of time.

A contemporary of Darwin, Charles Kingsley, said that it is "just as noble a conception of Deity, to believe that He created primal forms capable of self-development . . . as to believe that He required a fresh act of intervention to supply the lacunas [gaps] which He Himself had made."[85] Francisco de Ayala approvingly cites Aubrey Moore, a Protestant theologian

83. See R. Dawkins, *A Devil's Chaplain: Reflections on Hope, Lies, Science, and Love* (Boston: Houghton Mifflin, 2003), 173–79.

84. See S. Conway Morris, *Life's Solution: Inevitable Humans in a Lonely Universe* (Cambridge: Cambridge University Press, 2003).

85. C. Kingsley, *Letter to Charles Darwin,* November 18, 1959, in the University of Cambridge: Darwin Correspondence Project, available at http://www.darwinproject.ac.uk/entry-2534.

who in 1891 wrote: "Darwinism appeared, and under the guise of a foe, did the work of a friend. It has conferred upon philosophy and religion an inestimable benefit."[86]

CREATION, THE BIG BANG, AND THE BEGINNING OF THE UNIVERSE

Many explanations have been devised to account for the origins of the world as we know it. Authors speak of a cyclical universe, a self-contained universe, the steady state[87] continuous creation of matter, and so on. Among them, the big bang theory out of which the universe was born, has been of particular interest throughout the twentieth century. The names of Georges Lemaître, George Gamow, and Edwin Hubble, among others, come to mind.[88]

Until about a century ago, scientists, under the influence of the classical physics of Newton and others, for the most part took it that the world was more or less a fixed and static reality.[89] Things began to change in the 1920s as physicists attempted to explain the origin of the universe. The astronomer Edwin Hubble on the basis of novel telescopic observations came to the conclusion that nearly all galaxies in the universe were moving away from one another, and the farther away they went, the more they accelerated, the faster they were moving. In a 1929 paper summarizing his research he concluded that the universe, far from being static, is actually in a process of expansion.[90] This law had been discovered by the Belgian physicist and Catholic priest Georges Lemaître two years beforehand,[91] and is commonly called the law of Hubble-Lemaître.

86. See F. J. Ayala, *Darwin's Gift for Science and Religion* (Washington, D.C.: John Henry Press, 2007), 159. Ayala holds that intelligent design is potentially more atheistic than evolution.

87. F. Hoyle and J. V. Narlikar, "A New Theory of Gravitation," *Proceedings of the Royal Society A* 282, no. 1389 (1964): 191–207; "Cosmology and Action-at-a-distance Electrodynamics," *Reviews of Modern Physics* 67, no. 1 (1995): 113–55. Authors who deal with the issue include Herman Bondi and Thomas Gold.

88. See G. Gamow, *The Creation of the Universe* (New York: Viking Press, 1952).

89. S. Hawking and L. Mlodinow, *The Grand Design*, 2nd ed. (London: Bantham, 2012), which I have followed in the coming pages.

90. See E. P. Hubble, "A Spiral Nebula as a Stellar System, Messier 31," *The Astrophysical Journal* 69 (1929): 103.

91. G. Lemaître, "Un Univers homogène de masse constante et de rayon croissant rendant compte de la vitesse radiale des nébuleuses extra-galactiques," *Annales de la Société Scientifique de Bruxelles* 47 (1927): 49.

The fact that the universe is expanding means of course that in the past it was smaller than it is now. Extrapolating backward in time, all matter and energy at one stage must have been concentrated into a tiny space of extraordinary density and temperature, when the universe began.[92] When we say that the universe is in expansion this means that "the distance between any two points within the universe is growing."[93] The physicist Arthur Eddington in 1931 explained this with the image of an expanding balloon on whose surface each galaxy is situated.[94] As the balloon inflates each galaxy moves away from the others and does so at an ever increasing rate. Interestingly, he observed that the fact of expansion does not affect the size of the objects themselves (galaxies, stars, stones, atoms) because they are held together in a stable equilibrium by powerful gravitational forces. It is only because fixed objects retain their size that we are able to detect the expansion of the universe in the first place.

The Russian theoretical physicist Alexander Friedmann at the beginning of the twentieth century had already come to the conclusion that the universe began with infinitesimally small dimensions, and expanded until gravity slowed it down, and then, he predicted, it will eventually collapse back on itself. Lemaître came to a similar conclusion: if you trace the history of the universe backward into the past, it gets smaller and smaller until you arrive at an initial event, the big bang (a term coined derisively in 1949 by the astrophysicist Fred Hoyle). Hubble's and Lemaître's empirical proof for an expanding universe provided some support for what Albert Einstein's theoretical reflections on the matter had already suggested.

Direct observations in support of the big bang theory did not come until 1965 with the discovery at the Bell Laboratories by Robert W. Wilson and Arno Penzias of a faint background radiation of microwaves throughout the universe (called cosmic microwave background radiation).[95] In

92. Hubble-Lemaître's Law means that (1) objects observed in deep space—extragalactic space, ten megaparsecs or more—are found to have a redshift, interpreted as a relative velocity away from Earth, and that (2) this Doppler shift-measured velocity of various galaxies receding from the Earth is approximately proportional to their distance from the Earth for galaxies up to a few hundred megaparsecs away.

93. Hawking and Mlodinow, *The Grand Design*, 196.

94. See A. S. Eddington, *The Expanding Universe* (Cambridge: Cambridge University Press, 1933).

95. "One of the crucial differences between these scenarios was, respectively, the absence and the presence of a cosmic background of thermal radiation. It was just the direct observation of this background, discovered by Arno Penzias and Robert Wilson in 1965, that definitively confirmed one

the absence of alternative explanations, this radiation has been identified as being left over from the very hot and dense early universe. As the universe expanded it cooled down to a temperature just slightly above absolute zero. Some have also suggested that at its earliest stages, the universe would have been like a kind of fusion reactor. The explosion of the universe would cease with its expansion, and should have left a universe composed mainly of hydrogen and (to a lesser degree) helium, with traces of lithium; heavier elements would have been produced later. Studies of the composition of the universe substantially confirm these observations.

Still, the big bang need not be taken literally as a description of the origin of the universe. Einstein's theory of general relativity predicts there is a point in time when temperature, density and curvature of the universe are all infinite, what is called a singularity. But this does not explain how the universe actually got going and started expanding in the first place. For this reason it is not possible to apply the big bang picture right back to the beginning as a neat and definitive correlate or confirmation of creation.

Besides, in the proximity of an initial singularity, the temporal categories we commonly use are no longer applicable. Around a singularity there is a space-time horizon whose threshold generates a discontinuity in the time-scale. All this means that approaching a singularity could last an infinite time, thus making the very idea of a beginning *of time* problematic, and excluding the very notion of creation.[96] Thus when we say that the age of the universe, starting from the big bang, is about fifteen billion years, we are not giving a real measure of its duration. The situation is not comparable to when we say that a fossil is about a hundred million years old, for the whole range of the age of the fossil lies within a homogenous time-scale we are familiar with. But this is not the case regarding the origin of the universe. In other words the notion of the big bang cannot be taken as a demonstration of the absolute origin of the universe, and much less

---

scenario and disproved the other." M. Gasperini, *The Universe Before the Big Bang: Cosmology and String Theory* (New York: Springer, 2008), 196.

96. On the so-called Hartle-Hawking state, see J. B. Hartle and S. W. Hawking, "Wave Function of the Universe," *Physical Review* D28 (1983): 2960–75; S. Hawking, *A Brief History of Time* (New York: Bantam Books, 1988). As an example, a counter measuring time using the oscillations of a function y = sin (1/x) would describe the approach to a finite origin (x = y = 0) with an infinite number of oscillations.

of its creation *ex nihilo.*[97] Maurizio Gasperini suggests that "the Universe at the epoch of the Big Bang was not a newly born baby, but a rather aged creature, midway through an evolution of probably infinite duration."[98] Thus "the Big Bang could lose its rather mystical role as the beginning of everything, to become a more modest beginning of the current phase of the Universe, i.e., of the Universe as we currently know it, made up of radiation, matter, atoms, galaxies, and human beings."[99]

The physicist Edward Tryon made the proposal in 1973 that the universe as we know it is simply a quantum fluctuation within a complete vacuum that has failed to disappear for more than ten billion years. At the quantum level, on account of Heisenberg's uncertainty principle, he says that the law of the conservation of energy can be broken for just a brief moment, causing virtual particles to pop in and out of existence. The universe is such a virtual particle that has lasted for (a mere) ten billion years. He explains it as follows:

> Observations imply that a big bang occurred about 10^{10} years ago. One might suppose that the Universe has always existed, undergoing periodic expansions and contractions. There is, however, no known mechanism by which the Universe might bounce back from a contraction. Furthermore, to assume the Universe is infinitely old is to evade, rather than illuminate, the issues of its origin and quantum numbers . . . I assume the Universe to be undergoing its initial expansion, evidently having appeared as a fluctuation of the vacuum. The conservation laws of physics then imply that our Universe has the quantum numbers of the vacuum, including zero energy. Hence our Universe must be homogeneous, isotropic and closed, and must consist equally of matter and anti-matter.[100]

We may conclude by saying that the big bang, such as it is, may not be taken as an equivalent of creation of being in the Christian sense. Still less however can it be said that the physical explanations of the origin of the universe can dispense with a creator God who places it in existence in the

97. See G. Tanzella-Nitti, "Creation" (2002), available at https://doi.org/10.17421/2037-2329-2002-GT-3 and inters.org/creation. See also A. D. Hinks, "What Does Physical Cosmology Say about Creation from Nothing," in *Creation ex nihilo* (ed. Anderson et al.), 319–45; W. R. Stoeger, "The Big Bang, Quantum Cosmology and *creatio ex nihilo*," in *Creation and the God of Abraham* (ed. Burrell et al.), 152–75; S. Conway Morris, "What Is Written into Creation?," in ibid., 176–91.

98. Gasperini, *The Universe Before the Big Bang*, 15.

99. Ibid., 199.

100. E. P. Tryon, "Is the Universe a Vacuum Fluctuation?," *Nature* 246 (1973): 396–97.

first place. Philosophical and theological elements need to be applied, as I shall do now.

Creation, Faith, and Reason

We have already seen how ancient religions, such as Hinduism, Judaism, Islam, and modern scientific thought approach the reality of creation, the origins of the world. But how do Christian believers access the mystery of creation? How do they come to know for sure that the world was created *ex nihilo*? Is it by faith? Or by reason? Religion (and therefore faith) certainly plays a part. So does science, and therefore reason. The theological, philosophical, and scientific arguments have too often intersected and even conflicted throughout history to deny this. But do we know about the mystery of creation because God has revealed it to us? Or are we in a position to come to the knowledge of *creatio ex nihilo* through the powers of human reason alone? Is our rational knowledge of creation a kind of *praeambulum fidei*? Or is it, strictly speaking, an article of faith? In other words, although the study of creation clearly involves theological, philosophical, and scientific questions, we still may ask: is creation fundamentally a theological or a philosophical issue? Which of the two—philosophy or theology—is essential, and which is decorative? Which is primary and which is secondary? In general terms, we may say that we come to appreciate the mystery of creation in all its depth by means of God's word to which we respond in faith, as we shall see in the coming chapters. But reasoned philosophical inquiry would also seem to have an essential role to play in demonstrating creation. And if this is the case, if creation may be established by reason, what then does Christian faith "add" to this conviction? Does faith rest on reason therefore? Or does reason start where faith ends?[101]

101. See J. F. Anderson, *The Cause of Being: The Philosophy of Creation in St Thomas* (St. Louis, Mo.: Herder, 1952); J. A. Aertsen, *Nature and Creature: Thomas Aquinas's Way of Thought* (Leiden: E. J. Brill, 1988); M. F. Johnson, "Did Saint Thomas Attribute a Doctrine of Creation to Aristotle?," *New Scholasticism* 63 (1989): 129–55; S. Sanz Sánchez, "La creación, misterio de fe y verdad de razón según Santo Tomás. Algunas reflexiones epistemológicas," in *Fede e ragione. Le luci della verità. In occasione del decimo anniversario dell'enciclica "Fides et ratio,"* ed. A. Porras (Rome: Edusc, 2012), 65–79.

IS IT POSSIBLE TO KNOW CREATION BY REASON?

Peter Lombard in the *Sentences* was of the opinion that we come to know creation through faith; more specifically he holds that we cannot find support in either Aristotle or Plato for a creating God as a single principle of all that exists.[102] His position was probably based on Aristotle's conviction regarding the eternity of the world, which—Lombard argued—was opposed to the intrinsic finitude of the universe as revealed to us by scripture.[103] Bonaventure was of the same mind: we have access to the mystery of creation through faith, but not by reason.[104] Likewise Albert the Great was of the opinion that the notion of creation may be acquired not through philosophical reflection but from revelation alone.[105]

Thomas Aquinas however did state in his earlier works that the doctrine of creation—which he describes as "the emanation of the entire being from a universal cause"[106]—is in fact accessible to human reason. "Not only does faith hold but also reason proves there is creation,"[107] he says in his *Commentary on the Sentences.* "Reason shows and faith holds that all things have been created by God."[108] The sixteenth-century commentator

102. See Peter Lombard, *II Sent.*, d. 1, q. 1, a. 1., lib. 2.

103. See J. F. Wippel, *Metaphysical Themes in Thomas Aquinas* (Washington, D.C.: The Catholic University of America Press, 1984), 191–214.

104. See Bonaventure, *II Sent.*, d. 1, q. 1, a. 1, arg. 1, concl. He shows that it is contradictory to speak of an eternal creation in Averroes.

105. "It ought to be said that creation is properly a divine work. To us, moreover, it seems to be astounding in that we cannot conclude to it because it is not subject to a demonstration of reason. And so not even the philosophers have known it.... Some, to be sure, have found certain probable reasons, but they do not prove [it] sufficiently." Albert the Great, *I Sent.*, d. 8. See A. Rohner, *Das Schöpfungsproblem bei Moses Maimonides, Albertus Magnus und Thomas von Aquin: ein Beitrage zur Geschichte des Schöpfungproblems im Mittelalter* (Münster: Aschendorff, 1913), 137.

106. Aquinas says: "Emanationem totius entis a causa universali ... designamus nomine creationis" (*ST* I, q. 45, a. 1), that is, "to create is, properly speaking, to cause or produce the being of things" (*causare sive producere esse rerum*).

107. "Respondeo quod creationem esse non tantum fides tenet, sed etiam ratio demonstrat," *In II Sent.*, d. 1, q. 1, a. 2. On this text and others in the *Commentary on the Sentences*, see S. E. Baldner and W. E. Carroll, *Aquinas on Creation: Writings on the "Sentences" of Peter Lombard, Book 2, Distinction 1, Question 1* (Toronto: Pontifical Institute of Mediaeval Studies, 1997). Baldner and Carroll hold that "for Aquinas, reason alone can arrive at an understanding of the essential features of the doctrine of creation—of everything, that is, but the temporal beginning of the world" (ibid., 29).

108. "Sic ergo ratione demonstratur et fide tenetur quod omnia sint a Deo creata." *De Pot.*, q. 3, a. 5; *ST* I, q. 44, a. 1.

on Thomas's works, Francisco Suárez, also looked upon creation as a truth of reason.[109] Although some authors do not accept that Thomas looked on acceptance of creation as the result of philosophical reason,[110] others are convinced that he attributes a doctrine of creation to Aristotle,[111] which is therefore accessible to reason. Among the former, Étienne Gilson said that the eternal and necessary world of Greek philosophy is fundamentally different from the created world of Christian revelation.[112] But Lawrence Dewan says that Gilson misunderstood the position of Aquinas who clearly attributed the notion of creation to Aristotle.[113]

It is interesting to note, however, that in the corresponding place to his *Commentary on the Sentences* in the *Summa Theologiae*,[114] Thomas does not deal with the issue of access to creation by reason. It would seem he simply wishes to avoid this complex question in his mature work, the *Summa*.

But what does Thomas actually say about *faith's* contribution to our understanding of creation? He has the following to say in respect of the doctrine of the Trinity:

The knowledge of the divine persons was necessary for us ... for the right idea of creation. The fact of saying that God made all things by His Word excludes the error of those who say that God produced things by necessity. When we say that in Him there is a procession of love, we show that God produced creatures not because He needed them, nor on account of any other extrinsic reason, but because of the love of His own goodness. So Moses, when he had said, "In the beginning God created the heavens and the earth," he added, "God said, Let there be light," to manifest the divine Word; and then said, "God saw the light that it was good," to show proof of the divine love. The same is also found in the other works of creation. In another way, and principally, that we may think in a

109. See F. Suárez, *Metaph.*, d. 20, q. 1, nn. 1–14, as well as his *Comm. in S.Th.* I, q. 44.

110. See É. Gilson, *The Spirit of Mediaeval Philosophy (Gifford Lectures 1931–1932)* (New York: Charles Scribner's Sons, 1940), 438–41n4; A. C. Pegis, "A Note on St Thomas, 'Summa Theologica,' I, 44, 1–2," *Mediaeval Studies* 8 (1946): 159–68; J. F. Wippel, "Aquinas on Creation and Preambles of Faith," *The Thomist* 78, no. 1 (2014): 1–36.

111. M. F. Johnson, "Did Saint Thomas Attribute a Doctrine of Creation to Aristotle?," *New Scholasticism* 63 (1989): 129–55; J. F. X. Knasas, "Aquinas' Ascription of Creation to Aristotle," *Angelicum* 73 (1996): 487–506.

112. Gilson, *The Spirit of Medieval Philosophy*, 69.

113. See L. Dewan, "Thomas Aquinas, Creation, and Two Historians," *Laval théologique et philosophique* 50, no. 2 (1994): 363–87. The same position is argued in C. J. De Vogel, "*Ego sum qui sum* et sa signification pour une philosophie chrétienne," *Revue des sciences religieuses* 35 (1961): 337–55.

114. See Thomas Aquinas, *ST* I, q. 44, a. 2.

right manner concerning the salvation of the human race, accomplished by the Incarnate Son, and by the gift of the Holy Spirit.[115]

Some authors say that Aquinas in his analysis attempts to force metaphysics on scripture.[116] Leo Scheffczyk admits that "Thomas has deliberately placed the Biblical truth of creation within the conceptual forms of Aristotelianism."[117] However, Thomas's position is certainly nuanced: "faith presupposes natural knowledge, even as grace presupposes nature, and perfection supposes something that can be perfected. Nevertheless, there is nothing to prevent a man, who cannot grasp a proof, accepting, as a matter of faith, something which in itself is capable of being scientifically known and demonstrated."[118] He would seem to be saying that certain individuals may be able to reach the doctrine of creation by reason, whereas others must have exclusive recourse to faith. But what would such a rational process entail?

CONTINGENCY AND CREATION

Where the doctrine of creation *ex nihilo* arguably comes closest to philosophical analysis is in the area of metaphysical contingency.[119] John Damascene observed: "All that is out of nothing is changeable to nothing."[120] Thomas Aquinas relates contingency closely to creation *ex nihilo*.[121] The core of created being, in the words of the Thomist Bernard Delfgaauw, "lies simply and solely in the total dependence on God, the complete contingency of the creature, that can be and not be, in contrast to the being of God, that cannot not be."[122] Interestingly, many authors hold that the

115. Ibid., q. 32, a. 1, ad 3 (author's translation).

116. P. E. Persson, *Sacra doctrina* (Lund: CWK Gleerup, 1957), 297.

117. L. Scheffczyk, *Schöpfung und Vorsehung*, in *Handbuch der Dogmengeschichte 2,2,1* (Freiburg im Breisgau: Herder, 1963), 93.

118. Thomas Aquinas, *ST* I, q. 2, a. 2, ad 1.

119. On contingency in Aquinas, see C. Fabro, "Intorno alla nozione 'tomista' di contingenza," *Rivista di Filosofia neo-scolastica* 30 (1938): 132–49; J. De Finance, "Le contingence du monde et la liberté de la création," *Doctor Communis* 3 (1950): 201–4; M. Beuchot, "Necesidad y Contingencia en Aristoteles, Tomás de Aquino y Saul Kripke," *Revista Filosófica* 15 (1982): 211–30; T. F. Torrance, *Divine and Contingent Order* (Edinburgh: T and T Clark, 1998).

120. John Damascene, *De fide orth.* II, 3.

121. See Thomas Aquinas, *Summa contra Gentiles* [hereafter *SCG*] II.30.

122. B. Delfgaauw, *Thomas van Aquino* (Bussum: Het Wereldvenster, 1980), 63.

notion of contingency has a distinctly Christian provenance.[123] Others however take it that the notion of contingency may be fully found in Aristotle,[124] but it is clear that in medieval Christian thought, contingency takes on a much more radical meaning than it does in Aristotle, given the perspective of creation which now determines being as being.[125] So which comes first: the conviction of creation (through faith perhaps) which reinforces or radicalizes our idea of contingency, or the conviction of contingency (through reasoned observation) which makes it possible to speak philosophically of creation?

Contingency for Thomas indicates that beings neither persist of themselves nor possess the foundation of their own existence, for they are created out of nothing and are kept in being exclusively by God's will. It has been observed that the notion of contingency provided "perhaps the most far-reaching way in which medieval thought opposed itself to ancient thought."[126] It becomes central to the metaphysics of Duns Scotus.[127] There is an insufficiency that marks all things in this world and hence the world as a whole, which "lies in the contingency intrinsic to the being itself of all things . . . which appears as completely gratuitous."[128]

Two issues should be taken into account as regards the question of

123. Contingency according to H. Blumenberg is one of the few concepts of specifically Christian provenance in the history of metaphysics: *Religion in Geschichte und Gegenwart III*, ed. H. Campenhausen and K. Galling (Tübingen: Mohr, 1959), s.v. "Kontingenz." As a general mark of the Christian conception R. Panikkar suggests that "the horizon of mobility is altered into that of contingency. . . . This sense of contingency is in essence a feeling of creatureliness." *El concepto de naturaleza: análisis histórico y metafísico de un concepto*, 2nd ed. (Madrid: CSIC Instituto Luis Vives de Filosofía, 1972), 106.

124. The notion is to be found in Aristotle, *Perih.* I.9 as *endechomenon*. Boethius translated it as *contingens*.

125. See Aertsen, *Nature and Creature*, 240. Gilson considers that the metaphysical contingency of created beings is implied in the composition between *esse* and *essentia*, between being and essence. See his *Spirit of Medieval Philosophy*, 435n1.

126. L. M. D. Rijk, *La philosophie au Moyen Âge* (Leiden: E. J. Brill, 1985), 70.

127. C. Solaguren, "Contingencia y creación en la filosofía de Duns Escoto," in his *De doctrina Joannis Duns Scoti*, vol. 2 (Rome: Commissio Scotistica, 1968), 297–348. "Every being is essentially and existentially contingent" (ibid., 320).

128. D. M. D. Petter, *Naar het metafysische* (Antwerp: De Nederlandsche Boekhandel, 1972), 156. Aquinas says that contingency arises fundamentally from matter, for the contingent is what can be and not be, and potency belongs to matter. Necessity, however, results from the form: *ST* I, q. 86, a. 3. Some beings are necessary, but according to the *potentia Dei ordinata* (not *absoluta*); this is what Thomas in *De Pot.*, q. 5, a. 3, calls the *necessitas ex suppositione*. On this, see A. Hayen, *La communication de l'Être d'après saint Thomas d'Aquin* (Paris: Desclée de Brouwer, 1957), 2:153–77.

contingency and its relationship to creation. First, metaphysical contingency is a clear mark of all created beings, whether material or spiritual.[129] This would seem to indicate that they are all made *ex nihilo*. However, philosophical reflection, properly so-called, initiates with really existent beings that can only be known empirically; it can then move on to beings whose existence is inferred, though they are unknown empirically, such as God and angels, which we come to know about indirectly by means of efficient causality. But the point is that nothingness (*nihil*) by definition is unknowable because in no way does "it" register empirically with the knowing subject. At best, indirectly, we may arrive at the conclusion that *nihil* is a possibility, and thus that *creatio ex nihilo* is not a contradiction in terms. But we will never be in a position to attain empirical certainty of the priority of nothingness with respect to created being on purely philosophical grounds. Something (or someone) else will have to tell us about it. This is where faith comes in, of course.

The *second* issue is as follows. Even if it were possible to demonstrate by reason that the inherent contingency of creatures proves that the world came into being without presuppositions of any kind, *ex nihilo*, we would still have the problem of explaining why and how God made it in the first place. The original nothingness of creation posits some very serious questions in respect of the meaning of the world as it exists, questions that only God can answer. And God's mind can only be known when he speaks his word and we accept it in faith. As McFarland says, the notion of creation *ex nihilo* does not resolve the ultimate issue, "whether God can be trusted unreservedly; the doctrine of creation from nothing is of no help in answering this question because it presupposes that the question has already been answered, since creation from nothing is at bottom an account of *why* God can be trusted unreservedly."[130] Thus our understanding of creation is ultimately based on our faith in God who has revealed himself as just, all-powerful, provident, and redeemer.

129. Aertsen, *Nature and Creature*, deals with the issue.

130. McFarland, *From Nothing*, 188.

THE INTERACTION OF FAITH AND REASON

What I have just said sets the scene for the way that faith and reason interact in our knowledge of the mystery of creation, that is, the fact, the what, the how, the why the world exists. Ratzinger offers the following suggestion: "Even if reason itself cannot perhaps give an account of [faith in creation] it searches in faith and finds there the answer that it had been looking for."[131] We might say that faith in creation is a reasonable faith, a *fides quaerens intellectum*, for "the universe is not the product of darkness and unreason. It comes from intelligence, freedom and from the beauty that is identical with love."[132] Indeed human reason itself is a creature, made *ex nihilo.*

It should be clear that the key to discovering the truth and depth of the created world and human existence will be found in a proper confluence of faith and reason. Briefly put, we may say that faith opens reason out to the extraordinary amplitude of reality, indeed to the divine itself; yet reason in turn is meant to assimilate the nutrition faith provides it with. In that sense faith, a "pure" faith that excludes reason, produces nothing substantial in human thought, because what is revealed is not absorbed by the human mind nor does it form thought or culture; neither can it enter into dialogue with philosophy or science. Yet reason and culture and thought in the absence of faith will remain isolated, malnourished, diminished, and alone.[133] Sokolowski says that "the doctrine of creation is at the boundary between reason and faith in that it requires a radical distinction between the Creator and the creature, a distinction unknown, indeed unknowable, to pagan thought."[134]

As regards the contribution faith makes to reason, John Paul II's encyclical *Fides et Ratio* makes two points.[135] First, in the negative, faith purifies reason in a fallen humanity.

131. Ratzinger, *"In the Beginning,"* 21.

132. Ibid., 25.

133. See P. O'Callaghan, "L'incontro tra fede e ragione nella ricerca della verità," in *Fede e ragione: l'incontro e il cammino*, ed. G. Maspero and M. Pérez de Laborda (Siena: Cantagalli, 2011), 35–59.

134. Sokolowski, *Faith and Reason*, 112.

135. See O'Callaghan, "Cultural Challenges to Faith."

> As a theological virtue, faith liberates reason from presumption, the typical temptation of the philosopher.... The philosopher who learns humility will also find courage to tackle questions which are difficult to resolve if the data of Revelation are ignored—for example, the problem of evil and suffering, the personal nature of God and the question of the meaning of life or, more directly, the radical metaphysical question, "Why is there something rather than nothing?"[136]

In the words of Benedict XVI, "the humility of reason is always needed, man's humility, which responds to God's humility."[137]

Second, in the positive, faith provides the conviction that man himself, and everything that relates to his existence and life, is the coherent and reasonable fruit of God's creative action. If reason is truly created, then it is the fruit of a free, divine love, which can only be appreciated fully in the light of faith.

Seeing how faith enriches the endeavor of reason, Benedict XVI spoke on repeated occasions of "the great rationality" that is the fruit of faith, and of the need to "amplify the horizons of reason."[138] In effect, humans think—at least they should think—with their whole being and in rapport with others, and not merely with an isolated or individual "reason" capable of analyzing reality in computational and mathematical terms,[139] or as a separate "intellectual faculty."[140] Humans think at the same time that they open their hearts and minds in faith to what comes to them from beyond and above. In fact love and faith give wings to reason, challenging it, amplifying it, making it resourceful and creative.

Besides it should be remembered that without a rational complement, faith in creation would have no morally imperative force. If our knowledge of creation depended exclusively on faith, then the practical consequences, the Christian commitment and dedication that derive from it, natural law itself, would be the fruit of mere voluntaristic fideism. But because our

136. John Paul II, *Fides et Ratio*, Encyclical Letter, September 14, 1988, par. 76.

137. Benedict XVI, "Address to the Collège des Bernardins," September 12, 2008.

138. See Benedict XVI, "Address of His Holiness Benedict XVI to Participants at the Sixth European Symposium For University Professors," June 7, 2008; the theme of this symposium was "Widen the horizons of rationality. Perspectives for Philosophy." See also P. O'Callaghan, "Il compito della teologia: Porre domande o elaborare risposte?," in *Theo-loghía: Risorsa della Universitas Scientiarum*, ed. M. Sodi (Rome: Lateran University Press, 2011), 37–55, at 50.

139. See O'Callaghan, "L'incontro tra fede e ragione nella ricerca della verità," 37–39.

140. See G. Angelini, "Antropologia teologia. La svolta necessaria," *Teologia* 34 (2009): 322–49.

knowledge of creation depends also on reason, the "obedience of faith" becomes reasonable and morally binding.

As we shall see in chapter 2 (and elsewhere) faith and reason work in unison in the development and consolidation of the doctrine of creation. Throughout scripture we shall see how the perception of the power and word of God, made present in the books of the Old Testament and the New, challenges human reason in a wide variety of concrete ways, producing a series of eminently human reactions: rejection, rebellion, perplexity, reflection, contemplation, consolation, confirmation, and, ultimately, consolidated, serene conviction. Divine revelation received in faith opens the mind, stimulates reason, produces a response, and challenges certainties in such a way that over an extended period of time God's power, accepted in faith, transforms and elevates human thought-forms and reason itself. God perseveringly dialogues with humans, overcoming their reluctance, mistrust, and stubbornness, and brings them to accept him as their Lord, their Savior and creator, who offers them a *metanoia,* a new way of thinking about things. Divine revelation received in faith becomes incarnate, reasoned, personal, intimate, inculturated. Briefly put, the conviction that God has created the world develops and consolidates, through both Testaments, until it is clarified and declared definitively as a fundamental tenet of Christian identity and dogma in the second century. I will examine some of the stages of this process in the following four chapters.

PART 1

Unveiling the Christian Mystery of Creation

2

Creation in the Old Testament

THE OLD TESTAMENT begins with a clear affirmation that God created the world. In Genesis 1:1–3 we read the following solemn words: "In the beginning God created the heavens and the earth. The earth was without form and void, and darkness was upon the face of the deep; and the Spirit of God was moving over the face of the waters. And God said, 'Let there be light'; and there was light."

In this extensive chapter I shall attempt (1) to situate this complex text in the wider context of biblical hermeneutics, mythology, the scientific understanding of creation, and its possible philosophical implications. Then (2) I shall look into the doctrinal content of Genesis 1:1, "in the beginning God created the heavens and the earth." After that I shall consider other elements of the doctrine of creation present in the Old Testament: (3) the centrality of the Sabbath and (4) the link in historical and prophetic texts besides Genesis between creation and salvation. In effect, creation in the Old Testament is not an isolated doctrine but very much a foundational and integral part of the life and spirituality of the Jewish people with whom God established the covenant and for whom he continues to care. This will be followed up by (5) a reflection on the dynamics and understanding of creation and the created world in wisdom literature. The following chapter will look into creation in the New Testament, principally on the basis of the Christology found in the Synoptics, John, and Paul.

Situating the Doctrine of Creation in the Book of Genesis

It is of interest to note that the text just cited (Gn 1:1–3), though not among the earliest in scripture, was chosen by its redactors to preface the

Bible as a whole. It clearly sets the tone for all that follows: the divine covenant, the constitution of Israel, the history of salvation, the words and works of the prophets, wisdom literature, and the promise of the Messiah.

The *Catechism of the Catholic Church* puts it this way:

> Among all the Scriptural texts about creation, the first three chapters of Genesis occupy a unique place. From a literary standpoint these texts may have had diverse sources. The inspired authors have placed them at the beginning of Scripture to express in their solemn language the truths of creation—its origin and its end in God, its order and goodness, the vocation of man, and finally the drama of sin and the hope of salvation. Read in the light of Christ, within the unity of Sacred Scripture and in the living Tradition of the Church, these texts remain the principal source for catechesis on the mysteries of the "beginning": creation, fall, and promise of salvation.[1]

Several interesting points are made here. Genesis 1–3 clearly sets the tone for the doctrine of creation in the Bible as a whole. Besides, the *Catechism* refers to the question of the interpretation and sources of the text, to which I shall return presently. However it also says that Genesis—and other Old Testament works for that matter—are meant to be read in as wide a context as possible: fundamentally in the light of Christ and in the unity of scripture and church tradition. Joseph Ratzinger observed that in the past biblical exegesis frequently attempted "to read every text in itself, in its bare literalness. . . . But meanwhile it forgot the Bible as a whole. In a word, it no longer read the texts forward but backward."[2]

Four other issues should be kept in mind in order to provide a correct interpretation of the text, namely: (1) its literary genre, (2) its mythical quality, (3) its scientific content, or otherwise, and (4) its possible philosophical implications.[3]

1. *Catechism of the Catholic Church*, 2nd ed. (Washington, D.C.: United States Catholic Conference, 2000) [hereafter CCC], no. 289.

2. Ratzinger, *"In the Beginning,"* 17.

3. See H. Renkens, *Israel's Concept of the Beginning: The Theology of Genesis 1–3* (New York: Herder and Herder, 1964); C. Westermann, *Creation* (Philadelphia: Fortress Press, 1974); G. J. Wenham, *Genesis 1–15* (Dallas, Tex.: Word Books, 1987); E. McMullin, "Creation *ex nihilo*: Early History," in *Creation and the God of Abraham* (ed. Burrell et al.), 11–23; R. J. Clifford, "The Hebrew Scriptures and the Theology of Creation," *Theological Studies* 46 (1985): 507–23; "*Creatio ex nihilo* in the Old Testament/Hebrew Bible," in *Creation ex nihilo* (ed. Anderson et al.), 55–76; D. Bergant and C. Stuhlmueller, "Creation according to the Old Testament," in *Evolution and Creation*, ed. E. McMullin (Notre Dame, Ind.: University of Notre Dame Press, 1985), 153–75.

THE LITERARY GENRE OF GENESIS 1–3

There are older texts in the Book of Genesis dealing with the world and its creation. At the outset of Genesis in fact two versions of the creation narrative are provided, one after the other. One is Genesis 1–2:4a, which speaks of the creation of the world in seven days, of the creation of humans in the image and likeness of God. It is a theologically rich text, written with a cultual and liturgical purpose, which culminates in the creation of man and woman who, as God's image and likeness, are destined to exercise dominion over the earth. It is said to belong to the *Priestercodex* tradition (P), that is, the priestly narrative.[4] The other text is to be found in Genesis 2:4b–3:24. It is an older text, more anthropomorphic than Genesis 1, that describes the creation of humans as a composite of the dust from the ground (*'adam*, Gn 2:7) and divine spirit (*ruah*), thus becoming a living being (*nephesh*). It is claimed to belong to the J or Jahwist tradition. The two texts describe the creation of the world from clearly different, but mutually enriching, standpoints. The fact that they are so different in character, however, serves as a reminder that the task of interpretation is a complex one. "Fundamentalistic" readings, which attempt to understand the texts as if they were written as factual and historical descriptions proper to our own time and cultural context, must be excluded. Genesis provides a symbolic, prophetic, and sapiential narrative describing the beginning of the world. An example of this may be found the six days of creation, which some modern authors have attempted to read literally, although Church Fathers never did so.[5] By way of example the following text of Origen should suffice:

4. See W. H. Schmidt, *Die Schöpfungsgeschichte der Priesterschrift: Zur Überlieferungsgeschichte von Genesis 1,1–2,4a und 2,4b–3,24* (Neukirchen-Vluyn: Neukirchener, 1964).

5. This is the position assumed by the Pontifical Biblical Commission in a 1909 document (DH 3519). It should be noted that allegorical interpretations of the *Hexameron* (or six days of creation) were common among the Church Fathers, especially Basil, Ambrose, and Augustine. See, for example, M. Arranz-Rodrigo, "Interpretación agustiniana del relato genesíaco de la creación," *Augustinus* 33 (1988): 47–56. Augustine's interpretation of the opening chapters of Genesis became increasingly literal over time. The exegetical approach in the earlier work *In Genesi* (written in 388) and *Confessiones* (398), however, is largely figurative; that of the commentaries completed after the outbreak of the Pelagian controversy, including the *De Genesis ad litt.* (ca. 400–416) and *De Civitate Dei* (ca. 413–26), markedly less so. See I. A. McFarland, "Original Sin," in *T&T Clark Companion to the Doctrine of Sin*, ed. K. L. Johnson and D. Lauber (London: T and T Clark, 2016), 306–18, at 309n6.

What man of intelligence, I ask, will consider that the first and second and the third day, in which there are said to be both morning and evening, existed without sun and moon and stars, while the first day was even without a heaven? And who could be found so silly as to believe that God, after the manner of a farmer "planted trees in a paradise eastward in Eden" ... I do not think anyone will doubt that these are figurative expressions which indicate certain mysteries through a semblance of history.[6]

IS GENESIS 1–3 A MYTH?

Genesis should be considered in the wider context of mythical religious-cosmic visions typical of the time in which it was written. In fact, material coincidences with Mesopotamian, Babylonian, and Egyptian literature are notable, all of which provide useful elements for interpreting the text.[7]

Interesting parallels may be found between Genesis 1–11 and the epic Greek poetry of Homer and Hesiod.[8] The Akkadian cosmogony *Atrahasis*, written in the second millennium B.C., resembles Genesis very closely in plot and details, especially regarding the creation and flood, and can help us appreciate important elements of the content of Genesis.[9] Ugaritic texts, the product of Canaanite texts written in fourteenth- and thirteenth-century B.C., offer many parallels, linguistic and otherwise, to the biblical texts.[10] Interesting elements are also to be found in Egyptian literature.[11]

6. Origen, *De princ.* IV, 3.

7. See Clifford, "*Creatio ex nihilo* in the Old Testament/Hebrew Bible," 57–63; J. H. Walton, *The Lost World of Genesis 1: Ancient Cosmology and the Origins Debate* (Downers Grove, Ill.: IVP Academic, 2007).

8. See C. H. Gordon, "Homer and Bible: The Origin and Character of East Mediterranean Literature," *Hebrew Union College Annual* 26 (1955): 43–108; A. M. Jack, *The Bible and Literature* (London: SCM Press, 2012); R. K. Gnuse, "Greek Connections: Genesis 1–11 and the Poetry of Hesiod," *Biblical Theology Bulletin* 47, no. 3 (2017): 131–43.

9. See W. G. Lambert and A. R. Millard, *Atra-Ḫasīs: The Babylonian Story of the Flood* (Oxford: Oxford University Press, 1969). "In fact, the Atrahasis epic from the early second millennium shows that the basic plot of Gen 1–11 was already known then. The Atrahasis epic tells of the creation of mankind, then of various divine judgments on him, culminating in the flood which destroyed all but Atrahasis and his family, who escaped in a boat. As in Genesis they offer a sacrifice on leaving the ark. Clearly the Atrahasis epic shows that creation and flood were already part of a coherent story of world origins before Genesis was composed.... Atrahasis suggests rather that either J or P or J and P have second-millennium precursors.... It is quite improbable that there is direct literary dependence on Genesis on Atrahasis." Wenham, *Genesis 1–15*, xxxix and 8.

10. See R. J. Clifford, "Cosmogonies in the Ugaritic Texts and in the Bible," *Orientalia* 53 (1984): 183–201.

11. See for example A. Herrmann, *Altägyptische Liebesdichtung* (Wiesbaden: Otto Harrassowitz, 1959); R. Kilian, *Die vorpriesterlichen Abrahamsüberlieferungen* (Bonn: Hanstein, 1966); V. Notter, *Biblischer Schöpfungsbericht und Ägyptische Schöpfungsmythen* (Stuttgart: Katholisches Bibelwerk, 1974).

The Babylonian myth of *Enūma Eliš*[12] is of particular importance. It speaks of the origin of the world in terms of a battle between the elements. In its present form the world refers back to Mardoch, the god of light, who split the great dragon, the principle of evil, in two parts. One part now constitutes the heavens, the other the earth. Given their conflictive origin the two parts live in a perennial state of antagonism. The world is made up of the body of the dragon and in the veins of humans runs its blood. As a result, perpetual dualistic rivalry is present not only in the cosmos as a whole but also in the inner lives of human beings. And this accounts for the perennial human tendency to sin and rebel: what happened at the beginning determines what will take place for the rest of time. In reference to the *Enūma Eliš* Paul Ricoeur observes:

It will be seen that human violence is thus justified by the primordial violence. Creation is a victory over an Enemy older than the creator; that Enemy immanent in the divine will be presented in history by all the enemies whom the king in his turn, as servant of the god, will have as his mission to destroy. Thus Violence is inscribed in the origin of things, in the principle that establishes while it destroys.[13]

In fact several mythical elements may be found in the creation account of Genesis. Genesis 1:2 speaks of the primitive chaos or the waters out of which the world was made. This would seem to evoke the Greek notion of prime matter, older than the creator, out of which God made the world. Besides, Genesis 1:20–23 speaks of sea monsters (*tannin*) that are like similar figures in the *Enūma Eliš* as well as in other parts of scripture (Ps 74:13; Is 51:9). Likewise Genesis (6:1–4) speaks of marriage between the sons of God and the daughters of men—to all appearances in a positive light—a topic of clear mythical resonance.[14] Genesis 2–3 also gives an account of the primitive Fall of humans which gave rise later on to the doctrine of

12. See P. Talon (ed.), *The Standard Babylonian Creation Myth: Enūma Eliš* (Helsinki: Neo-Assyrian Text Corpus Progress, 2005), as well as E. McMullin, "Creation *ex nihilo*," 13: "The ancient *Enuma Elish* told of how the universe began from a chaos of waters, how the gods themselves then came to be from the waters, how Marduk gained supremacy among the gods, how he separated heavens and earth, and how he finally brought order to the gods in heaven and to those who worship him on earth."

13. P. Ricoeur, *The Symbolism of Evil* (Boston: Beacon Press, 1967), 182.

14. See U. Cassuto, "The Episode of the Sons of God and the Daughters of Man," *Biblical and Oriental Studies I* (Jerusalem: Magnes Press, 1973), 17–28; W. A. Gemeren, "The Sons of God in Gen 6:1–4," *Westminster Theological Journal* 43 (1981): 320–48; R. S. Hendel, "Of Demigods and the Deluge: Toward an Interpretation of Gen 6:1–4," *Journal of Biblical Literature* 106 (1987): 13–26.

original sin and redemption. There are important similarities between this text and that of Plato's *Timaeus* which likewise speaks of human fallenness in mythical terms. It would seem therefore that Genesis is not attempting to describe a historical and real event that had a powerful influence over the subsequent history of humanity and set the scene for salvation through Jesus Christ, but rather a mythical or historicized "event" to account for the present and perpetual fallen situation of humanity.

Not surprisingly, many authors take it for granted that Genesis offers a strictly mythical account of the creation of the world, no more and no less. Mark Robson put it as follows: "Creation, then, was not the unopposed, 'simple' act that follows from the doctrine of *creatio ex nihilo,* but a drama that took place in an environment where God triumphantly mastered forces that did not want order to be imposed on them."[15] According to Richard Clifford, Genesis 1 represents "God's easy mastery over unpromising matter, life on earth as self-renewing and ineradicable, the dignity of all humans as bearers of the image of God and rulers of the universe, and humans' mandate to continue in existence through having children."[16] And the Jewish author Jon Levenson has it that in the *midrashim,* or ancient commentaries of the Bible, "the exegesis of Genesis 1:1–2 is that God did not create the good world out of nothing, but out of a malignant substratum."[17]

So, should Genesis 1–3 be described as a creation myth? Let us first consider what myths are. Creation myths are usually presented as *narratives,* events or series of events. Their primordial purpose is not to describe historical happenings in objective terms, but rather to explain the *origins and nature* of reality at the hands of the *gods,* whether this refers to the world as a whole, or to a people, or a city, or whatever.[18] They attempt to express the *permanent truth* of reality, imperfectly perhaps, though

15. M. I. T. Robson, *Ontology and Providence in Creation: Taking* ex nihilo *Seriously* (London: Continuum, 2008), 155.

16. Clifford, "*Creatio ex nihilo,*" 64.

17. J. D. Levenson, *Creation and the Persistence of Evil: The Jewish Drama of Divine Omnipotence,* 2nd ed. (San Francisco, Calif.: Harper and Row, 1994), xx. The same idea may be found in H. G. Frankfurt, *Necessity, Volition, and Love* (Cambridge: Cambridge University Press, 1999), 119.

18. On mythology in general, see E. M. Berens, *The Myths and Legends of Ancient Greece and Rome* (New York: Maynard, Merill and Co., 1900); J. Daniélou, *Mythes païens, mystère chrétien* (Paris: A. Fayard, 1966); M. Eliade, *Myth and Reality* (New York: Harper and Row, 1963); W. Jaeger, *Paideia: The Ideals of Greek Culture,* 3 vols. (Oxford: Blackwell, 1946); H. Limet and J. Ries (eds.), *Le mythe: son langage et son message* (Louvain-La-Neuve: Centre d'Histoire des Religions, 1983).

comprehensibly. Myths are meant to be handed on intelligibly from one generation to the next, in that way giving a nation or people or humanity at large a sense of their enduring identity and purpose. In an important sense, myth is incompatible with history and progress, because the present and the future are already *determined* and described by what "happened" at the "beginning." Things are and will be what they always were. Change and progress are simply not envisaged. In their truest logic, myths are deeply "conservative."[19] Their purpose is not to objectively narrate the past and its influence on the present (what we normally call history), but rather to illuminate the present by means of a graphic historicizing of some permanent truth or value (a story).

Thus for mythological accounts, evil is as much a part of life as the good, for they coexist side-by-side from the moment the world is founded; they live out perennially on the same plane, though in perpetual conflict. In fact many myths provide a dualistic explanation of the world in which good and evil constantly battle for supremacy. Because the ultimate protagonists of myths are the gods, mythology in an ample sense may be considered a kind of theology through which we come to understand the actions of the divinity in our lives. And because the gods are immortal and unchangeable, myths explain and describe a reality that is immutable, determined forever.

Myths are to be found throughout the history of humankind for as long as we can remember. Perhaps it may be said that all humans possess a kind of mythical register by which they receive from those who went before them a map or plan or story of their origin and identity, a kind of narrative identity. Countries, communities, companies, corporations, and religious bodies all have their myths, their original narrative, upon which they live, rectify, adapt, and survive. It is interesting however to note that the term "myth" is nowadays understood in an ambivalent way: on the one hand, to say some person is mythical may be to speak highly of them, because it refers to a person of exceptional—archetypal—talent; on the other, to say something is mythical often means to disqualify it as not objective, as simply untrue.

19. See P. O'Callaghan, "Is the Christian Believer Conservative or Liberal?," *Church, Communication and Culture* 4, no. 2 (2019): 137–51.

Understandably perhaps, philosophers and scientists who seek after rational explanations have systematically attempted to eliminate myths and replace them with reasoned, empirically based, conclusions; a process that is commonly called demythologizing.[20] From what Plato told us, Socrates was a case in point. He was aware that public authorities habitually used (or abused) national myths in order to control and indoctrinate the general population, especially the youth. Yet he contested several mythical accounts on the basis of reason. But this was not tolerated by the authorities, which occasioned his death. Likewise theologians have attempted to rationally demythologize different accounts of the Christian message.

So we may return to the original question: *is Genesis a myth?* In an ample and structural sense it is, in that it describes the origins of the earth and the early history of God's chosen people, the people of the covenant. It provides the original, normative narrative for the people of Israel. Later generations systematically referred back to Genesis as well as to the Israel's exodus from Egypt to understand and live out their covenantal identity. In fact Jesus himself did so (Mt 19:4–5). Besides, as we saw, Genesis frequently employs terminology found in mythological texts.

However, in a more concrete sense Genesis 1–3 does not share many of the common features of mythological literature, principally because it does not accept the existence and action of the gods, for there is only one God, one Lord, Yahweh. Besides, humans under God act and react freely, giving rise to human history, real salvation history, that takes place in time. Indeed, they can change the course of history. In the Old Testament and the New, the human "mythical register" is now occupied by the history of salvation, which culminates in the coming of the Messiah, in such a way that with Julien Ries we can say that with Christianity "myth has given way to Christ."[21]

The mythical motifs present in Genesis give expression to human experience of the created world, and facilitate a better understanding on the part of the readers, many of whom were habituated to mythical accounts of the world's origin. For example, the primitive chaos that Genesis 1:2 speaks of may be said to refer to the human experience of the ordering

20. On Socratic mythology, see J. Pieper, *The Platonic Myths* (South Bend, Ind.: St. Augustine's Press, 2011).

21. J. Ries, *Il mito e il suo significato* (Milan: Jaca Book, 2005), 83 (author's translation).

work of God and of the possibility of sin, as he overcomes the reluctance and opposition of matter, what Clifford describes as "God's easy mastery over unpromising matter."[22] But no trace may be found in Genesis of an ongoing, life and death struggle between order and chaos, between good and evil. Time and again Genesis claims that all that God had created was good (Gn 1:4, 10, 12, 18, 21, 25, 31). In fact, "the *Eneuma Elish* presumes an epic battle between the God who will emerge as sovereign and the powers of chaos, while the Bible describes the creation of the world as taking place without any opposition."[23] Besides, the sea monsters Genesis speaks of (1:20–23) are not mythical in kind and are "created by God and wholly under his control."[24]

As regards the mythical elements present in the description of the marriage between the sons of God and the daughters of men (Gn 6:1–4), the writer's intent seems to have been to represent the historical, progressive, and deeply idolatrous sinfulness of humanity, of which God disapproved, which eventually would incur divine wrath with the flood (Gn 6:5).[25]

We may also observe that according to Genesis 1:14–18 the stars were created on the fourth day, before animals and plants and humans. Thus they cannot be considered as autonomous dispensers of life and light, as divinities, but rather as inferior to all living beings. The latter, biblical position was anything but common in the time the sacred texts were penned, but was typical in mythological accounts. According to Genesis on the contrary humans are not controlled by the stars (or by angels for that matter). Only the former have been created "in the image and likeness of God" (Gn 1:27), with the capacity and the divine blessing to "have dominion over the fish of the sea and over the birds of the air and over every living thing that moves upon the earth" (Gn 1:28).[26] Lastly, as we shall see in the final chapters, the Fall of humanity is not a cosmic or perennial motif, a permanent characteristic of the created universe or of human nature, but rather a spiritual one (the result of human sin) and a reparable one (an historical event).

The following observation of Gregory of Nyssa is worthy of note:

22. Clifford, *"Creatio ex nihilo,"* 64.

23. G. A. Anderson, "*Creatio ex nihilo* and the Bible," in *Creation ex nihilo* (ed. Anderson et al.), 15–35, at 17.

24. Ibid., 18.

25. See Wenham, *Genesis 1–15*, 139–44.

26. See O'Callaghan, *Children of God in the World*, 99–105.

"Sacred Scripture frequently uses certain profane myths, and admits without fear certain names from mythology, with a view to expressing as well as possible the thought to be communicated.... Does that mean that Scripture gives faith to such myths? On no account."[27] And David Bentley Hart concludes: "the pagan *mythos* was displaced by the Christian, and Christianity's immense epic of creation and salvation became for ancient men and women the one true story of the world, the conceptual shape of reality necessarily changed for them as well."[28] So we may conclude that Genesis 1 is a nonmythical text using a mythical language,[29] what Paul Ricoeur calls "a narrative interpretation of the enigma of existence."[30]

IS GENESIS 1–3 A SCIENTIFIC TEXT?

It has sometimes been suggested that Genesis be considered as a *scientific text* in the modern use of the word, providing empirical data and objective information on the created world. This position however is decidedly difficult to justify. Genesis does not attempt to provide an empirical, factual description of what happened as the world began. Rather it powerfully evokes the saving power and presence of God in the life of humans, a power and presence that is celebrated liturgically, that provides a realistic and satisfying explanation of the existing world and of humanity at large, with a wide variety of practical and ethical outworkings. Still it is fair to say that Genesis's doctrine of creation in many ways does prepare the way for a scientific consideration of the world and its origins.

In his discussion of evolution and creation, Wolfhart Pannenberg has the following to say:

27. Gregory of Nyssa, *In Cant. Cant.*, hom. 9.

28. D. B. Hart, *Atheist Delusions: The Christian Revolution and Its Fashionable Enemies* (New Haven, Conn.: Yale University Press, 2009), 201.

29. "If Gn 1–11 cannot be reduced to the category of myth, if, besides, the presence of mythical language is undeniable in these chapters, this brings us, in line with Gibert, to further considerations on the hermeneutic of the 'history of the origins.' According to Gibert, to affirm that Gn 1–11 is not a mythical text, even taking into account mythical language, means underlining more and more its relationship with history and emphasize its 'prescientific' character. In this way it will be possible to clarify further the notion of 'metahistorical etiology,' which ... is at the basis of a correct theological hermeneutic of Gn 1–11." L. Mazzinghi, *Quale fondamento biblico per il peccato originale?*, in *Questioni sul peccato originale*, ed. I. Sanna (Padova: Edizioni Messaggero, 1996), 61–80, at 74 (author's translation). The book Mazzinghi refers to is P. Gibert, *Bible, mythes et récits de commencement* (Paris: Seuil, 1986).

30. P. Ricoeur, *La symbolique du mal. Philosophie de la volonté. II. Finitude et culpabilité*, 3rd ed. (Paris: Aubier, 1988), 311.

Much more remarkable than the necessary revisions concerning the sequence of creative forms as reported in the first chapter of the Bible is the extent of substantial analogies between our contemporary and those ancient ideas about the origin and development of creation: the light in the beginning; human beings at the end of the sequence; the beginning of vegetation as a presupposition of animal life; the close kinship between human beings and mammals (the land animals) as creatures of one and the same, the sixth, day of creation. Above all, the scheme of a sequence of steps is still shared by the modern view. Certainly the sequence of steps appears from a modern perspective as an evolutionary process leading from primitive to more complex or higher organized forms. It is at this point that we identify the deepest difference between the biblical and modern conception of a sequence of forms in the process of the creation.[31]

According to Gasperini:

By carefully rereading the initial verses of the Holy Bible, we find a description of the birth and the first moments of our Universe which seems much closer to the pre-Big-Bang scenario than to the standard Big-Bang scenario. Indeed, there is no mention at all of an explosion, and no reference to any hot, dense, highly curved concentration of energy. What is described is rather an initial state that is completely quiet, deserted, dark, and lifeless, which just resembles the typical initial state of pre-Big-Bang models (described in poetic, but very appropriate, terms).[32]

And Wenham observes:

In more recent times Gn 1 provided the intellectual underpinning of the scientific enterprise. Its assumption of unity and order underlying the manifold and seemingly capricious phenomena of experience rests on Gn 1's assertion of the one almighty God who created and controls the world according to a coherent plan. Only such an assumption can justify the experimental method. Were this world controlled by a multitude of capricious deities, or subject to mere chance, no consistency could be expected in experimental results and no scientific laws could be discovered.[33]

Thus while Genesis 1–3 does not provide reliable scientific data describing the origin of the universe, it does offer elements that match up surprisingly well to what our scientific knowledge of the created world tells us.

31. Pannenberg, "The Doctrine of Creation and Modern Science," 19.

32. Gasperini, *The Universe Before the Big Bang*, 193.

33. Wenham, *Genesis 1–15*, 39.

DOES GENESIS 1–3 PROVIDE A METAPHYSICAL OR PHILOSOPHICAL DESCRIPTION OF THE WORLD?

It is fair to say that Genesis does not attempt to provide a *metaphysical or philosophical description* of the beginnings of the created world, as did Heraclitus, Parmenides, Plato, Aristotle, and the Stoics. In fact, a purely philosophical analysis of Genesis would make little sense. Yet it offers us important elements that allow believers, over time, to develop a systematic conviction and then a metaphysical vision of reality and the universe, a "Christian" or a "Jewish" metaphysics.[34] And that philosophical vision has been extraordinarily fruitful and important, for it has facilitated our reasoned identification with the word of God received in faith; it has contributed to the communication of God's word to humanity as a whole; and it has made it possible to establish a bridge between revelation and scientific explanations of the world.

What Genesis 1 Teaches about Creation

Genesis 1:1 reads as follows: *Ber'esith bara' Elohim shamayim 'aerez.* It is normally translated as follows: "In the beginning God created the heavens and the earth."[35] Four important terms are employed here.

First, the verb *bara',* usually translated as "created."[36] The term derives etymologically from a Semitic root that means to cut, to chop, to slash, to lacerate. It is used about fifty times in the Old Testament, more than ten times in the Book of Isaiah. The subject of *bara'* is always God, never the pagan deities, and invariably refers to an unexpected, uninvited action, without analogy in the world as we know it (see Nm 16:30; Is 43:18, 48:6–8,

34. See É. Gilson, *Thomism: The Philosophy of Thomas Aquinas* (Toronto: Pontifical Institute of Mediaeval Studies, 2002), 85–88, on the metaphysics of Exodus; C. Tresmontant, *La métaphysique du christianisme et la naissance de la philosophie chrétienne: problèmes de la création et de l'anthropologie, des origines à saint Augustin* (Paris: Seuil, 1961); N. Kretzmann, *The Metaphysics of Creation: Aquinas's Natural Theology in "Summa contra Gentiles" II* (Oxford: Clarendon Press, 1999). I entitled class notes I used for twenty-five years at Santa Croce *"La metafisica cristiana."*

35. See Wenham, *Genesis 1–15*, 13.

36. See P. Humbert, "Emploi et portée du verbe *bārā* (créer) dans l'Ancien Testament," *Theologische Zeitschrift* 3 (1947): 401–21; A. Angerstorfer, *Der Schöpfergott des Alten Testaments: Herkunft und Bedeutungsentwicklung des hebräischen Terminus [b-ar-a]* (bara) *"schaffen"* (Frankfurt a.M.: Peter Lang, 1979).

65:17–19). The term *bara'* is used for both cosmic (Is 40:28, 41:20, 42:5) and historico-salvific effects (Is 43:1–15, 44:2). In Psalm 51:10, for example, we read: "Create [*bara'*] for me a clean heart." It refers to a direct divine action, never impinging on preexistent matter or seeking out a subordinated instrumental cause. It is applied to the beginning and the end, it to be found in unexpected novelties, and every so often in relation to sea monsters (Gn 1:21), mountains (Am 4:13), and animals (Ps 104:30). Nonetheless, the term does not as such designate creation *ex nihilo* in the strict sense. It is used for example to express the creation of Israel (Is 43:15) and the salvation of believers; in both cases preexistent human beings were present. Nonetheless *bara'* does express the idea of "God's effortless, totally free and unbound creating, his sovereignty. It is never mentioned what God created out of."[37] The Jewish author Jon Levenson says: "in Genesis there is no active opposition to God's creative labor. . . . In fact, rather than *creatio ex nihilo*, 'creation without opposition' is the more accurate nutshell statement of the theology underlying the passage."[38] I shall consider this issue presently.

Second, Genesis 1:1 refers to the divine subject, *Elohim*, the God who creates. *Elohim* is present in the plural form, but is construed with a verb in the singular. This is not a plural of majesty or power, but is simply the ordinary word for God.[39] It is a general name for the divinity, not a personal one (such as *Yahweh, El Shaddai*, or *Mardoch*), what is normally expressed as "God" in the English language. In fact the title Yahweh—the name God revealed to Moses on Mount Sinai—is not used commonly to designate the God of Israel; thus *Elohim* expresses better the reality of God as a sovereign creator,[40] for the "God in Genesis 1 is one who acts and speaks."[41]

Third, the expression *bara' Elohim* is followed by the terms "heaven" and "earth" (respectively *shamayim* and *'aretz*), which designate in biblical language the whole of reality, both heavenly and earthly, physical and spiritual.[42] Heaven or "sky" is the abode of God, whereas earth or "world"

37. Schmidt, *Die Schöpfungsgeschichte der Priesterschrift*, 167.

38. Levenson, *Creation and the Persistence of Evil*, 122.

39. See J. L'Hour, "Elohim," *Revue biblique* 81 (1974): 524–56.

40. E. Jenni and C. Westermann (eds.), *Theological Lexicon of the Old Testament* (Peabody, Mass.: Hendrickson, 1997), *in hoc loco*.

41. C. Westermann, *Genesis 1–11* (Minneapolis, Minn.: Fortress Press, 1984), 100.

42. See J. C. M. Van Winden, "The Early Christian Exegesis of 'Heaven and Earth' in Genesis 1,1,"

is man's home. Thus Genesis 1:1 means simply that in the beginning God created the *universe*, everything that exists. The expression "heaven and earth" refers to a properly ordered cosmos with everything in its true place. The specific contents of the creation process, which occupy "heaven" and "earth," are filled out with their proper elements throughout the following "days" of creation. "The term *'aretz* means primarily the entire area in which man thinks of himself as living, as opposed to the regions of heaven (*shamayim*) or the underworld."[43] Whereas in the *Enūma Eliš* heaven and earth correspond to the two parts of the split-up body of the dragon, and express the dualistic tension between good and evil, in the biblical account God creates one and the other harmoniously. This principle is confirmed throughout the creation of the world in "six days": "heaven" is filled out on the first, second, and fourth days, respectively with the creation of the light, of the firmament, and of night and day, the two great lights; whereas the third, fifth, and sixth days belong properly speaking to the "earth," respectively to the separation of the dry land from the water, the creation of animals, and of humans.

Fourth and lastly, the very first word of the Bible, the term "in the beginning," *ber'esith*. The term, like all Hebrew words, is concrete, not abstract, and means literally "in the head," at the top. It has been translated and interpreted in three different ways throughout the history of biblical exegesis.

First, in an immediate or *literal* sense, "the beginning" of time refers to the world at the beginning (see, e.g., Dt 11:12 and Jer 26:1). This is the most common rendering of *ber'esith* in the translations of Genesis 1:1, and specifically in the Septuagint and the Vulgate. Likewise it is to be found in early Jewish exegetical commentaries.[44] Thus as a translation it will always retain its fundamental validity. This translation allows us to take Genesis 1:1 as an independent sentence describing the simple fact of creation, the different elements or stages of which are listed and detailed in Genesis 1:2 onward.

---

in *Romanitas et Christianitas*, ed. H. Waszink (Amsterdam: North-Holland, 1973), 371–82; L. I. J. Stadelmann, *The Hebrew Conception of the World: A Philological and Literary Study* (Rome: Pontificio Istituto Biblico, 1970), 1.

43. Westermann, *Genesis 1–11*, 127.

44. According to M. Kister, "*Tohu wa-Bohu*, Primordial Elements and *Creatio ex Nihilo*," *Jewish Studies Quarterly* 14 (2007): 229–56.

Second, the *mystical* sense, common among some Church Fathers, which links "in the beginning" of Genesis 1:1 with "in the beginning" (*en archē*) of John 1:1 ("In the beginning was the Word").[45] Thus Genesis 1:1 may be interpreted Christologically as follows: "In the Word God created the heavens and the earth." I shall return to this reading in the next chapter when considering the prologue of John's Gospel. In the words of McFarland, "John's 'in the beginning' does not merely echo Genesis 1 . . ., but interprets it."[46]

Third, we may speak of a *mythical* reading of Genesis 1:1. In the New American Bible and other modern translations Genesis 1:1–3 is rendered as follows:[47] "In the beginning, *when* God created the heavens and the earth, the earth was a formless wasteland (orig. *tōhû wābōhû*), and darkness covered the abyss, while a mighty wind swept over the waters. Then God said, 'Let there be light,' and there was light."[48] It may be noted that Wisdom 11:17 also speaks of creation out of "formless matter."

From a linguistic and structural standpoint this translation of Genesis 1 is legitimate, and makes better sense, besides, out of the terms that refer to the primitive "formless wasteland" and "darkness." The act of creation on the basis of previous formless reality, however, involves, in the words of Clifford, "a separation rather than a destruction, which is a mark of effortless divine action . . . [God continues to] to dismantle the chaotic mass, separating the unconfined, smothering waters into waters above (providing rain) and waters below (providing springs and wells)."[49] On the whole

45. This view is based on the understanding of Philo of Alexandria: see J. L. Moreno Martínez, "El logos y la creación: La referencia al Logos en el 'principio' de Gén. 1, 1, según Filón de Alejandría," *Scripta Theologica* 15 (1983): 381–419. The position may also be found in Justin, Athanasius, Ambrose, and Jerome, and more clearly in Origen, Basil, and Augustine. Origen has the following to say: "when Genesis speaks of the beginning, it is not referring simply to a temporal moment, but rather to the fact that in the Savior are produced the heavens, the earth and all created things" (*In Gen.* 1.1.9).

46. McFarland, *From Nothing*, 22. See P. Borgen, "Logos was the True Light: Contributions to the Interpretation of the Prologue of John," *Novum Testamentum* 14, no. 2 (1972): 115–30; G. Schwarz, "Gen 1,1–2,2a und Joh 1.1a.3a. Ein Vergleich," *Zeitschrift für die neutestamentliche Wissenschaft und die Kunde des Urchristentums* 73 (1982): 136–37.

47. This translation is accepted as valid by Anderson, *"Creatio ex nihilo,"* 16; J. M. Soskice, "Why *Creatio ex nihilo*"; May, *Creatio ex nihilo.*

48. On Gn 1:1, T. E. Fretheim, *God and the World in the Old Testament: A Relational Theology of Creation* (Nashville, Tenn.: Abingdon Press, 2005) offers four possible readings, and opts for Gn 1:1 as separate.

49. Clifford, *Creatio ex nihilo*, 65.

the text, thus translated, represents "the act of creation [taking] place by the effortless and uninterrupted speech of God."[50]

Still, the translation seems to be saying that dark, formless matter already existed *before* the world as we know it came into being, before it was created by God. Should this be the case, then God's work would not be one of *creation* but rather one of shaping, fashioning, or *modeling* what already existed. This of course would be unacceptable from the point of view of Christian faith and would ultimately amount to a denial of creation *ex nihilo*. In the context of other Old Testament texts, we shall see later on that this translation, though legitimate from a linguistic and structural point of view, does not correspond, if isolated, to the full import of the word of God.

The basic idea this translation contains is that creation, the overcoming of chaos, involves the gradual and eschatological establishment of divine mastery and dominion over the universe. The Jewish exegete Jon D. Levenson notes that the high point of creation doctrine in Genesis is the Sabbath, which has clearly eschatological connotations: "No wonder the Mishnah can call the eschatological future 'a day that is entirely Sabbath and rest for eternal life' and designate Psalm 92, the song 'for the Sabbath day,' as the special hymn for that aeon. The reality that the Sabbath represents—God's unchallenged and uncompromised mastery, blessing, and hallowing—is consistently and irreversibly available only in the world-to-come. Until then, it is only known in the tantalizing experience of the Sabbath."[51] Thus the primordial wasteland and darkness of the universe "is an element of the cosmos that not only is under God's providential power but can and will be eradicated at the close of the world's history."[52]

According to this position, Genesis 1:1 should be treated as a subordinate, temporal clause within the wider creation narrative, "but by the time we get to the seventh day (or the *eschaton*), this assumption must be qualified. In other words the close of the creation story forces the reader to go back and rethink what was described at the beginning."[53] That is to say,

50. Fergusson, "Creation," 73.

51. Levenson, *Creation and the Persistence of Evil*, 123.

52. Anderson, *Creatio ex nihilo*, 21.

53. Ibid., 22.

the forcefulness of Genesis 1:1–3 as an expression of God's total and definitive power over creation is not fully *perceived* until the end of the creation narrative, until the definitive Sabbath, the *eschaton,* presents itself openly, when God's name is proclaimed and he may be said to be, to borrow an expression from the New Testament, "all in all" (1 Cor 15:28). As the prophet Ezekiel repeats: "Then you will know I am the Lord" (24:24). In sum, we may say that at the level of *human perception,* the world as it is does not disclose its original utter nothingness until the Sabbath, but rather presents itself to us as a formless wasteland. After all, as we saw in chapter 1, we are simply incapable of directly knowing its "nothingness."

In brief terms, according to this translation, Genesis contains the *doctrine* of creation *ex nihilo* understood in terms of God's unchallenged mastery over the entire universe, although our knowledge or *perception* of that doctrine is focused eschatologically and not protologically, from the end (the Sabbath) and not from the beginning (*bara'*). This gradual unveiling of the doctrine of creation may be observed frequently throughout scripture, as we shall see in the coming sections.

Further Elements of the Genesis Narrative

Several other complementary aspects of the doctrine of creation may be found in Genesis 1. First, each stage of creation is described in terms of seven standard formulae of which God is the subject:[54] (1) the announcement, "God said"; (2) the command, "let there be"; (3) fulfillment, "it was so"; (4) execution of the command, "light"; (5) divine approval, "saw that it was good"; (6) the subsequent word, "God called"; and (7) lastly, the day number is appended.

In effect, each stage of creation involves the *word* and the *command* that is *fulfilled, executed,* and *approved,* for God creates the world through his word and with power. Genesis 1 speaks of God creating through his proffered word no less than ten times (Gn 1:6, 9, 11, 14, 20, 24, 26, 28, 29). This is the divine word of command that brings into existence what it expresses. In the Old Testament the word of God is "both creative and effective: it is the prophetic word that declares the future and helps it come into being."[55]

54. See Wenham, *Genesis 1–15,* 17–19.

55. Ibid., 18.

Second, of particular interest is the fact that God approved the world, he made it and declared it *good*. It is noticeable that no mention of sin and evil is made in Genesis 1: God's work is seen as perfect and holy and serene and transparent and positive from the outset. The goodness of creation is proclaimed on no less than seven occasions throughout the chapter (Gn 1:4, 10, 12, 18, 21, 25, 31). The last time it is mentioned, the expression used is "very good." It is as if the reader (or listener) is invited in a liturgical setting to exult along with the writer (or announcer) in proclaiming the goodness of the Lord who made the earth and filled it with good things. The same notion in a complementary form may be found in Genesis 2 which speaks of the earth as a paradise that God created for humans: "And out of the ground the Lord God made to grow every tree that is pleasant to the sight and good for food, the tree of life also in the midst of the garden" (Gn 2:9; see 2:8–15). "The concluding statement 'God saw all that he had made that it was very good' shows up the perfection of creation and its conformity to the divine will."[56] Wenham notes that "the Hebrew term 'good' [*tov*] as used by the Israelites is more closely related to the mind and opinion of God than is the English word. God is preeminently the one who is good, and his goodness is reflected in his works."[57] "No one is good but God alone" (Mk 10:18), Jesus said. The world is and presents itself as God made it; by definition the earth does not rebel against its creator, but joyfully reflects his goodness and power. The world is meant to praise God in all things; after all, as we have already seen, Genesis 1 is a liturgical text.[58]

A central aspect of the creation narrative—and this is the third element—is that man is created as *superior to all other beings,* for he is made "in the image and likeness of God," and is destined (as well as blessed) to exercise "dominion over the fish of the sea and over the birds of the air and over every living thing that moves upon the earth" (Gn 1:28). Man, in other words, cooperates in the supreme and exclusive sovereignty and dominion of God over the created world as his servant and ambassador.[59]

56. Ibid., 38.

57. Ibid., 18.

58. Ibid., 38: "Though there is little in the chapter that relates directly to worship, the prime interest of the P material, the references to the fixed times (v. 14), and to the seventh day (2:1–3) may be construed as hints of the editor's preoccupation with the cult." See also E. T. Mullen, *Ethnic Myths and Pentateuchal Foundations: A New Approach to the Formation of the Pentateuch* (Atlanta, Ga.: Scholars Press, 1997).

59. See O'Callaghan, *Children of God in the World,* 99–105, and chapter 10 below on ecology.

Fourth, there is the question of the Sabbath. The fact that humans exercise dominion over the earth as God's representatives does not mean that their creation marks the once-and-for-all high point of Genesis 1. This would provide an overly anthropocentric view of created reality out of keeping with the biblical text. Genesis makes it clear that the dominion humans are meant to exercise points to the proclamation of the divine goodness of creation. Thus it is more correct to say that the high point of creation in Genesis is *the celebration of the Sabbath*, which takes place on the seventh day. On the seventh day, we are told, once the creation of the heavens and the earth was concluded, "God rested from all this work which he had done" (Gn 2:2). And "so God blessed the seventh day and sanctified it, because on it God rested from all his work which he had done in creation" (Gn 2:3). Thus believers, who direct their lives to God (proclaiming that creation "was very good") and contribute to subduing the world God had made, are reminded to act always for God and under God. That is what it means to observe the Sabbath.[60] Thus the ultimate purpose and scope of creation is not the creation of man, even though he is made in the image and likeness of God on the sixth day, but God's Sabbath rest on the seventh, "the resting God, the celebrating God, the God who rejoices over his creation. . . . For it is only the sabbath which completes and crowns creation," in the words of Jürgen Moltmann.[61]

Celebration of the Jewish Sabbath means that the human activity of exercising dominion over the universe should cease in order for God's glory to be fully proclaimed. In the Book of Exodus we read significantly that at

60. On this text, see Wenham, *Genesis 1–15*, 36, "Positions."

61. "In the theological traditions of the Western churches creation is generally presented merely as 'the six days' work.' The seventh day, the sabbath, was often overlooked. Consequently God was presented throughout merely as the creative God: *Deus non est otiosus*. The resting God, the celebrating God, the God who rejoices over his creation, receded into the background. And yet it is only the sabbath which completes and crowns creation. It is only in his sabbath rest that the creative God comes to his goal, which means coming to himself and to his glory. When people celebrate the sabbath they perceive the world as God's creation, for in the sabbath quiet it is God's creation that they are permitting the world to be." J. Moltmann, *God in Creation: An Ecological Doctrine of Creation* (London: SCM Press, 1985), 6. Harmut Gese gives a clear ecological twist to this position: "The point of the sabbath is not primarily that human beings should rest from their labors. The main purpose is the non-intervention of human beings in the environment—the *restitutio in integrum* of creation. . . . In principle, what is at stake is the inviolability of creation, which at least on every seventh day is to be preserved from man, as a sign and symbol." H. Gese, *Zur biblischen Theologie: Alttestamentliche Vorträge*, 3rd ed. (Tübingen: J. C. B. Mohr, 1989), 79.

a certain stage "Moses finished the work" (Ex 40:33) that God had given him. The Jewish writer Abraham Heschel explains:

> The meaning of the Sabbath is to celebrate time rather than space. Six days a week we live under the tyranny of things of space; on the Sabbath we try to become attuned to *holiness in time.* It is a day on which we are called upon to share in what is eternal in time, to turn from the results of creation to the mystery of creation; from the world of creation to the creation of the world.[62]

The reason for this is a critical one: not only does the created world come entirely *from* God, but also, and perhaps more importantly, it must be directed totally back *to* him again, so that God may be glorified in everything.

As they work and subdue creation, humans may experience time as an oppressive, inhibiting tyrant; while living the Sabbath, however, time seems to expand into the joy of divine eternity. Romano Guardini explained it as follows: "The seventh day demands of man, as long as it lasts, that he lays down his dominion, in such a way that in the space of his silence the greatness of God may be elevated."[63] This is a classic idea already suggested by the fifteenth-century theologian Nicholas of Cusa, who extends the notion of the Sabbath to Christ in person, Lord of the Sabbath (Mt 12:8). For in real terms Christ, he says, is the "seventh day" of creation, in whom it finds its ultimate scope and consummation.[64]

In his theology of creation Joseph Ratzinger explains:

> To understand the account of creation properly, one has to read the Sabbath ordinances of the Torah. Then everything becomes clear. The Sabbath is the sign of the covenant between God and man; it sums up the inward essence of the covenant. If this is so, then we can now define the intention of the account of creation as follows: creation exists to be a place for the covenant that God wants to make with man. The goal of creation is the covenant, the love story of God and man. . . . If creation is meant to be a space for the covenant, the place where God and man meet one another, then it must be thought of as a space for worship.[65]

62. A. J. Heschel, *The Sabbath: its Meaning for Modern Man* (New York: Noonday Press, 1993), 19.

63. R. Guardini, *Der Anfang aller Dinge: Meditationen über Genesis Kapitel 1–3; Weisheit der Psalmen* (Mainz: F. Schöningh, 1987), 43.

64. Nicholas of Cusa, *Sermo* 125; see R. Haubst, *Die Christologie des Nikolaus von Kues* (Freiburg i.B.: Herder, 1956), 100.

65. J. Ratzinger, *The Spirit of the Liturgy* (San Francisco, Calif.: Ignatius Press, 2000), 26.

More specifically Ratzinger states: "Creation is designed in such a way that it is oriented to worship. . . . The creation accounts of all civilizations point to the fact that the universe exists for worship and for the glorification of God. . . . The danger that confronts us today in our technological civilization is that we have cut ourselves off from this primordial knowledge,"[66] that creation is meant to glorify the creator. It is not of course that "in worship the human being gives something to the gods that they themselves stand in need of. . . . Out of the pure relationship of love, which is what worship is supposed to be, there develops the manipulative attempt to seize control of the world."[67]

Ratzinger concludes: "In the creation account the sabbath is depicted as the day when the human being, in the freedom of worship, participates in God's freedom, in God's rest, and thus in God's peace. . . . The sabbath brings about universal equality"[68] among creatures. Rebelling against God, however, "the people had rejected God's rest, its leisure, its worship, its peace, and its freedom, and so they fell into the slavery of activity. . . . In their 'no' to the God-given rhythm of freedom and leisure they departed from their likeness to God and so did damage to the earth."[69] We shall return to the issue when dealing with the world being made for the glory of God in chapter 8.

Creation and Salvation in Scripture

Genesis 1 is a truly programmatic text. It presents a rich, unified, liturgically structured view of the divine project of creation, capable of providing a fundamental faith identity for the people of the covenant, centered on creation. But scripture speaks of creation on other occasions and in other ways.

Of particular interest is the way in which believers—whether Jews or Christians—are said to deepen their *conviction* of the truth about creation

66. Ibid., 27.

67. Ibid., 29. The text continues: "The Sabbath in its turn is the summing up of the Torah, the law of Israel. This means that worship has a moral aspect to it. God's whole moral order has been taken up into it; only this is it truly worship."

68. Ibid., 30.

69. Ibid., 32.

in two ways: through *reason* and on the basis of their *lived experience of divine salvation*. The *Catechism of the Catholic Church* puts it as follows:

> The truth about creation is so important for all of human life that God in his tenderness wanted to reveal to his People everything that is salutary to know on the subject. Beyond the natural knowledge that every man can have of the Creator (cf. Acts 17:24–29; Rom 1:19–20), God progressively revealed to Israel the mystery of creation. He who chose the patriarchs, who brought Israel out of Egypt, and who by choosing Israel created and formed it, this same God reveals himself as the One to whom belong all the peoples of the earth, and the whole earth itself; he is the One who alone "made heaven and earth" (cf. Is 44:24; Ps 104; Prv 8:22–31).[70]

In chapter 1, we considered our access to the mystery of creation through reason in a philosophical light. However, of considerable importance is the fact that we can also discover God as creator as we contemplate *the divine work of salvation* and the covenant that God established with Israel.[71] It should become clear in the forthcoming analysis that both ways—the philosophical and the experiential—are closely bound up with one another: God's people experience divine protection and salvation, they interiorize it through reason, and they proclaim it as (reasoned) faith in creation.

The Calvinist theologian Karl Barth famously stated that "creation is the external basis of the covenant and the covenant the internal basis of creation."[72] Interestingly, several Protestant theologians throughout the twentieth century have insisted on the notion of the history of salvation, at times to the neglect of the theology of creation understood in a strict sense. The former was considered to be biblically rooted, whereas the latter was considered to be philosophically and metaphysically justified and therefore tainted; the former was of faith, the latter of reason. Of particular interest here is the work of the Protestant exegete Klaus Westermann.[73]

Westermann argues that throughout the history of Christian theology the proper understanding of creation was lost. This happened firstly

70. *CCC*, no. 287.

71. See S. Sanz Sánchez, *La relación entre creación y alianza en la teología contemporánea:* status quaestionis *y reflexiones filosófico-teológicas* (Rome: Edusc, 2003); M. Á. Tábet, "Creazione e salvezza nella tradizione storico-narrativa del popolo d'Israele," *Creazione e salvezza nella Bibbia*, ed. M. V. Fabbri and M. Á. Tábet (Rome: Edusc, 2009), 17–48.

72. K. Barth, *Church Dogmatics III/1* (Edinburgh: T and T Clark, 1958), vii; see 94.

73. See Westermann, *Creation* and *Gen 1–12*.

because theology since the second century A.D. transformed the biblical account of *creation in praise of its creator* into a systematic doctrine of creation, a *new Christian metaphysics*. Second, creation lost its moorings because modern creation theology, philosophically developed, has showed itself incapable of positively confronting the conclusions of science and establishing a dialogue with it. And thirdly, Westermann says, modern theological reflection—especially with Schleiermacher and the school of Tübingen—has assimilated anew an allegorical-symbolic interpretation of Genesis typical of the Church Fathers.

In brief, Westermann says, the classical doctrine of creation had become a philosophical superstructure, badly integrated into the scriptural affirmation of the covenant with Israel and the history of salvation. The Christian understanding of creation has been distorted by reading revelation through the lens of Greek philosophy, thus becoming hellenized. Revelation, he says, only provides us with the certitude of divine protection, the love of God, salvation, etc., whereas believers extrapolated from the Bible a wide-ranging view of reality that found expression in philosophy, science, nature, and the cosmos. The Old Testament scholar Gerhard von Rad likewise teaches that scripture contains only a doctrine of the covenant and not one about the creation of the world.[74] Judeo-Christian personalism cannot be passed over in the name of Greek objectivism.

To some degree the position of these authors is acceptable, given that several modern metaphysical constructs—such as those of Wolff, Suárez, and others—had little in common with the living, dramatic, pulsating, tragic, existential, joyful dialogue between God and man that the Bible speaks about and theology is meant to reflect on. For that matter, neither had modern metaphysical systems much in common with those developed by Church Fathers and medieval authors. Creation was never meant to be an independent doctrine, for it is essentially subordinated to soteriological concerns, to God's continual intervention in the world,[75] to the profound interaction between faith and reason, and ultimately, to the eschatological consummation of the universe.

We considered the important issue of the natural knowledge of the

74. G. Von Rad, "The Theology of the Hexateuch," in *Old Testament Theology*, 16th ed. (New York: Harper and Row, 1983), 1:129–305.

75. See ibid.

creator through reason in chapter 1. Now we can consider how over a long period of its history Israel became more and more convinced that Yahweh was their creator because they experienced him as their Lord and Savior.[76] First of all I shall consider this in the Book of Exodus, then in the prophets, especially those of the post-exilic period. In chapter 3, I shall consider this idea in the Synoptic Gospels.

First we have the Book of Exodus, in which God is repeatedly said to protect and save his people from the slavery of Egypt, and other slaveries, with great power and a mighty hand. In this way he confirms time and again his covenant with them. The Israelites did not perceive God the creator in the context of the regularity of nature, the dawn and dusk, in the vicissitudes of the desert, the clouds, the heat and rain, of the cosmos, and so on. The Greek philosophers detected the presence of the divine in the regularity, harmony, and beauty of nature, but the Israelites did not. They saw God acting amidst the *exceptions* of nature, which were perceived as manifestations of God's glory: in the column of clouds by day in the desert, in the column of fire by night by which they were guided (Ex 12:21–22), in the dividing of the waters of the Red Sea (Ex 14:19–31), in the prodigious descent of the manna in the desert in response to their prayers and complaints (Ex 16). All these events were considered as concrete signs of God's favorable intervention in the life of his people, and also—crucially—in the material sphere. For God is Lord of the heavens and the earth, of the spiritual and the material universe.

In Exodus, God is not seen as the artificer of harmony, order, and consistency, as the guarantor of nature in its fixity and constancy (this approach would arise in the wisdom literature, later on), but rather as the one who acts in the midst of the exception, at times allowing the laws of nature be apparently violated or simply set aside. Interestingly, however, the divine interventions spoken of in Exodus are not of a magical kind as is common in mythological texts. They take place as it were in a natural way such that the laws and reality of nature are not definitively destroyed but ultimately perfected and fulfilled.[77]

76. See S. del Cura, "Creazione e salvezza in prospettiva trinitaria," *Lateranum* 75, no. 1 (2009): 199–243; S. Sanz Sánchez, "Creation and Covenant in Contemporary Theology: A Synthesis of the Principal Interpretative Keys," *Nova et Vetera* (English edition) 12, no. 1 (2014): 217–53.

77. On the "naturalness" of Christian miracles, see C. S. Lewis, *Miracles* (London: Macmillan, 1947), 136.

We may observe that the power of God as it is presented in the Book of Exodus is marked in two ways: by *depth* and *universality*, though both of them at a superficial level. In effect, the power of God is proclaimed, but his works seem to be of a kind with those of other gods, involving accidental and temporary modifications of the elements of nature, at the level of action rather than of being. That is, God's power as yet does not seem to reach the inner reality of creatures in all their *depth*. God is superior to the gods, but his actions are more or less of the same kind. This may be seen for example in the miracles/magic worked by Moses/Aaron and the Egyptian sorcerers in the presence of the Pharaoh (Ex 7:8–13). God's creative power is seen to be *limited in depth*. The same may be said of the *universality* of the power of God, who acts to guide, protect, and defend his own people, but not other peoples, at least ostensibly. In fact, the latter in some cases are badly treated in favor of the former.[78] God seems to have his favorites.

Second, we have the prophets. The same principle we find in the Book of Exodus—an almighty God who saves and cares for his people—may also be found in the writings of the prophets, especially those related to Israel's Babylonian exile. In effect, the years before and during the exile (which began in 587 B.C.) occasioned a very serious crisis for the people of Israel who sometimes came to doubt God's capacity to protect them and even his interest in doing so.

This phenomenon may be seen especially in the writings of Isaiah and Jeremiah and in the Book of Lamentations. The prophets admonished the people to return to the Lord and observe the Law, on the basis of a simple, often repeated, conviction: if God had saved them repeatedly in the past, he could do so now just as well. They may have been unfaithful, idolatrous, vain, and self-complacent. But God was faithful, always, and powerful besides. And just as he led them out of Egypt into the desert and eventually into the promised land, he would continue looking after his people for the rest of time. As Paul said to the Romans, "The gift and the call of the Lord are irrevocable" (Rom 11:29). And the reason why they should trust in God's saving power is a simple one: God is the creator of the universe, and

78. See G. Tanzella-Nitti, "Una immagine credibile di Dio. La rilettura della violenza nella Bibbia alla luce dell'evento di Gesù di Nazaret," *Annales Theologici* 28, no. 1 (2014): 85–121.

therefore its Savior. God can save his people because he is their creator in the first place. And he can do so with the greatest of ease. Let us consider some texts of Isaiah and Jeremiah.

The second part of the former, Deutero-Isaiah, aptly called the "book of consolation of Israel," provides an impressive overview of the doctrine of creation.[79] Resonances and similarities with Genesis 1 are frequent. The term *bara'*, "to create," is used frequently. The same message comes across in all the texts.

> Thus says God, the Lord, who created the heavens and stretched them out, who spread forth the earth and what comes from it, who gives breath to the people upon it and spirit to those who walk in it: "I am the Lord, I have called you in righteousness, I have taken you by the hand and kept you; I have given you as a covenant to the people, a light to the nations" (Is 42:5–6).

In other words, the God who creates is the one who saves.

> Thus says the Lord, your Redeemer, who formed you from the womb: "I am the Lord, who made all things, who stretched out the heavens alone, who spread out the earth – Who was with me? . . . Who says of Cyrus, 'He is my shepherd, and he shall fulfill all my purpose'"; saying of Jerusalem, "She shall be built," and of the temple, "Your foundation shall be laid" (Is 44:24–28).

That is, God is creator and all the authorities on earth are meant to obey him, for he is the only God. Elsewhere we read:

> I am the Lord, and there is no other, besides me there is no God; I gird you, though you do not know me, that men may know, from the rising of the sun and from the west, that there is none besides me; I am the Lord, and there is no other. I form light and create darkness, I make weal and create woe, I am the Lord, who do all these things. Shower, O heavens, from above, and let the skies rain down righteousness; let the earth open, that salvation may sprout forth, and let it cause righteousness to spring up also; I the Lord have created it (Is 45:5–8).

79. R. Rendtorff, "Die theologische Stellung des Schöpfungsglaubens bei Deuterojesaja," *Zeitschrift für Theologie und Kirche* 51 (1954): 3–13; C. Stuhlmueller, "The Theology of Creation in Second Isaiah," *Catholic Biblical Quarterly* 21 (1959): 429–67; P. B. Harner, "Creation Faith in Deutero-Isaiah," *Vetus Testamentum* 17 (1967): 298–306; R. J. Clifford, "The Hebrew Scriptures and the Theology of Creation," *Theological Studies* 46 (1985): 507–23; C. Streibert, *Schöpfung bei Deuterojesaja und in der Priesterschrift: eine vergleichende Untersuchung zu Inhalt und Funktion schöpfungstheologischer Aussagen in exilisch-nachexilischer Zeit, Beiträge zur Erforschung des Alten Testaments und des antiken Judentums* (Frankfurt a.M.: Peter Lang, 1993); S. Ausín, "Creación y Éxodo en Isaías: dos momentos claves de la acción salvífica de Dios," in *Creazione e salvezza nella Bibbia* (ed. Fabbri and Tábet), 49–76.

As a result, the phenomena of nature become a symbol of God's saving power, and God reminds his people of his power:

> Listen to me, O Jacob, and Israel, whom I called! I am He, I am the first, and I am the last. My hand laid the foundation of the earth, and my right hand spread out the heavens; when I call to them, they stand forth together.... Why, when I came, was there no man? When I called, was there no one to answer? Is my hand shortened, that it cannot redeem? Or have I no power to deliver? Behold, by my rebuke I dry up the sea, I make the rivers a desert; their fish stink for lack of water, and die of thirst (Is 48:12, 50:2).

So the creative power of God persists even when humans do not respond to his saving call.

In contrast with the almighty power of God represented in these serene and trusting words, the ruin of the impotent idols is inevitable.

> Bel bows down, Nebo stoops, their idols are on beasts and cattle; these things you carry are loaded as burdens on weary beasts. They stoop, they bow down together, they cannot save the burden, but themselves go into captivity ... "To whom will you liken me and make me equal, and compare me, that we may be alike? ..." "Remember this and consider, recall it to mind, you transgressors, remember the former things of old; for I am God, and there is no other; I am God, and there is none like me" (Is 46:1–2, 5, 8).[80]

The prophet Jeremiah speaks in a like way: "Ah, Lord God! It is you who have made the heavens and the earth by your great power and by your outstretched arm! Nothing is too hard for you, who show steadfast love to thousands, but requites the guilt of fathers to their children after them. O great and mighty God whose name is the Lord of hosts" (Jer 32:17–18). And elsewhere: "Thus says the Lord: 'If I have not established my covenant with day and night and the laws of heaven and earth, then I will reject the descendants of Jacob and David my servant and will not choose one of his descendants to rule over the seed of Abraham, Isaac, and Jacob. For I will restore their fortunes, and will have mercy upon them'" (Jer 33:25–26). Again we see that God's care for and salvation of his people is made possible by the fact that he governs the world as the one who made it from beginning to end.

80. See also Is 40:22–28 and 51:9–11.

Likewise, the prophet Nehemiah (9:6), in a text that evokes Genesis 2:1, proclaims the creating power of God alone and the duty of the people to recognize this and worship him and nobody else. "You are the Lord, you alone; you have made heaven, the heaven of heavens, with all their host, the earth and all that is on it, the seas and all that is in them; and you preserve all of them; and the host of heaven worships you."

The two motifs describing God's action found in the Book of Exodus may be detected again in the prophetic texts, namely, *depth* and *universality*. But now we can observe that the power of God penetrates more deeply into reality, especially into the mind and heart of humans. During the exile in Babylon the people of Israel bitterly experienced their nothingness and powerlessness to a greater degree than in Egypt, where at least they had enjoyed a certain prosperity, well-being, stability, and religious freedom. But as a people in Babylon they lost all their privileges and prestige, and were as "nothing" before the power of God and the tyranny of their rulers who enslaved them. They had to learn to depend on God alone. And the conviction the prophets reminded them of was that if God could save them from such a situation then he must be their creator in the most radical sense of the word. Something of a kind may be said of the *universality* of God's saving power. The fact is that the prophets, especially Isaiah, began to insist more and more that God's power is not limited to his chosen people but is destined to reach the whole of humanity, indeed the whole of reality.[81] The same logic may be found in the prophets as in Exodus: if God is (potentially) the Savior of all, then he must be the creator of each and every being. The same may be said, as we shall see presently, of the Synoptic Gospels.

Several books belonging to the Wisdom tradition in the Old Testament, for example Qoelet, Job, and some of the Psalms, likewise present the creating power of God in the context of the suffering, pessimism, injustice, and death that marks the created world; again, the creative and saving Lordship of God overcomes all possible obstacles. We shall return to them in the next section of this chapter.

Of particular interest in this context is 2 Maccabees 7:28–29.[82] This

81. See Is 2:2–4; 42:1–4, 6; 45:14–16, 20–25; 49:6; 55:3–5; Jer 12:15; 16:19–21; Zep 3:9 (before the Babylonian exile); and Zec 2:15; 8:20–23; 14:9, 16 (after the exile).

82. See U. Kellermann, *Auferstanden in den Himmel. 2 Makkabäer 7 und die Auferstehung der Märtyrer* (Stuttgart: Katholisches Bibelwerk, 1979).

text, originally written in Greek, speaks of the persecution of the Jews by the King Antiochus Epiphanes in the second century B.C. A brave Jewish mother encourages her seven sons not to accept the offers and threats of the king who is torturing them so that they eat unlawful meat. Her courage is based on her faith in creation and hope in final resurrection, elements which in the Old Testament clearly go together.[83] To the last of her sons she says:

> I beseech you, my child, to look at the heaven and the earth and see everything that is in them, and recognize that God did not make them out of things that existed [Septuagint: *ouk ex ontōn*]. Thus also mankind comes into being. Do not fear this butcher, but prove worthy of your brothers. Accept death, so that in God's mercy I may get you back again with your brothers (2 Mc 7:28–29).

In other words, the mother tells her son that if he holds on to faith in God who has created all things without exception, he should have no fear of death, of disappearing, of returning into nothing, for he is destined for resurrection, for life. Taken literally, it may be noted the expression "God did not make them out of things that existed" is not incompatible with the notion that God formed the world out of unformed matter. Thus the text does not strictly speaking provide a proof text for creation *ex nihilo*.[84] Greek authors of the same period use an almost identical idiom to describe the generation of children by their parents.[85] Nonetheless, a clear awareness of the doctrine of creation without material presuppositions of any kind may be detected in this text some two hundred years before the New Testament was penned.

Creation in Wisdom Literature

As regards the place occupied by wisdom literature in the theology of creation, Joseph Ratzinger has the following to say: "The Old Testament is not the end of the road. What is worked out in the so-called Wisdom literature is the final bridge on a long road that leads to the message of Jesus

83. See O'Callaghan, *Christ Our Hope*, 85.

84. For "God did not make them out of things that existed," the Vulgate has *ex nihilo fecit illa Deus*, whereas in the neo-Vulgate we read *non ex his, quae erant, fecit illa Deus*.

85. See May, *Creatio ex nihilo*, 8; Anderson, *Creatio ex nihilo*, 16.

Christ and to the New Testament. Only there do we find the conclusive and normative scriptural creation account."[86]

Doubtless, creation theology in Old Testament wisdom literature is different in tone from the teachings of Genesis, Exodus, and the prophets.[87] The latter invite the reader to look toward God who created this world, saves it, and exercises divine power over every ambit and aspect of life. In wisdom literature the essential novelty lies in the fact that *creation* (of humans and the world they live in) becomes *kosmos* (from the Greek term, which means "order"), that is, the unified and ordered totality of all created things which are the work and reflection of God's simple wisdom. God speaks; creation responds to its maker as a unified, harmonious whole. The harsh conditions that marked the life of God's people in Egypt, in exodus and in exile, do not seem to point to God's warm presence and consolation, but rather to his absence and changeableness. But with wisdom literature it is the created world itself, beautiful and harmonious, full of richness and mystery, that moves believers to think about God, filling them with a sense of wonder and praise. Divine omnipotence is no longer revealed in extraordinary interventions of divine power, in emergency situations, in the exception, but in the fact that God is perceived as the only creator of a unique and unitary cosmos.[88] Beforehand the world was viewed in an actualistic, historico-salvific way; now it is considered more in terms of objective, permanent greatness and harmony. No longer is biblical language primarily dramatic and tragic as in historical and prophetic works; in Wisdom books the life of the believer is presented in more horizontal and rational terms, and finds expression in a serene and confident dialogue, more in keeping with the Greek and oriental mentality.

86. Ratzinger, *"In the Beginning,"* 15.

87. See G. Von Rad, *Weisheit in Israel* (Neukirchen-Vluyn: Neukirchener, 1970); D. Winston, "The Book of Wisdom's Theory of Cosmogony," *History of Religions* 11 (1971): 185–202; H. J. Hermisson, "Observations on the Creation Theology in Wisdom," in *Israelite Wisdom: Theological and Literary essays in Honor of Samuel Terrien*, ed. J. G. Gammie and W. A. Brueggeman (New York: Union Theological Seminary, 1978), 43–57; L. G. Perdue, *Wisdom and Creation: The Theology of Wisdom Literature* (Nashville, Tenn.: Abingdon Press, 1994); J. Trublet (ed.), *La sagesse biblique: De l'Ancien au Nouveau Testament* (Paris: Cerf, 1995); M. V. Fabbri, *Creazione e salvezza nel libro della Sapienza: esegesi di Sapienza 1,13–15* (Rome: Armando, 1998); C. E. Deane-Drummond, *Creation through Wisdom: Theology and the New Biology* (Edinburgh: T and T Clark, 2000); A. Niccacci, "La teologia della creazione nei Salmi e nei Sapienziali," in *Creazione e salvezza nella Bibbia* (ed. Fabbri and Tábet), 77–117.

88. Interestingly the Old Testament contains no word strictly equivalent to the Greek word *cosmos*; it arises only in the wisdom literature.

This is not to say of course that wisdom literature provides a merely naturalistic account of the world, for God is still very much the ultimate point of reference. In fact wisdom in its ultimate source is to be found only in God; all true human wisdom points to his. In the Book of Proverbs we read: "And now, my sons, listen to me: happy are those who keep my ways. Hear instruction and be wise, and do not neglect it. Happy is the man who listens to me, watching daily at my gates, waiting beside my doors" (Prv 8:32–34). Wisdom literature does not involve a contamination of pure biblical religion by pagan or Hellenistic motifs. But there is a change of emphasis and tone from the vertical to the horizontal, from the dramatic to the harmonious, from the exceptional to the regular. The new miracle is the world itself in its stable greatness, in its noble majesty, in its enduring beauty. According to Leo Scheffczyk, in wisdom texts "we have a rational knowledge of the world. The divine transparency of the mysterious reality of the world is not denied; rather this reality relates to a kind of cosmological speculation, differently than when we understood creation from the point of view of the history of salvation."[89] Let us consider what the Books of the Psalms, Proverbs, and Wisdom, as well as the so-called mystical psalms, have to say about creation.

CREATION IN THE PSALMS

The Psalms contain frequent references to creation, almost always in a doxological context: our grasp of the truth of creation leads us by the hand as it were to praise and glorify the creator. The following examples may suffice to appreciate this. There are many others.

Psalm 136, called "the great Hallel," is an exuberant sung litany recounting the praise due to God for his providential care and great works, whether they be cosmic or historico-salvific. The following refrain is repeated time and again: "Give thanks to the Lord, for he is good, for his steadfast love endures for ever" (Ps 136:1).

Many psalms represent and repeat central aspects of the *hexameron*, or six days of Genesis 1. Among them, Psalm 148 sings out the praise of creation to its creator: "Praise the Lord! Praise the Lord from the heavens, praise him in the heights! Praise him, all his angels, praise him, all his host!

89. Scheffczyk, *Schöpfung und Vorsehung*, 10 (author's translation).

Praise him, sun and moon, praise him, all you shining stars!" (Ps 148:1–3).

In Psalm 74 we read:

> God my King is from of old, working salvation in the midst of the earth. You divided the sea by your might; you broke the heads of the dragons on the waters. You crushed the heads of Leviathan, you gave him as food for the creatures of the wilderness. You cleave open springs and brooks; you dried up ever-flowing streams. Yours is the day, yours also the night; you established the luminaries and the sun. You fixed all the bounds of the earth; you made summer and winter (74:12–17).

Likewise Psalm 104 follows the order and rhythm of Genesis 1. It is a hymn of exultation and joy for the great works of God, both cosmic and salvific. "O Lord, how manifold are your works! In wisdom have you made them all; the earth is full of your creatures" (Ps 104:24). The earth is considered as a living being, always awaiting the vivifying breath of its maker:

> These all look to you, to give them their food in due season. When you give to them, they gather it up; when you open your hand, they are filled with good things. When you hide your face, they are dismayed; when you take away their breath, they die and return to their dust. When you send forth your Spirit, they are created; and you renew the face of the earth (104:27–30).

Psalm 33 proclaims the faithfulness of God toward the work of creation, once again in a cosmic and salvific key.[90] "By the word of the Lord the heavens were made, and all their host by the breath of his mouth. . . . Our soul waits for the Lord; he is our help and shield. Yes, our heart is glad in him, because we trust in his holy name. Let your steadfast love, O Lord, be upon us, even as we hope in you" (Ps 33:6.20–22).

Psalm 8 is probably the best-known psalm that refers to creation. It gives expression to the believer's joy, amazement, and wonderment when faced with the greatness of God's work. "O Lord, our Lord, how great is your name in all the earth! . . . When I look at your heavens, the work of your fingers, the moon and the stars which you have established; what is man that you are mindful of him, and the son of man that you care for him?" (Ps 8:1, 3–4). The Psalmist goes on to contrast the greatness of

90. See S. Gahler, *Gott der Schöpfung – Gott des Heils. Untersuchungen zum anthologischen Psalm 33* (Frankfurt a.M.: Peter Lang, 1998).

humans and their insignificance, and concludes: "Yet you have made him little less than God [*Elohim*], and crowned him with glory and honor. You have given him dominion over the works of your hands; you put all things under his feet, all sheep and oxen, and also the beasts of the field" (Ps 8:5–7). As we can see, the text is closely tied in with the creation narrative of Genesis 1.

CREATION IN WISDOM LITERATURE

Chapter 8 of the Book of Proverbs provides a rich understanding of the relationship between Old Testament "Wisdom" and the existent cosmos. Clearly evoking Genesis 1, it describes the closeness of God to the world and his fatherly care for it in the following terms:

> When he [God] established the heavens, I [Wisdom] was there, when he drew a circle on the face of the deep, when he made firm the skies above, when he established the fountains of the deep, when he assigned to the sea its limit, so that the waters might not transgress his command, when he marked out the foundations of the earth, then I was beside him, like a *master workman*; and I was daily his delight, rejoicing before him always, rejoicing in his inhabited world and delighting in the sons of men (Prv 8:27–31).

The verbs used throughout the text are significant: God made firm, established, assigned a limit, marked out foundations. They express different aspects of God's joyful, decisive, fruitful creating action that takes place through and with eternal Wisdom whom he generated.[91] Besides, the latter is significantly described as a master workman, in Hebrew *'amon*,[92] an expression that evokes the Greek demiurge (*dēmiourgos*). Two further observations may be made on this text. First, it indicates that the world was not made from preexisting matter of any kind: "When there were *no depths*

91. Prv 8:22–26: "The Lord created me at the beginning of his work, the first of his acts of old. Ages ago I was set up, at the first, before the beginning of the earth. When there were no depths I was brought forth, when there were no springs abounding with water. Before the mountains had been shaped, before the hills, I was brought forth; before he had made the earth with its fields, or the first of the dust of the world."

92. The term *'amon* derives from Amon, an Egyptian god, originally the local deity of Thebes, but later promoted as the supreme god of the Egyptian pantheon, successor of the sun-god *Ra*. He was considered a secret god who hid himself and was difficult to find, and is translated as "master craftsman," "architect," or "little child." See R. B. Y. Scott, "Wisdom in Creation: the 'Āmôn of Proverbs viii.30," *Vetus Testamentum* 10 (1960): 213–23.

I was brought forth, when there were *no springs* abounding with water" (Prv 8:24). And second, it indicates that this teaching is not simply speculative in character, for it does not attempt to provide a scientific or philosophical view of the world, but a spiritual and ethical one.[93] In fact the text took on considerable importance in later speculation on the nature and role of the Logos or divine Word in the process of creation, which we shall consider in the next chapter.

A similar teaching may be found in the Book of Wisdom, written probably in the century before the coming of Christ. It is a beautiful and doctrinally mature document which invites the believer direct his attention to the creator who completely transcends the world.[94] And if humans are unable to detect the presence of the creator behind the appearances of the created world, the author tells us, this is fundamentally due to their moral depravity.

> For all men who were ignorant of God were foolish by nature; and they were unable from the good things that are seen to know him who exists, nor did they recognize the craftsman while paying heed to his works; but they supposed that either fire or wind or swift air, or the circle of the stars, or turbulent water, of the luminaries of heaven were the gods that rule the world. If through delight in the beauty of these things men assumed them to be gods, let them know how much better than these is their Lord, for the author of beauty created them. And if men were amazed at their power and working, let them perceive from them how much more powerful is he who formed them.... For if they [humans] had the power to know so much that they could investigate the world, how did they fail to find sooner the Lord of these things? (Wis 13:1–4, 8).[95]

We shall consider this text anew at the beginning of chapter 7.

93. Prv 8:32–34: "And now, my sons, listen to me: happy are those who keep my ways. Hear instruction and be wise, and do not neglect it. Happy is the man who listens to me, watching daily at my gates, waiting beside my doors."

94. See Wis 1:14; 6:7; 9:1–2, 9; 11:17, 21–26; 14:3; 19:6–9, 22. On these texts, see C. Larcher, *Études sur le Livre de la sagesse* (Paris: Gabalda, 1969); Winston, "The Book of Wisdom's Theory of Cosmogony"; Hermisson, "Observations on the Creation Theology in Wisdom"; G. Scarpat, *Libro della Sapienza* (Brescia: Paideia, 1989); Perdue, *Wisdom and Creation.*

95. See *Creazione e salvezza* (ed. Fabbri and Tábet).

THE CONTINUITY BETWEEN HISTORICO-SALVIFIC AND WISDOM TEXTS: THE MYSTICAL PSALMS

From a historico-salvific and prophetic view of creation typical of the early books of the Old Testament it may be observed here that the passage to a wisdom-based understanding in later works involves no special doctrinal novelty, for the simple reason that in both cases God alone created the world. This continuity between the historical/prophetic and wisdom texts may be affirmed for several reasons: first because wisdom texts regularly evoke Genesis 1, the text on which the doctrine of creation is based; second, insofar as soteriological motifs are present throughout wisdom literature, just as they abound in prophetic works; third, because the created world is seen to depend entirely on God, on the level of both being and action, and not just in a passing and occasional way, such as is the case with pagan divinities; and fourth, in that the incomprehensibility of God's ways are reflected in the historical and prophetic books of the Old Testament, but also in wisdom texts, especially when the tragic, futile, and mortal aspect of human life is considered in Qoelet, Job, and the mystical psalms.

The so-called mystical psalms deal impressively with the way in which the just man attempts to face up to the experience of injustice. The upright frequently find that whereas they suffer, sinners often prosper. And this produces indignation and discouragement. In the midst of their pain and dismay they gradually discover that the order is inverted: with the passage of time sinners will be punished and the just will flourish. In Psalm 37, we read:

> I have been young, and now am old; yet I have not seen the righteous forsaken or his children begging bread.... I have seen a wicked man overbearing, and towering like a cedar of Lebanon. Again I passed by, and he was no more; though I sought him, he could not be found. Mark the blameless man, and behold the upright, for there is posterity for the man of peace. But transgressors shall be altogether destroyed; the posterity of the wicked shall be cut off (Ps 37:25, 35–38).

But this serene conviction that justice will always be done is broken in Psalm 39, whose author is deeply disconcerted by the possibility that the sinner will be perpetually vindicated and the just man will continue suffering. "I was dumb and silent, I held my peace to no avail; my distress grew worse, my heart became hot within me. As I mused, the fire burned; then I spoke with my tongue: 'Lord, let me know my end, and what is the measure of my days; let me know how fleeting my life is!'" (Ps 39:2–4). The solution, as it were, to this arduous search for justice may be found in another mystical psalm, Psalm 73. Obviously it does not provide a rational, banal, technical, or practical solution to the dilemma, but rather a mystical and spiritual one, involving a renewed faith in God almighty, the creator and Savior of the universe, who promises justice through resurrection (Dn 12:1):

> All in vain have I kept my heart clean and washed my hands in innocence. For all the day long I have been stricken, and chastened every morning.... But when I thought how to understand this, it seemed to me a wearisome task, until I went into the sanctuary of God; then I perceived their end. Truly you set them in slippery places; you make them fall to ruin. How they are destroyed in a moment, swept away utterly by terrors! ... When my soul was embittered, when I was pricked in heart, I was stupid and ignorant, I was like a beast toward you.... Whom have I in heaven but you? And there is nothing upon earth that I desire besides you. My flesh and my heart may fail, but God is the strength of my heart and my portion for ever (Ps 73:13, 16–19, 21, 25).

Total faith or trust in God is made possible by the conviction that he is the creator of the universe.

3

Creation in the New Testament

It is undeniable that the New Testament speaks little about creation. And the reason for this is simple: the doctrine is taken for granted by the hagiographers. In the Acts of the Apostles we do read for example how Christian believers began their prayer of thanksgiving for the release of Peter and John with the following standard invocation: "Sovereign Lord, who did make the heaven and the earth and the sea and everything in them" (Acts 4:24; also 14:15, 17:24). Creation is an accepted truth of faith. It is a nonproblematic issue. In fact, many New Testament texts dealing with creation

> are to be found in the context of praise, proclamation of faith in the resurrection, of trust in God the Savior, and so on. Creation is never separate from the other works of God. Rather it is the presupposition of the latter, and even though creation has a relevance all of its own, it is not correct to speak of a solution of continuity between divine action "at the beginning" and the rest of God's action in benefit of humanity.[1]

I shall consider creation first in the Synoptics, then in Paul and in John.

Creation in the New Testament Synoptics

A few observations are worth making in respect of the New Testament doctrine of creation. First, on more than one occasion Jesus spoke of the beginnings, of the fact of creation in Genesis, as an authoritative point of departure (Mt 19:4), as if to confirm his own teaching, and that in spite of the fact that he frequently prefaced his teachings with the expression: "and

1. L. Ladaria, *Antropologia teologica* (Casale Monferrato: Piemme, 1982), 20 (author's translation).

I say to you."[2] Commenting of the promise of repudiation and divorce which Moses conceded to the Israelites on account of their hardness of heart, Jesus declared that "from the beginning it was not so" (Mt 19:8). On other occasions he spoke of what took place "before the foundation of the world" (Mt 13:35, 25:34; Mk 13:19; Lk 11:50).

Second, addressing the Pharisee who "was astonished to see that Jesus did not first wash before dinner," Jesus says: "Now you Pharisees cleanse the outside of the cup and of the dish, but inside you are full of extortion and wickedness. You fools! Did not he who made the outside make the inside also?" (Lk 11:38–40; Mt 23:25). For Jesus the rites of purification of objects and utensils are of secondary importance morally, for his Father created them all, and so the created world is good in every possible way.

THE PRESENCE OF GOD'S SAVING POWER IN ALL THINGS

The doctrine of creation in the Synoptics is to be found principally, though indirectly, in the fact that *God's saving power is present to all things that exist,* penetrating them in *depth* (this may be seen in Matthew and Mark) and *universality* (especially in Luke). I already noted this in respect of Exodus and the Babylonian exile prophets in chapter 2.

In effect, in the Gospel of Matthew, Jesus insists repeatedly on the importance of the *interior depth* of ethical life and spirituality as the fullest way of being faithful to the Law of the Old Testament. Jesus' disciples are invited not only to act in an upright way, externally, but also to act with an upright interior intention (Mt 5:17–48, 6:1–6). Rectitude does not depend so much on material factors or external actions but above all on the purity of intention (Mt 12:34; 15:11, 18). In Mark's Gospel we read that "there is nothing outside a man which by going into him can defile him; but the things which come out of a man are what defile him" (Mk 7:15; 7:19). This is an important affirmation: evil comes from within, not from without. It is clear that the saving power and word of Jesus do not remain on the surface but rather penetrate deeply into the mind and heart of humans. As the prophets often said, it is clear that God can save them from any kind of alienation—spiritual or material, forgiving sin or healing illness—because

2. An expression found over 150 times in the Gospels.

he created them entirely. God can save anything because he created all things, down to the very depths of their being.

Luke's Gospel speaks in a special way of the *universality* of salvation that derives from the life and words and saving work of Christ.[3] God is the merciful Savior of all humans, without exception, of the whole of humanity, of creation whole and entire, of every single being. The divine promise of universal salvation prophesied by Isaiah (Is 61:1) reaches its culmination in Luke's Gospel (4:18). The salvation offered by Christ is universal, in that nobody or nothing is excluded *a priori* from the abundance of divine mercy. We may say therefore that the insistence in the Synoptics on the intensive (Matthew) and extensive (Luke) presence of salvation provides a definitive expression of the conviction that God created all things without presuppositions of any kind, *ex nihilo*. Only a creating God can penetrate the depth of each and every being.

THE CHRISTOLOGICAL ARGUMENT FOR CREATION

The principles of depth and universality derived from Jesus' spiritual and moral teaching find a mystical fulfillment, if the term may be correctly used, in the death and resurrection of Jesus Christ.[4] Dying on the cross, Jesus willingly accepted the existential nothingness of death, of elimination, as he commended his life to his eternal Father, who gave it back to him definitively in the resurrection. He is the true martyr or witness not only to the Father's faithful love, but also to his omnipotence. The paternal power and the presence of God finds expression in both Jesus' assumed nothingness on the cross and in his fullness of life at the resurrection. And the fruit of his redeeming work reaches the *depth* of creatures (their material and spiritual being, their sin, even the possibility of condemnation) and the *universality* of creatures, of each and every creature, who in virtue of the redemption can open themselves to the universal power of salvation. In the words of McFarland, "it is in Christ that creation is revealed as a matter of grace alone, and thus as grounded solely in God's love."[5] He also explains in Christological terms that creation takes place from noth-

3. S. W. Hahn, "Christ, Kingdom and Creation in Luke-Acts," in *Creazione e salvezza* (ed. Fabbri and Tábet), 167–90.

4. O'Callaghan, *Christ Our Hope*, 88–91.

5. McFarland, *From Nothing*, 86; see also Barth, *Church Dogmatics III/1*, 40.

ing but God, that it is nothing apart from God, given besides that nothing limits God.[6] Besides, "the importance of Christ's resurrection for the doctrine of the creation lies in the fact that He rose in His earthly body and, at the ascension, took His risen body into the presence of the Divine Majesty."[7]

Creation in, through, and for Christ in the Pauline Corpus

There is a clear continuity between Old Testament teaching on creation and that of Paul in the New: God has created all things, without exception, and is therefore the Lord of the universe. Several interesting elements may be found throughout his writings.

PAUL'S TEACHING ON CREATION

First, on more than one occasion Paul refers to Genesis 1 as the basis of his own teaching. For example, 1 Corinthians 11:11 alludes to Genesis 1:27 on the creation of man and woman.[8] Second, he establishes a firm connection between creation and final resurrection, and explains that God "gives life to the dead and *calls into existence the things that do not exist*" (Rom 4:17).[9] God raises up and creates, or better, he raises up what he has created.

In the third place, Paul's first letter to the Corinthians draws practical consequences from the conviction that everything has been created by God. Specifically, Paul insists that the fact that some foodstuffs have been offered to idols is of no substantial importance. "Eat whatever is sold in the meat market without raising any question on the ground of conscience. For 'the earth is the Lord's, and everything in it'" (1 Cor 10:25, citing Ps 24:1). Paul was aware that some believers might interpret eating meat

6. McFarland, *From Nothing*, 85–107.

7. A. Ehrhardt, "Creatio ex nihilo," *Studia Theologica* 4 (1950): 13–43, at 40.

8. See G. Baumbach, "Die Schöpfung in der Theologie des Paulus," *Kairos* (1979): 196–205; U. Mell, *Neue Schöpfung: eine traditionsgeschichtliche und exegetische Studie zu einem soteriologischen Grundsatz paulinischer Theologie* (Berlin: W. de Gruyter, 1989); U. Vanni, "La creazione in Paolo. Una prospettiva di teologia biblica," *Recensioni di Teologia* 36 (1995): 285–325; R. Penna, "L'idea di creazione in Paolo e nel paolinismo: il ruolo di Cristo per un nuovo concetto di cosmo, di uomo e di chiesa," in *Creazione e salvezza* (ed. Fabbri and Tábet), 191–212.

9. J. D. G. Dunn, *Romans*, WBC 38A (Waco, Tex.: Word Books, 1988), 236.

offered to idols as a kind of collusion with pagan worship, but in real terms it is quite the opposite, insofar as it involves a faith-affirmation in the one God, who created the heavens and the earth and everything they contain. All foods are good because they have been created by God; the fact they might have been offered to idols carries no weight, for the simple reason that the idols to whom they are offered simply do not exist.

Fourthly, Paul says that sin is an obstacle to the clear knowledge we have of God through creation. He explains it in detail in Romans 1:17–32,[10] which clearly evokes Wisdom 13:1–9, considered above. He is convinced that the believer should be able to perceive that "the heavens proclaim the glory of the Lord" (Ps 19:1), to witness that the stars "shone with gladness for him who made them" (Bar 3:34), to apprehend the "eternal power and deity" (Rom 1:20) of God in created things, and thus to be convinced of the vanity of idol worship (Rom 1:18–23):

> For the wrath of God is revealed from heaven against all ungodliness and wickedness of men who by their wickedness suppress the truth. For what can be known about God is plain to them, because God has shown it to them. Ever since the creation of the world his invisible nature, namely, his eternal power and deity, has been clearly perceived in the things that have been made. So they are without excuse; for although they knew God they did not honor him as God or give thanks to him, but they became futile in their thinking and their senseless minds were darkened. Claiming to be wise, they became fools, and exchanged the glory of the immortal God for images resembling mortal man or birds or animals or reptiles.

The Stoics held that God may be known through creation in that "there is an innate rapport between the divine and the human because the divine logos immanent throughout the world is immanent also in man as the power of reason; and that consequently the invisible realities and eternal power of divinity behind the visible cosmos are clearly seen by the eye of understanding in and through creation."[11] And Paul applies this principle to humanity at large. J. D. G. Dunn glosses the text as follows:

10. G. G. Bornkamm, "The Revelation of God's Wrath (Romans 1–3)," *Early Christian Experience* (London: SCM Press, 1969), 47–70; C. Sanguineti, "La creazione nella lettera ai Romani: prima rivelazione di Dio, nel gemito e nell'attesa della gloria," in *Creazione e salvezza* (ed. Fabbri and Tábet), 305–12. See also W. Pannenberg, *Systematic Theology* (Edinburgh: T and T Clark, 1988), 1:73–82.

11. Dunn, *Romans,* 71.

Despite having this knowledge of God, despite knowing God insofar as he had made himself known to them, humankind refused that response. In consequence their reasoning became futile, their foolish heart darkened. That is to say, by closing the eye of understanding which has the capacity to receive and recognize God's self-revelation ... they shut off the light of the mind and left it fumbling with inane trifles and relatively worthless side issues. Their whole intellectual and emotional life ("heart") by thus demonstrating this foolishness became clouded and less capable of receiving or responding to that light.[12]

The power of salvation overcomes sin and blindness and makes it possible for us to perceive God as creator. In this text we can also see how our knowledge of the truth of creation is derived not only from faith but also from human reason.

Fifth, Paul speaks of a powerful eschatological tension present within the created world which "groans in travail." Thus, Romans 8:18–25:

I consider that the sufferings of this present time are not worth comparing with the glory that is to be revealed to us. For *the creation waits with eager longing for the revealing of the sons of God*; for the creation was subjected to futility, not of its own will but by the will of him who subjected it in hope; because the creation itself will be set free from its bondage to decay and obtain the glorious liberty of the children of God. We know that the whole creation has been groaning in travail together until now; and not only the creation, but we ourselves, who have the first fruits of the Spirit, groan inwardly as we wait for adoption as sons, the redemption of our bodies. For in this hope we were saved. Now hope that is seen is not hope. For who hopes for what he sees? But if we hope for what we do not see, we wait for it with patience.

This singular text expresses the living, dynamic quality of the created world and its eschatological destiny.[13] "Believers can be confident in the certainty (and imminence) of the eschatological climax because the work

12. Ibid.

13. On this text, see B. Rossi, *La creazione tra il gemito e la gloria (Rom 8,18–25)* (Rome: Dehoniane, 1992); A. Gieniusz, *Romans 8:18–30* (Atlanta, Ga.: Scholars Press, 1999); C. Sanguineti, "La creazione nella lettera ai Romani: prima rivelazione di Dio, nel gemito e nell'attesa della gloria." Sanguineti points out four aspects of the text: the dramatic, anxious waiting of creation, as a person, for the revelation of the children of God; the reason for this waiting is that creation has been subjected to futility, vanity, not of its own responsibility, but of one who submitted it (God who seals the rebellion of Adam); waiting takes on the form of hope of creation being freed from slavery, and this will involve common suffering and glory for which creation is suffering labor pains (315).

of eschatological liberation and renewal has already begun."[14] Here creation is in some ways personified, "full of wistful eager longing . . . all too acutely aware that its own fulfillment is bound up with the entry of God's sons upon their full inheritance—a transformed creation being part of that inheritance."[15] The reason why the created order awaits so intensely the redemption of humanity is "because creation itself is caught up in man's fallen state."[16] The result of this is that "there is an out-of-sortness, a disjointedness about the created order which makes it a suitable habitation for man at odds with his creator."[17] We can say, therefore, that creation not only refers to the beginning of the universe but to a process that reaches out to future eschatological consummation.

Sixth (and last), the principal teaching of Paul on creation involves the immediate *role of Christ* in God's work of creating the world.

THE ROLE OF CHRIST IN THE WORK OF CREATION

Paul explains the relationship between Christ and creation by using a series of functional creational prepositions which describe the way in which God's creative action relates respectively to the Father and to Christ. The Greek prepositions that relate divine action to the created world are principally the following: *ek* (from), *dia* (through), *eis* (for), although another two are also to be found: *epi* (above) and *en* (in).

Three Pauline texts are of particular interest here. First, Romans 11:36, which serves as a climax to a section of the letter to the Romans dealing with salvation and the Jews. Paul encourages believers to show appreciation for the gifts and hidden counsels of God and concludes: "For from [*ek*] him and through [*dia*] him and to/for [*eis*] him are all things. To him be glory for ever. Amen" (Rom 11:36). That is to say, the created world comes entirely from God and is always directed to his glory. He is "the source, medium and goal of everything, the beginning, middle, and end of all that is."[18]

14. Dunn, *Romans*, 486–92, at 487.
15. Ibid.
16. Ibid.
17. Ibid., 488.
18. Ibid, 704.

Second, in Ephesians 4:4–6 we read: "There is one body and one Spirit, just as you were called to the one hope that belongs to your call, one Lord, one faith, one baptism, one God and Father of us all, who is above [*epi*] all and through [*dia*] all and in [*en*] all." Again God, the one and only God, is seen to be the all-encompassing, transcendent creator, who is present in all things,[19] with an all-embracing closeness and action.

This doctrine is confirmed in a third text, 1 Timothy 6:13–15, in which we read that "God . . . gives life to all things . . . the blessed and only Sovereign, the King of kings and Lord of lords." The text also mentions Christ, not in the context of creation but as God's witness before Pontius Pilate (6:13). In these texts it may be said that the creational prepositions "from him," "through him," and "for him" are applied consistently to God the eternal Father. Things change in two more substantial texts in the Pauline corpus, 1 Corinthians 8:5 and Colossians 1:15–20.

First, the letter to the Corinthians. Speaking of the uniqueness of God,[20] Paul observes: "For although there may be so-called gods in heaven or on earth—as indeed there are many 'gods' and many 'lords'—yet for us there is one God, the Father, from whom [*ek hou*] are all things and for whom [*eis autou*] we exist, and one Lord, Jesus Christ, through whom [*di' hou*] are all things and through whom [*di' autou*] we are" (1 Cor 8:5–6).[21] The doctrine of Romans, Ephesians, and 1 Timothy is maintained: the world comes into being by and from God and is directed to him. But the *mediation* of creation and salvation (*di' hou*) is now attributed to Christ. This is a novelty not present in Romans, Ephesians, and 1 Timothy. The latter attributes salvation to Christ's mediation (especially 1 Tm 2:5), but not creation. In 1 Corinthians, however, creation is included in Christ's work. By implication Christ, in sharing the creational prepositions with God, is placed on the same plane as the Father, as there are no "gods" in the

19. Some authors understand "all" in the masculine and therefore apply the expression to the church, but the context here as well as other Pauline texts (1 Cor 8:6 and 15:28; Rom 11:36) indicate that "all" should be taken in the neutral sense, referred therefore to the created world. A. T. Lincoln, *Ephesians*, WBC 42 (Waco, Tex.: Word Books, 1990), 240.

20. Conzelmann put it as follows: "The gods become gods by being believed in, and faith in the one God and the one Lord creates freedom no longer to recognize these powers." H. Conzelmann, *1 Corinthians: A Commentary on the First Epistle to the Corinthians* (Philadelphia: Fortress Press, 1975), 145.

21. J. A. Fitzmyer, *First Corinthians, Anchor Yale Bible* (New Haven, Conn.: Yale University Press, 2008), 341–44.

strict sense, no intermediate beings, but only one, single divinity. And here Christ is presented as "the preexistent mediator of salvation."[22] Giacomo Biffi comments that "the extension of the intervention of Christ is not less ample than that which is attributed to the action and attraction of the Father; not only does the return of all humanity take place through Christ, but through Him passes the coming into existence of everything that finds its origin in God."[23] This position of course finds its roots in the Old Testament continuity between creation and salvation which I considered in the last chapter: the one who saves is the one who created us; God's work of creation finds its ongoing complement in salvation, one and the other taking place through Christ.

Second, the most extensive Pauline text on Christ and creation is to be found in the first chapter of the letter to the Colossians (1:15–20). It reads as follows:

He [Christ] is the image of the invisible God, the first-born of all creation; for in him [*en autō*] all things were created, in heaven and on earth, visible and invisible, whether thrones or dominions or principalities or powers—all things were created through him [*di' autou*] and for him [*eis auton*]. He is before all things, and in him [*en autō*] all things hold together [*sunestēken*]. He is the head of the body, the church; he is the beginning, the first-born from the dead, that in everything he might be pre-eminent. For in him [*en autō*] all the fullness of God was pleased to dwell, and through him [*di' autou*] to reconcile to himself all things, whether on earth or in heaven, making peace by the blood of his cross.

Some observations on these impressive words, probably of liturgical origin, are in order.[24] From the overall context it is clear that the subject

22. A. Lindemann, *Der Erste Korintherbrief* (Tübingen: Mohr Siebeck, 2000), 193; also G. De Virgilio, "Πᾶν κτίσμα θεοῦ καλὸν (1 Tm 4,4). La positività della creazione e la sua dimensione salvifica nelle Lettere Pastorali," in *Creazione e salvezza* (ed. Fabbri and Tábet), 361–76.

23. G. Biffi, *Approccio al cristocentrismo: note storiche per un tema eterno* (Milan: Jaca Book, 1994), 54 (author's translation).

24. A. Feuillet and Y.M.-J. Congar, *Le Christ sagesse de Dieu d'après les épîtres pauliniennes* (Paris: Librairie V. Lecoffre, 1966); P. Benoit, "L'hymne christologie de Col 1, 15–20. Jugement critique sur l'état des recherches," in *Christianity, Judaism, and Other Greco-Roman Cults: Studies for Morton Smith at Sixty*, ed. J. Neusner (Leiden: E. J. Brill, 1975), 226–63; J.-N. Aletti, *Colossiens 1, 15–20: genre et exégèse du texte: fonction de la thématique sapientielle* (Rome: Biblical Institute Press, 1981); L. R. Helyer, "Arius Revisited: the Firstborn over all Creation (Col 1:15)," *Journal of the Evangelical Theological Society* 31, no. 1 (1988): 59–67; C. Basevi, "Col 1, 15–20: Las posibles fuentes del 'himno' cristológico y su importancia para la interpretación," *Scripta Theologica* 30 (1998): 779–802; S. M. McDonough, *Christ as Creator: Origins of a New Testament Doctrine* (Oxford: Oxford University Press, 2009), 172–91.

of the text is Christ.[25] However a certain confusion results from the fact that in other passages (considered above) the creational prepositions (*en, dia, eis*) are applied also to the Father. Perhaps the most important theological novelty in Colossians lies in the fact that a double role is attributed to Christ that in other texts was attributed to the Father, "all things were created through him and for him" (v. 16). Besides, this clearly finds expression in verse 17: "in him all things hold together." The latter text connects directly with Hebrews 1:3: "He [Christ] reflects the glory of God and bears the very stamp of his nature, upholding [*pherōn*] the universe by his word of power." As a result, "from the highest to the lowest, all creatures alike are subject to Christ."[26] André Feuillet sums up Colossians 1:15–20 by saying that Christ "as divine Wisdom, is the mirror in which God has contemplated the plan of the cosmos."[27]

The text also explains why the creational prepositions may be "transferred" from the Father to Christ. Christ is "the image of the invisible God" (Col 1:15),[28] a way of speaking that finds deep roots in the Old Testament, especially in Proverbs (8:22, 30),[29] in Wisdom (7:25), and to a degree in Genesis itself (1:27), although it is clear that the "image of God" in the first book of the Bible refers only to humans, and not to the divinity. In fact, being the "first-born of all creation" does not make Christ a mere creature, but rather the eternal Son in whom and through whom and for whom creation takes place, because in him God's image is perfect. Christ "reflects the glory of God and bears the very stamp [*charaktēr*] of his nature" (Heb 1:3). Thus he is the creator, along with the Father, of all things, heavenly and earthly, including the angels: "all things were created, in heaven and on earth, visible and invisible, whether thrones or dominions or principalities or powers—all things were created through him and for him" (v. 16).

In comparison with the prologue of the Gospel of John, which express-

25. Ladaria, *Antropologia teologica*, 23; A. Grillmeier, *Christ in the Christian Tradition, vol. 1: from the Apostolic Age to Chalcedon* (Atlanta, Ga.: John Knox Press, 1975), 144.

26. P. T. O'Brien, *Colossians, Philemon* (Waco, Tex.: Word Books, 1982), 47.

27. Feuillet-Congar, *Le Christ Sagesse*, 365.

28. On the interpretation of "image of the invisible God" in Col 1:15, see J. R. Strawbridge, "The Image and Unity of God: The Role of Colossians 1 in Theological Controversy," in *The Bible and Early Trinitarian Theology*, ed. C. A. Beeley and M. Weedman (Washington, D.C.: The Catholic University of America Press, 2018), 172–90.

29. Scott, *Wisdom in Creation*.

es the presence and mediating role of Christ in creation in the past tense, as a former event (see the third section of this chapter), Paul insists besides on the present action of Christ: "in him all things hold together." This suggests that Christ constantly conserves all things in their very existence, cohesion, and harmony (the term used is *sunestēken*, "to bring together").[30] Christ may not simply be considered as a static exemplar of what the world always was and always will be. This position is close to what the Stoics and other Greek philosophers taught.[31] In Colossians a linguistic bridge with the Stoics may be found, of course, but Paul's thought is not pantheistic as is that of the Stoics. The Stoic philosopher and emperor Marcus Aurelius, who of course is posterior to Paul, put it this way: "O Nature . . . all things come from you, subsist in you, go back to you."[32]

Another important novelty of the Colossians text lies in the affirmation that the world was created *for* Christ: 1 Corinthians 8:6 spoke of God "for whom we exist." And O'Brien observes: "The teaching that Christ is the ultimate goal of all creation has no parallel in the Jewish Wisdom literature or indeed any other Jewish source. The very one who was crucified as a common criminal, that is Jesus Christ, is the very person to whom the whole of creation, and therefore history as well, moves."[33] Yet McDonough points out that "a messianic reading of the passage fits well with frequent Jewish assertions that the world was created 'for the sake of' Moses or whomever."[34]

All in all, we may say that Christ is, to use the technical term, the *final cause* of the entire created universe. The same doctrine may be found, substantially, in Ephesians 1:9, which says: "For he [Christ] has made known to us in all wisdom and insight the mystery of his will, according to his purpose which he set forth in Christ as a plan for the fullness of time, to unite all things in him, things in heaven and things on earth." "To reconcile

30. W. Bauer, F. W. Danker, W. F. Arndt, and F. W. Gingrich (eds.), *A Greek-English Lexicon of the New Testament and Other Early Christian Literature*, 3rd ed. (Chicago: University of Chicago Press, 2000) [hereafter BDAG], 972, s.v. συνιστημι.

31. The term *sunestēkenai* can be found in Plato, *Republic* 530a; Ps.-Aristotle, *Mund.* 6; Philo, *Rer. Div. Her.* 281 and 311.

32. Marcus Aurelius, *Meditations* IV, 23 (author's translation).

33. P. T. O'Brien, "Colossians," in *New Bible Commentary*, ed. D. Guthrie, D. A. Carson, R. T. France, J. A. Moteyer and G. J. Wenham, 4th ed. (Leicester: InterVarsity, 1994), 1259–75, at 1265.

34. McDonough, *Christ the Creator*, 186. This author refers to *b. Sanh.* 98b, where the world is variously said to be created for David, Moses, and the Messiah.

to himself all things" (v. 20) is the translation of the Greek term *anakephalaiōsasthai,* often rendered as "recapitulation."[35] In effect, the union or coming together of all things in Christ and under Christ is the ultimate purpose and thrust of the created universe, the reason why it exists, the reason why the Father created it. The notion is present in verses 19–20: "For in him all the fullness of God was pleased to dwell, and through him to reconcile to himself all things, whether on earth or in heaven, making peace by the blood of his cross." Only with the final triumph of Christ will the Father be fully glorified.

But what does this involve theologically? It means that just as creation has a beginning, it will also have an end, a fulfillment, an ultimate purpose, and on the same terms. Just as the Son, the perfect image, was present, actively present, at the beginning, and present throughout history, he will also be so at the end, when God through him will be "all in all things" (1 Cor 15:28). In Christ, God's Word/Wisdom has taken on the dominion, the control, the reins, and the meaning of the entire universe, of the whole of history, in all its height and depth, in its intricate dynamism and dramatic realism. Christ, the beginning of all things, the eschatological judge of history in its final fulfillment, was present at the beginning of creation, is now and ever shall be present. Present *actively,* not as a mere spectator. Christ is never lost, or relativized, or emptied, or surpassed "on the way" as it were, whether by history, by reason, by progress, by the Enlightenment, by technology, by humans. He is, always was, and always will be the Lord of history and judge of the universe. Everything that exists tends toward him, whether it is aware or not of the fact.

In the Old Testament we could observe the dependence of the mystery of salvation on that of creation. Here again, when we say that Christ is the mediator of salvation, he is so on account of being the mediator of creation. Thus creation takes place *through* Christ and *for* Christ, and thus, ultimately *in* Christ. He is not a simple static model, not just a prototype of abstract, atemporal rationality. Creatures depend on him just as they do on God. Because he is their Lord he is also their Savior. Giacomo Biffi says this in the following words: "Everything derives its nature from him, the exemplar principle; everything derives its very existence from him,

35. O'Callaghan, *Children of God in the World,* 129–31; BDAG 65, s.v. ἀνακεφαλαιόω.

the efficient cause. Everything is a fragment of immeasurable value gathered together in him; every single thing receives from him alone its proper meaning. We are all fruit of his act of love, which mysteriously humanizes the ineffable act of divine love that is at the source of the existence of every creature."[36]

Creation through the Word/Son in the Gospel of John

John's theology of creation is situated principally in the prologue of his Gospel (1:1–18). It is based on two motifs with deep roots in the Old Testament: the power of the word and the personification of Wisdom.[37]

JOHN, THE WORD, AND WISDOM

In effect, scripture on repeated occasions tells us that God creates *through the word.* The "word" in scripture is not a simple means by which an abstract idea is communicated; it is the sign and powerful expression of the presence and activity of God (Gn 1:6, 9, 11, 14, 20, 24, 26, 28, 29). Isaiah tells us that the word is *the vehicle of divine power* (Is 55:10). By means of the word God *called* Israel and at the same time *constituted* it as his people. Hence creation is a product of the divine word. "Let all your creatures serve you, for *you spoke, and they were made.* You sent forth your Spirit, and it formed them; there is none that can resist your voice" (Jud 16:14). "My hand laid the foundation of the earth, and my right hand spread out the heavens; when I call to them, they stand forth together" (Is 48:13). "Let all the earth fear the Lord, let all the inhabitants of the world stand in awe of him! For he spoke, and it came to be; he commanded, and it stood forth" (Ps 32:8). The notion of word coming from the "mouth" of God fits well with the revealed doctrine of creation, for God when he creates does not merely give "instructions" to a previously existing messenger or worker who goes on to construct the universe out of previously existing matter, which is what the Greek explanation of the Demiurge entails, but rather

36. Biffi, *Approccio,* 80 (author's translation).

37. A. Bottino, "*Logos,* Sapienza, Creazione," in *Creazione e salvezza* (ed. Fabbri and Tábet), 377–86.

he carries it out himself, directly, personally, with his own power, without intermediaries.

Not unrelated to creation through the word is *creation through Wisdom*.[38] I have already considered the singular power and personality attributed to "wisdom" in the Old Testament, which teaches that God creates the world, his world, *through Wisdom*. We can sum up this teaching as follows. First, creation takes place through wisdom (Ps 8; Prv 8:27, 29–31). Second, Wisdom penetrates the whole of reality, complete and entire.[39] In the third place, Wisdom is superior to the created world (Bar 3:29–31). Fourth, Wisdom, though eternal, is described as distinct from God and at the same time made by him.[40] Fifth and last, scripture presents a deep and powerful *mutual* relationship between God and Wisdom (Bar 3:31; Jb 28:23–27). Johann Auer describes the passage between Old and New Testaments as follows: "In the place of the created wisdom of the Old Testament appears the eternal Son of the eternal Father, as principle, center and end of the history of salvation."[41]

The similarities of Wisdom with the Word through whom all things

38. On Wisdom in scripture, see M. Silva (ed.), *New International Dictionary of New Testament Theology and Exegesis*, 2nd ed., 5 vols. (Grand Rapids, Mich.: Zondervan, 2014) [hereafter *NIDNTTE*], 4:330–40, s.v. σοφία.

39. "For wisdom, the fashioner of all things, taught me. For in her there is a spirit that is intelligent, holy, unique, manifold, subtle, mobile, clear, unpolluted, distinct, invulnerable, loving the good, keen, irresistible, beneficent, humane, steadfast, sure, free from anxiety, all-powerful, overseeing all, and penetrating through all spirits that are intelligent and pure and most subtle. For wisdom is more mobile than any motion; because of her pureness she pervades and penetrates all things. For she is a breath of the power of God, and a pure emanation of the glory of the Almighty; therefore nothing defiled gains entrance into her. For she is a reflection of eternal light, a spotless mirror of the working of God, and an image of his goodness. Though she is but one, she can do all things, and while remaining in herself, she renews all things; in every generation she passes into holy souls and makes them friends of God, and prophets; for God loves nothing so much as the man who lives with wisdom. For she is more beautiful than the sun, and excels every constellation of the stars. Compared with the light she is found to be superior, for it is succeeded by the night, but against wisdom evil does not prevail" (Wis 7:22–30).

40. "All wisdom comes from the Lord and is with him for ever . . . Wisdom was created before all things, and prudent understanding from eternity. The root of wisdom – to whom has it been revealed? Her clever devices – who knows them? There is One who is wise, greatly to be feared, sitting upon his throne" (Sir 1:1, 4, 6–8). "Then the Creator of all things gave me a commandment, and the one who created me assigned a place for my tent. And he said, 'Make your dwelling in Jacob, and in Israel receive your inheritance.' From eternity, in the beginning, he created me, and for eternity I shall not cease to exist" (Sir 24:8–9).

41. J. Auer, *Die Welt – Gottes Schöpfung*, 2nd ed. (Regensburg: F. Pustet, 1983), 38 (author's translation).

were made (John's prologue), and with the Christ through whom, for whom, and in whom the world was created (Paul), are quite obvious. Wisdom, though used in the feminine in the Old Testament (*chokhmah* in Hebrew, *sophia* in Greek) and in general usage,[42] becomes fully personified[43] in the New. Indeed it becomes a Messianic title. Christ identifies himself with it (Mt 23:34; Lk 11:49–50).[44] Interestingly, Church Fathers hesitated between attributing the term to Christ or to the Holy Spirit. But with time the former prevailed.[45] Christ is the eternal Wisdom of the Father.

CREATION THROUGH THE WORD IN THE PROLOGUE OF JOHN

The relevant texts of John's prologue (Jn 1:1–18) read as follows (beginning with vv. 1–5):[46]

In the beginning was the Word, and the Word was with God, and the Word was God. He was in the beginning with God; all things were made through him, and without him was not anything made that was made. In him was life, and the life was the light of men. [Notably, vv. 3–4 may alternatively be translated as follows: *All things were made through him and without him nothing was made. All things made in him were life, and life was the light of men*]. The light shines in the darkness, and the darkness has not overcome it.

42. Von Rad, *Weisheit in Israel*; E.-B. Allo, "Sagesse et Pneuma dans la première épître aux Corinthiens," *Revue Biblique* 43 (1934): 321–46; L. Bouyer, *Sophia, ou, le monde en Dieu* (Paris: Cerf, 1994); Trublet (ed.), *La sagesse biblique*; M. Cimosa (ed.), *La sapienza nella Bibbia* (Rome: Borla, 2013).

43. A. M. Sinnott, *The Personification of Wisdom* (Aldershot: Ashgate, 2005).

44. S. Kim, *The Origin of Paul's Gospel*, 3rd ed. (Tübingen: J. C. B. Mohr, 1985), 173–339; Feuillet-Congar, *La Christ sagesse.*

45. Theophilus (*Ad Autolycum* II.15) and Irenaeus (*Adv. Haer.* IV, 20:1–3) both apply the term "Wisdom" to the Holy Spirit, whereas Augustine (*De Trinitate* VII, 3:5) and Thomas Aquinas (*ST* I, q. 38, a. 8; III, q. 3, a. 8) identify it with the Son.

46. M.-É. Boismard, *Le prologue de saint Jean* (Paris: Cerf, 1953); A. Feuillet, *Le prologue du quatrième Evangile: étude de théologie johannique* (Paris: Desclée de Brouwer, 1968); G. R. Beasley-Murray, *John*, WBC 36 (Waco, Tex.: Word Books, 1987), 1–15; E. L. Miller, *Salvation-History in the Prologue of John: The Significance of John 1:3–4* (Leiden: E. J. Brill, 1989); M. Endo, *Creation and Christology: A Study on the Johannine Prologue in the Light of Early Jewish Creation Accounts* (Tübingen: J. C. B. Mohr, 2002); D. J. MacLeod, "The Creation of the Universe by the Word," *Bibliotheca Sacra* 160 (2003): 187–201; R. Fabris, "Creazione nel *Logos* e nascita da Dio in Giovanni," in *Creazione e salvezza* (ed. Fabbri and Tábet), 213–25; P. Borgen, *The Gospel of John: More Light from Philo, Paul and Archaeology: The Scriptures, Tradition, Exposition, Settings, Meaning* (Leiden: Brill, 2014); J. G. Van der Watt, R. A. Culpepper, and U. Schnelle (eds.), *The Prologue of the Gospel of John: Its Literary, Theological, and Philosophical Contexts* (Tübingen: Mohr Siebeck, 2016).

Verses 6–8 recount the witness of John the Baptist to the light. The text continues (vv. 9–11):

> The true light that enlightens every man was coming into the world [*kosmos*]. He [the Word] was in the world, and the world was made through him, yet the world knew him not. He came to his own home, and his own people received him not.

Verses 12–13 explain John's understanding of divine filiation. Then comes the culmination of the prologue (v. 14):

> And the Word became flesh and dwelt among us, full of grace and truth; we have beheld his glory, glory as of the only Son from the Father.

Verse 15 provides the second witness of John the Baptist stating that Jesus was "before [*prōtos*] him." John continues (vv. 16–18):

> And from his fullness have we all received, grace upon grace. For the law was given through Moses; grace and truth came through Jesus Christ. No one has ever seen God; the only Son, who is in the bosom of the Father, he has made him known.

On this singularly beautiful, dense, and important text of the New Testament Augustine made the following comment:

> And I sought a way of acquiring strength sufficient to enjoy You; but I found it not until I embraced that "Mediator between God and man, the man Christ Jesus" (1 Tim 2:5), "who is over all, God blessed forever" (Rom 9:5), calling unto me, and saying, "I am the way, the truth, and the life" (Jn 14:6), and mingling that food which I was unable to receive with our flesh. For "the Word was made flesh" (Jn 1:14), that Your wisdom, by which You created all things, might provide milk for our infancy.[47]

And Edwin C. Hoskyns explains the teaching the fourth Gospel in the following terms: "That Jesus once spoke is more fundamental for the understanding of the *Logos* than is the history of Greek philosophy, or the story of the westward progress of oriental mysticism, more fundamental even than the first chapter of Genesis or the eighth chapter of Proverbs."[48]

The teaching of John's prologue may be presented briefly in the follow-

47. Augustine, *Confessions* VIII, 18:24.

48. E. C. Hoskyns, *The Fourth Gospel*, 2nd ed. (London: Faber and Faber, 1948), 137.

ing five stages: (1) God and the Word are one and the same (vv. 1, 12, 14, 18), although (2) there is a personal difference between the Father and the Son (vv. 1, 18); (3) but the Word is particularly present to creation, because "all things were made through him" (v. 3) and "in him was life and the life was the light of men" (v. 4), the play of words between "life" and "light" offering a key insight into the kind of presence the Word enjoys among creatures; (4) the Word, coming into the world created through him is not recognized by the world (vv. 10–11), and especially by his own people, on account of the darkness and gloom introduced by sin that kills life and quenches light; and (5) for this reason the Word, life and light, became flesh to save the world, reveal Wisdom, and bring creation back to the Father (vv. 1, 4, 9, 14, 17). Again, as we saw in other biblical passages, creation is totally tied up with salvation.

As regards John's doctrine of creation in the prologue, the following seven observations may be made. First, that creation is an entirely divine work; creatures have no involvement whatsoever in bringing it into existence. The Word is not a mere intermediate instrument, a Demiurge, a first creature, a created creator. Rather he is with God and is God. The text does not say that the Word was a god,[49] such as might suggest a lesser, intermediate being. In fact the Word's divinity is clearly affirmed here and elsewhere throughout John's Gospel: "before Abraham was, I am" (Jn 8:58).

Second, God created the world through the Word. The expression applied by Paul to Christ, *dia autou*, is employed here. Thus the Word is presented as the "mediator" of creation. Certainly John uses terminology that is frequent in Greek philosophy, that of Plato and Philo especially. This is of help in understanding the text, although the prologue goes beyond the tenets of the philosophers on many fronts. Besides, the prologue evokes Genesis, as we saw already,[50] as well as Proverbs and Wisdom. This helps us to situate and understand the text, which is ultimately meant to present the person and saving work of Jesus Christ, the Son of God, eternal Word of God made man.

In the third place, because the Word is *one with God*, as we have just seen, then his mediating role cannot be merely passive or passing; the

49. Beasley-Murray, *John*, 10.

50. Borgen, *The Gospel of John*; Schwarz, "Gen 1, 1–2,2a und Joh 1.1a.3a."

Word is not a mere created, temporary intermediary. It is not as if the Word offers the Father a series of possible blueprints which God could then choose from and follow in making the universe. In effect, the mediation of the Word is not accidental, occasional, or temporary, one that comes to a close as soon as the work of creation is over. Rather, the Word's mediation is as continuous, profound, and direct as it is divine. Perhaps for this reason the Book of Revelation—close to the Johannine corpus—speaks of Christ as the origin or principle (*archē*) of creation (Rv 3:14),[51] as "the Alpha and the Omega, the beginning and the end" (Rv 21:6; 22:13). The idea that God is the beginning and end of the universe is common in religious visions contemporaneous with Christianity.[52] But here the Word's mediation is both *profound* on account of the divinity of the Word, and *concrete* due to the fact of the incarnation. In brief terms, we may say that the creative mediation of the Word is active, enduring, and dynamic, not merely passive, accomplished, and static, because creation takes place not only through the Word but also in the Word.

Fourth, created entities receive existence, permanence in being, intelligibility, and vitality from the inexhaustible existence, permanence, intelligibility, and vitality of the Word, that is, they *receive life* from the one who has received it from the Father. Indeed, the Word's mediation may be expressed as a kind of continuous vivifying presence. In presenting the text of the prologue I mentioned a variant in the translation of verses 3–4: "All things made in him were life."[53] The variant brings out an important aspect of role the Word plays in creating the world, which is more than that of an architect or a teacher; in fact, he is *the living source of all life*, a doctrine confirmed later on in John's Gospel: "For as the Father raises the dead and gives them life, so also the Son gives life to whom he will. . . .

51. C. F. Burney, "Christ as the APXH of Creation," *Journal of Theological Studies* 17 (1926): 160–77; C. Doglio, "La creazione 'nuova' secondo l'Apocalisse," in *Creazione e salvezza* (ed. Fabbri and Tábet), 227–67.

52. "Zeus is the beginning, Zeus is the middle, all things are fulfilled by Zeus." Orphic poem, *Derveni papyrus*, 350 B.C., cited in Aune, *Revelation 1–5*, 1126. Hippocrates, imitating Heraclitus, refers to the beginning and end as a kind of unbroken circle (Diels-Kranz, *Die Fragmente der Vorsokratiker*, 1:189): "The beginning of everything is one and the end of everything is one and the end and the beginning are the same." The emperor Marcus Aurelius says that the soul "that knows the beginning and the end" knows the *Logos* that penetrates the universe, that is, God (*Meditations* 5:32).

53. On the correct translation of the text, see I. De la Potterie, "De interpunctione et interpretatione Jo 1, 3–4," *Verbum Caro* 9 (1955): 193–208, and Feuillet, *Le prologue*, 37–64.

For the Father has life in himself, so he has granted the Son also to have life in himself" (Jn 5:21, 26). The God of the Old Testament of course is the God of life, the one who has life in fullness and communicates it to us with almighty power.[54] Pagan gods on the contrary are primarily receptive to life and thus incapable of natively imparting it; unable to take care of themselves, they are the work of human hands, standing in need of human support, with no vital power of their own. Yet the life Christ has received from the Father he divinely imparts it to creatures: he is the only Lord.

Fifth, whereas according to Colossians 1:16 the world was made for Christ, John's Gospel does not clearly say that the world was made *for* the Word. Still, the Book of Revelation, which is closely associated with the Johannine corpus, does say that the Word incarnate is the one who has obtained sovereignty over the world by means of his voluntary immolation on the cross (Rv 4–5). This may be seen in Revelation 4:11: "Worthy are you, our Lord and God, to receive glory and honor and power, for you created all things, and by your will they existed and were created."[55] Besides, it says, Christ is "the Alpha and *the Omega*, the beginning [*archē*] and the end [*tēlos*]" (Rv 21:6). The hymn of praise that constitutes the high-point of the Book of Revelation presents Christ as Lord and goal of creation. So creation may be said to take place not only through the Word, or in the Word, but also for the Word, the ultimate source of life at every stage of the existence of the universe.[56]

Sixth, sin obscures human awareness of the living presence of the Word in creation. "He was in the world, and the world was made through him, yet the world knew him not. He came to his own home, and his own people received him not" (Jn 1:10–11). This text resonates openly with Wisdom 13:1–9 and Romans 1:18–22, which speak of the "obviousness" of

54. F. Mussner, *Zoë: Die Anschauung vom «Leben» im vierten Evangelium unter Berücksichtigung der Johannesbriefe. Ein Beitrag zur biblischen Theologie* (Munich: K. Zink, 1952); F. Asensio, *Trayectoria teológica de la vida en el AT y su proyección en el Nuevo* (Madrid: CSIC, 1968).

55. Rv 4:11: "Worthy are you, our Lord and God, to receive glory and honor and power, for you created all things, and by your will they existed and were created." As regards the question of the pre-existence of creation, "one of the major difficulties of this clause, reflected in the variety of textual variants extant, is the apparently illogical order of the verbs ἦσαν, 'they were,' ie, 'they existed,' and ἐκτίσθησαν, 'they were created'; ie, the 'existence' of everything seems to precede creation. This can perhaps be explained as an instance of *hysteron-proteron*, ie, the inversion of events, which sometimes occurs in Revelation." Aune, *Revelation 1–5*, 312, with references to Rv 3:17; 5:2, 5; 6:4; 10:4, 9; 19:13.

56. McFarland, *From Nothing*, 34–42.

God's presence in creation and the blindness in humans induced by sin. Through the incarnation God wanted to bring the world back to himself by vivifying our awareness of the Word already present among and within creatures. Thus through the faith involved in conversion, *life,* the life given to the world by the Word, becomes *light.* Life becomes anew the light of men (v. 4), overcoming the darkness of sin (v. 6). Again, creation and salvation are seen to relate closely to one another.

Seventh and last, the earthly life and death of Jesus on the cross provides a definitive manifestation of divine Wisdom and understanding of creation.[57] It might seem that the incarnation of the Word hides wisdom behind the weakness of the flesh[58] rather than actually revealing it. However, God wished to reveal his wisdom precisely in and through the smallness, weakness, and ordinariness of the life of Christ: his birth in Bethlehem, the flight into Egypt, the long, work-filled, "irrelevant" years in Nazareth, the opposition and scandal occasioned by his preaching, and eventually the betrayal and ignominious death on the cross. To human eyes this was scandalous: divine Wisdom, God's Word and intelligence, made common cause with fragility, weakness, and mortality.

The divine logic of the incarnation is shown in two ways. On the one hand, it shows that God's self-giving and revelation in Christ has become extraordinarily direct and accessible to humanity. The beauty and light and approachability of Jesus' words and life are undeniable. On the other hand, the incarnation of the Word in weak and mortal flesh provides perhaps the true key to understanding the reality of divine Wisdom, God's own Word: the word of God and his wisdom speak with greater power through the death and apparent weakness of Christ, for they do not impose but rather convince. The deepest knowledge of the interior reality of the created world, of its total dependence on God, of its "own" nothingness and inner orientation toward a transcendent end, derives from and is revealed in Christ. And this is Christ on the cross, the Word through whom, in whom, and for whom the world was made. Christ, dying on the cross, renounced, in order to do the will of his Father, the greatest and most noble created good, human life itself, in that way showing not only the fidelity and

57. On the motif of "Christ reveals man to man" from Vatican Council II, *Gaudium et Spes,* December 7, 1965 [hereafter *GS*], no. 22, see O'Callaghan, *Children of God in the World,* 64–85.

58. On the notion and role of flesh in scripture, see ibid., 411–13.

intensity of his love for humanity (Jn 15:13), but also the inner reality of the created world.

Christ and the Mystery of Creation

In the words of Ethelbert Stauffer, in Christ God "destroys his creation, in order to erect it again to perfection."[59] The death of Christ reveals the nothingness of the universe, while his glorious resurrection reveals its divine origin, the inexhaustible power of the creator, the purpose of the universe and its eternal vocation. Speaking of Athanasius's presentation of creation, Khaled Anatolios observes: "Death is a recurring demonstration of creation's being from nothing, in the negative mode of its sinful being-towards-nothing, *creatio ad nihilum*."[60] And finally, in the words of Giuseppe Colombo: "Jesus Christ is the demonstration of the possibility of creation understood as the *ad extra* communication of God's being. In this way Jesus Christ reveals the meaning of creation; he reveals, that is, that creation is the action of God to communicate Trinitarian life *ad extra*."[61]

59. E. Stauffer, *Die Theologie des Neuen Testaments,* 3rd ed. (Stuttgart: W. Kohlhammer, 1947), 206.

60. K. Anatolios, "*Creatio ex nihilo* in Athanasius of Alexandria's *Against the Greeks–On the Incarnation,*" in *Creation ex nihilo* (ed. Anderson et al.), 119–49, at 145. See also Anatolios, *Athanasius: The Coherence of His Thought* (London: Routledge, 1998).

61. G. Barbaglio and G. Colombo, "Creazione," in *Nuovo Dizionario di Teologia,* ed. G. Barbaglio and S. Dianich (Milan: Paoline, 1979), 184–210, at 201 (author's translation).

4

The History of the Doctrine of Creation

The New Testament confirms the profound conviction present throughout the Old to the effect that God created the universe, whole and entire, without presuppositions of any kind. It adds little to our understanding of the *fact* of creation, but does provide decisive indications as regards the *how* and the *why* of creation. Granted, Old Testament teaching on the word of God and on Wisdom paves the way for what Paul and John teach about creation through Christ and for Christ. But the true contribution of the New Testament lies in *how* creation takes place and *why* God brings it into existence in the first place: through, in, and for the incarnate Word, Jesus Christ. Interestingly David Fergusson notes that "the scientific account of the *how* of creation can . . . sit alongside the theological account of its *why*."[1]

In the present chapter, however, we shall consider the principal moments of the development of the fact of creation over the centuries, from the earliest times, through the Church Fathers; through medieval and modern theologians in dialogue with Platonism, Gnosticism, pantheism, and contemporary ontologies; and finally in official church teaching.[2] The next chapter will examine a specific issue—particularly present among Church Fathers—of the creation of the world through the divine *Logos* who became flesh in Jesus Christ.

1. Fergusson, "Creation," 74.
2. See esp. Scheffczyk, *Schöpfung und Vorsehung*.

Early Church Fathers on Creation

Admittedly, the apostolic Church Fathers added little to the biblical message.[3] They probably did not feel the need to do so. The *Shepherd of Hermas* (150 A.D.) gave expression to the Christian understanding of creation on the basis of 2 Maccabees 7:28, saying: "first of all believe that there is one God who created and finished and made all things out of nothing, he is able to contain the whole, but himself cannot be contained."[4] The *Didaché* has the same teaching.[5] The *Letter to Barnabas* offers the following prescription to believers: "You shall love Him that created you: you shall glorify Him that redeemed you from death."[6]

The apologists in the second and third centuries insist more openly on the doctrine of creation in the context of preaching the Christian gospel to the Greeks. Olof Gigon describes the view of Greek philosophers contemporaneous with early Christendom in the following terms.

> Coming to existence is for ancient thought always an arising "out of self," not a being created by some superior, already subsisting, reality. The idea of a Creator is in no way Greek, even though approximations may have been made to it.... What we call "creator" would be understood in Greek thought as putting something already existing in movement.... There is no creator in the strict sense of the term since the Greeks did not want to accept the idea of a being arising out of nothing.... What makes the concept of creation impossible for Greek thought is that the origin is always thought of objectively and never personally.[7]

That is to say, for the Greeks one thing gives rise to another, but not a person to the whole.

Stoics and Middle Platonists taught that God was the origin of the universe, the principle of all that exists.[8] But with Philo of Alexandria, a Jewish philosopher and contemporary of Jesus, and others, they began to

3. See P. Bouteneff, *Beginnings: Ancient Christian Readings of the Biblical Creation Narratives* (Grand Rapids, Mich.: Baker Academic, 2008).

4. Shepherd of Hermas, *Commands* 1.

5. *Didaché* 1:2 and 5:2.

6. *Letter to Barnabas,* 19:2.

7. O. Gigon, *Der Ursprung der griechischen Philosophie: von Hesiod bis Parmenides* (Basel: Benno, Schwabe and Co., 1945), 33, cited by C. Schönborn, "Catechesi della creazione e teoria dell'evoluzione (dalla tregua al conflitto costruttivo)," *Communio (ed. italiana)* 15, no. 100 (1988): 30–46, at 31.

8. See Aristides, *Apol.* 1:2–3; Justin, *2 Apol.* 6:10; Tatian, *Or. ad Graecos* 4:3.

insist on the mediating function of the *Logos* (or Word) in creation, understood of course in a subordinationist key, for the *Logos* was considered as inferior to God. Early Christian writers tended to follow them on this.[9] I shall consider these authors in greater detail in the next chapter.

Yet what gave life and depth and precision to the Christian doctrine of creation in the second and third centuries A.D. was the challenge presented by different forms of dualism and Gnosticism. Claude Tresmontant observed that "the first heresy, the fundamental heresy of Christianity, is not related to doctrines on the Son, or the theology of the Trinity or the Incarnation; but rather it is the heresy about God as Creator."[10] Hans Urs von Balthasar points out that the acceptance of God as the creator of *matter* was "the greatest scandal for the mind" during the early centuries of Christianity.[11] Christoph Schönborn, speaking again of the creation of matter, puts it as follows: "no aspect of Christian doctrine of creation encountered so much resistance as this one; no point was defended by Christian theologians more vehemently than this one.... The question of the creation of matter in a certain sense was the key to grasping the entire Christian message."[12]

The Orthodox theologian Georges Florovsky is even more radical:

> The idea of creation is alien to "natural" consciousness. Classical, Hellenistic thought did not know it. Modern philosophy has forgotten it. Given in the Bible it is disclosed and manifested in the living experience of the Church.... Creation is neither self-existent being, nor transitory becoming; neither eternal "substance," nor illusory "appearance." In creaturehood a great wonder is revealed: the world also might not have existed at all. And that which might not have existed, for which there are no inevitable causes or bases, does exist. This is a riddle, a "foolishness" for "natural" thought.[13]

9. See Justin, *Dial.* 61:3–4; Theophilus of Alexandria, *Ad Autoclycum* 1:3.

10. Tresmontant, *La métaphysique du christianisme,* 89.

11. Cited by Schönborn, "Catechesi della creazione," 34.

12. Ibid., 32.

13. G. Florovsky, "Creation and Creaturehood," in his *Creation and Redemption* (Belmont, N.Y.: Nordland, 1976), 51.

Irenaeus, Theophilus, and Later Church Fathers on Creation *ex nihilo*

The two principal defenders of the doctrine of creation *ex nihilo*, "from nothing," were Irenaeus of Lyons and Theophilus of Antioch.[14] Both of them held that if God had not created the world from nothing, then he would no longer be sovereign over creation. Irenaeus, an important second-century adversary of Gnosticism, stated the doctrine of God the creator as follows. "This is the methodical teaching of our faith, the basis of its edification, the foundation of salvation. God the Father, who is not created, not generated, is the Creator of all: this is the first article of our faith."[15] He teaches that the profession of faith in creation from nothingness (*ex nihilo*) is an exact complement of the teaching of God's perfect sovereignty over all things. The world is created *ex nihilo* because God is the only Lord of the universe. Irenaeus is convinced that this article of the creed on its own is capable of destroying Gnosticism entirely. To retain that matter,

> the visible world is a *fructus labilis*, fruit of the fall, that it is *ignorantia prolatio*, the product of ignorance, is for Irenaeus "the great blasphemy," because this would mean that the forces that made the world did so out of ignorance.... A world that has been produced out of complete ignorance cannot in any way exist for the glory of the Creator, it is blind and without light, it is a place of darkness, created out of *vacuitas*, emptiness, and it will eventually turn back to nothingness.[16]

That is to say, creation *ex nihilo* and divine omnipotence are doctrinally equivalent to one another.[17] The following three texts of Irenaeus's *Adversus Haereses* are indicative of this position.

14. J. C. O'Neill, "How Early is the Doctrine of *Creatio ex Nihilo*?," *Journal of Theological Studies* 58 (2002): 449–65, holds that *creatio ex nihilo* is already to be found in the New Testament.

15. Irenaeus, *Demonstr.* 6; see A. Orbe, "San Ireneo y la creación de la materia," *Gregorianum* 59, no. 1 (1978): 71–127.

16. Schönborn, "Catechesi della creazione," 34.

17. See Irenaeus, *Adv. Haer.* II, 1:1; 10:4; IV, 20:1. See R. F. Brown, "On the Necessary Imperfection of Creation: Irenaeus' Adversus haereses IV, 38," *Scottish Journal of Theology* 28 (1975): 17–25; Orbe, "San Ireneo y la creación de la materia"; J. Fantino, "La création 'ex nihilo' chez saint Irénée," *Revue des sciences philosophiques et théologiques* 76, no. 3 (1992): 421–42; M. C. Steenberg, *Irenaeus on Creation: The Cosmic Christ and the Saga of Redemption* (Leiden: E. J. Brill, 2008); S. O. Presley, *The Intertextual Reception of Genesis 1–3 in Irenaeus of Lyons* (Leiden: E. J. Brill, 2015). On the nature of divine omnipotence, see also P. O'Callaghan, "Un'onnipotenza paterna o una paternità onnipotente?," *PATH* 17 (2018): 35–47.

I should begin with the first and most important principle, that is, God the Creator, who made the heaven and the earth, and all things therein ... and to demonstrate that there is nothing either above Him or after Him; nor that, influenced by any one, but of His own free will, He created all things, since He is the only God, the only Lord, the only Creator, the only Father, alone containing all things, and Himself commanding all things into existence.[18]

For, to attribute the substance of created things to the power and will of Him who is God of all, is worthy both of credit and acceptance. It is also agreeable [to reason]. ... While men, indeed, cannot make anything *out of nothing,* but only out of matter already existing, yet God is in this point pre-eminently superior to men, that He Himself called into being the substance of His creation, when previously it had no existence.[19]

God is so great that it is He who by Himself has established, and selected, and adorned, and contains all things; and among all things, both ourselves and this our world. We also then were made, along with those things which are contained by Him. ... For God did not stand in need of these [beings] ... as if He did not possess His own hands. For with Him were always present the Word and Wisdom, the Son and the Spirit, by whom and in whom, freely and spontaneously, He made all things.[20]

Robin Lane Fox is quite correct to note that, among the authors of the second century, "it is the Christians who are most confident and assured," and that the "magnificent optimism" of Irenaeus of Lyons and the almost innocent cheerfulness of Justin Martyr stand out as distinctively and unmistakably Christian characteristics.[21]

The second-century bishop Theophilus of Antioch considers the question of creation in depth, in the context of the Platonic conviction that matter exists eternally. He opposed an important work by the Gnostic author Hermogenes,[22] likewise criticized by Tertullian.[23] Hermogenes defended the Platonic principle of eternal unformed matter out of which

18. Irenaeus, *Adv. Haer.* II, 1:1.

19. Ibid., II, 10:4.

20. Ibid., IV, 20:1.

21. See R. Lane Fox, *Pagans and Christians in the Mediterranean World* (San Francisco, Calif.: Harper and Row, 1986), 331, cited by Hart, *Atheist Delusions,* 144.

22. Eusebius refers to a work of Theophilus, *Against the Heresy of Hermogenes,* in his *Eccl. Hist.* 4:24.

23. See Tertullian, *Adv. Hermog.* 2.

God made the world. But Theophilus rejected this because otherwise matter would be placed on same plane with the divinity, whose sovereignty would be compromised. The dilemmas faced by Christians are clarified in the following extensive citation of Theophilus.

Plato and those of his school acknowledge indeed that God is uncreated, and the Father and Maker of all things; but then they maintain that matter as well as God is uncreated, and teach that it is coeval with God. But if God is uncreated and matter uncreated, God is no longer, according to the Platonists, the Creator of all things, nor, so far as their opinions hold, is the sovereignty of God established. And further, as God, because He is uncreated, is also unalterable; so if matter, too, were uncreated, it also would be unalterable, and equal to God; for that which is created is mutable and alterable, but that which is uncreated is immutable and unalterable. And what great thing is it if God made the world out of existent materials? For even a human artist, when he gets material from some one, makes of it what he pleases. But the power of God is manifested in this, that *out of things that are not* He makes whatever He pleases; just as the bestowal of life and motion is the prerogative of no other than God alone. For even man makes indeed an image, but reason and breath, or feeling, he cannot give to what he has made. But God has this property in excess of what man can do, in that He makes a work, endowed with reason, life, sensation. As, therefore, in all these respects God is more powerful than man, so also in this; that *out of things that are not* He creates and has created things that are, and whatever He pleases, as He pleases.[24]

Contemporaries of Irenaeus and Theophilus, such as Aristides[25] and Tatian,[26] confirmed this position, associating creation *ex nihilo* with divine sovereignty and freedom in the act of creation.

The same position as regards creation *ex nihilo* is held consistently by other Church Fathers. Tertullian developed it, and coined the Latin expression *creatio ex nihilo*.[27] Origen said he was amazed that anybody might claim that that matter existed eternally.[28] John Chrysostom taught that Moses "eradicates all the heresies that swarm in the Church when he

24. Theophilus, *Ad Autocl.* II, 4.

25. See Aristides, *Apol.* I, 4.

26. See Tatian, *Or.* 5, 7. See M. Elze, *Tatian und seine Theologie* (Göttingen: Vandenhoeck and Ruprecht, 1960).

27. See May, *Creatio ex nihilo*, 145–47.

28. See Origen, *De principiis* II, 1:4.

says 'In the beginning God created the heavens and the earth.' If a Manichaean comes to tell you that matter pre-existed, or Marcion or Valentinus, or a pagan, just say to them: 'In the beginning God created the heavens and the earth.'"[29]

And Augustine,[30] who was profoundly familiar with Platonic doctrine, says in his *Confessions*: "For you, Lord, have made the world of a formless matter, *that almost nothing you made from nothing*, out of which to make those great things which we, sons of men, wonder at."[31] "Why, therefore," he continues, "may I not consider the formlessness of matter—which You had created without shape, out of which to make this shapely world—to be fittingly intimated unto men by the name of earth invisible and formless?"[32] A similar position to that of Augustine may be found in the words of the first century Rabbi Gamaliel II to a philosopher who says to him: "Your God was indeed a great artist, but surely He found good pigments which assist him." To which the Rabbi replied: "God made the colors, too!"[33]

But we may still ask what was the doctrine of Irenaeus and Theophilus, of Tatian and Aristides, of Tertullian and Origen and Augustine reacting to? Let us examine that now.

Situating Christian Doctrine on Creation: Platonism, Gnosticism, Pantheism

Christian thinkers, as we have just seen, took a stance and developed their theology with respect to and in contrast with three understandings of reality and the origin of the world in vogue: the Platonic (or spiritualist), the Gnostic, and the pantheistic. To the latter may be appended other contemporary ontologies. Let us consider them briefly.

The Orthodox theologian John Zizioulas says:

29. John Chrysostom, *Hom. 11 in cap. 1 Gen.*, 3.

30. See J. C. Cavadini, "*Creatio ex nihilo* in the Thought of Saint Augustine," in *Creation ex nihilo* (ed. Anderson et al.), 151–71, holds that creation *ex nihilo* is very central for Augustine. See also J. Torchia, Creatio ex nihilo *and the Theology of St. Augustine: The Anti-Manichaean Polemic and Beyond* (New York: Peter Lang, 1999); R. D. Williams, "'Good for Nothing'? Augustine on Creation," *Augustinian Studies* 25 (1994): 9–24.

31. Augustine, *Confessions* XII, 8 (emphasis added).

32. Ibid., 4.

33. Cited by Soskice, *Creatio ex nihilo*, 33.

The Christian doctrine of creation began in response to Gnosticism and Platonism. To Gnosticism, the Church responded by linking the "Creator" to the "Father" to stress the direct involvement of God in creation. The Church responded to Platonism with the expression "creation from nothing," meaning "from no existing material or ideas." It responded to middle Platonism and Neoplatonism by stating that the world did not eternally exist as a thought of the mind (*nous*) of God, but that its existence was the result of the will of God. Because this will was related to the Son of God, the *Logos*, creation took place and the world became a real entity through a relationship of love, without ever constituting a necessity for God.[34]

PLATONISM

The philosopher Plato was particularly interested in the spiritual and religious aspect of human life and the world.[35] The same may be said of Platonic thought as a whole. Platonism inquired into the invisible world of Forms and therefore into the spiritual relationship between humans and the divinity. Key to Plato's philosophy is his search for endurance, for permanence, for immortality. Philosophy—the love of wisdom—is meant to train humans to obtain eternal happiness. According to Platonists, humans are meant to strive to identify with all that is permanent, lasting, spiritual, and divine. But that is no easy task, for immortality and permanence are hidden, deformed, or dispersed on account of the material world in which reality is immersed. At best our encounter with matter offers us the occasion to awaken a reminiscence of what the spirit originally contemplated in the world of Forms, a remembrance lost due to the fall of the human soul into the darkness of matter, as Plato recounts in his work *Timaeus*. Humans are thus invited to live a virtuous life, heroically if needs be, detaching themselves from everything that is changeable, material, corruptible, everything that can weaken their union with the divine. According to John Zizioulas the Platonic world should "be perceived as an extension of God . . . who is the logical and cohesive force contained within nature."[36]

34. Zizioulas, "Creation and Salvation," 88.

35. See M. V. Fabbri, "Creatore e demiurgo: fede biblica e platonismo a confronto," in *Creazione e salvezza* (ed. Fabbri and Tábet), 119–65, esp. 119–34. Plato is a complex and highly influential author. I will not be studying Plato the philosopher in detail in these pages, but rather his philosophy, Platonism, and those aspects of his thought which principally impacted later authors and influenced thought forms.

36. Zizioulas, "Creation and Salvation," 84.

Besides, continues Zizioulas, "the laws of space and matter resist the Creator's efforts to conform them completely to the perfect forms."[37] In fact, the Greeks "made no radical distinction between created and uncreated. When they talked about the creation of a thing, they meant only that it used to exist in a form different from its present form."[38]

In spite of his penchant for personal spirituality, Plato pays considerable attention to life in society, the *polis,* to human development and shared happiness, to politics, insofar as it plays an essential part in the life of humans, in the process of "salvation" and immortality, which involves permanent union with the divine. But on the whole he neglects the material side of things; for this reason he considers scientific investigation a vain pursuit.[39] This superiority of the eternal, of the spiritual, and of the immortal over the mutable and the material that Plato defends is present to some degree in the theological and pastoral view inherited by many Church Fathers, among them Clement of Alexandria, Origen, and Augustine.

Let us consider the Platonic view of the origin of the world in respect of three elements: the divinity, the *human soul,* and the *material cosmos* and evil. Plato was unsure what to say about divine nature. "It is a hard task to find the maker and father of this universe," he says speaking of the Demiurge who gives shape to the world, "and having found him it would be impossible to proclaim him to humanity."[40] The God of Plato—whom he calls the Good—is not a personal, active, transcendent, and unique divinity. Humans enjoy different degrees of access to numerous divinities and finite personifications of the divine: the Demiurge, the cosmic Soul, gods, the souls of heroes and humans. The reason why humans can know the divine to an important extent lies in the fact that they, or better their soul (*psyche*), is a part, or product, or emanation of the divine.[41] The spiritual knows the spiritual. In fact a hint of pantheism may be found here. A solid hierarchical structuring may be found between all the different elements that go to make up the universe, starting from the supreme divinity right

37. Ibid., 85.

38. Ibid., 92.

39. See Plato, *Phaedo* 98.

40. Plato, *Timaeus* 28c.

41. Philo applies the term "emanation" to creation, as does Gregory of Nyssa (*Vita Moysis* I, 24) and in his own way, Thomas Aquinas (*ST* I, q. 45, a. 1).

down to worthless matter. True philosophers are meant to actualize or enliven the divinity of their own soul as they distance themselves ever more from matter.[42]

The *material cosmos*, however, is marked by obscurity, mutability, and corruptibility. It cannot share in the soul's union with the divine. This was something Plato simply took for granted. Union with the divine involves necessarily detaching oneself from the material world, because its mutability and corruptibility contrast with the immortality and spirituality the soul aspires to. This may be explained in the following four stages. First, material things are changeable and ephemeral; hence they are unreal, or at best, they enjoy a minimum level of existence, as the neo-Platonist Plotinus holds. Second, the senses give us the impression that *spirit is unreal* and that *matter is real*. But in fact matter is unreal, because it does not possess the features of true reality that belongs fundamentally to the spiritual, as we just saw; hence the senses are not dependable insofar as they fool us. Third, matter is simply nondivine. Plato detected some intelligibility in material entities, although he held to the existence of *prime matter*, a permanent, noncreated, independent substrate on which the divine forms are impressed. Fourth, concrete things, once-off actions, temporality, history, all that is specific, limited, and linked with the material . . . all this belongs to a transient world and is of little theological or spiritual importance. Material things are apparent, fleeting, negative. At best, single actions enter into the vast cycles of the eternal return and are lost within them. Their peculiarity and individuality come and go within an eternal dialectic, as parts that disappear in order to constitute the whole, not having any value or consistency on their own.

It may be noted that, for obvious reasons, Plato was unaware of an element that was very central in the Christian view of things, which is that salvation, or union with the divine, and the reception of immortality, are all the *work of divine grace*, God's own work. For Platonists humans had to establish their union with the divine through their own efforts. For Christians of course this is the result of grace received in faith. The difference between the two positions is fundamentally, of course, insurmountable. As Josef Pieper concludes, any attempt at "making Plato a Christian shows

42. On the soul, see O'Callaghan, *Children of God in the World*, 408–30.

simply that you have become a pagan."[43] For Plato the soul is divine and matter is corruptible, whereas for Christians both are equally creatures, created *ex nihilo*. In the coming chapter, I shall consider some elements of the contrast between the Platonic and Christian view of origin of the cosmos.

GNOSTICISM

Let us now consider the position of Gnostic thinkers. The Platonic idea that the soul in some ways is part of the divinity may be found anew in this important philosophical and theological movement that was very influential in early Christianity during the second century A.D. It is commonly called Gnosticism.[44] Other factors contributed to the development of this view—it "began from the premise that the world we know is fraught with evil, which reflected the widespread pessimism of the time"[45]—but a clear continuity with Platonic dualism and disdain for matter may be detected. From a doctrinal standpoint it was probably the gravest threat that nascent Christianity suffered, and it left a very clear mark on the consolidation of the doctrine of creation.

The Gnostic cosmology of the second-century philosopher Marcion was determined by his rejection of the Old Testament, which, he claimed, is definitively outstripped and supplanted by the New. With this move the economy of the Law of Christ takes over from the Torah and the prophets. According to Marcion, with the New Testament the merciful God revealed in Jesus Christ replaces the just and angry God of the old covenant, the Savior takes over from the creator. Besides, he holds that the material world was not created by God at all but by an evil spirit, a malevolent demiurge. Hence, because matter supposes a hindrance for human freedom and the development of the spirit, it must be eliminated and overcome. As

43. See J. Pieper, *Scholasticism: Personalities and Problems of Medieval Philosophy* (London: Faber and Faber, 1960), 86.

44. For a brief introduction to Gnosticism, see H. Cornélis and A. Léonard, *La Gnose éternel* (Paris: D. Roge, 1960); K. Rudolph, *Gnosis: The Nature and History of Gnosticism* (San Francisco, Calif.: Harper and Row, 1983); A. H. B. Logan, *Gnostic Truth and Christian Heresy: A Study in the History of Gnosticism* (Edinburgh: T. and T. Clark, 1996); G. Lettieri, "Lo gnosticismo: La sua essenza e le sue origini," *Lateranum* 64 (1998): 629–48. See also Congregation for the Doctrine of the Faith, Letter *Placuit Deo* (2018), nos. 3, 11, 14.

45. Zizioulas, "Creation and Salvation," 83.

we saw earlier on, it is not that the New Testament denies the doctrine of creation; it is just that the Old Testament teaches it so clearly that the New takes it for granted, usually in the context of redemption and "new creation." But above all, the God and Father of Jesus Christ *is* the God of the Old Testament. "Concerned to preserve God's purity and transcendence," however, Gnostics claimed the world "was created by another being. . . . But the Church declared that the very opposite was true: it was God himself who had created the world. . . . The relationship that God has with the world is direct and immediate . . . whereas Gnosticism isolated God from the world."[46]

Gnostic anthropology is decidedly elitist and dualist. Marcion takes it that the "natural" man (who is carnal, not spiritual, but rather immersed in and suffocated by matter), typified by the Old Testament, cannot perceive grace, cannot live a spiritual life. But others, the "spiritual" ones, in the depths of their being are like spiritual fragments originally belonging to the divine fullness, or *plērōma*, but now detached from their origin and fallen into the darkness and alienation of matter. Hence, in order to be saved the soul must flee from matter, from all the bonds that shackle it to the world. This would involve salvation of humans *from* the world, but not salvation *of* the world. It would take place not as a work of divine grace received in faith, but as an acquiring of knowledge (*gnosis*) by which the "spiritual" ones with notable fatigue find their way back, through a detailed knowledge of a myriad of celestial places and beings and names, to their original moorings in the divinity. Christianity was considered by Gnostics to be a pure doctrine of salvation with negligible creational or cosmological implications.

Gnostic theology, particularly that of Marcion, was soundly and deeply criticized by Irenaeus in his major work *Adversus Haereses*; earlier on we saw several texts of his that powerfully affirm the fundamental place occupied by the doctrine of creation. Tertullian also criticized the Gnostics, saying in relation to Marcion that "I venerate the whole of Sacred Scripture, through which God reveals to me both the Creator and things he has made. But in the Gospel I find, besides, the One who is the minister and mediator of the Creator of the world."[47] The novelty of the New

46. Ibid.
47. Tertullian, *Adv. Hermog.* 22:3.

Testament in other words is the distinct existence of the Word/Son, not the doctrine of salvation, which was fully present in the Old, along with creation.

Both Platonism and Gnosticism are characterized by dualism, that is, that the world has a double origin. Creation in the Christian sense does not mean that all duality is absent from created reality: it is obvious that the created world involves a wide variety of polar opposites.[48] Dualism means that there are two alternative and conflictive origins to the world, God on the one hand, and the Demiurge or devil on the other. Their dialectic relationship shows up in the perennially discordant relations between different aspects of the created world, in particular between spirit and matter. And in real terms it would seem that the world will never be free from evil, for the latter is an intrinsic part of its structure. "The binary, if it is one, in *creatio ex nihilo* is not between the material world and an immaterial God," Janet Soskice observes, "but between the Creator and *everything else*—space, time, angels, souls, and so on."[49] From the metaphysical standpoint angels are much more like rocks than like God.

Likewise Platonism and Gnosticism share a doctrine of emanation, which means that the spiritual world is a product of the very substance of the divinity, belonging to it and destined to amalgamate with it anew. Whereas, as Florovsky writes, "creating is an act, and is not done out of the creator's own substance; therefore creation is heterogeneous to its creator."[50] And Richard Wallis notes: "The generation of Reality by the One is described by the Neoplatonists in terms of their well-known image of emanation. The image's underlying principle is summarized in the Scholastic maxim that 'good diffuses itself' (*bonum diffusivum sui*). In other words, entities that have achieved perfection of their own being do not keep that perfection to themselves, but spread it abroad by generating an external 'image' of their own identity."[51] But this position is not held by orthodox Christianity, for God creates the world freely, and the latter is not an extension of God.

48. On the question of polar opposites, see O'Callaghan, *Children of God in the World,* 2–5.
49. Soskice, "Why *creatio ex nihilo,*" 49.
50. Florovsky, "Creation and Creaturehood," 48, on Cyril of Alexandria, *Thesaurus* 15.
51. R. T. Wallis, *Neoplatonism,* 2nd ed. (Indianapolis, Ind.: Hackett, 1995), 61.

PANTHEISM

After Platonism and Gnosticism, I shall now consider pantheism. Both Platonists and Gnostics teach that certain elements of the created world, principally those of a spiritual kind, belong originally to the divine substance. Yet Christian thought, deeply rooted in the Old Testament, insisted time and again that divine ontology differs radically from created ontology, that God completely transcends the created world and is not conditioned by it in any way. Still, the very closeness of God to created reality (usually referred to as his "immanence" in the world), confirmed by the incarnation of God's own Word, tempted Christian thinkers to think of the relationship between creator and creature in somewhat mutual terms. In other words, just as creatures depend on God for everything, so also it might be said that God depends on the creature, because at heart creator and creature belong to one another, they are identified, they share in the oneness of being. This position is usually called pantheism, from the Greek terms *pan-theos*, "all is god."[52]

Certain Eastern religions, especially Hinduism of the Vedanta school, as well as the Buddhism of the Brahmins, have a strong pantheistic flavor. But Church Fathers and the great theologians, deeply rooted in the teachings of scripture, were clearly opposed to any kind of pantheism. However during the Middle Ages several authors began to focus things in a pantheistic way (Scotus Eriugena to some degree, then David of Dinant and Amalric of Bena). This developed and was radicalized throughout the modern period, especially in the philosophy of Baruch Spinoza and Georg Hegel, who were followed by Friedrich Schelling, Karl Marx, and other authors.

Some traces of pantheism may be found during the early Middle Ages in the writings of the ninth-century philosopher and mystic John Scotus Eriugena, which speak of a kind of coincidence between God and the world. Eriugena, whose work *De divina natura* is complex and not always easy to interpret, considers God not only as the efficient and exemplar cause of the universe, but also in a sense its material cause; in other words,

52. See F. C. Schalk, "Pantheisme," in *Dictionnaire de théologie catholique*, ed. A. Vacant and E. Mangenot (Paris: Letouzé et Ané, 1908–72), 11:1855–74.

God is the one out of which the world is made.[53] This would seem to exclude the teaching of creation *ex nihilo*.

Two minor twelfth-century authors, David of Dinant and Amalric of Bena, addressed the issue of pantheism openly.[54] David situates his explanation within the important medieval debate on the notion of universals. He says there are three kinds of beings: bodies (or matter), spirits, and God. Now whereas the human process of knowing seems to distinguish between the three elements, in real terms human intelligence is directed toward finding the unitary intelligibility of all things, seeking out their foundational unity. And it would be possible for this process to take place only if the three types of being were not really distinct, but coincide with one another. Every human being therefore is a part of God; if he were not, then he could know neither himself nor other things. Amalric drew the practical conclusions from this reasoning process: because humans are a part of God, there is no real polarity or distinction between the two.[55] Therefore there is neither sin, nor merit, nor guilt, nor redemption, nor good, nor evil.

Amarlic was condemned as mentally unbalanced at the Fourth Lateran Council in 1215.[56] Pantheism was an unthinkable proposal. The fact is that the theologians of that period of history, among them Thomas Aquinas, insisted strenuously that pantheism was unacceptable. God is not one more being among the rest. God is being itself, and the source of all being.

The first author who may be considered a pantheist in the full sense of the word is the seventeenth-century Dutch Jew Baruch Spinoza. He identifies God with the world in an explicit and consistent way. All that exists, he says, belongs to the "substance," which is necessary, infinite, unique, and all-embracing. The first axiom of his work *Ethics* is: "all that is, either is in

53. Scotus Eriugena, *De divina natura* 3:19. See U. Galeazzi, "Dio e mondo in Giovanni Scoto Eriugena," *Rivista di filosofia neo-scolastica* 58 (1966): 629–52; J. F. Ortega, "El panteísmo de Juan Escoto Eriúgena," *La Ciudad de Dios* 198 (1985): 33–70. It may be said that for Eriugena nothingness is present in God, insofar as God does not stay undefined and indeterminate in his own infinity; hence there is clear bond between creator and creature.

54. See É. Gilson, *A History of Christian Philosophy in the Middle Ages* (London: Sheed and Ward, 1955), 240–44.

55. G. C. Capelle, *Amaury de Bène, étude sur son panthéisme formel* (Paris: J. Vrin, 1932); J. B. Russell, *The Influence of Amalric of Bene in Thirteenth Century Pantheism* (Berkeley: University of California Press, 1957).

56. DH 808.

itself or in another." But if there is nothing other than the substance, he asks, how do differences arise among individual beings? He replies that

> particular things are nothing but states of God's attributes, or ways [modes] by which God's attributes are expressed in a certain and determinate way.... By nature viewed as active [*natura naturans*] we should understand that which is in itself, and is conceived through itself, or those attributes of substance.... By nature viewed as passive [*natura naturata*] I understand all that which follows from the necessity of the nature of God, or of any of the attributes of God, that is, all the modes of the attributes of God, insofar as they are considered as things which are in God, and which without God cannot exist or be conceived.[57]

In real terms for Spinoza all things converge on God, described as *Deus, sive Substantia, sive Natura*, "God, or substance, or nature." His position is not far from David of Dinant's: the object of human intelligence is the unification of the multiple, and this is only possible if all things are in reality one in spite of the appearance of multiplicity. In other words, there is a perfect and mutual coincidence between the human mind and reality, as Spinoza himself says: "The order and connection of ideas is the same as the order and connection of things."[58]

For Spinoza there is no real distinction between God and the world, there is no polarity between the divine and the creature which would find expression in faith, or sin, or pilgrimage, or redemption, or repentance, or recognition, or adoration, or dialogue. His teaching renders the notion of creation *ex nihilo* simply superfluous.[59] He insists on Parmenides's principle: *ex nihilo nihil fit*, "out of nothing can come nothing."[60] It made sense that Spinoza should be excommunicated by the Jews, the people of the covenant, the pilgrim people, who consistently recognized the total otherness and transcendence of God with respect to the world. However, in spite of being rejected by Judaism and the weight of Christian tradition, the influence of his doctrine on modern philosophy was powerful, especially among German Idealists, and in particular in Goethe.[61] Henri Berg-

57. B. Spinoza, *Ethics I*, theorema 25 and 29.

58. Ibid., 7.

59. See C. O'Regan, "Spinoza and the Eclipse of Creation from Nothing," in *Creation ex nihilo* (ed. Anderson et al.), 233–73.

60. See ibid., 237.

61. See R. Scruton, *Spinoza* (Oxford: Oxford University Press, 1986), 110–12. Goethe writes: "What kind of God would push only from outside, letting the cosmos circle round his finger? He likes

son said on one occasion that all modern philosophers have two philosophies: their own and that of Spinoza.[62]

It may be observed that Spinoza's position, though all-encompassing and attractive, is simplistic and one-sided. The explanation leaves important aspects of reality unresolved and unexplained, given that no relevance may be attached to change, corruptibility, movement, human freedom, history, and polarity. Nearly two centuries later, Hegel would make the first serious attempt at incorporating everything, literally everything, into the divine, with a thoroughgoing pantheism.

The nineteenth-century philosopher Georg W. F. Hegel shared the idealistic-romantic optimism of modern authors, Spinoza and Goethe among them, as regards the real human capacity of explaining definitively and entirely the internal laws of every single aspect of reality. He strove to overcome the deterministic view of reality typical of the Platonists, the closed and immutable metaphysics of Wolff and Suárez, the skepticism of the empiricists, and the "bloodless categories" of the Kantians. As a point of departure he accepted the perfect, mutual, active, and productive relationship between human thought and reality, between Reason and Nature, between ideas and the world. This brought him to identify *progress in thought* with *progress in reality*. And progress was what he was principally interested in, for he realized that philosophers before him, especially Spinoza, had not managed to *integrate* into a single explanation of all things the reality of *time, matter, progress,* and *history*.

When we attempt to give a rational account of something we realize quickly enough that our explanation is incomplete, imperfect, inadequate. In fact we often discover that the full truth about something requires us to say the very opposite of what we had previously said. We can say for example "the sea is vast." But then, from another angle, we realize that the

to drive the world from inside, harbors the world in Himself, Himself in the world, so all that lives and weaves and is in Him, never wants for his power or his spirit." *Goethe. The Collected Works*, vol. 1: *Selected Poems*, ed. C. Middleton (Princeton, N.J.: Princeton University Press, 1983), 227 (author's translation). "If the eye were not sun-like, how could it ever spy the sun? If God's own power lay not inside us, how could divinity delight us?" (179).

62. See H. Bergson, Letter to Brunschvicg in *Mélanges* (Paris: PUF, 1972), 1483. See V. T. Thayer, "A Comparison of Bergson and Spinoza, with Reference to the Conceptions of Reality and Knowledge," *Monist* 21, no. 1 (1919): 96–105; S. Mariani, "Bergson duplice. Spinoza nemico-amico della filosofia della durata," *Lo Sguardo* 26, no. 1 (2018): 149–62.

statement needs to be complemented in order for it to adjust more fully to reality, and so we say the very opposite: "the sea is small." This is an essential aspect of the human thought process, what is called the dialectic aspect. The synthesis that best adapts to reality is the result of combining the thesis ("the sea is vast") with the antithesis ("the sea is small"). Affirmation and negation are an essential aspect of the human process of knowing. Their fruit is the synthesis.

However, Hegel attempts to apply the dialectic logic not only to our knowledge of the world but also to reality itself, with a view to overcoming both rationalism and empiricism. The rationalist, confident in his capacity to know reality, will say that reality may be measured (this is the thesis). But the empiricist responds saying that reality cannot be measured (the antithesis). Hegel says that the whole truth may be found in the synthesis of the two, overcoming at once the imperfection of one and the other. However, for Hegel, this is not just a description of the laws of thinking or criticism, but rather the fundamental law of reality as a whole and its development in every single stage. He argues that the dialectic is present not just in the thinking process but in the whole of reality, both material and spiritual. His understanding may be described in four stages.

First, following the ontologism of Malebranche and Spinoza, Hegel takes it that human thought, in its content and development, is nothing other than a direct participation in divine thought itself. Humans, when they think, actualize divine thought, they experience the mind of God directly. God thinks in them and through them.

Second, the phenomenology of the human spirit demonstrates—in the opinion of Hegel—that thought develops continually, from primitive, imperfect, semi-conscious, fragmentary, individual, inexpressible, and athematic forms (typical of primitive peoples) to the developed, perfect, fully conscious, unitary, universal, perfectly expressed, and thematic forms (typical of advanced peoples).

Third, progress in human thought does not consist for Hegel in a mere accumulation of data and information which generations hand on one to the next, typified in the French Encyclopedic movement. Rather it involves reality as such: the history of thought and the world has a single, true subject, someone who thinks it, identifies with it, and lives it out.

Fourth and last, the subject in question cannot be particular human beings who are born, die, and disappear, but rather the Absolute Spirit, equivalent for Hegel to God; this makes sense when we appreciate that human thought is nothing other than an experience of divine thought, as we saw in the first stage above. The growth and consolidation of our knowledge and understanding of reality, and of reality itself, therefore, consists simply of a transitory and partial stage in the development of the "coming-to-consciousness-of-the-Absolute-Spirit." The development of the universe coincides with a true development of God. But what place do matter and Nature occupy in this process?

Hegel insisted on the need to overcome Platonic spiritualism and avoiding what Bradley called the "fantastic ballet of the bloodless categories" typical of Kant. He spoke of a dialectical rapport between thoughts and things, between the subjective-spiritual and objective-natural. In keeping with idealistic philosophers, the Idea is the thesis, but Nature is the antithesis, and Spirit is the synthesis of the two. The Idea needs a material objectification or a concrete incorporation in order to be an idea. In Hegel's language, the Idea becomes an object as Nature, and returns to itself as Spirit, or absolute subject. In a less precise or technical way we might say that the idea pressurizes nature, and nature, which is material, historical and changing, in turn pressurizes the idea, bringing about the synthesis, the Absolute Spirit.

The disciples of Hegel applied his principles to just about everything: anthropology, theology, science, politics, law, work, society. He managed to do what nobody had done before him, bringing together the divine and the human in the spiritual, the material, the temporal, the historical in a single synthetic panorama: God himself partakes directly in time and history, and submits himself to them to transform them and to realize his own being. What may we say of Hegel's construct? Three critiques are in order, one metaphysical, another anthropological, and a third theological.

First, the metaphysical. The dialectic process as we saw above can well be applied to the reasoning process, for it is a sign of the spirituality of the human mind; the mind can think about black and white simultaneously without the colors becoming mixed, without producing grey. But the dialectic principle cannot be applied in the same way to the whole of reality as such, and especially to the material world, without introducing a principle of destruction or contradiction in it. The fact of a universal dialectic could easily turn into a duty of promoting the dialectic within society, an ideology, as Marxism has often done. In brief terms, what is applicable to the human mind (the principle of contradiction, logical negation) may not be applied to reality as a whole.

Second, the anthropological critique. If man and God coincide at the deepest level of being, what value does the individual human being have? Hegel does say that certain individuals throughout history have played a singular role in the coming to consciousness of the Absolute Spirit (Alexander the Great, Julius Caesar, Napoleon), and thus their behavior may not be judged by the criteria that are commonly applied to others. But the rest of humanity, made up of the vast majority of individuals, is irrelevant and destined to perish forever. Kant had insisted on the value of individual and personal conscience; Hegel rejected it. Kierkegaard vociferously critiqued Hegel on this front and insisted on the importance of the individual human being, of human singularity.[63]

Third, from the theological standpoint, we may add that Hegel's manipulation of man in his inalienable individual dignity easily leads to the manipulation of the divinity itself. He forcefully claimed he was not an atheist, saying in fact that only God exists. But of course because God is fully identified with the world and with man, it is just as easy to say that only man exists or that only the world exists. Pantheism easily leads to humanism or atheism.

CONTEMPORARY EXPLANATIONS OF THE ORIGIN AND DEVELOPMENT OF THE WORLD

Hegel's pantheism left its mark in several different explanations of the cosmos, its origins and development, among them (1) philosophical evolutionism (already considered in chapter 1), (2) process theology, and to some degree, (3) God as the basis of being (Tillich) and (4) God as the one who makes space for being within himself (Moltmann).

One of the most influential twentieth-century philosophical movements in the English-speaking world goes by the name of process theology.

63. See O'Callaghan, *Children of God in the World,* 24 and 456.

Inspired by Hegel, its defenders—Alfred N. Whitehead, Charles Hartshorne, John B. Cobb, and others—hold that God is present in the world in a fully immanent way.[64] God is not the cause of the universe, nor is he transcendent nor separate nor distinct from it. Rather he partakes directly in the world's own development or process, in which finite creatures contribute actively to the divine essence through a process of interchange. The world in that sense may be described as God's body. Thus it makes no sense to speak of creation *ex nihilo* or of the omnipotence of God over the cosmos. Man cooperates with God more or less as he cooperates with other humans.[65] God persuades humans but does not impose on them. David Fergusson observes that process theology "accentuates the divine influence through allurement as opposed to the sheer sovereignty of the *ex nihilo* tradition. Creation is to be understood better as a gradual evolving of patterns of order from chaos—patterns which realize values such as consciousness, pleasure, freedom, and love."[66]

These authors consider that the notion of divine omnipotence is morally problematic (its possible arbitrariness makes human evil unintelligible), scientifically incredible (for the present situation we live within would be the fruit of billions of years of evolution), and incompatible with meaningful creaturely freedom. Moreover, process theology is clearly not in keeping with Christian teaching on divine omnipotence and creation *ex nihilo*. But is it possible to respond to the difficulties and challenges it attempts to grapple with? Later on, in chapter 9, which deals with providence, I shall attempt to do so.

A not unrelated position is held by the twentieth-century American Protestant theologian Paul Tillich, according to whom God should not be called the creator of the world but rather the basis or ground of being.[67]

64. See A. N. Whitehead, *Process and Reality: An Essay in Cosmology* (New York: Social Science Book Store, 1941); J. B. Cobb and D. R. Griffin, *Process Theology: An Introductory Exposition* (Philadelphia: Westminster, 1976).

65. See McFarland, *From Nothing*, 15–18.

66. Fergusson, "Creation," 82. See also D. B. Burrell, "Does Process Theology Rest on a Mistake?," *Theological Studies* 43 (1982): 125–35; D. R. Griffin, "Creation out of Nothing. Creation out of Chaos and the Problem of Evil," in *Encountering Evil: Live Options in Theodicy*, ed. S. Davis (Louisville, Ky.: Westminster John Knox, 2001), 108–25.

67. See J. H. Thomas, "Some Comments on Tillich's Doctrine of Creation," *Scottish Journal of Theology* 14 (1961): 113–18; J. L. Illanes, "Teología Sistemática de Paul Tillich," *Scripta Theologica* 6 (1974): 711–54.

It is possible to speak of God in a meaningful way only in the context of finite creatures, he argues, and "the Christian doctrine of *creatio ex nihilo* affirms that there is an element of nonbeing in all finite existence."[68] Tillich associates *nihil* with what he calls "the heritage of nonbeing,"[69] a concept clearly inspired in Heidegger, a kind of hypostatization of negation.[70] Tillich says that if we speak of God in personal terms, this does not mean that God is a person in the normal sense of the word, but rather that he is the basis or foundation of everything that is personal. This would seem to compromise divine freedom of creation in the work of creation.

Something of a kind may be said of the theology of the Lutheran Jürgen Moltmann.[71] On the basis of Jewish mystical medieval speculations, called the Kabbalah,[72] Moltmann explains that the nothingness out of which the world is created is a kind of space that God makes within himself, retreating back into his own being (this is what the Jewish texts called *zimsum*). He cites Gershom Scholem: "In the self-limitation of the divine Being which, instead of acting outwardly in its initial act, turns inwards towards itself, Nothingness emerges. Here we have an act in which Nothingness is called forth."[73] As Moltmann himself puts it: "Where God withdraws himself from himself to himself, he can call something forth which is not divine essence or divine being."[74] The same idea is to be found in Robert Jenson: "for God to create is for him to open a place in his triune life for others than the three whose mutual life he is."[75] And likewise Hans Jonas who, after the terrible experience of Auschwitz, held that divine omnipotence should be considered incompatible with divine goodness and

68. Thomas, "Some Comments," 113. Ehrhardt holds that Tillich's use of the expression *creatio ex nihilo* is contradictory of the biblical notion of creation: A. Ehrhardt, "Creatio ex nihilo," *Studia Theologica* 4 (1950): 13–43, at 14.

69. P. Tillich, *Systematic Theology*, 1:253.

70. Thomas, "Some Comments," 116.

71. See Moltmann, *God in Creation*, 86–93. In support of this position he cites Nicholas of Cusa, Schelling, Brunner, and others.

72. See G. Scholem, *Origins of the Kabbalah* (Princeton, N.J.: Princeton University Press, 1962); J. Maier, *Die Kabbalah. Einführung – Klassische Texte – Erläuterungen* (Munich: C. H. Beck, 1995); D. M. Wexelman, *Kabbalah: The Splendor of Judaism* (Northvale, N.J.: J. Aronson, 2000).

73. G. Scholem, "Schöpfung aus Nichts und Selbstverschränkung Gottes," *Eranos-Jahrbuch* 25 (1956): 87–119, at 117, in Moltmann, *God in Creation*, 87.

74. Moltmann, *God in Creation*, 87.

75. R. W. Jenson, "Aspects of a Doctrine of Creation," in *The Doctrine of Creation: Essay in Dogmatics, History and Philosophy*, ed. C. E. Gunton (Edinburgh: T. and T. Clark, 1997), 17–28, at 24.

rationality. God, in conceding humans their freedom, renounced his own power, and allowed the world to exist.[76]

The position just described may be helpful if taken in an existential way. If understood in a strict metaphysical way, however, it would seem to allow creatures to occupy an autonomous space beside God who self-limits his own being. This would mean that God and the creature occupy the same metaphysical space, in other words that they share the same ontology, and God has decided simply to move over in order to leave space for creatures. This position of course is not easy to accept.[77]

The Church's Teaching on Creation

The principal official declaration of the church on creation may be found in the Vatican Council I dogmatic constitution *Dei Filius* (1870), which provides the following profession of faith:

> There is one God, true and living, Creator and Lord of heaven and earth, almighty, eternal, immense, incomprehensible, infinite in his intellect and will and in all perfection. As he is one unique and spiritual substance, entirely simple and unchangeable, we must proclaim him distinct from the world in existence and essence, most happy in himself and of himself [*in se et ex se beatissimus*], ineffably exalted above all things that exist or can be conceived besides him. This one and only true God, of his own goodness and almighty power, not for the increase of his own happiness, nor for the acquirement of his perfection, but in order to manifest his perfection through the benefits which he bestows on creatures, with absolute freedom of counsel [*liberrimo consilio*], "from the beginning of time made at once out of nothing both orders of creatures, the spiritual and the corporeal, that is, the angelic and the earthly, and then the human creature, who as it were shares in both orders, being composed of spirit and body."[78]

The Vatican I text speaks for itself. The triune God is perfect and self-sufficient, standing in no need of any complement or assistance from outside factors. In creating the world God neither increases his happiness nor

76. See H. Jonas, *Der Gottesbegriff nach Auschwitz: Eine jüdische Stimme*, 2nd ed. (Frankfurt a.M.: Suhrkamp, 1987).

77. See Robson, *Ontology and Providence*, 133–36. See the critique by A. J. Torrance, "*Creatio ex nihilo* and the Spatio-Temporal Dimension, with special reference to Jürgen Moltmann and D.C. Williams," in *The Doctrine of Creation* (ed. Gunton), 83–103.

78. DH 3001, citing DH 800.

augments his perfection. The purpose of creation is one of manifesting his goodness *ad extra,* beyond the bounds of his own being. In other words, creation is an entirely free act of the divinity, the most free or unconditioned act imaginable. "In Christian belief we understand the world as that which might not have been, and correlatively we understand God as capable of existing, in undiminished goodness and greatness, even if the world had not been."[79]

In the years after this Council the doctrine of creation received little direct attention in official church teaching; during Vatican Council II in fact it seems to have been simply taken for granted. But in more recent times two important sources of church teaching should be noted. First, the extensive catechesis of John Paul II in 1986, which deals with the mystery of creation, providence, angels, and original sin in thirty-six audiences,[80] and second, the *Catechism of the Catholic Church,* nos. 279–421. Both documents present what the church has understood about the mystery of creation in comprehensive terms, and I shall refer to them frequently in the coming pages.

However, Vatican I's solemn declaration marks a high-point in church teaching on creation. It draws on (1) a variety of Symbols of faith from the first millennium of Christianity, (2) different official documents also situated in the first millennium, and (3) three church councils: Fourth Lateran (1215), Florence (1442), and a diocesan Synod in Cologne in 1860, held just ten years before Vatican I. Vatican I also takes position on (4) the issue of pantheism. Let us consider them one by one.

CREATION IN THE SYMBOLS OF FAITH

Christian teaching on creation may be found in early church professions of faith, called Symbols or creeds. In them from the earliest times the church attempted, in a series of short, clear formulae, to summarize the biblical message of salvation through Jesus Christ.[81] The best known Symbol, which went through many versions, was the Apostles' Creed, used principally in the baptismal liturgy.[82] Of great weight besides is the

79. Sokolowski, *The God of Faith and Reason,* 19.

80. The catechesis took place from January 8 to December 17, 1986.

81. See J. N. D. Kelly, *Early Christian Creeds,* 3rd ed. (New York: Longman, 1995).

82. See P. O'Callaghan, "The Bangor Antiphonary Creed: Origins and Theology," *Annales*

Nicene-Constantinopolitan Creed prepared at the Councils of Ephesus (325 A.D.) and Constantinople (381 A.D.),[83] a text commonly used in the Eucharistic celebration.

The earliest Symbols pay little attention to the doctrine of creation as such. But they do speak clearly of God as all-powerful:[84] *omnipotens* (all-powerful),[85] *pantocratōr* (a Greek term meaning "universal sovereign," often used in the Book of Revelation),[86] *omnium*—or *universi*—*dominatorem.*[87] These terms, which include the notion of conservation (Augustine translates *pantocratōr* as *omnitenens*),[88] speak little however about the work of creation and refer, rather, to the One who creates. In effect, by reciting the Creed, Christians professed belief in the *God who creates,* not so much in his work of creation.

As regards the created world itself some early versions of the Symbol, following Genesis 1:1, speak of the Father as *caeli et terrae creator,*[89] creator of heaven and earth. This formula is used frequently in different forms.[90] The following text is attributed to Justin Martyr: "we believe that God is one, from the beginning he is creator and demiurge of the whole world, of things visible and invisible."[91] Eastern redactions of the Creed likewise duplicate the result or product of creation: heaven *and* earth, things visible *and* invisible. They use the term "author" or "builder" of the universe (Greek, *poiētēs*), whereas Latin authors use the word *creator.*[92] Several redactions of the Symbol of faith make specific mention of the creating role of the Son and the Spirit. The cosmic role of Christ is central in these

Theologici 6 (1992): 255–87; L. H. Westra, *The Apostles' Creed: Origin, History, and Some Early Commentaries* (Turnhout: Brepols, 2002).

83. See Scheffczyk, *Schöpfung und Vorlesung,* 23–29.

84. See A. De Halleux, "Dieu le Père tout-puissant," *Revue Théologique de Louvain* 8 (1977): 401–22.

85. See DH 3, 4, 10, 12, etc.

86. See DH 2, 11, 40, etc.

87. DH 1 and 5.

88. See Augustine, *Confessions* XI, 13:1.

89. From the *Explanatio Symboli* attributed to Nicetas of Remesiana (DH 19).

90. For example, "universorum creatorem, regem saeculorum, immortalem et invisibilem" (DH 21–22); and from ca. fifth- or sixth-century North Africa, "creatorem caeli et terrae" (DH 27, 28, 30, 37). This formula was taken up by the *textus receptus* of the Apostles' Creed; "omnium creaturarum visibilium et invisibilium conditorem" (DH 29).

91. G. Krüger, *Akten Justins und seiner Genossen* (Tübingen: J. C. B. Mohr, 1929), 2.5 and 15.32–16.1.

92. Kelly, *Early Christian Creeds,* 373.

documents: Christ is not only Savior but also Lord of the universe. Besides, the same texts that speak of the Son as *dominum et salvatorem (nostrum)*, also speak of the Holy Spirit as *omnia vivificantem*, or *vivificantem universam creaturam*.[93]

In the context of the Arian controversy, Eastern creeds insist besides on the distinction between the generation of the Son and the creation of the universe.[94] Latin versions of the Creed do not for the most part attribute any creative role to the Holy Spirit, but the Eastern ones do: the Spirit is said to "vivify every creature."[95] The profession of the *Fides Damasi* (fourth century) teaches:

> For it is written: "By the Word of the Lord the heavens were made," that is, by the Son of God, "and all their host by the breath of his mouth" (Ps 33:6); and elsewhere: "When you send forth your Spirit, they are created, and you renew the face of the earth" (Ps 104:30). Therefore, in the name of the Father and of the Son and of the Holy Spirit we confess one God, for the term "God" refers to power, not to personal characteristics."[96]

OTHER FIRST-MILLENNIUM CHURCH TEACHINGS

Apart from the general affirmations of church creeds in respect of creation *ex nihilo* and its immediate implications, three other issues related to creation were dealt with in official church documents in the early centuries, related in the main to neo-Platonism and Gnosticism (which were considered earlier on in this chapter).

First, insistence is made on the absolute transcendence of God, which is shared consubstantially by the Son and the Holy Spirit. That the Word/Son who became incarnate in Jesus Christ is fully divine was taught unequivocally by the Council of Nicaea in 325 A.D. against Arius. Thus God is considered as supreme over all creatures, which depend entirely on him. Creatures depend on him but he does not depend on them. The Platonic notion of a connected hierarchy of being is set aside: the divine and the created realms are separate and incomparable. On no account is the Word/

93. DH 3–4.
94. DH 40.
95. DH 4.
96. DH 71.

Son subordinate to the Father, as Arius taught. Speaking of the Gnosticism of the second-century author Valentinus or his disciples, Pope Leo the Great wrote in the fifth century:

> And besides this one consubstantial, eternal, and unchangeable Godhead of the most high Trinity there is nothing in all creation which, in its origin, is not created out of nothing.... No man is truth, wisdom, justice; but many are partakers of truth, wisdom, and justice. But God alone is exempt from any participating: and anything which is in any degree worthily predicated of Him is not an attribute, but His very essence. For in the Unchangeable there is nothing added, there is nothing lost.... Thus abiding in Himself He renews all things (Rv 21:5), and receives nothing which He did not Himself give.[97]

Second, church documents speak of the *creation of the human soul.* In the context of Platonic and Gnostic explanations of the world and of humans, the church has repeatedly taught that the soul is made by God, *immediate,* directly, without intermediaries,[98] from nothing;[99] that the soul is not a part of God,[100] nor is it of the divine substance;[101] that souls do not exist *ab aeterno,* from time immemorial, in such a way that the presence of the soul in the body would be due to the Fall, as Origen suggested.[102] The First Council of Toledo in 400 A.D. sums up this position as follows: "The human soul is not of the divine substance, nor is it a part of God, but rather it is a creature according to the will of God."[103]

And third, the church has repeatedly insisted on the *goodness of matter,* marriage, and the body, against Gnostic devaluations of all three. It confessed the original goodness of the material world, and specifically of the institution of matrimony. This was on account of the Gnosticism of Prisciallian in the fourth century. The latter taught that the devil, the malign principle, had created matter, whereas the soul was divine, though in bondage to material nature as a punishment for sins committed as a pure spirit.

The following positions were rejected at the First Council of Braga in 561:

97. Leo the Great, *Letter* 15:6 to Thuribius of Asturias (DH 285).

98. DH 190, 360, 3896.

99. DH 190, 360, 685.

100. DH 190, 201, 685.

101. DH 190, 201, 285, 455.

102. DH 403 and 456.

103. DH 190.

> [Any teaching to the effect that] the devil was not first a good angel created by God, or that his nature was not the work of God, but that he emerged from darkness, and had no creator but is himself the principle and substance of evil; [Any teaching that] condemns human marriage and despises the procreation of children; that the formation of the human body is the work of the devil and the conception of children in their mothers' womb is brought about through the activity of the devil, and for this reason does not believe in the resurrection of the body; the creation of all flesh is not the work of God but of bad angels.[104]

The same principle was applied during the Middle Ages when the Gnostic antimaterialism of Albigensians and Waldensians was condemned at the Fourth Lateran Council.[105]

REFERENCE POINTS FOR VATICAN I

A key reference point for Vatican I's teaching on creation may be found in the declaration made at the Fourth Lateran Council in 1215, centered on the oneness of trinitarian action. The latter was explained by Augustine and Peter Lombard with the aid of the expression *inseparabilia sunt opera Trinitatis*, "the works of the Trinity are inseparable," against the position of Joachim of Fiore, and the rejection of all dualism in the origin of the universe (against Albigensians and Waldensians).[106] Fourth Lateran used the term *de nihilo* for the first time in a conciliar document. In fact Vatican I cites the central passage of Fourth Lateran directly, with one important novelty: the inclusion in Vatican I of the expression *liberrimo consilio*, "with absolute freedom of counsel." This was probably due to Vatican I's effort to avoid neo-Hegelian pantheism that denied divine freedom. In effect, God created the world with utter freedom, in a totally free decision, without limitations of any kind.[107] In Fourth Lateran we read:

104. Council of Braga, canons 7 and 11–13 (DH 457 and 461–63).

105. See Fourth Lateran Council (1215), in DH 802; Council of Florence (1442), in DH 1333. See M. Rainini, "Creazione e tempo nella Costituzione I del Concilio Lateranense IV. Prime ricognizioni intorno alle urgenze e alle contingenze della stessa," *Divus Thomas (Piacenza)* 47 (2007): 119–50; N. Ciola, A. Sabetta, and P. Sguazzardo (eds.), *Il Concilio Lateranense IV a 800 anni dalla sua celebrazione: una rilettura teologica* (Vatican City: Lateran University Press, 2016).

106. See Ciola, Sabetta, and Sguazzardo (eds.), *Il Concilio Lateranense IV*, esp. 229–31. The following *professio fidei* was prescribed for the Waldensians by Innocent III in 1208: "We believe with our heart and confess with our tongue that Father, Son, and Holy Spirit are one God . . . creator, maker, ruler and provider of all things, corporeal and spiritual, visible and invisible. We believe that one and the same God is author of the Old and New Testaments" (DH 790).

107. On the centrality of divine freedom in creation at Vatican I, see J. Rebeneck, "Die

We firmly believe and confess without reservation that there is only one true God, eternal, infinite and unchangeable, incomprehensible, almighty and ineffable, the Father, the Son and the Holy Spirit.... They are the one principle of the universe, the creator of all things, visible and invisible, spiritual and corporeal, who by His almighty power from the beginning of time made at once [*simul*] out of nothing [*de nihilo*] both orders of creatures, the spiritual and the corporeal, that is, the angelic and the earthly, and then the human creature, who as it were shares in both orders, being composed of spirit and body.[108]

The Council of Florence in 1442 insisted, in response to the Gnosticism of the time, on the goodness of created reality, especially matter, in that it is created by God.

The Church most firmly believes, professes and proclaims that the one true God, Father, Son, and Holy Spirit, is the creator of all things, visible and invisible, who, when He so willed, out of His bounty made all creatures, spiritual as well as corporeal. They are good since they were made by Him who is the highest good, but they are mutable because they were made out of nothing. She asserts that there is no such thing as a nature of evil, because all nature, as nature, is good.[109]

Lastly we may mention a diocesan Synod held in Cologne in 1860, held just ten years before Vatican I. The Synod prepared the way for the Council on this issue, as it attempted to clarify church teaching on creation in the light of the neo-Hegelian positions of two Catholic nineteenth-century authors, Georg Hermes and Anton Günther.[110] The Synod taught that nothing outside God forced or conditioned him to create the world, for he stands in no need of anything outside himself. As regards the scope or purpose of creation the Synod stated that God wished to bring creatures

Lehrentscheidungen des Vatikan Konzils über der Freiheit des Schöpfers," *Scholastik* 32 (1957): 565–669.

108. DH 800.

109. Decree for the Jacobites (DH 1333).

110. On this Synod and the importance of Thomas Aquinas in its formulations, see H. Schauf, "Thomas als theologischer Kronzeuge auf dem Kölner Provinzialkonzil von 1860," in Pontificia Accademia di san Tommaso, *San Tommaso: Fonti e riflessi del suo pensiero* (Rome: Città Nuova, 1974), 317–24. On Hermes, see K. Eschweiler, *Die zwei Wege der neueren Theologie: Georg Hermes, Matth. Jos. Scheeben: eine kritische Untersuchung des Problems der theologischen Erkenntnis* (Augsburg: B. Filser, 1926); on Günther, see L. Orbán, *Theologia Güntheriana et Concilium Vaticanum: Inquisitio historico-dogmatica de re Güntheriana iuxta vota inedita consultoris J. Schwetz actaque Concilii Vaticani exarata,* 2 vols. (Rome: Gregoriana, 1949).

to partake in the good, to manifest divine perfection, and above all to share in the power, wisdom, and goodness of God. This divine manifestation is usually referred to as the eternal glory of God because on account of it God is praised by creatures. Connected with God being glorified is the salvation of humanity. So, the Synod concludes, the ultimate purpose of creation is the glorification of God (*gloria Dei*), whereas the happiness of creatures and especially of humans (*salus animarum*) must be directed to that end.[111]

THE CHURCH'S TEACHING ON PANTHEISM

Pantheism, which I considered earlier in this chapter, was not an issue for the greater part of the history of Christianity. As we saw earlier on, the Fourth Lateran Council rejected the pantheistic position of the medieval author Almaric of Bena not only as heretical, but as insane.[112] Pantheism of course became central for several modern philosophies, especially those of Spinoza, Hegel, Marx, and Schelling.

In 1861 the ontologist position of Malebranche and Leibniz, which held that human thought is nothing but a passive reflex of divine thought, was declared unacceptable by the Holy Office.[113] The issue of pantheism was directly dealt with at Vatican Council I in 1870. The principal *rapporteur* of the Council, Vincent F. Gasser, stated that the Council's rejection of pantheism referred mainly to that of Hegel and Schelling,[114] as well as to the position of the Catholic theologian Anton Günther, with his mitigated version of Hegelianism.[115]

The following theses were rejected at Vatican I: that "the substance and essence of God and of all things is one and the same"[116] and that "finite beings, the corporeal as well as the spiritual, or at least the spiritual ones, have emanated from the divine substance, or that the divine essence becomes all things by self-manifestation or self-evolution; or lastly that God is the universal or indefinite being which, by self-determination, constitutes

111. See J. D. Mansi, *Sacrorum Conciliorum Nova et Amplissima Collectio* (Graz: Akademische Druck- und Verlagsanstalt, 1961), 48:87–91.

112. See DH 808.

113. See DH 2842–43.

114. See Schalk, "*Panthéisme*," 1872.

115. See DH 2828–31.

116. DH 3023.

the universality of beings differentiated into genera, species and individuals."[117] Lastly, the Council rejects the position of those who "refuse to confess that the world and all things contained in it, the spiritual as well as the material, were in their whole substance produced by God out of nothing, or says that God created not by an act of will free from all necessity, but with the same necessity by which He necessarily loves Himself; or denies that the world was made for the glory of God."[118]

117. DH 3024.
118. DH 3025.

5

The Logic of Creation and the Divine *Logos* in the Patristic Period and Middle Ages

IN THE ORDER, unity, goodness, beauty, and harmony of nature, in its "logic" as it were, Christian authors have always detected traces of God's action in and through the eternal Word, through whom all things were made. *Semen omnium Christus,* said Ambrose: "Christ is the seed of all things."[1] In chapter 3, we saw how this doctrine is developed throughout the New Testament, especially in Paul and John. For Paul, all things are made through Christ and for Christ, and for John, all things were made through the Word, all things made in him were life. The Old Testament roots for these positions are situated especially in wisdom literature, in particular, the Books of the Psalms, Proverbs, and Wisdom.

Biblical and patristic understandings of the "logic" of the universe developed principally in an intentional dialogue between Jewish and Christian believers on the one hand and Greek philosophers on the other. Content-wise, the Christian end-product differed clearly from Platonism, Stoicism, and Aristotelianism, as may be seen in the declarations made at the Council of Nicaea in 325 A.D. Yet the language and philosophical concepts of Greek and Christian thought had a great deal in common. Besides, the concern of philosophers was not substantially different from that of Christian theologians: to understand what God did in creating the world, why he did it, and the kind of mediations he employed in doing so.

Throughout the chapter we shall consider the position of four philosophers who dealt with the issue of the creation of the world through the

1. Ambrose, *In Ps.* 43, 39.

mediation of an intermediary being (*Logos*, Demiurge): (1) Plato, (2) Philo of Alexandria, (3) Plotinus, and (4) Arius. Others could certainly have been chosen, for example, Origen or Clement of Alexandria, but I consider the four to be sufficiently representative of the variety of positions present in the debate. Then we shall look into (5) the teaching of Athanasius and the Council of Nicaea, as well as that of (6) Augustine and Thomas Aquinas. In their reflection the first four authors prepare the theological ground for understanding the role Christ played in creating and redeeming the world, which I shall consider systematically in chapter 6.

Plato

As we saw above, Plato considers as true and real what is divine. And to be divine means above all to be immortal, that is, permanent, eternal, perfect, and immaterial. And yet divinities are to be found everywhere throughout the whole world. "The world is full of gods," he says.[2] The supreme divinity, which maintains all the rest in unity and provides the center point in the hierarchy of beings, is designated as the Good. In itself, however, the Good is unreachable and virtually unknown to all the other creatures, for it has no direct contact with the world, with mortals, with matter and the senses. The reason for this is simple: matter cannot enter into contact with the divinity, for spirit and matter are antithetical to one another. Hence a mediation between the two orders is provided, Plato says, by the so-called Demiurge, from the Greek term *dēmiourgos*, which means "public worker."[3]

The Demiurge divinity is unique, eternal, inalterable, invisible, intelligent, full of knowledge and power. In the *Timaeus* Plato explains that it shapes the world in two stages, first by contemplating the world of Forms,[4] and then by organizing and constructing visible things on the basis of prime matter, that is, preexisting nonformed matter. The world produced by this process is called *kosmos*,[5] which literally means "order."[6] Thus prime

2. Plato, *Laws* 899b.

3. *NIDNTTE* 1:682, s.v. Δημιουργός. The term is to be found only once in the New Testament (Heb 10:11), but is not referred to creation. K. Murakawa, "Demiurgos," *Historia* 6 (1957): 385–415; A. Douda, "Platons Weltbaumeister," *Altertum* 19 (1973): 147–56; E. Lévy, "La dénomination de l'artisan chez Platon et Aristote," *Ktema* 16 (1991): 7–18.

4. Plato, *Timaeus* 29a.

5. BDAG 56:1–3, s.v. Κόσμος.

6. Plato, *Timaeus* 30a.

matter is the substrate of all beings, of every generation,[7] it is the receptacle of all forms,[8] the undifferentiated subject awaiting to be shaped and formed. Given its mediating role, the Demiurge is often considered as a god and as provident for this world. Yet its role is limited in two ways: (1) by the Form, a kind of eternal and preexistent exemplar, which it must contemplate and imitate, and (2) by matter, both chaotic and stubborn, besides being preexistent. Thus the Demiurge may form matter, shape or fashion things material, but on no account does it *create* or give existence to things. It is to be understood as a kind of second-god, intermediate and instrumental, inferior to the Good who produces and generates it and with which it acts in continuity. The reason for its existence is to make or fabricate the world.

In the words of Zizioulas, for Plato

> the Creator [demiurge] did whatever the ideas directed him to; they dictated the form of creation, although matter prevented creation from achieving the perfect correspondence with the ideas ... Philo [of Alexandria] realized that these theories were not suited to the freedom of God, so he modified Platonism by transferring these ideas into the mind of God.... In this way he solved the problem of God's freedom with respect to the ideas.[9]

Let us now consider Philo.

Philo of Alexandria

The philosophy of the Jew Philo of Alexandria, a contemporary of Christ's, is of particular importance in understanding the Christian doctrine of creation.[10] He attempted to establish a synthesis between Old Testament revelation and the cosmological vision of Platonists and Stoics. Taking up the position of the latter, he provided an explanation that overcomes

7. Ibid., 49a.

8. Ibid., 50c.

9. Zizioulas, "Creation and Salvation," 85.

10. On Philo, G. M. Pozzo, "Filone di Alessandria," in *Enciclopedia Filosofica* (Milan: Bompiani, 2006), 2:393; R. Radice (ed.), *Platonismo e creazionismo in Filone di Alessandria* (Milan: Vita e pensiero, 1989); J. Daniélou, *Philo of Alexandria* (Cambridge: James Clark, 2014); G. Reale, "Filone di Alessandria e la prima elaborazione filosofica della dottrina della creazione," in *'Paradoxos politeia.' Studi patristici in onore di Giuseppe Lazzati*, ed. R. Cantalamessa and L. F. Pizzolato (Milan: Vita e pensiero, 1979), 247–87.

an important lacuna in Plato's understanding of the Demiurge, especially in respect of the intrinsic intelligibility of created things.[11] Besides, as a Jew he held that the transcendent God of the Old Testament is truly the creator of the world,[12] and that he created matter *ex nihilo*.[13] "For God called the non-existent into being, order out of disorder, quality out of unqualified matter, similarities out of dissimilarity.... [To create is] to introduce the non-existent into existence."[14]

Philo uses the Greek term *ktizein* to designate God's action ("create," the standard translation of *bara'*), and not *poiein* (to "make") as Plato does. In effect, for Plato the intelligibility or "form" of things is not inherent in them but belongs to the divine realm. At best, for Plato, finite beings are occasions with which the human mind contemplates the world of Forms; as we saw earlier on, knowledge involves remembering what was once seen or contemplated in the world of Forms. It does not involve abstracting inherent intelligible content from things, what Aristotle referred to when speaking about the *entelechia* present in beings, and the Stoics called the *logoi spermatikoi*, or seminal reasons. Philo however holds that between the Platonic Demiurge (intelligibility on God's side as it were, the *logos*

11. "Philo realized that there were problems with Plato's account because it assumed that God was confronted by the existence of matter as by a given. Who created matter? Philo took the step of declaring matter to be a creation of God.... For Plato, ideas also just existed, so God found them ready-made. Philo's solution was to turn the ideas into the thoughts of God. The ideas were not above God but within him." Zizioulas, "Creation and Salvation," 85.

12. The issue is controversial among experts, as we have just seen with Zizioulas. See also Soskice, *Creatio ex nihilo*, 33, who says that Philo "is not entirely consistent, but the basic tenets of *creatio ex nihilo* are already present in his writings: God created the world out of non-being, creating as well as moulding formless matter. God, he believes, has created time itself." And as Philo writes: "God was not only demiurge but also creator" (*Somn.* 1:76). See also Philo, *Legum Allegoriae* 3; *De Fuga et Inventione* 46; *De Vita Moysis* II, 267.

13. Philo is somewhat ambiguous as to whether God creates primary matter in *De Opificio Mundi*. On creation of matter in Philo, see G. E. Sterling, "'The Most Perfect Work.' The Role of Matter in Philo of Alexandria," in *Creation ex nihilo* (ed. Anderson et al.), 99–118. On the debate regarding whether matter is created or eternal, see G. Scarpat, *Libro della Sapienza* (Brescia: Paideia, 1989), 1:129; May, *Creatio ex nihilo*, 8–22; Radice, *Platonismo*, 28–45. As regards 2 Mc 7:28, J. A. Goldstein, "The Origins of the Doctrine of Creatio ex Nihilo," *Journal of Jewish Studies* 35 (1984): 127–35; G. Reale, "Filone di Alessandria e la prima elaborazione." Philo never says that matter existed from all eternity, which Plato does clearly in *Timaeus*. Besides, "before the creation of the cosmos there was nothing beside God" (Philo, *Leg. All.* 2:2). So Plato is reformed as it were by Philo: "God gives rise to the intelligible cosmos, then to matter, and last of all to the sensitive cosmos, making use of the ideas and of matter." Fabbri, "Creatore e demiurgo," 155.

14. Philo, *Spec. Leg.* 4, 187; *De Opif. Mundi* 31.

theios) and the intelligibility inherent in things (the *logos spermatikos*) there is an intermediate being, called the *Logos*, or Word. By means of the *Logos*, Philo says, God created the cosmos and continues his action in the world.

Philo compares God with the architect who, wanting to found a great city, "first thought the types and with them formed the intelligible cosmos to then produce the sensitive cosmos, using the former as a model."[15] He explains:

> Now he by whom a thing originates is the cause; that from which a thing is made is the material; that by means of which it was made is the instrument; and why, is the object.... What things must meet together, that any house or city may be made? Must there not be a builder, and stones, and timber, and tools? What then is the builder, but the cause by whom the house or city is built? And what are the stones and timber, but the materials of which the buildings is made? And what are the tools, but the things by means of which it is made? And for what reason is it built, except to serve as a shelter and protection? This is the object. Now passing on from these particular buildings, consider the greatest house or city, namely, this world, for you will find that *God* is the cause of it, by whom it was made. That the *materials* are the four elements, of which it is composed [earth, air, fire, water]; that the *instrument* is the word [*logos*] of God, by means of which it was made; and the object of the building you will find to be the display of the goodness of the Creator [*dēmiourgos*].[16]

Philo identifies the *logos* with Wisdom or Reason. Using biblical terminology he likewise describes the *logos* as the Son, the Angel, the High Priest, the image, the model and idea of the world, its living law, its vital power, the bond between all the different elements it is made up of, and thus the instrument or mediator of creation. He expresses this mediating role in the following powerful words:

15. Philo, *De Opif. Mundi* 19. "For Plato, the demiurge looks up towards Principles and Ideas, which measure/control his creative action. The God of Philo has nothing above him. The demiurge looks at intelligible world of Ideas, but this is ontologically inferior to God." Fabbri, "Creatore e demiurgo," 151.

16. Philo, *De cherubim* 12, 5–7. See also *De Opif. Mundi* 24: "The intelligible cosmos is nothing other than the divine Logos already involved in the act of creation. In fact the conceived city in thought is not other than the calculated reasoning of the architect, when he is already planning to found the city.... All is God's grace: earth, water, air, fire, sun, stars, heaven, all the animals and plants. God gives no grace to himself, because he has no need for it, but gives the world to the world, but also gives the parts to the parts themselves, and reciprocally, one to the other, and besides, to all."

The Father who created the universe has given to his archangelic and most ancient Word [*logos*] a pre-eminent gift, to stand on the confines of both, and to separate that which had been created from the Creator. And this same Word is continually a *suppliant* to the immortal God on behalf of the mortal race, which is exposed to affliction and misery; and is also the *ambassador*, sent by the Ruler of all, to the subject race. And the Word rejoices in the gift, and, exulting in it, announces it and boasts of it, saying, "And I stood in the midst, between the Lord and you" (Nm 16:48), *neither being uncreated as God, nor yet created as you, but being in the midst between these two extremities*, like a hostage, as it were, to both parties: a hostage to the Creator, as a pledge and security that the whole race would never fly off and revolt entirely, choosing disorder rather than order; and to the creature, to lead it to entertain a confident hope that the merciful God would not overlook his own work.[17]

Still, in this mediating process Philo is aware of the tension between what the Stoics called the *logos endiathetos* and the *logos proforikos*.[18] The first refers to divine thought itself, the *logos* on God's side of things, as it were; the second to expressed (or proffered) thought present in creatures, in the "world soul." Yet he does not quite manage to overcome the tension. The *logos* is tugged at from one side to the other in a perpetual dialectic between the eternal and the temporal, between the spiritual and the material. It is neither divine nor created; as the above text says, the *logos* is "neither uncreated as God, nor yet created as you, but being in the midst between these two extremities."

It is commonly held that Philo made a direct contribution to the development of Christian theology in respect of the identity and creative role of the divine *Logos*, although not all authors hold this position.[19] Zizioulas acutely observes: "Although Philo had tried to free God from creation, he had actually confined him to it. Philo made the world necessarily present to God, ever-present within him in the form of the *logoi*, the thoughts of God."[20] The *Logos* of Philo is divine, but subordinate; in the words of

17. Philo, *Quis rerum divinarum heres sit* 205 (emphasis added).

18. Similar to the *logos theios* and the *logos spermatikos*, respectively. A. Kamesar, "The *Logos Endiathetos* and the *Logos Prophorikos* in Allegorical Interpretation: Philo and the D-Scholia to the *Iliad*," *Greek, Roman, and Byzantine Studies* 44 (2004): 163–81.

19. See McDonough, *Christ as Creator*, 135–49. "The idea that Philo's writings contributed directly to the doctrine of Jesus' agency in creation cannot be proven" (ibid., 149). See also Fabbri, "Creatore e demiurgo," 149–57.

20. Zizioulas, "Creation and Salvation," 86.

Grillmeier, "in accepting gradations between God and the world into his Judaistic monotheism, Philo would feel less threatened than a Christian theologian who designated Christ (and the Pneuma) as God."[21]

Plotinus and the Neo-Platonists

Another important figure to understand the Christian doctrine of creation is the third-century neo-Platonic philosopher Plotinus. Two terms mark his understanding of the world, its creation and dynamics: emanation (in Greek, *aporroia*),[22] and as a result hierarchy (*ieros*).[23] The term "emanation" is used only once in the Old Testament: "For she [Wisdom] is a breath of the power of God, and a pure *emanation* of the glory of the Almighty" (Wis 7:25), but is typical of Platonic thought. In Plotinus emanation refers to the production of one reality from another, and in this case the production of the world from the substance of the divine; this is Plotinus's equivalent to creation,[24] what may be called integral emanation.[25] In real terms emanation is a kind of halfway-house between generation and creation.[26] And the world that results from the process of emanation is clearly hierarchical, connected, and subordinated. Plotinus's emanationist hierarchy[27] is composed of five elements.

At the top of Plotinus's hierarchy is the supreme divinity, the One; below the One is the *Nous*, thought or Mind, which represents the intelligible world, and suggests Plato's Demiurge. The One without the *Nous* is unthinkable, says Plotinus: "just suppress otherness and all you get will be indistinct unity and silence."[28] "The *Nous* is therefore the *Logos* of the

21. Grillmeier, *Christ in the Christian Tradition*, 1:224.

22. I. Ramelli, "Emanatismo" in *Enciclopedia filosofica* (Milan: Bompiani, 2006), 3315–18. In Plotinus a more precise term might be "procession" (*prōodos*). J. Trouillard, *La procession plotinienne* (Paris: PUF, 1955).

23. BDAG 470, s.v. ἱερός.

24. F. Ricken, "Emanation und Schöpfung," *Theologie und Philosophie* 49 (1974): 483–86; L. P. Gerson, "Plotinus's Metaphysics: Emanation or Creation?," *Review of Metaphysics* 46 (1992): 559–74; "Eternal Truth: Plotinus, Aquinas, and James Ross," *Proceedings of the American Catholic Philosophical Association* (1993): 143–50.

25. J.-M. Narbonne, "Plotinus and the Secrets of Ammonius," *Hermathena* 157 (1994): 117–53.

26. Ramelli, "Emanatismo," 3317.

27. G. Scholem, *Major Trends in Jewish Mysticism* (London: Thames and Hudson, 1955), vii, 256.

28. Plotinus, *Enneads* V, 1:4.

One,"[29] God's intelligibility as it were. Below the *Nous* is situated the *psyche,* the soul, equivalent to Plato's world-soul, which serves as a connecting link between the higher world and the world of the senses, "a mediating reality, looking at once upwards and downwards."[30] Below again is the *physis,* or nature, the soul of the material world into which the human soul has fallen. At the bottom of the hierarchy, in the fifth place, is matter itself which is equivalent to nothingness (in Greek, *to me on,* relative nothingness) when it is without form, just as light gets weaker and weaker the further it gets from the source, until it simply disappears.[31] In the *Enneads* Plotinus says that "the entire intellectual order may be figured as a kind of light with the One in repose at its summit as its king."[32]

Colin Gunton notes the continuity between Plato and Plotinus: "What we have in Plotinus is the world view of the *Timaeus* almost entirely freed of the mythological background which still pervades that work."[33] Some authors argue that Plotinus's process of emanation—his equivalent to creation—takes place necessarily,[34] others that it is spontaneous.[35] Whatever the case, the production of the universe may not be looked upon as an act of the divine will in the Christian sense, for the triad which structures reality—the One, the Mind, and the soul—is not equivalent to the Christian Trinity of persons which serves as an interpersonal locus for free divine action. In the words of Gunton:

> The real contrast [between Plotinus and the Christian understanding of the world] is between the flowing forth of the lower from the higher, in which the material order is grudgingly given a small place, and the personal act of creation which affirms the whole of the world, matter and spirit alike. It is between creation as the result of the One's concern with itself, and the triune God's love of that which is not himself.[36]

29. G. Faggin, "Plotino," in *Enciclopedia filosofica,* 8701–12, at 8704.
30. C. E. Gunton, *The Triune Creator: A Historical and Systematic Study* (Grand Rapids, Mich.: Eerdmans, 1998), 34.
31. J. Opsomer, "Proclus vs Plotinus on Matter," *Phronesis* 46 (2001): 154–88.
32. Plotinus, *Enneads* V, 2:2.
33. Gunton, *The Triune Creator,* 35.
34. Copleston, *History of Philosophy,* 1:467.
35. J. M. Rist, *Plotinus: The Road to Reality* (Cambridge: Cambridge University Press, 1967), 72.
36. Gunton, *The Triune Creator,* 36.

For Plotinus's emanation the divinity is conditioned, we may say; for Christianity's creation, it is not.

Plotinus is important in his own right, as the maximum representative of the neoPlatonic philosophical movement. But he is of particular importance because his works, like those of Philo, were influential in the writings of Christian authors, especially Dionysius the Areopagite and Augustine, but also in Origen, Clement of Alexandria, and Arius, who set the scene for Christology as well as trinitarian and creation theology during much of the critical fourth century. Each one of them developed in different ways a theology of the *Logos* in its mediating role between God and the created world. Let us now examine one of them, Arius.

Arius of Alexandria

Given his particular influence, the position of the early fourth-century Alexandrian presbyter Arius should be taken especially into account.[37] On the basis of a series of important biblical texts, Arius took it that the Word/Son, made incarnate in Jesus Christ, was subordinate to the Father in such a way that "there was a time in which he [the Word] did not exist."[38] In a nonextant work attributed to him, the *Thaleia*, we read: "The Son has age and magnitude from the will of God. His origin from God has a 'from when,' a 'from which' and a 'from then.'"[39] This understanding of the Son is structurally similar to Plato's *Timaeus* Demiurge. Besides, it is fair to say that the writings of Plotinus paved the way for Arius.[40] According to his adversary Athanasius, Arius said that "the Father is alien in being to the Son, and he has no origin. Know that the monad [a single subject, the Father] was, but the dyad [a double subject, the Father and the Son] was not, before it came into being."[41] In other words, God once existed as one,

37. G. Bardy, *Recherches sur saint Lucien d'Antioche et son école* (Paris: Beauchesne, 1936); T. E. Pollard, "The Origins of Arianism," *Journal of Theological Studies* 9 (1958): 103–11; L. W. Barnard, "The Antecedents of Arius," *Vigiliae Christianae* 24 (1970): 172–88; Grillmeier, *Christ in the Christian Tradition*, 1:219–48; R. D. Williams, *Arius: Heresy and Tradition*, 2nd ed. (London: Darton, Longman and Todd, 2001), 181–98.

38. According to the historian Sozomen, *Hist. Eccl.* 1:15, and Athanasius, *Contra Arianos* I, 5, who quotes Arius's *Tales*.

39. Athanasius, *Synod.* 15.

40. Grillmeier, *Christ in the Christian Tradition*, 1:224.

41. Athanasius, *Synod.* 15.

but subsequently the Son came into being, giving rise to a twosome, or dyad.

The following text attributed to Arius expresses his position well.

We know *only one God,* who alone is uncreated [unbegotten], who alone is eternal, who alone is without origin, who alone is true, who alone possesses immortality, who alone is wise, who alone is good: the sole ruler, the judge of all, the ordainer and governor, unchanging and immutable, righteous and good, the God of the Law and the prophets of the New Covenant, who *brought forth the only-begotten Son* before eternal times, by whom he created the aeons and all things ... as God's perfect creature, but not as one of the creatures; brought forth, but not as others are brought forth.... For he is not eternal or as eternal or as uncreated as the Father, nor does he have identical being with the Father ... rather, as monad and *archē* [origin] of all, he (the Father) is God before all. So he is also before the Son.[42]

Unlike Plato and Plotinus, the Christian Arius holds to the doctrine of God's creation of the world *ex nihilo.* But this means of course that the created world is clearly distinct from the divinity. So a question arises that did not arise for Plato and Plotinus: which side of the divide is the Son on—God or creation? Arius concludes that the Word is clearly on the side of creation, a supreme creature, but a creature nonetheless. Grillmeier comments that, for Arius,

the gulf between creation and the transcendent God is unbridgeable, because the "Son" too is on the other side of the gulf and therefore cannot know the Father as he is in himself, but only in the way in which he has the right, that is only with creaturely knowledge ... Arius would have found it difficult to lay the foundations for a theology of revelation. He sees the Son chiefly as the mediator of creation ... his *Logos* doctrine is determined cosmologically.[43]

42. Letter of Arius to Alexander of Alexandria, cited in Grillmeier, *Christ in the Christian Tradition,* 1:226n25 (emphasis added). Elsewhere Arius says: "Thus God himself, insofar as he is, is inexpressible for all, he is inexpressible (even) for the Son. For he (the Father) is what he is for himself, that is (he is) unutterable, so that the Son cannot express any of the statements which encompass (God's being). For it is impossible for him to search out the Father who is in himself." *Thaleia,* in Athanasius, *Synod.* 15, 3, in Grillmeier, *Christ in the Christian Tradition,* 1:228. "Everything we have from Arius professes the creation of the Son as an act of the Father's will." R. C. Gregg and D. E. Groh, "The Centrality of Soteriology in Early Arianism," *Anglican Theological Review* 59, no. 3 (1977): 260–78, at 266.

43. Grillmeier, *Christ in the Christian Tradition,* 1:228.

For Arius the *Logos* has to belong to the creaturely realm, "for an immanent principle of form, movement and order cannot belong to the sphere of the transcendent creator God."[44] "If only the divine monad [the Father] was considered 'uncreated,' the Son or the *Logos* (as mediator of creation) had to be transferred into the realm of that which had 'come into being,'" observes Grillmeier.[45] It is clear that for Arius the *Logos* is on the side of the created world: "the Son does not exist of necessity, but only in dependence on a decision by the Father."[46] When Arius speaks of the relationship between the Father and the Son, he is really talking of a relationship between God and the world.[47]

When God wanted to create nature and bring it into being, he saw that it could not participate in the unmixed hand of the Father and his creation; therefore first of all he created and made only the sole, unique one and called this the Son and *Logos*, so that he might be the middle one (i.e. intermediary in a cosmological sense); in this way the rest of the universe could come into being through him.[48]

In the *Thaleia* Arius draws the following conclusion:

"God was not always a Father." But "at one stage God was alone, and not yet a Father, but afterwards He became a Father." "The Son was not always the Son," for, whereas all things were made out of nothing, and all existing creatures and works were made, so the Word of God Himself was "made out of nothing," and "once He was not," and "He was not before His origination," but He as others "had an origin of creation." "For God," he says, "was alone, and the Word as yet was not, nor was Wisdom. Then, *wishing to form us, thereupon He made a certain one*, and named Him Word and Wisdom and Son, that He might form us by means of Him."[49]

And why then did God generate the Son? Clearly because "the *Logos* is only created *when the Father wanted to create us.*"[50]

This position of course marks a significant departure from the proper

44. F. Ricken, "Nikaia als Krisis des altchristlichen Platonismus," *Theologie und Philosophie* 44 (1969): 321–41, at 326.

45. Grillmeier, *Christ in the Christian Tradition*, 1:230.

46. Ibid.

47. Ibid., 1:231.

48. Cited by Bardy, *Recherches sur saint Lucien*, fr. IV, 263. Athanasius, *Contra Arianos* I, 24.

49. Cited by Athanasius, *Contra Arianos* II, 5 (emphasis added).

50. Cited by Bardy, *Recherches sur saint Lucien*, fr. IV, 262.

understanding of the Trinity and creation: according to Arius, the Father's prime intention was one of creating the world, of forming humans, and for that to take place he created the *Logos*. In God's mind the existence and activity of the *Logos*/Son is subordinated to the work of creation. In other words, we may say that the Word's sonship is instrumentalized for the sake of the fabrication of the world.[51] It is true that several earlier Christian authors likewise situated the generation of the Word principally in function of creation.[52] But with Arius the theological conclusions are better delineated; according to Alexander of Alexandria, Arius said that "He (the Son) was created *for our sake*, so that God might create us *through him* as through an instrument; and he would not exist if God had not wanted to create us."[53]

On Arius, Athanasius has the following to say: "And just as the sun is only one of the luminaries in the visible sphere, but lights the whole world according to the ordinance of the one who made it, so too the Son, who is one among the intelligible natures, appears and illuminates all that is in the known cosmos [*noetos kosmos*]."[54] And Grillmeier comments: "The Son of the baptismal creed has become the created mediator of creation. His exclusive pre-eminence consists in the fact that he alone was created directly by the Father, the only true God. So everything else was created through him.... True, Arius assigns the created Logos the role of demiurge. But in his view ... this demiurge is created."[55] And in the words of

51. O'Callaghan, *Children of God in the World*, 255–62.

52. Something of a kind may be found in Justin's *Dialogue* 55:8 and 60:1, which teaches that the procession of the Word, the Wisdom of the Father, took place only for the purpose of creating the world: Scheffczyk, *Schöpfung und Vorlesung*, 36; G. Aeby, *Les missions divines de S. Justin a Origène* (Fribourg: Editions Université de Fribourg, 1958), 6–15. The result in practical terms is the subordination of the Word: *Apol.* I, 63. That is to say, both the being of the Son and the purpose of his existence are subordinate to the Father. Theophilus puts it this way: "When God wished to make all that he determined on, he begot this Word, uttered, the first-born of all creation, not himself being emptied of the Word" (*Ad autol.* II, 22). But the procession of the Word and creation of the world are due to the free will of the Father. Also Tatian holds that the Word proceeds from the Father with creation as the ultimate object (*Or. ad graecos*, 5). For the apologists, the world is created for man, *di' anthropōus*, a typically Stoic position according to M. Spanneut, *Le stoïcisme des Pères de l'Église: De Clément de Rome à Clément d'Alexandrie* (Paris: Seuil, 1957), 380. Thus in Justin, *Apol.* I, 10; Clement, *1 Clem.* 33:4; Theophilus, *Ad Autol.* I, 4 and II, 10; Aristides, *Apol.* I, 3; *Letter of Diognetus* IV, 2. Scheffczyk, *Schöpfung und Vorlesung*, 38, states that the Christological purpose of creation is simply missing in this early period.

53. Cited by Grillmeier, *Christ in the Christian Tradition*, 1:231n43.

54. Cited by Bardy, *Recherches sur saint Lucien*, 343.

55. Grillmeier, *Christ in the Christian Tradition*, 1:232 and 236. Arians also speak of the *logos-sarx*

Rowan Williams: "The *Logos,* as mediator, principle of plurality, source of intelligible structures, exists primarily for the sake of creation, and has no discernible role prior to the Father's decision to create.... It could be said by a hostile reader (like Athanasius) that the creation is the sole *raison d'être* of the Logos."[56]

Nicaea and Athanasius on the Consubstantiality of the Father and the Son

It is clear that Platonic and neo-Platonic thought and terminology had been employed by Church Fathers from the beginning with a view to understanding Christian revelation properly and communicating it effectively. Justin, Irenaeus, Clement of Alexandria, Origen, Eusebius of Caesarea, Arius, Athanasius, Hilary, the Cappadocians, and others contributed to this process. In a variety of different ways they employed the idea, already broached in the New Testament, of Jesus Christ as the Demiurge or *Logos* or mediator not only of redemption but also of creation. From a Christian standpoint the issue, though complex in detail as we have seen throughout this chapter, is quite straightforward in general terms: does Christ, the Word, in his inner essence, belong to the realm of God, or to that of creation? Or is he an intermediate being, not fully divine, not entirely created? Put in another way, is Christ—the Word, the Son—to be understood in the light of revelation, of God's word, that is of scripture and the living tradition of the church, or, rather, in the light of the philosophy of the time, which was of course predominantly Platonic and neo-Platonic?

Arius as a Christian believer could not easily accept the notion of an intermediate being, neither fully divine nor completely created, as Plotinus had suggested, because he took it that the world had been created *ex nihilo,* and so had to posit a clear distinction between God and creation. But it would seem that his understanding of Christ borrowed more heavily from the dominant philosophy than from revelation. In the words of Leslie W. Barnard, Arius's "system was simply one of philosophical dual-

Christology, according to which Christ had no human soul: "The Logos has taken over the place and function of the soul" (238).

56. Williams, *Arius,* 190 and 196.

ism—although not without a biblical coloring in its idea of the Sole, Unoriginate God."[57] Thus the Word/Son belongs primordially to the realm of creatures, and though the highest of them, is *subordinate* to the Father. Arius insisted on this, as we saw, because he wished to hold on to the unassailable oneness of God and the realism of the incarnation of the Word: if God is one and the incarnation is real, then the Word must be intermediate, situated between one and the other, though clearly on the side of creatures.

And Athanasius with the Council of Nicaea would oppose him on this very front. Grillmeier observes that "the Nicenes will be the better theologians—and philosophers. They rule out the middle sphere which Arius occupied with his created Logos and pneuma, and thus reject the Middle Platonic picture of the world."[58] The Council of Nicaea taught in the following terms: "One Lord Jesus Christ, the Only Begotten Son of God, born of the Father before all ages. God from God, Light from Light, true God from true God, begotten, not made, consubstantial [*homoousios*] with the Father; through him all things were made. For us men and for our salvation he came down from heaven. And by the Holy Spirit was incarnate of the Virgin Mary, and became man."[59]

The text makes it quite clear that Jesus in his inner essence belongs fully to the realm of the divine, for he is consubstantial with the Father. It adds of course that "through Him" all things were made, in keeping with the New Testament, and that he became flesh in the power of the Holy Spirit in order to save us. Thus only in an ample sense may it be said that Christ is the mediator of creation, for mediation normally involves a certain distance from the extremes mediated, as Plato, Philo, Plotinus, and Arius explained in a variety of different ways.[60]

57. L. W. Barnard, "The Antecedents of Arius," *Vigiliae Christianae* 24 (1970): 172–88, at 187.

58. Grillmeier, *Christ in the Christian Tradition*, 1:243. He also asks whether "the incarnation was not rather the starting point for the whole Arian system. Could not the heresy of the creatureliness of the Logos have been occasioned by the doctrine of the incarnation, at least in so far as through it the Alexandrian subordinationism was extended to the teaching of the Logos as a creature?" (246). He adds: "Arians say to their Nicene opponents, 'How dare you say that the Logos shares in the Father's existence, if he had a body so as to experience all this.' Behind their objection there is probably the notion that a really transcendent Logos cannot enter into a body-soul conjunction with the human sarx of Christ" (ibid., 247).

59. DH 150 (emphasis added).

60. This is also the position of Athanasius, according to J. M. Robertson, *Christ as Mediator: A*

The principal opponent of Arius of course was Athanasius.[61] The latter explains the role of the Word (*Logos*) in creation in a highly vivid way, as a divine principle of inner cohesion and life in the world, entirely on the side of the God the creator. The following extensive text from his *Contra Gentes* shows this.

The Father of Christ, most holy and above all created existence, who like an excellent pilot, by his own Wisdom and his own Word, our Lord and Savior Christ, steers and preserves and orders all things.... But if the world subsists in reason and wisdom and skill, and is perfectly ordered throughout, it follows that the one that is over it and has ordered it is none other than the Word of God. But by Word I mean ... the living and powerful Word of the good God, the God of the Universe, the very Word which is God, who while different from things that are made, and from all Creation, is the One own Word of the good Father, who by his own providence ordered and illumines this Universe. For being the good Word of the Good Father he produced the order of all things, combining one with another things contrary, and reducing them to one harmonious order.... The holy Word of the Father, then, almighty and all-perfect, uniting with the universe and having everywhere unfolded his own powers, and having illumined all, things both seen and invisible, holds them together and binds them to himself, having left nothing void of his own power.[62]

Athanasius goes on to explain the role of Christ as that of a musician performing harmoniously:

There is nothing that is and takes place but has been made and stands by him [the Word] and through him, as also John 1:1 says, "In the beginning was the Word ..." For just as though some musician, having tuned a lyre, and by his art adjusted the high notes to the low, and the intermediate notes to the rest, were to produce a single tune as the result, so also the Wisdom of God, handling the Universe as a lyre, and adjusting things in the air to things on the earth, and things in the heaven to things in the air, and combining parts into wholes and

Study of the Theologies of Eusebius of Caesarea, Marcellus of Ancrya, and Athanasius of Alexandria (Oxford: Clarendon Press, 2007), 172–74.

61. On Athanasius, the bibliography is vast. See, for example, Anatolios, *Athanasius*; G. Florovsky, "The Concept of Creation in Saint Athanasius," *Studia Patristica* 6, ed. E. A. Livingston (Berlin: Akademie, 1962), 36–57; J. Roldanus, *Le Christ et l'homme dans la théologie d'Athanase d'Alexandrie. Étude de la conjonction de la conception de l'homme avec sa christologie* (Leiden: E. J. Brill, 1977); A. Pettersen, *Athanasius, Outstanding Christian thinkers* (London: Geoffrey Chapman, 1995); T. G. Weinandy, *Athanasius: A Theological Introduction* (Aldershot: Ashgate, 2007).

62. Athanasius, *Contra Gentes*, 40.

> moving them all by his beck and will, produces well and fittingly, as the result, the unity of the universe and of its order, himself remaining unmoved with the Father while he moves all things by his organizing action, as seems good for each to his own Father.... All things according to their several natures are quickened and organized by him, and he produces as the result a marvelous and truly divine harmony.... For with the single impulse of a nod as it were of the Word of God, all things simultaneously fall into order, and each discharge their proper functions, and a single order is made up by them all together.

And in even greater detail, he continues:

> For by a nod and by the power of the Divine Word of the Father that governs and presides over all, the heaven revolves, the stars move, the sun shines, the moon goes her circuit, and the air receives the sun's light and the ether its heat, and the winds blow: the mountains are reared on high, the sea is rough with waves, and the living things in it grow, the earth abides fixed, and bears fruit, and man is formed and lives and dies again, and all things whatever have their life and movement; fire burns, water cools, fountains spring forth, rivers flow, seasons and hours come round, rains descend, clouds are filled, hail is formed, snow and ice congeal, birds fly, creeping things go along, water-animals swim, the sea is navigated, the earth is sown and grows crops in due season, plants grow.[63]

For Athanasius, the divine Word of the eternal Father is the One who makes the world go around.

Christ and Creation in Augustine and Aquinas

Similar explanations to that of Athanasius may be found often among Church Fathers and theologians. "For Athanasius, the Cappadocians, John Damascene, and Augustine it was precisely *creatio ex nihilo* which slipped the chains of the destructive dualism prevalent in late antiquity where matter was bad and spirit was good," in the words of Janet Soskice.[64] Bonaventure, during the Middle Ages, spoke of *mundum quasi carmen pulcherrium*,[65] the created world as a most beautiful song. Likewise Augustine speaks of creation as a beautiful hymn.[66] His position is expressed in

63. Ibid., 42–44.
64. Soskice, "Why *creatio ex nihilo*," 49.
65. Bonaventure, *II Sent.*, d. 13, q. 1, a. 2.
66. Augustine, *De Civ. Dei* XI, 18.

the following terms in his commentary on John's prologue, translated as "that which was made in him [the Word] was life" (Jn 1:3).

A carpenter makes a box. First he has the box in design; for if he had it not in design, how could he produce it by workmanship? But the box in theory is not the very box as it appears to the eyes. It exists invisibly in design, it will be visible in the work. Behold, it is made in the work; has it ceased to exist in design? The one is made in the work, and the other remains which exists in design; for that box may rot, and another be fashioned according to that which exists in design. Give heed, then, to the box as it is in design, and the box as it is in fact. *The actual box is not life, the box in design is life*; because the soul of the artificer, where all these things are before they are brought forth, is living. So . . . because the Wisdom of God, by which all things have been made, contains everything according to design before it is made, therefore those things which are made through this design itself are not immediately life, but *whatever has been made is life in Him*. You see the earth, there is an earth in design; you see the sky, there is a sky in design; you see the sun and the moon, these also exist in design: but externally they are bodies, *in design they are life*.[67]

Thomas Aquinas develops the ideas of Augustine further in his commentary on John 1:3–4, paying special attention to the expression "all things that were made in him were life." He excludes the interpretation of the Manicheans who said that all life is at heart none other than divine life, for there is such a thing as created life.[68] Likewise he avoids the position of Scotus Eriugena who—in his view—gives a similar, quasi-pantheistic interpretation of John,[69] and says that all things "are life" in the Word because "the cause of all effects produced by God is a life and an art full of reasons or living ideas."[70] Rather he follows the position of Augustine that the above citation refers to. In effect, created things may be considered in two ways, either as they are in themselves (some are alive, some or not), or as they are in the Word. In the latter sense all things are alive insofar as their ideas are spiritually present in living divine Wisdom and are identified with it. *Creatura in Deo est creatrix essentia,* concludes Thomas: "In

67. Augustine, *In Tr. Io.* 1:17 (on Jn 1:3). See G. Remy, *Le Christ médiateur dans l'oeuvre de Saint Augustin,* 2 vols. (Paris: H. Champion, 1979).

68. Thomas Aquinas, *In Io.* I, 2 (no. 89).

69. Scotus Eriugena, *Hom. super Prol. Io.,* in J.-P. Migne (ed.), *Patrologiae cursus completus,* series latina (Paris: 1844–64) [hereafter PL], 122:288.

70. Thomas Aquinas, *In Io.* I, 2 (no. 90).

God, the creature is the creating essence."[71] As far as God is concerned the creature is identified with the creator. Thomas explains this at length in the *Summa contra Gentiles*:

Consideration should also be given to this: A thing made by an understanding pre-exists in the plan understood even before it is in itself, for the house exists in the understanding of the architect before it is brought to actuality. Now, the Word of God is the knowledge of all those things which are made by God.... Necessarily, then, all those things which are made by God have pre-existed in the Word of God even before they are in their own proper nature. Now, what is in something is in it in the way proper to that in which it is; it is not in that thing in its own proper manner, for the building in the mind of the architect exists intelligibly and immaterially. Things must, therefore, be understood to have pre-existed in the Word of God in the manner of the Word Himself. The manner of the Word Himself is this: He is one, simple, immaterial, and *not only living but even life*, since He is His own being. Necessarily, then, the things made by God have pre-existed in the Word of God from eternity, immaterially, without any composition. Moreover, they can be nothing else in Him but the Word Himself who is life. For this reason, we read: "that which was made in Him," that is, in the Word, "was life" (Jn 1:3).[72]

When we say that the world was made "through him," this does not mean, for Aquinas, that the Word is a kind of inert instrumental cause (a Demiurge) which acts in a way extrinsic to the efficient cause, as a blueprint for an artifice, as an agent in building, as a pilot for a boat, as a map for a journey, but rather that the living God creates by Wisdom and for Wisdom. Augustine had already said as much: "the Word is art, full of the ideas of all living things."[73] As a result of this living presence of the Word in the world, Thomas adds, each and every creature becomes *vox Verbi*,[74] "the voice of the Word." In fact G. K. Chesterton called Aquinas *Thomas a Creatore*, because he saw that creation was at the very heart of his work, indeed of his metaphysical construct.[75]

71. Ibid. (no. 91). See Remy, "Le Christ Médiateur."

72. Thomas Aquinas, *SCG* IV.13.10.

73. Augustine, *De Trin.* VI, 10:11.

74. Thomas Aquinas, *I Sent.*, d. 27, q. 2, arg. 3, ad 3.

75. G. K. Chesterton, *St. Thomas Aquinas* (London: Hodder, 1947). See especially J.-M. Vernier, *Théologie et métaphysique de la création chez Saint Thomas d'Aquin* (Paris: P. Téqui, 1995).

PART 2

The Theology of Creation

6

Christ and Creation

HAVING PRESENTED the principal moments in the history of the dogma of creation—scripture, patristic witness, official church teaching, and philosophical background—I shall now turn to different aspects of the systematic theology of creation. In this chapter, in continuity with the previous one, I shall consider what it means for the created world to have been created in and through and for the Word. In the following two chapters I shall consider the purpose of creation, why the universe was made, from two perspectives: that of divine freedom as trinitarian love (chapter 7) and that of the glory of God (chapter 8). After that I shall look into some specific aspects of the mystery of creation: the conservation of the created world, *concursus*, providence, and time (chapter 9), the material world and ecology (chapter 10), and the spiritual world of angels and demons (chapter 11).

Confronting the Greek and the Christian Understanding of the *Logos*

In the previous chapter I considered the role of the *Logos*/Demiurge in the making of the world proper to the Platonic tradition in four authors: Plato, Philo, Plotinus, and Arius. Other authors could have been examined. However, in spite of the differences and shifts between and among each of these authors, a basic structure emerges regarding the relationship and mediation between God and the world, what I shall refer to in general terms as the "Greek *Logos*," which is situated between the creator and the creature. A similar structure may be found within Christian theology, developed in Old Testament wisdom literature, in Paul and John, with Irenaeus and Justin, with Origen and Athanasius, with Augustine and Thomas (as we saw in chapters 2–4). I shall refer to this in general terms as the "Christian *Logos*."

Important confrontations have taken place between the two positions that served to enrich and clarify both sides. Yet it became quite clear during the Arian controversy and at the Council of Nicaea that the positions, though not dissimilar linguistically, were simply irreconcilable with one another at a philosophical level, involving a different understanding of the divinity, of the created world, of metaphysics, of revelation and of salvation.

T. E. Pollard sums up the contrast between Arius and Athanasius in the following terms.

> Over against the metaphysical monotheism of the Arians, for whom the essence of the godhead is to be without beginning and unoriginate, Athanasius sets the biblical concept of the living and loving God, the Father of Jesus Christ. Over against the concept of a God who is remote, inaccessible and incapable of entering into direct relations with the created world, Athanasius sets the Church's faith in a God who condescends continually to man in creation, revelation, redemption and sanctification; who, in Jesus Christ his Son, becomes man for the salvation of men. The God of the Arians neither creates, nor reveals himself, nor redeems man. "Arius never speaks of the love of God." . . . There is no room in Athanasius' conception of God for the lifeless, impersonal, privative attributes derived from extra-biblical sources, which the Arians ascribe to the godhead. The difference between Athanasius and Arius is the difference between a living religion and an intellectualistic philosophy, between salvation and speculation, between the evangelical faith in God who reveals himself as Father through his Son Jesus Christ and flights of metaphysical fancy into the realm of the unknown and unknowable. "The sin of Arianism is that it shifts the centre of interest from the hope of salvation to the hope of explanation."[1]

Christoph Schwöbel observes that the Nicene affirmation of the equality of the Word with the Father directly involves the doctrine of creation *ex nihilo*: "The *homoousios* of trinitarian theology depicting the relationship of Father and Son as one of ontological coequality here plays a critical role

1. T. E. Pollard, *Johannine Christology and the Early Church* (Cambridge: Cambridge University Press, 1970), 192. Pollard cites two authors within this text: H. M. Gwatkin, quoted by D. M. Baillie, *God Was in Christ: An Essay on Incarnation and Atonement* (London: Faber and Faber, 1948), 70, and W. Temple, *Christus Veritas* (London: Macmillan, 1926), 13.

in determining the ontological status of the world as one of contingent, that is created, being."[2]

Drawing on what was explained in chapter 5, and simplifying somewhat the two positions—one centered on what we called the Greek *Logos* and the other on the Christian *Logos*—we may contrast and explain them as follows on the basis of five elements: the function of the *Logos* with respect to the creation of the world; the kind of continuity between God and the world that the *Logos* expresses; the relationship between the *Logos* and God; the divinity of the *Logos*; and, last of all, the purpose of the existence of the *Logos* (see table 6-1).

As was said above, the positions mentioned represent the Greek and the Christian understanding of the identity of the divine *Logos* in respect of the creation of the world in generic and approximative terms. Several fundamental observations may be made in respect of the Christian understanding of creation and the created world, as follows: whether or not God uses instruments in the creation of the world, the diversity and unity within the created world, the ultimate purpose of creation, the transcendence of God and his immanence in respect of the created world, and the role of the Holy Spirit in the work of creation.

The Role of Instruments in Creation

From what we have seen, the work of creation is undertaken by God alone without instruments of any kind. The church has always taught that God is the one and only origin of the universe.[3] If the divine Word is directly involved in the work of creation, this can only mean that he is fully divine, "God from God, Light from Light, true God from true God," as the Nicene creed says. The non-Christian Greek *Logos* or Demiurge on the other hand involves a clearly instrumental role of mediation for the Word, situated between the sovereignty and transcendence of the divinity and the deficiency of matter. Of course in the work of revelation, of redemption, of salvation, and of providence, God does use instruments, as we shall see presently. But in that of creation, it may be said that each and every creature

2. C. Schwöbel, "God, Creation and the Christian Community: The Dogmatic Basis of a Christian Ethic of Createdness," in *The Doctrine of Creation* (ed. Gunton), 149–76, at 156.

3. See DH 800 and 3005.

TABLE 6-1. GREEK LOGOS AND CHRISTIAN LOGOS

Topic Area	The Role of the Greek *logos*	The Role of the Christian *Logos*
The function of the *logos* in respect of the creation of the world	The function of the Greek *logos* is one of giving form, of shaping, of ordering the prime matter that already exists; in that sense the *logos* does not give existence to things *ex nihilo*.	God creates the world through the *Logos*, the perfect Image of the Father, giving it existence *ex nihilo* directly by means of the Word.
The kind of continuity between God and the world expressed by the *logos*	The Greek view envisions a profound though hierarchical continuity between all the different elements of reality: between the supreme divinity (the Good or the One) at the top, then the demiurge, the *Logos*, the World Soul, the souls of heroes and humans, right down to the purely material world.	For Christianity, there is a clear and insuperable distinction between the divine and the created sphere, involving two completely distinct ontologies. No ontological continuity—whether hierarchical or otherwise—may be posited between God and the world. All finite beings share the created condition.
The relationship between the *logos* and God	Within this hierarchy, the Greek mediating *logos* is inferior or subordinate to God, because God cannot enter directly into contact with preexisting matter, or with matter of any kind.	The Christian *Logos* is consubstantial with the Father, and through the incarnation has direct contact with the created world, both material and spiritual, without modifying the nature of either.
The divinity of the *logos*	The Greek *logos* is not fully divine because it is limited on the one hand by the world of *ideas* to which it refers, and on the other hand by the facticity and opacity of preexisting *matter*.	The *Logos* is limited neither by God (because everything the Father has, the Son also has), nor by preexisting matter (because matter comes into being, whole and entire, at the moment of creation).
The purpose of the existence of the *logos*	The Greek *logos* was made or created *on account of the world*, because God, the Good or the One, wished to provide harmony, goodness, beauty, and light to all that was disorderly, chaotic, ugly, and dark; this provides a cosmocentric or anthropocentric vision of humanity and the created world.	The world was made *on account of the Logos*, the Son, and not the other way around; in that sense the Christian vision of the world is logocentric, or better Christocentric; it is neither anthropocentric nor cosmocentric. In fact the created world need never have existed.

is touched by the hand of God, or to use the terminology of Irenaeus, by the *hands* of God, the Son and the Holy Spirit.[4] Thomas Aquinas explains why no instruments whatever were or could be involved in the work of creation. He offers two arguments.[5]

On the one hand, he says, creation is the production of all things *ex nihilo*. This operation requires the infinite power of God, not so much in respect of the finite creature made (what is called the *terminus ad quem* of creation), but in respect of what Thomas calls the *id ex quo fit*, "that from which it is made," the *terminus a quo*, which is sheer nothingness, total absence of being. Creation after all is the gift of existence and so anything that has *received* being does not have nor will ever have the *native* capacity to communicate or donate it further to others. No creature, no matter how exalted, can be an instrument for the creation of another creature. "The earth is the Lord's and the fullness thereof" (Ps 24:1).

On the other hand, Thomas explains that the very nature of instrumental causality means that no creature could be an agent in the creation of others. The operation proper to an instrument, a brush for painting, a hammer for putting in a nail, a pen for writing, according to Aquinas, is *dispositive operari*:[6] the instrument acts on the object preparing it for the action of the efficient cause, disposing, facilitating, directing. But because creation involves an action that literally initiates with nothing, there is nothing whatsoever to prepare or to dispose of in the first place. The only thing that makes creation possible is the direct, immediate, and exclusive action of almighty God who brings things into being. And this is so for both material and spiritual beings.

Diversity and Unity in Creation

For the Greeks, hierarchy is written into reality, from beginning to end: beings are ontologically situated within a clearly defined hierarchy. That is the way things are made and the way they will always be. Superior beings determine the destiny of inferior ones; the latter exist for the sake of the former. In the Christian context, however, an important consequence of

4. See Irenaeus, *Adv. Haer.* V, 6:1.
5. See Thomas Aquinas, *ST* I, q. 45, a. 5.
6. Ibid., co.

the fact that each creature has been created by God, without instruments, directly, might be termed the democracy of creation. Each and every created being, from the last electron lost in space to the highest angel glorifying the Trinity, has been equally created by God *ex nihilo*. Equally created, of course, does not mean created equal. But the point is an important one: God commits himself with each and every creature, down to the last detail. All of them have in common that they are loved into existence by the creator. Obviously God gives each being its own nature and power and destiny, but each and every one has been touched directly by the hand of God, as it hovers perpetually over the metaphysical abyss of nothingness. But this brings us to ask: what is the meaning of the differences between created beings? All are created, certainly, but not all are equal in their nature. So, what is the meaning of this inequality?

Thomas Aquinas puts it as follows. He says that God

> brought things into existence so that his goodness might be communicated to creatures and reenacted through them. And because it was not possible for his goodness to be represented through any single creature, he produced many different ones, so that what was wanting in one expression of divine goodness might be supplied by another; for goodness, which in God is single and united, in creatures is multiple and divided. Hence the whole universe shares and represents his goodness less incompletely than any one creature by itself.[7]

We can see that the diversity present in creation is a sign of God's transcendence:[8] all things are one in God because God is infinite and the source of all the diverse things. Diversity is not a problem for a Christian believer.

The fact of God-created diversity may be seen in different biblical texts, and especially in Genesis 1 and 1 Corinthians 15:39–41. Genesis 1:2 does speak of a primordial, undifferentiated uniformity, yet the divine work of creation in all its variety "depicts such diversifying as a deliberate and benevolent process of ordering and enrichment, rather than as an accident that would better have been avoided."[9] McFarland writes: "Contemporary science also derives the complexity of the present universe from an earlier state of relative homogeneity (the first fractions of a second), it ascribes

7. Thomas Aquinas, *ST* I, q. 47, a. 1.

8. See McFarland, *From Nothing*, 67–72.

9. Ibid., 70.

the resulting diversification of creatures—from galaxies thousands of light-years across to atomic nuclei many orders of magnitude smaller than a grain of sand—to the accumulated effects of the mutual interaction of forces and particles over billions of years through cosmological and biological evolution."[10]

According to Genesis 1 it would seem that God creates this diversity. Still, there is a problem here, what might be termed the disanalogy between divine and creaturely productivity, which McFarland explains as follows: "Whereas the Trinitarian diversification of the Godhead entails neither diminution of the Father as source nor competition among the hypostases that are constituted through the acts of begetting and proceeding, the dynamics of creaturely diversity entails both: the flourishing of some creatures invariably comes at the expense of others."[11]

Scripture does suggest a kind of universal, harmonious vegetarianism, the absence of all hostility and adversity within created nature (Gn 1:29; Is 11:6–9, 65:25), as an ideal at least. However the view that the Bible seems to present "does not reflect the structure of any ecosystem that has existed during the half a billion years of multicellular life on earth."[12] Modern evolution is generally considered as a zero-sum affair, in clear contrast with divine life, for God is inexhaustible in riches, whereas "creaturely begetting entails a reallocation of resources that diminishes the parent and represents a threat to others of the same species."[13] This may be seen in the phenomena of predation and parasitism among creatures. Specifically, as we can see, "no two creatures can occupy the same space,"[14] for *perichoresis* (the mutual presence of the divine persons to one another) is to be found fully only in God and not in creatures. Some see this as a sign of the brutality of cosmic life,[15] others as an indication of a self-regulating system moving toward homeostasis, that is, a stable equilibrium between interdependent systems.[16]

10. Ibid.

11. Ibid., 71.

12. Ibid.

13. Ibid.

14. Ibid., 72.

15. See R. Dawkins, *The Selfish Gene*, 3rd ed. (Oxford: Oxford University Press, 2006).

16. See J. E. Lovelock, *Gaia: A New Look at Life on Earth* (Oxford: Oxford University Press, 2000).

However, many Church Fathers speak of the unity of the cosmos as God's great work, Irenaeus for example,[17] and Athanasius in his musical analogy as we saw in the previous chapter. Augustine, for one, waxes eloquent on the unity of the cosmos:

> Seven times I have counted Scripture saying you saw that what you made is good. But on the eighth occasion when you saw all that you had made, it says they were not merely good but "very good"—as if taking everything at once into account. For individual items were only "good," but everything taken together was both "good" and "very good." This truth is also declared by the beauty of the bodies. A body composed of its constituent parts, all of which are beautiful, is far more beautiful as a whole than those parts taken separately; the whole is made of their well-ordered harmony; though individual, the constituent parts are also beautiful.[18]

But Christians also recognize the God-willed variety, diversity, and lack of uniformity present among creatures.[19] Thomas Aquinas explains the God-given nature of variety and diversity as follows: "Divine wisdom is the cause of the distinction present in things on account of the perfection of the universe; the same may be said of inequality."[20] The perfection of the universe, he says, actually requires variety and diversity among created beings. Michael Welker speaks of creation as "the construction and maintenance of associations of different, interdependent creaturely realms . . . such that God creates by bringing different creaturely realms into fruitful associations of interdependent relations that promote life."[21]

17. See Irenaeus, *Adv. Haer.* II, 25:2.

18. Augustine, *Confessions* XIII, 43.

19. See McFarland, *From Nothing*, 73–83.

20. Thomas Aquinas, *ST* I, q. 47, a. 2, co. See O'Callaghan, *Children of God in the World*, 507–12.

21. M. Welker, *Creation and Reality* (Grand Rapids, Mich.: Fortress Press, 2000), 13. In the words of D. B. Hart, "On the older model, the actual distinction between the Father's generation of the Son and God's creation of the world was somewhat indiscernible; the Logos was, in some sense, merely the first movement in a kind of cascading pullulation of lesser beings, each level of existence ever more remote and estranged from its highest source. Now, however, with God's full transcendence and creation's inherent integrity both established, as it were, it was no longer necessary to think of this world as a distortion or dilution of divine reality, which must be negated or forsaken if the divine is to be known in its own nature" (*Atheist Delusions*, 207).

The Ultimate Purpose of Creation

The last of the five points mentioned in table 6.1 is of particular relevance. From the standpoint of Christian faith, we have seen that the work of creation should be considered as logocentric or Christocentric (or perhaps theocentric), rather than cosmocentric or anthropocentric (closer to the Greek understanding). What does this involve?

For the Greeks, the *Logos* or Demiurge was produced by the supreme divinity with a view to putting order (*kosmos*) on unruly preexistent matter. In doing so the *Logos*/Demiurge was not fully free in making or shaping the world, but was conditioned to some degree by factors beyond himself. God's hand was forced, to some extent at least, to give life to an intermediate first-being that would build or shape up the world as we know it. That is, the *Logos*/Demiurge exists in function of the world and not the other way around. In other words, the world is necessary and the *Logos*/Demiurge is contingent, for it must look toward and obey the eternal Platonic Forms.

For the Christian understanding, conversely, the consubstantial *Logos*/Son who became flesh exists with the Father for all eternity, in the absence of matter or created objects of any kind. The world therefore is simply and solely the fruit of a completely free act of God through and for the *Logos*/Son, Jesus Christ, an entirely unconditioned creative action. That is to say, the world exists on account of the *Logos*/Son—that is, Christ—and not the other way around. In effect, from the standpoint of Christian faith, the world is fundamentally contingent and completely dependent, whereas the *Logos*, Christ the eternal Son, is necessary and eternal, as necessary as God himself is.

This explains why scripture speaks not only of the mediating or exemplary role of the *Logos* in the work of creation, but also of Christ as the final cause or purpose of the created world, a position that is particularly clear in Paul's letter to the Colossians: "all things were created *through* him and *for* him" (1:16). Arius saw things differently in his work *Thaleia* in a text already cited: "'God was not always a Father,' but 'once God was alone, and not yet a Father, but afterwards He became a Father.' 'The Son was not always the Son' ... but He as others 'had an origin of creation.' 'Then, *wishing to form us*, thereupon He made a certain one, and named Him Word and

Wisdom and Son, that He might form us by means of Him.'"[22] As a result, in the words of Arius, "the *Logos* is only created when the Father wanted to create us."[23] For Arius, in the words of his bishop, Alexander of Alexandria, "He (the Son) was created *for our sake,* so that God might create us *through him* as through an instrument; and he would not exist if God had not wanted to create us."[24] The position of Arius, as we saw above, owes more to the Greek view of the origin of the world than to the Christian one.

Tertullian, as he contemplated God patiently modeling the body of Adam, reflected: "For, whatever was the form and expression which was then given to the clay (by the Creator) Christ was in His thoughts as one day to become man, because the Word, too, was to be both clay and flesh, even as the earth was then."[25] Irenaeus says the same thing: "For inasmuch as He had a pre-existence as a saving Being, it was necessary that what might be saved should also be called into existence, in order that the Being who saves should not exist in vain."[26] From the time of the creation of Adam, in other words, God looked forward toward the birth of the Savior.[27] It is a common position among Christian thinkers.[28]

According to Maximus the Confessor, the work of creation is directed to Christ and not to creation itself.[29] McFarland observes that

> Maximus's interpretation of humanity's role in creation does not involve any appeals to [human] lordship, sovereignty, or the manipulation of other creatures. Instead, he depicts humanity more as the keystone to creation's order than as its master (or even its steward). As in a round arch, where the keystone's role is a matter of relative position rather than any intrinsic properties of the stone itself, humans' special status seems to derive from their location in the overall structure and thus is primarily a function of their relation to other creatures rather than evidence of any inherent superiority.[30]

22. Athanasius, *Contra Arianos* I, 5.

23. Cited in Bardy, *Recherches sur saint Lucien,* 262–63.

24. Cited in Grillmeier, *Christ in the Christian Tradition,* 1:231n43.

25. Tertullian, *De res. carnis* 6.

26. Irenaeus, *Adv. Haer.* III, 22:3.

27. See ibid., 21:10; *Epideixis* I, 2:22.

28. Bonaventure for example saw Christ as the "absolute final cause of creation," Bonaventure, *III Sent.,* d. 1, q. 2, a. 2. See Scheffczyk, *Schöpfung und Vorlesung,* 88.

29. See Maximus the Confessor, *Quaest. ad Thalass.* 2. See T. T. Tollefsen, *The Christocentric Cosmology of St. Maximus the Confessor* (Oxford: Oxford University Press, 2008).

30. McFarland, *From Nothing,* 80.

Commenting the parable of the mustard seed (Mt 13:31–32), Maximus teaches that the world, grounded in the eternal divine Word, gives rise to a varied multitude of creatures:

> The Word of God is like a grain of mustard seed: before its cultivation it appears to be very small, but when it has been properly cultivated, it shows itself to be so big that the noble *logoi* of sensible and intellectual creatures, like birds, find rest in it. For the *logoi* of all things, as finite beings, are set in [the Word], but it is limited by any of them.[31]

All beings share the fact of being, all are necessary parts of the whole: so, we must grasp the one divine *Logos* as the source and end of all.[32] McFarland comments on Maximus's position: "all *logoi* abide equally in the one divine *Logos*, and none provides access to the *Logos* apart from the grace of divine illumination. . . . In short, the light streaming from Christ enables us to understand the world as God's creation, thereby confirming Jesus as the necessary reference point for all human knowledge of God and the world alike."[33] And he concludes: "Because the unity of creation can be established only in the *Logos* and not through reference to any feature of created being considered in itself, it is not enough to say that God created the world, but it is necessary to specify that God created it *from nothing*."[34] I shall return to this issue in chapter 8, on the glory of God.

The Transcendence and Immanence of God in Respect of Creation

God, through the prophet Isaiah, declares that "my thoughts are not your thoughts, neither are your ways my ways, says the Lord. For as the heavens are higher than the earth, so are my ways higher than your ways and my thoughts than your thoughts" (Is 55:8). God in his being and action is completely transcendent to creatures. John Damascene says that God "is in his own place, filling all things and being above all things and himself

31. Maximus the Confessor, *Capita* 2:10.

32. See McFarland, *From Nothing*, 82.

33. Ibid., 82. So, "the point of the Incarnation is not for Christ to displace other creatures as the object of our vision, but rather to enable the mind 'to see with knowledge what is already in front of it'" (ibid.). See also A. Louth, *Maximus the Confessor* (London; New York: Routledge, 1996), 107.

34. McFarland, *From Nothing*, 83.

maintaining all things ... all things are distant from God not by place but by nature."[35] Anselm speaks of God as "that than which nothing greater can be conceived."[36] Thomas says that *Deus non est in genere*,[37] "God does not belong to any species." That is to say, God is not a being like any other. He is not one more being. Thus his very existence destabilizes any conceptual system we may attempt to develop with a view to understanding reality in general.[38] This is what the *transcendence* of God means: God is not one more among the rest, not even is he the pinnacle of beings; rather he is totally above and beyond all beings.

Macarius the Great says: "He is God, and she [the soul] is non-God. He is the Lord, and she the handmaid; He the Creator, and she the creation; He the Architect, and she the fabric; and there is nothing in common between Him and her nature."[39] John Damascene observes that whereas "generation means producing from the substance of one who generates an offspring similar in substance to the begetter, creation ... is the bringing into being, from outside and not from the substance of the creator, an actor of something, entirely unlike [by nature]."[40] Florovsky explains these words as follows: "There is an infinite distance between God and creation, and this is a *distance of natures*. All is distant from God and is remote from him not by place but by nature ... [this is] the living duality of God and creation."[41] Zizioulas puts it simply: "Everything that exists is either created or uncreated. There is no intermediate category.... In our case existence is forced. It is easy to assume that if it is necessary for us, existence must be necessary for the one who has brought us into existence, but we cannot infer one from the other."[42] According to Sokolowski, "in Christian faith God is understood not only to have created the world, but to have permitted the distinction between himself and the world to occur ... God is understood as distinct from the world, not the best thing in it."[43]

This fundamental affirmation could give the impression that God is

35. John Damascene, *De fide orth.* I, 13.
36. Anselm, *Proslogion* 2.
37. Thomas Aquinas, *ST* I, q. 3, a. 5.
38. See McFarland, *From Nothing*, 30.
39. Macarius of Egypt, *Hom.* 49:4.
40. John Damascene, *De fide orth.* I, 8.
41. Florovsky, "Creature and Creaturehood," 46.
42. Zizioulas, "Creation and Salvation," 91.
43. Sokolowski, *The God of Faith and Reason*, 33 and 47.

distant from creatures, unconnected from and disinterested in them, but scripture assures us that the creator God is also infinitely close to created beings: God is said to be immanent to created reality. God is the one who "gives life to everything" (Neh 9:6) in the present moment. In the Book of Job, God is the one who generates earthquakes (Jb 9:5–6), brings about eclipses (9:7), wraps up water in the clouds (26:8), spreads his clouds over the moon (26:9), brings down hail and snow from his storehouses (38:22), and molds Job himself like clay (10:9). In the New Testament the emphasis shifts to Christ the Word of God, in whom and through whom the whole created order exists (Jn 1:3). "He is before all things, and in him all things hold together" (Col 1:17). The Son is the one who "sustains all things by his powerful word" (Heb 1:3).

This is a paradox in many ways, and a very important one. Creatures have literally nothing purely of their own to fall back on, except nothingness, *nihil*. God alone is the support of their being and action. Nothing whatever escapes divine lordship. As we shall see in detail in chapter 9, God not only creates the world, but conserves it in being at every moment, moves each being to act according to the nature given to it, and brings it to plenitude. Nothing escapes the hand of God. God is truly omnipresent. Speaking of the human heart, Augustine says that God is *intimior intimo meo*, "closer to me than I am to myself."[44]

But how do God's transcendence and immanence combine? The impression could be given that if God is completely transcendent to the created world, then he is distant from it, disconnected from it, disinterested in it. God would have to come down from his throne of glory, as it were, in order to be close to creation. Anderson puts this apparent objection in the following way: "In a world in which matter stands over against God, God is necessarily limited by the constraints it imposes. Though divine transcendence is not at risk, the degree of intimacy [immanence] that God can have with the world is severely qualified."[45] Such explanations of course involve an anthropomorphic and materialistic view of reality in which God and creatures are taken equally as beings that can be compared with one another within a hierarchy. It would seem that God can in some

44. Augustine, *Confessions* III, 6:11.

45. Anderson, *"Creatio ex nihilo,"* 23.

way be enriched by, or affected by, created beings.[46] If this were the case, God would have to distance himself from the created world in order to affirm his transcendence and sovereignty, just as a human authority needs to establish a certain distance from his or her subjects in order to be able to command over them.

It should be said however that divine transcendence is what makes immanence possible in the first place. If God were metaphysically comparable to creatures then he would have something in common with them, and something not in common. But God has nothing in common with created beings: he keeps them in being and action without being in any way identified or confused with them. God alone is good, indeed, is Goodness itself, the source of all goodness, even though he creates good beings. Thomas Aquinas puts it as follows: "God is not present to things as if he was mixed with them: he is neither the matter or form of anything, but is present in his works as agent cause."[47] And Régis Jolivet says: "Divine transcendence is not a spatial beyond, but rather absolute independence. Immanence is not a mixing of divine Being with created things, but rather a kind of spiritual presence."[48] The doctrine of creation, according to Kathryn Tanner, is precisely what "explains how the Bible can speak of God's utter transcendence from and immanence to the world in a non-contradictory fashion."[49]

God in fact is pure Spirit, which means that he is infinitely close to the material world without being a part of it. That is just what spirit means: it permeates reality without losing its own identity.[50] Richard Norris put it succinctly: "What makes God different from every creature—his eternal and ingenerate simplicity—is thus . . . precisely what assures his direct and

46. See P. O'Callaghan, "Can God Be Enriched? On the Metaphysical Underpinnings of Von Balthasar's Theology," *Irish Theological Quarterly* 84, no. 2 (2019): 175–94.

47. Thomas Aquinas, *SCG* II.68.

48. R. Jolivet, *Métaphysique*, 5th ed. (Paris: Emmanuel Vitte, 1955), 497.

49. Tanner, *God and Creation in Christian Theology*. See also J. M. Soskice, "Creation and the Glory of Creatures," *Modern Theology* 29 (2013): 172–85.

50. McFarland observes that "transcendence and immanence do not stand in this sort of zero-sum relationship in the Christian doctrine of creation from nothing, because the nature of God's difference from creatures—precisely as the One who transcends all categories—cannot be defined in terms of the categorical differences of kind (vis. *this* rather than *that*) by which creatures are distinguished from one another" (*From Nothing*, 105).

intimate involvement with every creature."[51] Transcendence is the very thing that makes immanence possible.

One result of this is that the radical quality of creation is what makes the life of grace eminently necessary for the salvation of creatures. Sokolowski observes: "If human agency could, on its own terms, achieve or at least initiate the divine life in man, as the Pelagians and Semi-Pelagians held, then that divine life would be something achievable within the powers of nature and the world, and God would not be distinguished from the world in the way Christian faith understands him to be."[52] McFarland, speaking of the pre-Judeo-Christian mythological creation accounts, observes that "these cosmogonies share the presupposition of a fundamental ontological continuity between Creator and creature: the world and its inhabitants derive from divinity in such a way that the visible cosmos includes traces of divinity, however obscure or deformed these may be." According to Theophilus and Irenaeus, he adds, "it is precisely the metaphysical *discontinuity* between Creator and creature . . . that becomes for them the basis for God's ability to interact directly with creatures."[53] And in the words of David B. Hart:

> The doctrine of creation *ex nihilo*, by God's free action, raised the principle of divine transcendence to an altogether vertiginous height. It produced a vision of this world as the gratuitous gift of divine love, good in itself: not merely the defective reflection of a higher, truer world, not a necessary emanation of the divine nature or a sacrificial economy upon which the divine in some sense feeds, but an internally coherent reality that by its very autonomy gives eloquent witness to the beauty and power of the God who made it.[54]

In practical terms the working out of divine transcendence and immanence should be understood in a Christological way: the incarnate Word in person provides the maximum revelation of what it means for God to be united to the creature, without compromising the proper nature of either. Reading the relationship transcendence-immanence from a Christological standpoint helps us understand that God's very self-sufficiency is

51. R. A. Norris, *God and World in Early Christian Theology: A Study in Justin Martyr, Irenaeus, Tertullian and Origen* (London: A. and C. Black, 1966), 86. He refers here to Irenaeus.

52. Sokolowski, *The God of Faith and Reason*, 37.

53. McFarland, *From Nothing*, xii and 19.

54. Hart, *Atheist Delusions*, 201.

what makes his love for creatures possible[55] and his will to make them flourish.[56] In effect, God's love for creatures does not depend on their nature, on their poor contribution, but entirely precedes their existence and essence and action. Sokolowski writes: "the distinction between God and the world, the denial that God in his divinity is part of or dependent on the world, was brought forward with greater clarity through the discussion of the way the Word became flesh."[57] In fact the distinction that creation establishes between God and creatures is the very thing that makes the mysteries of the Trinity, of grace and of sacraments possible.[58] "What occurs in a sacrament can be understood only in the context in which the world is seen as created and as distinguished from the Christian God. If this setting is not appreciated, the sacraments become simply commemorations of a past event, signs of a community's decisions, expressions of someone's dispositions, or symbols of principles or truths."[59] Sacraments are much more than that; like the incarnation, they give expression not only to the union between God and creature that they bring about, but also of their absolute distinction.

55. The following words of the abbess Julian of Norwich should be noted: "[The Lord] showed me something small, no bigger than a hazelnut, lying in the palm of my hand, as it seemed to me, and it was round as a ball. I looked at it with the eyes of my understanding and thought: What can this be? I was amazed that it could last, for I thought that because of its littleness it would suddenly have fallen into nothing. And I was answered in my understanding: It lasts and always will, because God loves it; and thus everything has being through the love of God. . . . In this little thing I saw three properties. The first is that God made it, the second is that God loves it, the third is that God preserves it. But what did I see in it? It is that God is the Creator and the protector and the love." *Showings V*, trans. E. Colledge and J. Walsh (New York: Paulist, 1978), 183.

56. McFarland insists on this point. "Interpreting creation *from nothing* as meaning that in the beginning there is nothing but God, that there is created *nothing apart from God,* and that in creation *nothing limits God*—this interpretation in the first instance suggests very traditional views of divine self-sufficiency, omnicausality, and sovereignty, respectively. Read within the specifically christological framework suggested by the opening verses of John's gospel, however, these forbidding-sounding attributes acquire a rather different spin: *Nothing but God* points to the fact that divine self-sufficiency takes the form of love that is realized in the mutual communion of the Father with the Son in the power of the Spirit. *Nothing apart from God* proposes a vision of divine omnicausality as the extension outside of God of the sharing of being that constitutes God's own triune life. *Nothing limits God* means that divine sovereignty is perfected in God's making the life of a creature to be God's own, as a means of ensuring creation's flourishing. Viewed in this threefold, christological mode, the point of creation from nothing is not, as the doctrine's critics fear, to affirm God's ultimate indifference to creatures but rather God's total and unrestricted dedication to them" (*From Nothing,* 106).

57. Sokolowski, *God of Faith and Reason*, 37.

58. Ibid., 38.

59. Ibid., 146.

Creation in the *Logos* and the Holy Spirit

Throughout the Arian controversy that followed the Council of Nicaea, Church Fathers came to realize more and more that the truth about the *Logos* incarnate, who is consubstantial with the Father, could hold up only by means of a thorough reflection on the person and action of the Holy Spirit, third person of the trinitarian triad.[60] Within the Platonic/Greek understanding of the *Logos,* which I considered in chapter 5, nothing comparable to the Spirit may be found. The triad of Plotinus—One, Mind, and soul—is hierarchical in character and clearly nonmutual; it certainly involves no consubstantiality of persons. However, the Nicene-Constantinopolitan creed insisted on the full divinity of the Spirit who is coeternal with the Father and the Son, alongside them is adored and glorified as the one true God, and is the Lord and giver of life.[61] Just as the Son reveals the truth of the Father, the Holy Spirit reveals the truth of the Son (and thus of the Father), because the *Logos* is not just the perfect image of the Father, but also the firstborn, the beloved Son, loved in the Holy Spirit. Thus the creation of the world is not just the work of the Father through the Son, but that of the Father through the Son in the Holy Spirit. This brings us consider now what the purpose, or the "why," of creation, is. Creation in other words does not simply involve a *that* or a *how,* but also a *why.* And that "why" is love, the love of God, the work of the Spirit. I shall consider this further in the coming two chapters.

60. Grillmeier, *Christ in the Christian Tradition,* 1:153–63.
61. DH 150.

7

The Purpose of Creation

THE MEANING OF DIVINE FREEDOM AS TRINITARIAN LOVE

WE HAVE CONSIDERED in previous chapters the *fact* of creation, that God has created the world *ex nihilo,* without presuppositions of any kind. In the previous chapter, I examined the question of the *how* and the *what* of creation, the source and intelligibility and rationality of the created world in God's *Logos,* the Son/Word made incarnate in Jesus Christ, and several other consequences of this. But it is not sufficient to establish and describe the *fact* and *logic* of creation, that it is and how it works. Greek philosophers could stop there, perhaps, because they took it for granted that the world simply existed, as necessarily as God does. Why it existed was of little interest to them. However, for a Christian, the world, literally, might have never existed. Or it might have been made in a different way, with a completely different logic, for example without time, or without matter, or without interaction between the elements, or without diversity, or anything else imaginable. The question asked by Leibniz in respect "the best of all possible worlds" is meaningless in a Christian context. As is Schopenhauer's rejoinder "the worst of all possible worlds."[1] The world is simply as God wanted it to be; thus there is no ultimate model with which it can be compared as being better or worse. Because the fact of creation is rooted in a completely free act of God, and because the world might have been structured by a different logic than the one it has, a further, more fundamental, question must be asked of the God who made the world: *why* did he make it in the first place? What was his *purpose* in

1. Schopenhauer, *Welt als Wille und Vorstellung,* §71.

making the world as it is now? Why does it exist anyway? Where is it heading? What is it meant to achieve?

In this chapter I shall consider the following five issues: (1) the way in which God's creative freedom is challenged by the experience of suffering and evil in the world; (2) situating the creation of the world between necessity and arbitrariness; (3) the motivation or purpose of God's creative act; (4) the inner meaning of God's freedom as love; and (5) the trinitarian structure of creative action.

The Dilemma of Suffering and Evil

The total dependence of a freely created world on God occasions an acute dilemma in the context of common human experience of pain and suffering, of evil in the world. If God created the world, whole and entire, as it is, then how can we explain the mystery of suffering and evil? The notion of evil arises in our lives at an elementary level when we detect a discrepancy between the way we experience reality and the expectancy we have of it. A lot of the time there may be little or no discrepancy between how we experience things and what we expect them to be: things turn out to be more or less what (we think) they should be. This leaves us happy, at peace with the world. But then comes the change, the exception, things that are out of place, and this causes bother, disturbance, suffering, reactivity, a desire to defeat the discrepancy. And we ask: why this change? Why are things like this when they should be different? Why does this happen to me? Who is responsible for this situation?

Indeed, our common human experience shows up evil as *that which should not be*. "Evil is not an entity,"[2] Gregory Nazianzen says. "It has no substance," adds John Damascene.[3] And Gregory of Nyssa states that evil "in its very non-being it has its being."[4] Florovsky, summing up these authors, says that "evil has a negative and privative character, it is the absence and privation of true being.... The root and character of evil is delusion and error."[5] Augustine and Aquinas both speak of evil in terms of the *priva-*

2. Gregory Nazianzen, *Or. 40 in S. Bapt.* This and the following texts are taken from Florovsky, "Creation and Creaturehood," 50.

3. John Damascene, *C. Manich.* 14.

4. Gregory of Nyssa, *De anima et res.*

5. Florovsky, "Creation and Creaturehood," 50.

tio boni,[6] the privation of the good, although Thomas specifies the expression as *privatio debiti boni,*[7] the privation of *due* good. The philosopher Maurice Blondel explains this even more radically.

Ontology does not consider evil except under one aspect, in which, not having positive existence, or, in other words, not being a creature of God, is the result of a conflict between ends proposed to the option of freedom, but in which the infinite good has been denied; in such a way that the end preferred to the infinite brings with it a loss without human compensation, the privation of all good: *malum est debitae aut oblatae perfectionis privatio.*[8]

In spite of its nothingness, however, evil plays an extraordinarily important role in the life of humans. In principle the experience of good things should move the Christian believer to recognize God as the source of all good, to a sense of amazement and wonderment when faced with the marvels of the created world (Wis 13; Rom 1). But the experience of evil is never far behind; like the good, the experience of evil induces the believer to inquire into its ultimate origin, but often with greater urgency and immediacy than in the case of the good. In effect, experience of the good often produces complacency and smugness, that of evil perplexity and fluster. It might be said that without some experience of evil as the lack or loss of the due good, humans might well just get accustomed to holding on to the created goods they enjoy, basking in the positive experience they receive, yet seeing no need to direct their lives in appreciation and gratitude to a divine principle who is the living source of all created goods. In other words, the good things we perceive refer us more easily to something greater and more foundational mainly when we perceive them in their fragility, tenuousness, nonultimateness, and unreliability—and that perception often comes through the experience of evil present in the created world. In other words, the experience of evil has a place to play in our appreciation of the good.

But we may still ask the question: how is it that humans have *become accustomed to* the good in the first place, adoring God with an effort out of keeping with their inclinations, and stand in need of its absence in order to appreciate its reality and source? What has happened to the human heart

6. Augustine, *Confessions* VII.

7. Thomas Aquinas, *ST* I, q. 48, a. 1, ad 4.

8. M. Blondel, *L'Être et les êtres* (Paris: PUF, 1963), 488.

that has rendered it incapable of—spontaneously, joyfully—recognizing the source of good in the absence of the tangible, painful loss of good things? I shall return to the issue at a theological level in the final chapter when examining the mystery of original sin.

The issue of evil and our experience of it becomes particularly important in the context of the Christian conviction that God has created the *whole* world without presuppositions of any kind. Throughout history philosophers have attempted to explain away the presence of evil by systematically exonerating the divine, and attributing evil to the cosmos or to humans. The philosopher Epicurus presents the following panorama:

> The gods can either take away evil from the world and will not, or, being willing to do so cannot; or they neither can nor will, or lastly, they are able and willing. . . . If they have the will to remove evil and cannot, then they are not omnipotent. If they can but will not, then they are not benevolent. If they are neither able nor willing, they are neither omnipotent nor benevolent. . . . Lastly, if they are both able and willing to annihilate evil, why does it exist?[9]

The question must be addressed to the God of revelation: if God is able and willing to eliminate evil, why does it exist? Six common ways of explaining the origin evil may be noted.[10]

First, many ancient authors attempt to explain evil away by saying that it simply does not exist or that it is just apparent. This is particularly so with the Stoic philosophers. Cleanthes says: "O Lord, you have gathered up all things, together, in harmony, good and evil, in such a way that there is only one reason [*logos*] by which all things exist and live."[11] And Marcus Aurelius exhorted his readers as follows: "Willingly accept everything that happens, no matter how hard it appears to be, thinking that it contributes to the health of the world and to the good outcome of the purposes of Jove. Because it would never have happened were it not convenient for the whole."[12]

Second, some more modern positions—those of Schopenhauer and Leopardi—see evil as the most authentic mark of the universe we live in. The latter writes:

9. Epicurus, *Physica*, fr. 374, in H. Usener (ed.), *Epicurea* (Cambridge: Cambridge University Press, 1887), 252.

10. G. Morra and C. Ciurco, "Male," in *Enciclopedia filosofica* (Milan: Bompiani, 2006), 6930–43.

11. Cleanthes, *Hymn to Zeus* 19–21.

12. Marcus Aurelius, *Meditations* V, 8.

> Everything is evil. That is to say, everything that is, is evil; each thing that exists is an evil; each thing exists only for an evil end; existence is an evil and made for evil; the end of the universe is evil; the order and the state, the laws, the natural development of the universe are nothing but evil, and they are directed to nothing but evil. There is no other good except non-being; there is nothing good except what is not; things that are not things: all things are bad.[13]

Doubtless, a simplistic and deeply pessimistic view of human life is involved here.

Third, the position typical of antiquity, specifically of Gnosticism, is that whereas the spirit was created by God, matter was made by the evil Demiurge. To all appearances this exonerates God from responsibility for evil, for the latter is situated in matter, that has not been created by God. This is what is usually called dualism. From the Christian standpoint, however, it is an unacceptable position because God has created everything that exists, literally, both the material and the spiritual.

In the fourth place, it is suggested at times that *society* as such is the source of evil in human life. We observe that evil and uncontrolled, destructive inclinations arise and abound often in conflictual situations of a social kind. When there is nothing to eat, people rebel, the personal thus finding expression in the collective: the eruption of evil seems to coincide with the socialization of humans. It would seem that the more people organize their lives, the more they socialize, the more they ruin themselves, the more they suffer. This substantially is the position of Jean-Jacques Rousseau.[14] Likewise Jean-Paul Sartre famously stated that "hell [where evil belongs] is other people."[15] This position however mistakenly confuses context and cause. Evil may emerge powerfully or become apparent in a social context, but that does not mean that socialization as such is the *cause* of evil. We may say that society simply manifests the evil present previously in the lives and hearts of human individuals. This is where the search for the origin of evil must be undertaken.

It is quite common to distinguish between *physical* and *moral* evil, a dis-

13. G. Leopardi, *Zibaldone,* ed. M. Cesar and F. D'Intino (New York: Farrar, Straus and Giroux, 2013), no. 4174.

14. This position may be found in J.-J. Rousseau, *Emile or On Education* (Basic Books: New York, 1979) and other works of his.

15. From Sartre's drama *Huis-clos.*

tinction developed especially by Augustine.[16] Physical (or metaphysical) evil is really a good, he says. But *malum culpae,* the evil of guilt, sin, deriving from free human will, is a different matter. In effect, many painful experiences seem to derive from physical nature itself, from matter, from society, from the outside, anonymously: we suffer evil uninvited. But it is clear to us that evil may be inflicted by one human being on another: one person may injure, hurt, or kill another person. Clearly the ultimate source of this evil is not merely physical, but moral, deriving ultimately from the will of another spiritual being. As Socrates says, it is better to suffer injustice than to commit it.[17] In attempting to understand the origin of evil, physical evil retains its own consistency and dynamic, but the finger points inevitably to moral evil, to those who inflict evil and suffering on others. This brings us to consider whether evil derives from the divine or the human will.

Fifth, if evil cannot be attributed to the material world or to society as such, then perhaps evil derives directly from *God,* or from the deepest grounds of being. Now it cannot be denied that God's power to create involves him taking on responsibility for the world he created whole and entire, as well as for the evil it contains. This is what gives meaning to the doctrine of redemption for which God sent his only Son (Jn 3:16), who mysteriously identifies himself with sin (2 Cor 5:21) to save the world from evil and corruption. Mark Robson goes so far as to suggest that "whatever evil is cannot be known by God unless we assert that evil is, in some way, an emanation or a copying of something in God."[18]

However, Christians cannot really accept this position at a substantial level, for God is the all-powerful source of all the goodness and beauty and harmony that exists in the universe. Besides, should God be to blame in any way for evil then certainly humans are not. But if evil is not from God, then we can say at least that it takes place with God's *permission,* although as van Inwagen suggests, perhaps not each and every bad thing is planned or permitted by God.[19]

Sixth and last, the only feasible alternative left seems to be that, ulti-

16. Augustine, *Confessions* VII.

17. Plato, *Gorgias* 469a–479e.

18. Robson, *Ontology and Providence,* 143.

19. P. Van Inwagen, *God, Knowledge and Mystery: Essays in Philosophical Theology* (Ithaca, N.Y.: Cornell University Press, 1995), 65.

mately, sin and evil derive from the human *will* which, instead of seeking the good which is God himself, makes common cause (or finds its ultimate end) with a created good, thus becoming perverted and producing evil. For Clement of Alexandria, evil can only come from man.[20] It is simply privation of the good,[21] mere negativity, lack of light, darkness.[22] God by his very nature is extraneous to evil, says Basil,[23] although he is capable of drawing good from evil.[24]

But even this explanation, which finds substantial confirmation in Christian experience and moral theology, does not fully explain how and why the spiritual, willing, conscious but transitory actions of humans can powerfully influence the world around them, emptying it of its being and life. In fact not all philosophers equate evil with simple privation, for the simple "lack of due good" does not do justice to the real energy of evil, to its active, destructive, and often intelligent power.[25]

The nineteenth-century philosopher Arthur Schopenhauer has the following interesting observation to make: "I know no greater absurdity than that absurdity which characterizes almost all metaphysical systems: that of explaining evil as something negative. For evil is precisely that which is positive, that which makes itself palpable; and good, on the other hand, that is all happiness and gratification, is that which is negative, the mere abolition of a desire and the extinction of a pain."[26] In other words, for Schopenhauer, evil is active, and goodness passive. I noted this at the beginning of this section: the experience of goodness easily induces complacency and narcotizes people, whereas evil often provokes and stimulates us.

In effect, those who act freely—whether well or badly, whether constructively or destructively—commonly claim that they are drawn along by the world around them. Hence humans at a subjective level often experience evil as a positive, enabling, preexistent, malefic power, deriving from something or someone, that oppresses them and seems to *control* their will. Now we have established by elimination that evil derives funda-

20. Clement of Alexandria, *Stromata* IV, 13.
21. Origen, *In Io.* II, 7; *Contra Celsum* VI, 53.
22. Gregory of Nyssa, *Orat. Catech. Mag.* 7.
23. Basil, *Quod Deus auctor mali non sit* 7.
24. Boethius, *De consol. phil.* IV, 1–2.
25. J. Hick, *Evil and the God of Love* (New York: Harper and Row, 1966), 62–64.
26. A. Schopenhauer, *On the Suffering of the World* (London: Penguin, 2004), 4.

mentally from the human will. Thus the question as regards the origin of evil is placed even further back: how can the human will (or any will for that matter) produce an evil that attempts to oppress or destroy itself and others? Is there no power in evil? Is there solidarity in evil?

Clearly the foregoing analysis, based on a kind of *phenomenology of evil* to situate our consideration of its origin, essence, and fruits, has not provided a satisfactory explanation. The mystery of evil still has to be considered in the light of revelation and faith, as we contemplate the One who "reveals man to man,"[27] Jesus Christ, the Savior of the world. Only in that way can we discover how evil relates to both God and humans, and how sin is understood as an offense to the creator. We shall return to this in chapter 13.

The Creation of the World between Necessity and Arbitrariness

We have seen that our inquiry into the logic of creation leads us by the hand to reflect on the *why and wherefore* of creation. The question regarding the *why* of creation is directly related to the meaning of *divine freedom* in creating the world. In fact the *why* of creation is situated entirely within the divinity itself, for nothing outside God can bring him to create, to desist from creating, or to create in one way or another. The world depends purely and simply on the divine will. This fundamental (Christian) conviction brought Feuerbach to take it that the world as we know it is "a momentary, arbitrary, unreliable, i.e., unreal existence."[28] If the world depends on God and God does not exist . . . then?

Some would say that God created the world out of *necessity* (Aristotle among them), others in an *arbitrary* way (Ockham and the Nominalists). For some, creation is something God *had* to do. For others, God created just because the idea popped into his mind out of the blue, as it were.

27. *GS*, no. 22. O'Callaghan, *Children of God in the World*, 64–85.

28. Feuerbach puts it as follows: "The will has called it into existence—the will calls it back again into nothing. When? The time is indifferent: its existence or non-existence depends only on the will. But this will is not its own will—not only because a thing cannot will its non-existence, but for the prior reason that the world is itself destitute of will. Thus the nothingness of the world expresses the power of the will. The will that it should exist is, at the same time, the will—at least the possible will—that it should not exist. The existence of the world is therefore a momentary, arbitrary, unreliable, i.e., unreal existence." L. Feuerbach, *The Essence of Christianity* (Buffalo, N.Y.: Prometheus Books, 1989), 63.

McFarland observes that in a sense "a genuine gift must be arbitrary.... Otherwise the giver will always be suspected of a self-interest that vitiates the purity of the gift."[29] So what "happened" in God for creation to take place? Perhaps we will never know. But Sokolowski does speak of the "dilemma between arbitrariness that appears to undercut necessity, and necessity that appears to dominate the creator."[30] This brings us to consider what it means for God to be truly free in creating the world.

As regards the *wherefore* of creation, we may say the following. Not only does the world come from God, reaching out as it were into the depths of time-space and seeking its own life and autonomy. Besides, it is directed—in Christ—back to God. The world comes from the creator, finds its meaning in the creator, and goes back the creator. The world can acquire no meaning of its own outside the God who gives it existence and significance, and brings it back to himself. I shall consider this question in the coming chapter on the glory of God. The *why* and the *wherefore* of creation, what it came from and where it is going, point to God himself, to God's freedom and his glory respectively, that is, to God's inner life. Many aspects of the mystery of creation may be clarified by philosophical and scientific discourse, principally the *what* and the *how*, for example, but these particular aspects, the *why* and the *wherefore*, require, besides, a careful consideration of the mystery of divine revelation. Let us consider now what it means to say that God created the world freely.

NECESSITY AND FREE WILL IN CREATION

Two positions emerge in respect of the motivation of creation, one related to necessity and the other to free will. The notion that creation is as necessary as God himself is, is not only to be found in Aristotle.[31] Metho-

29. McFarland, *From Nothing*, 20, who refers to J. Derrida, *Given Time, vol. 1: Counterfeit Money* (Chicago: University of Chicago Press, 1991). McFarland continues: "Anything other than God exists only because God brings it into being. That God should do so is a matter of grace, since there is neither any power external to God nor any deficiency internal to God that could render creation necessary to God. At the same time, creation is not arbitrary because it is grounded in the expressive character of God's own life in and as the Word, so that the graciousness of creation itself is a reflection of the gracious character of God's own triune existence as loving and unstinting gift of being" (ibid., 92).

30. Sokolowski, *The God of Faith and Reason*, 44.

31. Copleston, *History of Philosophy*, 1:314–15: "[Aristotle's] First Mover is not a Creator-God: the world existed from all eternity without having been created from all eternity. God forms the world,

dius of Olympus had a similar position.[32] Origen put it as follows: "It is alike impious and absurd to say that God's nature is to be at ease and never to move, or to suppose that there was a time when Goodness did not do good and Omnipotence did not exercise its power."[33] Thus God was always a creator. And he continues: "Just as nobody can be a father without having a son, nor a lord without holding a possession or a slave, so too we cannot even call God Almighty if there are no creatures over whom he can exercise his power . . . [otherwise he would] become *Pantocrator* afterwards, and Almighty from the time be began to have creatures over whom he could exercise power."[34] Following the principle of Dionysius and Platonists, *bonum est diffusivum sui,*[35] the good diffuses itself, some would say that God's goodness necessitates creation. Aquinas uses this formula but avoids a necessitarian view.[36]

Sokolowski observes: "Through his doctrine of the divine ideas Aquinas avoids the alternative between natures arbitrarily constructed and natures determined independently of God."[37] In any case, says Florovsky, "God is forced to think of and contemplate himself as a creative principle and as the source of the world."[38] The same may be said of divine providence, Florovsky says: "The divine economy of the world, the unchanging and immutable Providence of God, conveys—to our vision—perfect stability and wise harmony—and also a kind of necessity,"[39] that reflects the mind of God. So "we cannot conceive the world as non-existing without introducing a kind of impious fortuitousness or arbitrariness in its existence and genesis."[40] God

but did not create it, and He forms the world, is the source of motion, by *drawing* it, i.e. by acting as final cause."

32. Methodius, *De creatis.*

33. Origen, *De prin.* III, 5:3.

34. Ibid., I, 2:10.

35. N. Kretzmann, *The Metaphysics of Theism: Aquinas's Natural Theology in "Summa contra Gentiles I"* (Oxford: Oxford University Press, 1997), 224, though he recognizes that Aquinas disavows the position.

36. For example, Thomas Aquinas, *SCG* I.37.5 and III.24.8.

37. Sokolowski, *The God of Faith and Reason,* 45.

38. Florovsky, "Creation and Creaturehood," 55.

39. Ibid.

40. Ibid. Florovsky adds: "The idea of the world, God's design and will concerning the world, is obviously *eternal,* but in some sense *not co-eternal,* and *not conjointly everlasting* with Him, because 'distinct and separated' as it were from his 'essence' by his *volition*" ("Creature and Creaturehood," 56). So, a distinction arises between nature and will of God. "The idea of the world has its basis *not in the essence, but in the will* of God" (ibid.). God could have not created the world: "any such refraining from

creates by *thought*, and the thought becomes *deed*, John Damascene would say.[41]

And secondly, a willing or voluntarist position emerged in the late Middle Ages in a clearly Christian context. Duns Scotus explains the act of creation as follows: "The creation of things proceeds from God, not by necessity, or essence, or knowledge, or will, but from mere freedom, which is not moved or much less necessitated by anything outside of himself."[42] William of Ockham[43] holds that the omnipotence of God cannot be demonstrated by reason. But this takes away from creation its rational basis. Ockham borrows from Peter Aureolus and Durandus the argument that ideas are placed freely by God within creatures that do not have any internal relationship to the divine essence.[44] This results in a radical contingency for all things that exist, the arbitrariness of the creation of the world.

---

creation would in no way alter or impoverish the Divine nature, would mean no diminution, just as the very creation of the world does not enrich the Divine Being" (ibid.). "Creative revelation is not something imposed upon God by his goodness. It is executed in perfect freedom" (ibid., 57).

41. John Damascene, *De fide orth.* I, 2. "In creation there is projected from out of nothing a new reality which becomes the bearer of the Divine idea, and must realize this idea in its own becoming," as cited in Florovsky, "Creation and Creaturehood," 61. "The *created nucleus* of things must be rigorously distinguished from the *divine idea* about things. . . . The divine pattern in things is not their 'substance' or 'hypostasis'; it is not the vehicle of their qualities and conditions" (ibid.). Then Florovsky speaks of the distinction between essence and energies: "The divine energies are that aspect of God which is turned towards creation" (ibid., 67). For Athanasius there is no Demiurge within the divine being: "the generation of the Word does not presuppose the being—and not even the design—of the world. Even had the world not been created, the Word would exist in the completeness of His Godhead, because the Word is Son by nature" (cited in ibid., 70). "The creation presupposes the Trinity, and the seal of the Trinity lies over the whole creation; yet one must not therefore introduce cosmological motifs into the definition of the intra-Trinitarian Being" (ibid.).

42. "Procedit autem rerum creatio a Deo, non aliqua necessitate, vel essentiae, vel scientiae, vel voluntatis, sed ex mera libertate, quae non movetur et multo minus necessitatur ab aliquo extra se ad causandum," Duns Scotus, *IV Sent.*, a. 1, nos. 3–4. On Scotus, see A. Broadie, *A History of Scottish Philosophy* (Edinburgh: Edinburgh University Press, 2009), 18–25, and the same author's "Scotistic Metaphysics and Creation *ex nihilo*," in *Creation and the God of Abraham* (ed. Burrell et al.), 53–64. According to Gunton, *The Triune Creator*, the contribution of Scotus lies in the idea that God creates things and their forms. "Forms are not so much in the divine mind, so partaking of a form of eternity, as more clearly a part of the created world. This, in turn, leads to a new stress on particularity, with all its long-term epistemological implications. Scotus' doctrine of *haecceitas*, or 'this-ness,' implies that the ultimate reality of a thing is to be found in its being what it is rather than in it instantiating general notions of forms. This means, as T. F. Torrance has pointed out, that a knowledge of particulars is prior to a knowledge of abstractions.'" Ibid., 118, citing T. F. Torrance, *The Hermeneutics of John Calvin* (Edinburgh: Scottish Academic Press, 1988), 4.

43. See William of Ockham, *Quodl.* I, 1; McFarland, *From Nothing*, 95.

44. See William of Ockham, *I Sent.*, d. 35, q. 9, a. 5.

Of course there was a price to pay for the Nominalist disconnect: the loss of the internal relationship of creatures with the divine essence as exemplar. Created beings would simply say nothing to us *about* God, and this is not biblical. The result is a radical, perhaps dualistic, separation between God and the world: agnosticism. This may be seen for example in the anthropology of the thirteenth-century philosopher Peter John Olivi, based on the opposition between matter and spirit, insofar as the rational soul cannot inform matter immediately and of itself.[45] The same thing happens with the moral order, in such a way that the Decalogue is not to be considered immutable or rationally necessary: things are right and wrong because God has simply decided things that way.[46] This provides an individualist and voluntarist account of the world, destroys the medieval notion of the *ordo* of the universe in such a way that the relationship between God and world takes place only through the express, concrete, and punctual will of God. Faith is easily identified with blind submission to authority, thus becoming fideism. This of course paved the way for the Protestant Reformation, and later on, to the process of secularization.

A strange coincidence may be found between the two seemingly opposed explanations when taken to the extreme: the necessitarian and the arbitrary. When God creates he does so, it is commonly said, on the basis of eternal ideas or concepts identified with his own being. We might say that the world already fully exists in his mind, in his thought, in the Word. This position is commonly called *panentheism*, meaning "all is in God."[47] All God would have to do at the moment of creation is to snap it into existence by an act of the divine will. In that sense the nature of the world is *necessary* as a reflection of God's mind, whereas its real existence is *arbitrary* in that God might not have created it at all. The fact of its existence adds nothing substantial to the eternal essence in the divine.[48] Or so it would seem. Church Fathers were aware of the problem, which Athanasius

45. See O'Callaghan, *Children of God in the World*, 423–25; DH 1311.

46. See Peter John Olivi, *IV Sent.* 14.

47. E. Tiefensee, "Pantheismus," in M. Buchberger and W. Kasper (eds.), *Lexikon für Theologie und Kirche*, 3rd. ed., 11 vols. (Freiburg i.B.: Herder, 1993–2001), 7:1318; J. Macquarrie, "Panentheismus," in *Theologische Realenzyklopädie*, vol. 25, ed. G. Krause and G. Müller (Berlin: De Gruyter, 1995), 611–15. Soskice says that "creation *ex nihilo* rules out panentheism, for the world is in no sense part of God's body" (*Why Creation ex nihilo?*, 50).

48. See O'Callaghan, "Can God Be Enriched?"

expressed in the following terms: "For no part of creation is left void of him [the Word]: he has filled all things everywhere, remaining present with his own Father."[49]

Likewise, medieval authors battled with the issue.[50] *Either* creation starts with rationality (and thus knowability) and this seems to necessarily demand its existence (Aristotle and his commentators), *or* the contingency of the universe which results from its being freely created seems to lead to arbitrariness, and ends up in irrationality. What is logical would not be free, what is free would not be logical. The world would therefore be either rational and necessary or irrational and free. Can we overcome this dichotomy? Can we consider the creator at once as free but not arbitrary, as rational but not necessary?

Among modern philosophers, for Leibniz creation means the passage from possibility to actuality, putting eternal essences into existence; this leads to essentialism, in which the essence or nature of things is superior to their existence. Several authors in recent times have contested the identification of creation as God giving existence to a set of eternal ideas, because in that way the temporality of the world and the freedom of spiritual creatures are rendered commonplace and banal. Let us consider the issue in greater detail.

THE ETERNAL IDEAS IN GOD AS THE SOURCE OF CREATION

Zizioulas poses the question of creation and the divine ideas as follows: "If ideas were thoughts in the mind (*nous*) of God, the world would always have existed in God's thoughts. If the thoughts of God are eternal, and the world exists as the thoughts of God, this makes the world eternal too."[51] Likewise, Robson considers the possibility of creation in terms of

49. Athanasius, *Contra gentes* 8:1.

50. Bonaventure spoke of the fruitfulness and active character of ideas, they are *expressio*, or *similitudo expressiva* (*I Sent.*, d. 35, q. 1, a. 1, concl.). Things in their essence are expressive forms of the divine being, shadows, vestiges, or images of God. Bonaventure, *I Sent.*, d. 3, q. 1, a. 1, concl.: "creation is thus a hierarchical kingdom of analogies." "Each substance shows in the triad of matter, form and composition, a reflection of the divine Trinity, whose basis is the Father, image the Son and bond the Holy Spirit" (Scheffczyk, *Schöpfung und Vorlesung*, 88). See also Bonaventure, *Coll. In Hexaem.* II, 23; *Itinerarium mentis* I.

51. Zizioulas, "Creation and Salvation," 87.

God who "copies out his ideas and places them outside of himself."[52] But he says that he "finds this model of creation completely unsatisfactory. All that is happening is relocation and duplication. . . . It is hard to see how this avoids a kind of emanationism."[53] Christoph Schwöbel put it as follows: "creation as absolute giving excludes an understanding of creation that reduces it to the actualization of individual essences already existing as ideas in the divine mind."[54] In such a system, "creation *ex nihilo* is again rendered as something inferior to absolute giving, since the possible individuals already are what they are before they are actualized."[55]

Different suggestions have been made to overcome the dilemma, principally in the direction of understanding free divine action in terms of a work of art, of love, of chance, of risk, that goes beyond a mere fabrication of the world on the basis of a previous model or design. Teilhard de Chardin says that creation does not refer so much to divine freedom, but to divine commitment and dedication, what scripture normally calls love. Creation does not take place "in absolute freedom, but it represents a work of almost absolute interest."[56] Moltmann likewise says that God creates the world out of love.[57] Zizioulas considers the position of Maximus the Confessor[58] and sums it up as follows:

> There is a relationship of love between God and his Word, the Father and his Son, and the world is created in and through this Word. The relationship between God and the world is now freely willed. God's will is eternal, but this does not mean that God's thought is instantly extended. Maximus refers to the *logoi* as the wills of God, not the *thoughts* of God. . . . Thus existence is not an extension of the thoughts of God.[59]

In other words, God loves the world into existence, not just thinks it into existing.

52. Robson, *Ontology and Providence*, 135.

53. Ibid., 137.

54. Schwöbel, "God, Creation," 163.

55. Ibid.

56. Teilhard de Chardin, *L'union creatrice* (1917), cited by A. Glässer, *Konvergenz: die Struktur der Weltsumme Pierre Teilhards de Chardin* (Kevelaer: Verlag Butzon and Bercker, 1970), 219.

57. "This criticism of an arbitrary God is justified. So when we say that God created the world 'out of freedom,' we must immediately add 'out of love.'" Moltmann, *God in Creation*, 75.

58. Maximus the Confessor, *Ad Thalass*. 60.

59. Zizioulas, "Creation and Salvation," 87.

Mark Robson makes the following, somewhat anthropomorphic, proposal:

It seems to me that the artist loves her own work, not because it merely copies something that was previously mental, but because it was created by herself and has emerged as a new object that has no previous counterpart. It is an *other* that can be loved. . . . It is precisely because it is not divine and is new that the possibility of non-egocentric love can come about. . . . These natures are not chosen by God, but arise determinately from his indeterminate creative capacities.[60]

He goes on to suggest that God *took a chance* on creation,[61] following a suggestion of Peter van Inwagen,[62] and is opposed to those who say that God micromanages every last detail.[63] He holds that God has left chance within the evolving process, and this is not something Christians should be wary of.[64] According to D. J. Bartholomew chance is part of God's plan for the world: it fosters freedom and creativity, while also producing order and regularity.[65] Robson goes so far as to say: "God does not know what he is going to make. There is an unavoidable—logically unavoidable—indefiniteness in God's decree 'Let there be light.'"[66] Similar positions may

60. Robson, *Ontology and Providence*, 138–40.

61. Ibid., 144.

62. Inwagen, *God, Knowledge and Mystery*, 56. See also ibid., 147: "I see no reason as a theist, or as a Christian, to believe the existence of humans as a part of God's plan. This may seem a shocking statement. Let me attempt to palliate the shock. First, I do not claim to *know* that the existence of our species is not part of God's plan. Secondly, I am sure that the existence of animals made in God's image—that is, rational animals having free will and capable of love—*is* a part of God's plan. I am simply not convinced that He had any *particular* species in mind."

63. For example, John Calvin, *Institutes* I, 16:2. "God does not take risks in governing the world because God micromanages every detail." J. Sanders, *The God Who Risks: A Theology of Divine Providence*, 2nd ed. (Downers Grove, Ill.: IVP Academic, 2007), 211.

64. W. G. Pollard, *Change and Providence: God's Action in a World Governed by Scientific Law* (London: Faber and Faber, 1958).

65. D. J. Bartholomew, *God, Chance and Purpose: Can God Have It Both Ways?* (Cambridge: Cambridge University Press, 2008). He suggests that chaos theory eventually points to the existence of a more or less Christian God.

66. Robson, *Ontology and Providence*, 153. He goes on to say: "They want God to be free, not only of external constraints, but also of internal ones" (ibid., 181). "The utter self-sufficiency of God is not the absolute 'existential' freedom of inventing the nature of the divine reality." The thesis of Robson is as follows: "God ventures into novelty, and novelty cannot be completely foreknown" (ibid.). Robson asks why did God create freedoms, with his own creative capacity? "Out of love; out of a desire for freshness and newness; out of pure generosity; out of sheer exuberance; but, as we have seen, no complete answer can be given since it is of the nature of the spontaneity of creative freedom and grace that no absolute rationalization can be given" (ibid., 182). At creation "God is not thinking a thought

be found in the writings of Hausman, Bergson, Pannenberg, Tanner, and others.[67] A variety of other suggestions have been made to explain the work of creation, also in the area of process theology.[68]

McFarland puts it this way:

that has *emerged* ... God is expanded as it were by the activity of creation" (ibid., 202). "When God created Adam, thoughts about Adam became possible. Then and only then were thoughts about Adam possible. Then and only then did Adam-thoughts become meaningful" (ibid., 204). "For as Dorothy Sayers pointed out, the characters created by the author of a novel begin, in her experience, to take on a certain life of their own which reacts upon their author as a constraint upon his development of the plot." A. R. Peacocke, *Theology for a Scientific Age* (Minneapolis, Minn.: Fortress Press, 1993), 171. Robson develops the artistic analogy in *Ontology and Providence*, 186–89. McFarland speaks of divine generosity in considering the world "less in its implications for divine power than in what it says about God's generosity" (*From Nothing*, 186).

67. See C. R. Hausman, *A Discourse on Novelty and Creation* (The Hague: Martinus Nijhoff, 1975), 79: "novelty is occasioned by God's creativity and not destroyed by his omniscience." The same may be said of Bergson, according to Robson, *Ontology and Providence*, 167: "nothing possible precedes its realization. A new thing is thus not the actualization of something pre-existent, but the genuine evolution of something that had no precedents. Bergson thus distinguishes between an 'unfurling' and 'evolution.' An unfurling is 'a rearrangement of the pre-existing,' while evolution ... is the emergence of the 'radically new.'" See especially H. Bergson, *The Creative Mind* (New York: Philosophical Library, 1946), 21. See Robson, *Ontology and Providence*: "While human creativity squeezes newness from so much, God pours novelty out of nothing.... As we argued when we criticized Ockham's doctrine of divine ideas, God has no need of determinate models in order for Him to create rationally.... Because God is the source of rationality, of reason itself. He has within Himself all the resources to create rationally" (172). The same idea may be found also in Pannenberg, *Systematic Theology* (Edinburgh: T and T Clark, 1994), 2:26. See also D. B. Burrell, *Freedom and Creation in Three Traditions* (Notre Dame, Ind.: University of Notre Dame Press, 1993), against L. Zagzebski, "Individual Essence and the Creation," in *Divine and Human Action: Essays in the Metaphysics of Theism*, ed. T. V. Morris (Ithaca, N.Y.: Cornell University Press, 1988), 119–43. See also K. E. Tanner, *Christ the Key* (Cambridge: Cambridge University Press, 2010), 9: "What creatures get from God pre-exists in God in exemplary fashion, and therefore when they participate in God in virtue of their creation creatures also image God."

68. K. Ward, *Divine Action* (London: Collins, 1990), offers four reasons God may have for creating: so that there might be subjects capable of valuing their own existence; that values lived by finite beings would never have been lived had there been no creation; God himself will come to know as actual the finite values he chooses to create; and the essential creativity of God overflowing into a created expression. D. Turner, *Faith Seeking* (London: SCM, 2002), 32, speaks of the reality of giftedness in the world. Process theologians such as C. Hartshorne speak of "a continuing desire for newness and freshness and originality" (Robson, *Ontology and Providence*, 178). P. Clayton speaks of an open kenotic panentheism, "Creation *ex nihilo* and Intensifying the Vulnerability of God," in *Theologies of Creation: Creatio ex Nihilo and Its New Rivals*, ed. T. J. Oord (New York: Routledge, 2015). Something of a kind may be found in Moltmann. "In the panentheistic view," he writes, "God, having created the world, also dwells in it, and conversely the world which he has created exists in him" (*God in Creation*, 98). He writes of God "making space," a nothing (*nihil*) to which God gives being (*creatio ex nihilo*). "God does not create merely by calling something into existence.... In a more profound sense he 'creates' by letting-be, by making room, by withdrawing himself" (ibid., 88).

God is free precisely as one whose divinity is, and therefore may be, shared without loss or diminishment. . . . That God's freedom is exercised in the mode of the Father's giving the Father's own life to the Son in the Spirit means that God's life is essentially a matter of generosity, or of grace, which, in the light of the character of the Trinity, may be defined as freedom lived out in love.[69]

And Rowan Williams has it that God's desire for creatures "is groundless, in the sense that nothing other than God causes it, but it is not arbitrary, because there is no extraneous or random element within God's own being."[70] Provocatively he says that "creation is 'good for nothing': its point is not to serve a divine need."[71] And finally, in the words of Brian Horne:

The creation of the world and the building of Grand Central Station both arise out of freedom, but arise quite differently. The creation of the world is the act of absolute freedom; it comes into being out of nothing; it is not the re-ordering of pre-existent material; it is not God wrestling meaning out of recalcitrant nature. There are no constraints upon this act: God expresses nothing but himself for there is nothing else to express.[72]

The Motivation of God's Creative Action

What can we say then about the motivation of God's free creative action? In a human context we usually distinguish between a subjective and an objective motivation for our actions. Let us consider by way of example the hobby of fashioning clay models. The *subjective* motivation, why we do it, may be related to rest, to relaxation, to overcoming stress or boredom, to developing friendships, to earning some extra money. The activity in itself is instrumental as it were in producing effects which are basically unconnected with the nature of the object fashioned. The *objective* motivation in exercising this hobby coincides simply with the use of the model in question: in benefit of other people, for decoration, for its artistic value, etc. In the case of most hobbies the objective motivation is usually subordinate to the subjective one. In fact, if the person is unsatisfied with the product of their efforts, nobody will think twice if they destroy or abandon them. After all, the primary function of the hobby has been achieved.

69. McFarland, *From Nothing*, 48.

70. R. D. Williams, *On Christian Theology* (Oxford: Blackwell, 2000), 73.

71. Williams, "'Good for Nothing'?," 19.

72. Horne, "Divine and Human Creativity," 146.

In other human activities it may happen the other way around: the subjective is subordinated to the objective. By way of example, a man or woman gets married to found a family. They work off a subjective motivation, certainly, wanting to be happy, fulfilled, situated in life. And off an objective one as well, that of establishing a stable conjugal relationship with their spouse and have children, thus founding a new family. From the fact that both motivations are deeply bound up with one another we may infer that the founding of a family through marriage belongs to the very essence of being human. The eventual breakup of the marriage involves not only the separation of the members of the family, but also, in most cases, the impairment of the happiness and life project of the spouses. Of course it could happen that someone might focus on marriage and family as a mere hobby, or for that matter turn their hobbies obsessively into life-projects with which they identify completely and excessively. But the driving force in marriage is to make things work, the objective motivation.

At an intuitive level it should be clear enough that the distinction between subjective and objective motivations is not applicable to God's work of creation. Contemplating the crucifixion and resurrection of the Son of God incarnate we can understand that the world, the created universe, humanity as a whole, has been taken very seriously by God. Creating the world is certainly not an arbitrary or sideline activity; it is not a mere divine hobby with no objective purpose, a way for a bored and eternal God to find entertainment and amusement. In effect, God created the world freely. He might not have created it at all. But he did create it and made it as he wished it to be. This is how Vatican Council I explained creation, in an 1870 text already cited:

> This one and only true God, of his own goodness and almighty power, not for the increase of his own happiness, nor for the acquirement of his perfection, but *in order to manifest his perfection through the benefits which he bestows on creatures*, with *absolute freedom of counsel*, "from the beginning of time made at once out of nothing both orders of creatures, the spiritual and the corporeal, that is, the angelic and the earthly, and then the human creature."[73]

As we saw above, Vatican I added to the medieval Fourth Lateran Council the expression *liberrimo consilio*: God created the world with an utterly

73. DH 3002, citing the Fourth Lateran Council (emphasis added).

free counsel, with a completely free decision. The position is to be found in scripture. "Our God is in the heavens; he does whatever he pleases" (Ps 115:3). "Whatever the Lord pleases he does, in heaven and on earth, in the seas and all the depths" (Ps 135:6). "In him [God], according to the purpose of him who accomplishes all things according to the counsel of his will" (Eph 1:11). "Worthy are you, our Lord and God, to receive glory and honor and power, for you created all things, and by your will they existed and were created" (Rv 4:11). Vatican I's teaching on the motivation of creation reflects what Irenaeus says: "in the beginning, therefore, did God form Adam, not as if He stood in need of man, but that He might have [some one] upon whom to confer His benefits."[74]

Irenaeus is very clear that creation was not occasioned by the Fall of man. Augustine says that the world "cries out that it has been created – it cries out that it did not create itself: I exist because I am created; and I was not before I came to be, and I could not issue from myself."[75] And Florovsky concludes: "The world exists. But *it began* to exist. There is no necessity whatever for the existence of the world."[76] The creation of the world is an act of the divine will: "Will and volition precede creating. Creating is an act of will, and therefore is sharply distinguished from the divine generation, which is an act of nature."[77] God wanted the world and wanted it as it is. But how can we understand the inner significance of God's creating action?

The Inner Meaning of God's Freedom as Love

What can we say of the true meaning of God's freedom in creation?[78] By studying created beings we can discover how God wanted things to be: we get to know the mind of God, to a certain degree, by studying the *Logos*, the logic, of creation. But knowing the nature of things does not explain necessarily *why* they exist in the first place, what the purpose and scope of the created world actually is. Apart from the fact that we cannot fully understand the nature of things unless we understand their ultimate

74. Irenaeus, *Adv. Haer.* IV, 14:1: "non quasi indigens Deus hominibus, sed ut habebat, in quem collocaret sua beneficia."

75. Augustine, *Confessions* XI, 4.

76. Florovsky, "Creation and Creaturehood," 45.

77. Ibid., 48, citing Athanasius, *Contra Arianos* 3.

78. See P. Ganne, *La Création* (Paris: Cerf, 1979).

scope and purpose, it must be said that only through divine revelation we can really come to know something of God's personal attitude toward the world he created, his hidden counsel, his deepest hopes and aspirations and dreams, if such words are appropriate.

Is God's fundamental attitude toward the world hostile, tolerant, benign, or paternal? "It is not merely a question of knowing when and how the cosmos began and man appeared," says John Paul II. "It involves discovering the meaning of such an origin, and whether it was presided over by chance, by blind destiny, or by a transcendent Being, intelligent and good, called God."[79] McFarland asks the following question: "How do we know that in creation, God is seeking the benefit of creatures? This question can only be answered by attending to the character of Divinity, showing what *kind* of creator this God is.... Evaluating what God does is inseparable from knowing who God is."[80] Only by divine revelation, in other words, can we come to fully know the mind and heart of God as regards creation.

THE BIBLICAL WITNESS

The following words of the prophet Jeremiah give us some idea to start with: "For I know the plans I have for you, says the Lord, plans for welfare and not for evil, to give you a future and a hope" (Jer 29:11). And shortly afterward: "The Lord appeared to him from afar. I have loved you with an everlasting love; therefore I have continued my faithfulness to you" (Jer 31:3). God's plans for the world do not promise conflict and evil, Jeremiah tells us, but a future full of hope, based on an everlasting love and rock-like faithfulness. The prophet Isaiah continues in this direction: "For a brief moment I forsook you," God says,

> but with great compassion I will gather you. In overflowing wrath for a moment I hid my face from you, but with everlasting love I will have compassion on you, says the Lord, your Redeemer. For this is like the days of Noah to me: as I swore that the waters of Noah should no more go over the earth, so I have sworn that I will not be angry with you and will not rebuke you. For the mountains may depart and the hills be removed, but my steadfast love shall not depart from you, and my covenant of peace shall not be removed, says the Lord, who has compassion on you (Is 54:7–10).

79. John Paul II, "The Mystery of Creation," General Audience, August 1, 1986, par. 1.

80. McFarland, *From Nothing*, 21 and 23.

As in Jeremiah, the love of God for humans and for creation is enduring and purposeful, the very antithesis of arbitrariness.

In the New Testament the divine attitude toward creation is definitively revealed: it is one of love, of eternal, divine love.[81] For God in his inner essence is love, John tells us repeatedly (1 Jn 4:8, 16). And this is revealed above all, tangibly, in the incarnation of the Word. Here the love of God is not merely proclaimed or promised, as a mere word, but is made concrete in divine flesh, in the divine Word that has identified with humanity: the Word becomes flesh.

Throughout the history of salvation, the evangelist John situates the incarnation of the Word as the high point, the definitive revelation of God's attitude of paternal and benevolent affection for the world. "For *God so loved the world* that he gave his only Son, that whoever believes in him should not perish but have eternal life" (Jn 3:16). Or in the negative: "For God sent the Son into the world, not to condemn the world, but that the world might be saved through him" (Jn 3:17). In the words of Augustine, the Word "without losing what he had, wanted to become what he had done"[82]—the creator wished to identify with the creature.

In the words, in the life and willing death of Christ on the cross for love of the Father and of humans we can contemplate tangibly the power and perseverance and realism of the love of God for humanity. This comes across powerfully in Romans 8:31: "What then shall we say to this? If God is for us, who is against us? He who did not spare his own Son but gave him up for us all, will he not also give us all things with him?" And shortly afterward in the same letter this conviction comes across as follows: "For I am sure that neither death, nor life, nor angels, nor principalities, nor things present, nor things to come, nor powers, nor height, nor depth, nor anything else in all creation, will be able to separate us from the love of God in Christ Jesus our Lord" (Rom 8:38).

Paul explains why Christ casts a definitive light on the faithful yet hidden counsel of God in the Old Testament. In the letter to the Romans, speaking of the chosen people, the Jews, he says: "As regards the gospel they are enemies of God, for your sake; but as regards election they are

81. See L. Scheffczyk, "La creación como revelación del amor de Dios," in *Dios y el hombre: VI Simposio Internacional de Teología*, ed. A. Aranda (Pamplona: Eunsa, 1985), 353–65.

82. Augustine, *Sermo* 192:1.

beloved for the sake of their forefathers. For the gifts and the call of God are irrevocable" (Rom 11:28). And elsewhere: "He [God] chose us in him [Christ] before the foundation of the world, that we should be holy and blameless before him" (Eph 1:4).

However, the great New Testament witness to the solidity and fidelity of the love of God for man in creation and redemption is to be found principally in the Johannine letters.[83] In Christ, in the incarnation of God's Word, believers obtain a concrete assurance of what the Old Testament had only insinuated, hoped for, and desired in respect of God's love for and fidelity to the created world and humanity. John explains that the essence of the gospel and Christian faith lies in the full acceptance of the love of God. "See what love the Father has given us, that we should be called children of God; and so we are. The reason why the world does not know us is that it did not know him.... By this we know love, that he laid down his life for us; and we ought to lay down our lives for the brethren" (1 Jn 3:1, 16). This principle is confirmed in the Gospel: "Greater love has no man than this, that a man lay down his life for his friends" (Jn 15:13).

The central text of John in this regard is the following:

> Beloved, let us love one another; for love is of God, and he who loves is born of God and knows God. He who does not love does not know God; for God is love. In this the love of God was made manifest among us, that God sent his only Son into the world, so that we might live through him. In this is love, not that we loved God but that he loved us and sent his Son to be the expiation for our sins.... So we know and believe the love God has for us. God is love, and he who abides in love abides in God, and God abides in him. In this is love perfected with us, that we may have confidence for the day of judgment, because as he is so are we in this world. There is no fear in love, but perfect love casts out fear. For fear has to do with punishment, and he who fears is not perfected in love (1 Jn 4:7–10, 16–18).

A full acceptance of the greatness, sincerity, and fidelity of God's love for us is not something superficial, sentimental, or secondary for a Christian, but goes to the very heart of the act of faith. With faith we accept not only the conceptual content of revelation but more fundamentally we come to trust unreservedly the love of God, that God loves the creature into existence.

83. See Hans Urs von Balthasar, *Love Alone Is Credible* (New York: Herder and Herder, 1969); John Paul II, *Dives in Misericordia*, Encyclical Letter, November 30, 1980, par. 7.

At the core of Christian faith is not to be found a resigned and indifferent acceptance typical of the Stoics faced with the determinism of nature; not a trace is there of the bitter and sterile heroism of atheistic existentialists facing down the progressive invasion of nothingness. Rather, Christian believers experience that sense of marvel when faced with the goodness and power of God. "I was beside him, like a master workman; and I was daily his delight, rejoicing before him always, rejoicing in his inhabited world and delighting in the sons of men" (Prv 8:30). The same message is to be found in the Book of Wisdom: "For you love all things that exist, and loathe none of the things which you have made, for you would not have made anything if you had hated it. How would anything have endured if you had not willed it? Or how would anything not called forth by you have been preserved? You spare all things, for they are yours, O Lord who loves the living" (Wis 11:24–26). Of course this love is manifested especially and definitively in the life, death, and resurrection of Christ. As John Paul says in *Dives in Misericordia*, "Believing in the crucified Son means 'seeing the Father' [Jn 14:9], it means believing that love is present in the world and that this love is more powerful than any kind of evil in which individuals, humanity, or the world are involved."[84]

THE DYNAMIC OF DIVINE LOVE

How can we describe the dynamics of divine love?[85] Four elements may be found in a free, good act by which we (the self) love someone else (the other): first, the improvement of the other (an increase in their happiness or virtue); second, the improvement of self; third, the progressive identification of the other with an ideal we have for them; and finally, the progressive identification of the self with that same ideal. But what happens if these four elements are applied to God's act of creation?

Obviously the act of creation does not as such involve just an *improvement* of the other, for before creation takes place the other simply does not exist; rather it involves the donation of being itself, without presuppositions of any kind, a true divine *agape*, deriving from a pure, disinterested

84. John Paul II, *Dives in Misericordia*, par. 3.

85. See J. P. Moreland and D. Willard, *Love Your God with All Your Mind: The Role of Reason in the Life of the Soul* (Colorado Springs, Colo.: Navpress, 1997).

love.[86] God in that sense does not desire something already existent and waiting for improvement, but rather he loves reality itself into existence.[87]

The improvement of self does not take place as the result of divine creation, for God does not improve or self-realize as he gives himself. After all, as Vatican I says, God creates "not for the increase of his own happiness, nor for the acquirement of his perfection, but in order to manifest his perfection through the benefits which he bestows on creatures."[88]

In creation there is identification of the other, the created world, with the ideal present in self, the creator. This identification of human nature with what God wants takes place in a special way with the creation of man "in God's image and likeness" (Gn 1:26), although it will not be complete until the end of time, eschatologically, when God will be "all in all" (1 Cor 15:28). After all, God loves the created world in keeping with the nature he gave it, which is strictly temporal and historical.

Lastly, as regards the identification of the loving self with the self-same ideal: this does not take place with God, because God is perfect, and the source of all perfection. In that sense God does not have a mutual or dialogical relationship with creation, ontologically at least. God is not enriched by the created world.[89] Man is made in the image of God, but God is not made in the image of man. Creation depends on God but God does not depend on creation.

Summing up, we may say that God creates the world freely, not arbitrarily, but as an act of love. Were it made arbitrarily, creation would not identify with the (eschatological) ideal God has for it. But God creates out of love, a patient, respectful, passionate, persevering love. God creates the world, giving existence freely, lovingly, altruistically, magnanimously. He obtains no recompense for himself in doing so because the created universe

86. Aquinas writes: "since to love anything is nothing else than to will good to that thing, it is manifest that God loves everything that exists. Yet not as we love. Because since our will is not the cause of the goodness of things, but is moved by it as by its object, our love, whereby we will good to anything, is not the cause of its goodness; but conversely its goodness, whether real or imaginary, calls forth our love, by which we will that it should preserve the good it has, and receive besides the good it has not, and to this end we direct our actions: whereas the love of God infuses and creates goodness" (*ST* I, q. 20, a. 2, co.; see q. 32, a. 1, ad 3).

87. Thomas Aquinas, *In I Sent.*, d. 1, q. 2, a. 1.

88. DH 3002.

89. See O'Callaghan, "Can God Be Enriched?"

is intrinsically incapable of giving back to God something it has already received from him. Only a perfectly happy God can love disinterestedly in such a way that creation is a total gift existing in conformity with its maker.

If, hypothetically, God was less than happy in himself, then the inhabitants of a created world might suspect that his intentions and declarations in creating them are not as pure and transparent as they are said to be, for he would be seeking something for himself in creating the world. As a result, we can say that the real content and fruit of God's creating freedom is not arbitrariness, chaos, and disorder, but rather the ultimate conformity of the universe to God's loving plan, at the beginning, in its development and in its eschatological fullness. We may say that the purpose or scope of the work of creation is God himself, yet not as if creation was something he would benefit from, but rather because the entire destiny and dignity of the universe lies in its conformity with God's design, with his will, with the *Logos*.

God Creates the World through the Son in the Holy Spirit

Because God is a Trinity of Persons, it is clear that the work of creation must reflect trinitarian life in a significant way. Thomas after speaking of the eternal processions in God—generation and spiration—describes creation as a *processio creaturaum a Deo,* the procession of creatures from God.[90] He says that "just as the flow of water comes from the river, so the temporal procession of creatures derives from the eternal procession of the persons."[91] Thus the root of creation may be found in trinitarian life: "the processions of the persons are in a sense the cause and reason of creation."[92] In fact he goes so far as to apply the neo-Platonic term "emanation"[93] to the act of creating.[94]

90. See Thomas Aquinas, *ST* I, q. 44. On the theology of creation in Thomas and Bonaventure, see J. P. Wawrykow, "Aquinas and Bonaventure on Creation," in *Creation ex nihilo* (ed. Anderson et al.), 173–93.

91. Thomas Aquinas, *In I Sent.*, prol.

92. Thomas Aquinas, *ST* I, q. 45, a. 7, ad 3.

93. See Burrell, "The Act of Creation," 43–45, who holds that the act of emanation is equivalent to that of creation in Plotinus and Gregory of Nyssa (citing Ramelli, "Emanatismo," 3317). See also M. Harl, "À propos d'un passage du Contre Eunome de Grégoire de Nysse, ἀπόρροια et les titres du Christ en théologie trinitaire," *Recherches de science religieuse* 55 (1967): 217–26; H. A. Wolfson, "The Identification of *Ex Nihilo* with Emanation in Gregory of Nyssa," *Harvard Theological Review* 63 (1970): 53–60.

94. Thomas Aquinas, *ST* I, q. 45.

AUGUSTINE'S PSYCHOLOGICAL REPRESENTATION OF DIVINE PROCESSIONS AND CREATION

Augustine describes the divine processions with the aid of human psychology. This position was amply accepted by later theologians, especially in the medieval period, though it has been questioned of late.[95] The following, approximate reflections may be made as regards the role of the three divine Persons in the work of creation.[96] Of course the ensuing reflection does not amount to a kind of proof of the existence of a Trinity of Persons on the basis of rationality and human experience. Rather it involves a detection of traces of the life of the Trinity—known to us only through revelation—within a world created by God.[97] Augustine himself says: "We are speaking of God; is it any wonder if you do not understand? For if you understand, it is not God. Let there be pious confession of ignorance, rather than a rash profession of knowledge. To reach by the mind in any measure is great blessedness, but to comprehend him is altogether impossible."[98] Four stages may be mentioned.

First, when we know things, we form of them a concept, a mental word, which we may use later on in order to know other things of a similar kind.

95. It is common nowadays to recognize the limits of Augustine's psychological explanation of the Trinity and (by implication) of the divine work of creation. It is suggested that Augustine emphasizes the unity of the Trinity over its triune character, to the detriment of the realism of the divine relationships and the true nature of divine unity (as a unity of three). H. U. von Balthasar insists that the core of the generation of the Son is not knowledge but love, thus calling into question Augustine's explanation. "If we reflect once more on the process of the intra-divine processions, two approaches are barred to us: the idea of a Father who generates the Son in order to come to know himself as God, and the idea of a Father who, because he has already known himself perfectly, generates the Son. The first position would be Hegelianism, the second, thought through consistently, would be Arianism. For this reason, the immemorial priority of the self-surrender or self-expropriation thanks to which the Father *is* Father cannot be ascribed to knowledge but only to groundless love, which proves the identity of love as the 'transcendental par excellence.'" *Theo-Logic* (San Francisco, Calif.: Ignatius Press, 2000), 2:177. Lewis Ayres says: "The use of psychological analogies pushes Augustine increasingly clearly towards a monistic account of God in which the distinctions between the persons—and their specific roles in the drama of salvation—are downplayed." *Augustine and the Trinity* (Cambridge: Cambridge University Press, 2010), 22. See also D. O'Byrne, *"For Us and Our Salvation": On the Dogmatic Grounds for a Trinitarian Anthropology* (Rome: Urbaniana University Press, 2018), 187.

96. Augustine, *De Trin.* IX, 2:2 and XIV, 16:22. See also J. Galot, *Découvrir le Père: esquisse d'une théologie du Père* (Louvain: Sintal, 1985), 80–82.

97. "So created entities are understood to participate in the eternal kenosis of the persons of the Trinity by continually giving themselves to be seen, known, understood and delighted in." Oliver, "Trinity, Motion and Creation *ex nihilo*," 145.

98. Augustine, *Sermo* 117:3.5.

This happens also with our knowledge of self. In effect, we have a kind of concept-of-self, a mental word that expresses our identity, an image of what we are and of what we aspire to be. This of course will always be an imperfect concept, more or less true, more or less complete, a work in progress. Yet the content of our actions depends critically on this identity, which we project onto other people, onto society, onto the problems we have to solve.

Second, applying this explanation to the triune God, while keeping in mind the ineffability of the divine mystery, we can say the following. When God knows himself and confers with himself as it were, there is no imperfection whatever in this process, no deception, no progress, no change—characteristics all of which belong to the created condition. God has a perfect concept of himself, a faithful and perfect image of what and who he is. And this Augustine applies to the second Person of the Trinity, eternal Wisdom, the Word, the perfect image, the Son: God's self-knowledge is so perfect and transparent and true that it may be identified with the divine substance and nature and is presented as one of the divine Persons. This of course does not constitute a proof that there is a multiplicity of Persons in God; but once we know by revelation that there are three Persons in God, one of whom is called the Word and Wisdom, then it is legitimate at a hypothetical level to identify God's self-knowledge (or self-concept) with the Word.

Third, returning to the human situation we may say that from self-knowledge comes forth self-love, that natural love—desire, not sinful egoism—that brings us to act according to what and how we are and what we aspire to be. The human will is always moved by the good that it knows, Augustine says. Our own willing, our free actions depend directly on our own self-knowledge.

Fourth, within God something of a kind happens. God loves himself necessarily, as the only adequate object of his own will; that is, he loves the Word, the perfect image, and that love is so real, so constant, so faithful, so eternal, so perfect and necessary that, again, it must be identified with the simple divine substance and nature. For this reason we can say as Christians that God is love (1 Jn 4:7). Following on from the reflection of Augustine, therefore, it is legitimate to identify this love between the Father and the Son with the Holy Spirit, the third Person of the Trinity, the gift in person. Again, this does not *prove* the personal existence of the Spirit *a priori*, for this can only be known through revelation. But it provides *a posteriori* a way of understanding the nature of the second procession and the relation between the Father and the Son.

And this love the Father has for the Son in the Holy Spirit is what makes the creation of the world possible.

CREATION AS THE WORK OF THE TRINITY

That creation is the work of the Trinity may be found in the writings of many Church Fathers and theologians. The following texts may be mentioned. There are many other possible ones.

Gregory of Nyssa describes the unity of God's work in the following terms:

> But in the case of the Divine nature we do not similarly learn that the Father does anything by Himself in which the Son does not work conjointly, or again that the Son has any special operation apart from the Holy Spirit; but every operation which extends from God to Creation, and is named according to our variable conceptions of it, has its origin from the Father, and proceeds through the Son, and is perfected in the Holy Spirit . . . the Holy Trinity fulfills every operation in a manner similar to that of which I have spoken, not by separate action according to the number of the Persons, but so that there is one motion and disposition of the good will which is communicated from the Father through the Son to the Spirit.[99]

Basil explains the trinitarian mystery of creation in a similar way:

> For the first principle of existing things is One, creating through the Son and perfecting through the Spirit. The operation of the Father who works all in all is not imperfect, neither is the creating work of the Son incomplete if not perfected by the Spirit. The Father, who creates by His sole will, could not stand in any need of the Son, but nevertheless He wills through the Son; nor could the Son, who works according to the likeness of the Father, need co-operation, but the Son too wills to make perfect through the Spirit.[100]

Likewise Gregory Nazianzen speaks of the one, single act of creation, in which the Father makes the decision, the Son carries it out in cooperation with the Father, and the Holy Spirit vivifies the created world.[101] Gregory also says that from all eternity the divine mind

99. Gregory of Nyssa, *Ad Ablabius* 9.
100. Basil, *De Spiritu Sancto* 16:38.
101. Gregory Nazianzen *Oratio theol.* 2:1 (= *Oratio* 28:1).

contemplated the desirable light of His own beauty, the equal and equally perfect splendor of the triple-rayed Divinity. . . . The world-creating Mind in his vast thoughts also mused upon the patterns of the world which He made up, upon the cosmos which was produced only afterwards, but which for God even then was present. All, with God, lies before his own eyes, both what shall be, and what was, and what is now. . . . For God, all flows into one, and all is held by the arms of the great Divinity.[102]

Augustine explains the mystery as follows on the basis of the teaching of John and Paul:

Also, when the same apostle says, "But to us there is but one God, the Father, of whom are all things, and we in Him; and one Lord Jesus Christ, by whom are all things, and we by Him" [1 Cor 8:6], who can doubt that he speaks of all things which are created; as does John [1:3], when he says, "All things were made by Him"? I ask, therefore, of whom he speaks in another place: "For of Him, and through Him, and in Him, are all things: to whom be glory forever. Amen" [Rom 11:36]. For if of the Father, and the Son, and the Holy Spirit, so as to assign each clause severally to each person: of Him, that is to say, of the Father; through Him, that is to say, through the Son; in Him, that is to say, in the Holy Spirit – it is manifest that the Father, and the Son, and the Holy Spirit is one God, inasmuch as the words continue in the singular number, "To whom be glory forever" [Rom 11:36].[103]

Augustine says: "The Catholic faith does not say that God the Father made something, and the Son made something else; but rather that what the Father made, that also the Son made, that also the Holy Spirit made."[104] Yet in the following text from *De Civitate Dei* Augustine admits to the complexity of the question:

And as to these three answers which I formerly recommended when in the case of any creature the questions are put: Who made it? By what means? Why? That it should be replied, God, by the Word, because it was good—as to these three answers, it is very questionable whether the Trinity itself is thus mystically indicated, that is, the Father, the Son, and the Holy Spirit, or whether there is some good reason for this acceptation in this passage of Scripture; this, I say, is questionable, and one cannot be expected to explain everything in one volume.[105]

102. Gregory Nazianzen, *Carm. Theol.* IV; *De mundo* 67.
103. Augustine, *De Trin.* I, 6.12.
104. Augustine, *In Io. Ev. Tr.* 20, 3.
105. Augustine, *De Civ. Dei* XI, 23.

Ambrose of Milan said the following: "Since I have Christ, even though I have nothing, I have everything. Everything is to be found in Christ, in the power of whom all things exist and in whom all things subsist. Having all things in him, I seek no more gain, because he is the gain of all things."[106] And in brief words: *semen omnium Christus*,[107] "Christ is the seed of all things."

The Second Council of Constantinople (553) has the following brief formula: "There is only one God and Father, from whom all things come, and one Lord, Jesus Christ, through whom all things are, and one Holy Spirit, in whom all things are."[108] And John Damascene explains the mystery of creation as follows:

> Since, then, God, Who is good and more than good, did not find satisfaction in self-contemplation, but in His exceeding goodness wished certain things to come into existence which would enjoy His benefits and share in His goodness, He brought all things out of nothing into being and created them, both what is invisible and what is visible. Yes, even man, who is a compound of the visible and the invisible. And it is by thought that He creates, and thought is the basis of the work, the Word filling it and the Spirit perfecting it.[109]

In the early Middle Ages, Rupert of Deutz, glossing Genesis 1:2, says that the Father is source of the created world, the Son is the causing reason, and the Holy Spirit is the *formatio* and *exornatio*,[110] that is, the one who forms and embellishes creatures. Thierry of Chartres in the twelfth century attributes the following elements to the divine Persons: to the Father, efficient causality, to the Son, formal causality, and to the Spirit, final causality.

Bonaventure sees created things, in their unity, truth, and goodness, as marks (*vestigia*) of the *Trinitas fabricatrix*; specifically, spiritual creatures are the image of the Trinity (following Augustine's scheme of memory, intellect, and will) as well as likeness (by grace).[111] In the same line, Bernard speaks of "the creating Trinity, Father and Son and Holy Spirit, from whom fell the created trinity, memory, reason and will."[112]

106. Ambrose, *De interpell. David* III, 28.

107. Ambrose, *In Ps.* 43:39.

108. Council of Constantinople II, canon 1 (DH 421).

109. John Damascene, *De fide orth.* 2:2.

110. Rupert of Deutz, *De Trinitate et operibus eius* I, 8.

111. Bonaventure, *Breviloquium* 2, 12:1. L. Mathieu, *La Trinité Créatrice d'après saint Bonaventure* (Paris: Les Éditions Franciscaines, 1992), 11.

112. Bernard of Chiaravalle, *Sermo XLV: De varia Trinitate, Dei scilicet et Hominis* 6 (PL 183:669).

Thomas Aquinas has a particularly interesting observation to make:

> The Father loves not only the Son, but also Himself and us, by the Holy Spirit; because ... to love, taken in a notional sense, not only involves the production of a divine person, but also the person produced, by way of love, which has relation to the object loved. Hence, as the Father speaks Himself and every creature by His begotten Word, inasmuch as the Word "begotten" adequately represents the Father and every creature; so He loves Himself and every creature by the Holy Spirit, inasmuch as the Holy Spirit proceeds as the love of the primal goodness whereby the Father loves Himself and every creature. Thus it is evident that a relation to the creature is implied both in the Word and in the proceeding Love, as it were in a secondary way, inasmuch as the divine truth and goodness are a principle of understanding and loving all creatures.[113]

Also during the Middle Ages, Meister Eckhart offered the following reflection on the Trinity's work of creation:

> When he [the Father] says the word, he speaks to himself and to all things in another Person and gives him the same nature that he himself has, and speaks to all spiritual beings with reason in the same word as equal [essentially] to the same word of the image, in the measure that it remains interiorly non-equal, however, to the same word in every way, in the fact that it radiates in the measure therefore in which each one has a separate being for itself.[114]

The Calvinist theologian Karl Barth puts it in brief terms: "The decisive anchorage of the recognition that creation and covenant belong to each other is the recognition that God the Creator is the triune God, Father, Son and Holy Spirit."[115]

McFarland says that "creation from nothing is fundamentally a trinitarian doctrine, since *nothing apart from God* is equivalent to the claim that not one thing came into being apart from the Word." And then he explains:

> Just as the Son, by virtue of the Father's gift, does nothing without the Father and yet is by the same token empowered to do everything the Father does, so creatures that have everything from the Son are thereby empowered to do everything they can. Once again, the divine is not something that needs to be taken or hoarded, which is how we fallen and finite creatures tend to conceive of

113. Thomas Aquinas, *ST* I, q. 37, a. 2, ad 3.

114. Meister Eckhart, "Sermon *Intravit Jesus*," in his *Meister Eckharts Traktate*, ed. J. Quint (Stuttgart: W. Kohlhammer, 1954) (author's translation).

115. Barth, *Church Dogmatics III/1*, 48.

power; rather, it is exercised in giving. God is supremely powerful as the one who bestows power. This bestowal happens within God in the generation of the divine persons and outside of God in God's bringing into existence creatures who have their own, non-divine spheres of power.[116]

The doctrine of the Trinity clarifies the relationship between God's power to create and God's identity. God's own life takes the form of a sharing of existence, as the Father eternally begets the Son in the power of the Holy Spirit; and in creation this same threefold structure is reflected in God's external action, as the Father brings the world into being through the Son (Jn 1:1–4) and sustains it through the Spirit (Ps 104:29).[117]

John Paul II in his catechesis puts it this way:

Creation is the work of the Triune God. The world "created" in the Word-Son, is "restored" together with the Son to the Father, through that Uncreated Gift, the Holy Spirit, consubstantial with both. In this way the world is created in that Love, which is the Spirit of the Father and of the Son. This universe embraced by eternal Love begins to exist in the instant chosen by the Trinity as the beginning of time.... In this way the creation of the world is the work of Love. A created gift, the universe springs from the Uncreated Gift, from the reciprocal Love of the Father and Son, from the Most Holy Trinity.[118]

And elsewhere:

The creation of the world finds its *model* in the eternal generation of the Word, of the Son, who is of the same substance of the Father. Creation finds its *source* in the Love which is the Holy Spirit. This Love-Person, consubstantial with the Father and the Son, together with the Father and the Son, is the source of the creation of the world from nothing, that is, of *the gift of existence to every being*. The whole multiplicity of beings, "visible and invisible," participate in this gratuitous gift.[119]

Finally, in the *Catechism of the Catholic Church*, citing the Byzantine liturgy, we read: "The Word of God and his Breath are at the origin of the being and life of every creature. It belongs to the Holy Spirit to rule, sanctify, and

116. McFarland, *From Nothing*, 96.

117. Ibid., 187.

118. John Paul II, "Creation Is the Work of the Trinity," General Audience, March 5, 1986, par. 8.

119. John Paul II, "Creation Reveals God's Glory," General Audience, March 12, 1986, par. 2 (emphasis added).

animate creation, for he is God, consubstantial with the Father and the Son.... Power over life pertains to the Spirit, for being God he preserves creation in the Father through the Son."[120]

Summary

Summing up what we have seen in this chapter, we may say the following: the Son proceeds from the Father, is generated as perfect Word, image, and Son; the Holy Spirit who proceeds from the Father and the Son is the love the Father has for the Son and the Son for the Father. On the basis of the revelation God has provided of himself in Christ and the Spirit, we can understand that everything that takes place within the divine life, *ad intra,* is a constant, infinite, and living communication between the Father, the Son, and the Holy Spirit. This finds expression in the operation *ad extra* of creation: in the words of Athanasius, "the Father does all through the Word in the Holy Spirit."[121] We may say that God in the Word (the Son, the image) sees the universe in time and space as a possible moment of his self-knowledge and life, and loving it with the same love with which he loves the Son, that is, in the Holy Spirit, he creates the world in complete freedom, giving it existence, by the Spirit, uncreated gift. And he creates it so that it lives out its existence in conformity with the Word or image in such a way that the created world is loved by the Father in a way analogous to the way the Father loves the Son in the Spirit. This does not take place once and for all at the very inception of creation, but throughout time and history, eschatologically.

The Father loves the Son in the Holy Spirit and the free result *ad extra* of this love is the created universe. The latter is therefore (1) entirely under the dominion of God, (2) completely steeped in God's love, the Holy Spirit, who from the beginning "was moving over the face of the waters" (Gn 1:2), and (3) with the vocation or destiny of being and becoming more and more like the Word/Son. God perpetually seeks out with love (in the Holy Spirit) his own Son (the Word) in the whole of creation. Thus when God made the world, and especially when he gave life to certain

120. *CCC*, nos. 291 and 703.
121. Athanasius, *Ad serap.* 28.

creatures in his image and likeness, they became as it were brothers of the Word and sons of the Father.[122]

God looks upon his created children, indeed upon the entire universe, with paternal pride as he seeks out the Son in each person and each element. For this purpose he sent his only Son (Mt 21:33–41; Jn 3:16) to reconcile humans from their sinful alienation and learn to live like brothers of his (Rom 8:29) and children of God (Gal 4:5). Creation was designed and projected and made by God so that it would exist in conformity with the Son; in other words it was made on account of the Son and through the Son. This powerful "desire" of the Father gives life to the work of the Holy Spirit, who forges the filial conformity of creation to the Word. "We know that the whole creation has been groaning in travail together until now; and not only the creation, but we ourselves, who have the first fruits of the Spirit, groan inwardly as we wait for adoption as sons, the redemption of our bodies" (Rom 8:22), in such a way that at the end of time, when the Word who created all things will judge everyone,[123] the Father can look at the Son and verify the conformity that should exist between the eternal divine project and the reality of the universe, and truthfully exclaim "this is my beloved Son in whom I am well pleased" (Mt 3:17) with all the intensity and incisiveness that marks the fatherly love that awaited the return of the prodigal son (Lk 15:20).

122. See O'Callaghan, *Children of God in the World*, 262–68.

123. On the trinitarian aspect of eschatological judgment, see O'Callaghan, *Christ Our Hope*, 156–58.

8

The Purpose of Creation

THE GLORY OF GOD

IN THE PREVIOUS CHAPTER we saw that God created the world out of love in such a way that it would become more and more identified with the Word/Son in the power of the Holy Spirit. This response of the created world to divine power involves a clear affirmation of time, history, and the ultimate eschatological realization of the created universe. Still, because the world was created through the Word in the power of the Spirit, its purpose or scope is, to an important degree, already written or hard-wired into its very structure, into its nature. Created things reflect more or less—or at least they should reflect—the mind of God, the will of God, the power of God, the glory of God. After all, creation is God's own work: "The earth is the Lord's and its fullness" (Ps 24:1).

Situating the Notion of the Glory of God

We have already seen that God did not make the world for his own benefit or gain; God is not enriched by creating the world.[1] The beneficiaries of creation in an absolute sense are creatures themselves who come into existence as living and good. They are not merely improved by creation but are actually given being by God. As Irenaeus said, *gloria Dei vivens homo*,[2] the glory of God is the living man. Thomas Aquinas says: *Deus suam gloriam non quaerit propter se sed propter nos*,[3] "God does not seek his

1. See O'Callaghan, "Can God Be Enriched?"
2. Irenaeus, *Adv. Haer.* III, 20, 2.
3. Thomas Aquinas, *ST* II-II, q. 132, a. 1, ad 1.

glory for himself, but for us." And McFarland notes that "the glory of God in creation consists precisely in the graciousness of God's giving existence to that which is not God."[4]

In this chapter I shall consider the classical affirmation that the universe was made for the glory of God.[5] At the level of practical spirituality, however, a certain ambivalence may be detected in the expression, a tension between humans acting for the glory of God and humans acting simply in their own interest. The former would bring believers to give glory to God by carrying out his will no matter what the cost, by teaching and manifesting his word and nothing else, by making sure nothing gets in the way of God's actions, even to the point of renouncing personal happiness to ensure that God's will is done and his decrees fulfilled. The latter approach, on the contrary, could lead humans to give glory to God in the wider context of seeking out their own peace, or joy, or happiness, directly perceived, for example by rejecting a vocational commitment that might seem to be incompatible with their personal freedom and happiness. Perhaps the biblical image that best describes this attitude is that of the rich man with the abundant harvest (Lk 12:16–21). "Soul, you have ample goods laid up for many years; take your ease, eat, drink, be merry" (Lk 12:19). The former approach to giving glory to God, we might say, is radical and God-centered; the latter rather more self-indulgent and man-centered.

Among pagan religions the dilemma between the achievement of divine glory and the attainment of human happiness did not arise because most humans were convinced that their personal lives were of little or no importance at a religious or cosmic level anyway. At best they could live and survive thanks to the precarious benevolence of some second-rate divinity. The gods after all looked after their own interests, not those of humans, although they stood in need of the support of humans on account of which they contributed toward their protection. Yet the cosmos on the whole is not particularly concerned about individual humans, who have to be satisfied with looking after themselves as best they can. Plato has it that

4. McFarland, *From Nothing*, 63.

5. See Z. Alszeghy and M. Flick, "Gloria Dei," *Gregorianum* 36 (1955): 361–90; J. Morales, *El misterio de la creación* (Pamplona: Eunsa, 1994), 161–72; D. Mollat, "Gloire," in *Théologie biblique*, ed. X. Léon-Dufour (Paris: Cerf, 1970), 504–11; *NIDNTTE* 1:761–67, s.v. δόξα.

the cosmos does not exist on account of humans, but the latter on account of the cosmos.[6]

But Christian faith teaches that God made humans, male and female, in his image and likeness; he wants them to live as his children, and destines them, one by one, to everlasting life in personal communion with the Trinity.[7] Genesis tells us that man was created on the sixth day, just before the Sabbath, whereas all the stars that fill the universe, and were traditionally considered as deities controlling the world's destiny, were made on the fourth (Gn 1:14). It may be that the Jewish and Christian view of human dignity has traditionally given fallen humans a disproportionate idea of their value and dignity at the center of the universe. Yet this is due in good measure to the fact that they have consistently challenged the idea that the world exists for the benefit of the God who made it.

However, in saying that the world is made *propter gloriam Dei*, for the glory of God, as Vatican Council I clearly does, the impression is given that the created world should be sacrificed in order to ensure that the proclamation of the absolute transcendence and magnificence of God is fully affirmed. The latter position is typical of traditional evangelical Protestantism, specifically of John Calvin, who insisted, in his work *The Institutes*, that all has to be done and (if needs be) sacrificed for the glory of God. And this has manifested itself at times as a severe, austere, excessively rigorous Puritanism. The Protestant theologian Karl Barth, paraphrasing the teaching of Calvin, said that the only reason that justifies the existence of the world is that of "serving as a theater of the glory of God."[8]

Some modern philosophies, reflecting a more liberal kind of Protestantism, have shifted attention away from God as the center of the universe toward humans. This has occasioned a systematic anthropocentric shift in theology and spirituality in recent centuries. The best-known example of this phenomenon is the philosopher Immanuel Kant who, in his *Critique of Practical Reason*, explains that ethics are not relevant at a transcendent level, in relation to God. Ethical life relates to humans themselves, and they are its only point of reference. The maxim he proposes is as follows:

6. See Plato, *Laws* X, 903c–d.

7. See O'Callaghan, *Children of God in the World*, 215–46.

8. K. Barth, *Dogmatik im Grundriss: im Anschluss an das apostolische Glaubensbekenntnis* (Stuttgart: W. Kohlhammer, 1947), 73.

"I am never to act otherwise than so that I could also will that my maxim should become a universal law."[9] In other words, the only criterion for judging whether life is lived out ethically or not is the good of humans, or more precisely, the good of humans as perceived and determined by humans themselves. God is not directly involved in this process, but is considered simply as the guarantor of the established order, a postulate of pure practical reason.[10] Elsewhere Kant speaks of the practical imperative that should guide human action: "man and generally any rational being exists as an end in himself, not merely as a means to be arbitrarily used by this or that will, but in all his actions, whether they concern himself or other rational beings, must be always regarded at the same time as an end."[11]

Doubtless Kant intended here to defend human dignity, the dignity of each person. And his affirmations to the effect that the human being is an absolute and untouchable reality, source of the supreme law of moral action, make considerable sense. He was convinced that no human has the right to arbitrarily use another human as a mere means for personal benefit. But where does this leave God, the creator of the universe? If the only absolute criterion for moral action stops at man himself, as perceived by himself, whether individually or collectively, then the role and position of God would seem to be excluded. When the Catholic Kantian Anton Günther said that the *gloria Dei* should be considered secondary and extrinsic with respect to the intrinsic good of creation, and Georg Hermes suggested God's action should be understood in the light of the moral demands of practical reason (given that the world is the ultimate end of man),[12] Vatican Council I responded by teaching that the world has been created *propter gloriam Dei*, for the glory of God.[13] After all, man does not have the last word, only God does. Man was not created on the last day, but on the second last. The last day was for God's rest, for the proclamation of God's glory. Let us consider now how scripture and theology understands the glory of God.

9. I. Kant, "Fundamental Principles of the Metaphysic of Morals I," in his *Critique of Practical Reason* (London: Longmans, Green, and Co., 1898), 18.

10. See ibid., 220–29.

11. Ibid., 46.

12. Morales, *El misterio de la creación*, 166; L. M. Armendáriz, "Fuerza y debilidad de la doctrina del Vaticano I sobre el fin de la creación," *Estudios eclesiásticos* 45 (1970): 359–99.

13. DH 3025.

The Glory of God in Scripture

Scripture speaks extensively of the glory of God. The term used is *kābôḏ Yahweh* in Hebrew, *doxa tou Theou* in Greek, and *gloria Dei* in Latin.[14]

THE GLORY OF GOD IN THE OLD TESTAMENT

At a purely linguistic level, an important difference may be noted between the Hebrew and the Greek versions of the term *glory*. The Greek *doxa* evokes the notion of brightness and light, and generally refers to the opinion of one person about another person or situation: it is equivalent to fame, reputation, esteem, honor, credibility, etc. The Hebrew term *kābôḏ*, on the other hand, evokes solidity, and refers to an objective and untouchable quality present in beings, quite independently of human opinion. *Doxa* is usually used in a profane and intellectual sense among Greek authors. But in the Septuagint it is used to translate *kābôḏ* and is applied to God, specifically to his great and marvelous deeds,[15] but more fundamentally to his very being. The root of *kābôḏ*, *kbd*, is to be found in different adjectives and verbs that indicate gravity, weight, and solidity;[16] it is also applied to demanding work (Ex 5:9), to the stubbornness of an intractable people (Nm 11:14), to Abraham who was said to be heavy in gold and cattle (Gn 13:2). *Kābôḏ* indicates a situation of privilege for humans (Gn 45:13), for kings (1 Sm 15:30), for man as the lord of creation (Ps 8:6). It is also applied to the cedars of Lebanon (Is 35:2) and to the prosperity of the city of Tyre (Ezek 27:25–36).

Thus *kābôḏ* refers to something solid, inherent, and preexisting in things, to something that awakens respect and admiration in humans, who attribute to things weight, importance, celebrity, or prestige. At the same time glory is always something fragile, ambivalent, and passing in the created order: "Be not afraid when one becomes rich, when the glory of his house increases. For when he dies he will carry nothing away; his

14. See BDAG 256–58, s.v. δόξα; *NIDNTTE* 1:761–67, s.v. δόξα.

15. See H. Brockington, "The Septuagintal Background to the New Testament Use of δόξα," in *Studies in the Gospels: Essays in Memory of R. H. Lightfoot*, ed. D. E. Nineham (Oxford: Blackwell, 1955), 1–8.

16. See 1 Kgs 12:4, 10, 11; Prv 27:3; Ps 37:5; Lam 3:7.

glory will not go down after him. Though, while he lives, he counts himself happy, and though a man gets praise when he does well for himself, he will go to the generation of his fathers, who will never more see the light" (Ps 49:17–18). In 1 Pt 1:24 we read: "All flesh is like grass, and all its glory like the flower of the field; the grass withers, and the flower wilts, but the word of the Lord abides forever" (citing Is 40:6–9).

The principal subject of *kāḇôḏ* in the Old Testament of course is God. Humans in different ways can perceive the *kāḇôḏ Yahweh*.[17] "Arise, shine; for your light has come, and the glory of the Lord has risen upon you. For behold, darkness shall cover the earth, and thick darkness the peoples; but the Lord will arise upon you, and his glory will be seen upon you" (Is 60:1–2). The external and ephemeral glory of creation is based entirely on the immutable inner glory of God. John Paul II explains this as follows:

> The Glory of God is first of all in himself. It is the "interior" glory, which fills the unlimited depth and infinite perfection of the one divinity in the Trinity of Persons. Inasmuch as it is the absolute fullness of being and holiness, this infinite perfection is also the fullness of truth and of love in the mutual contemplation and giving (and hence in the communion) of Father, Son and Holy Spirit.[18]

When the interior glory of God is manifested externally, through creation, we are told that the world becomes full of his glory (Nm 14:21; Is 6:3; Ps 72:19).[19] Particularly graphic is what we read in Psalm 18:2: "The heavens are telling the glory of God; and the firmament proclaims his handiwork." The same message may be found elsewhere throughout the psalms. "God's interior glory springs from the mystery of the divinity," John Paul II says. "Through the work of creation, it is in a certain sense transferred 'outside'—in the creatures of the visible and invisible world, in proportion to their degree of perfection. . . . A new dimension of God's glory begins with the creation of the visible and invisible world."[20]

God's glory of course is identified with his very being, in that it belongs to his interior, trinitarian, life, yet it may be hidden, ambivalent, and frag-

17. See B. Stein, *Der Begriff Kebod Jahweh und seine Bedeutung für die alttestamentliche Gotteserkenntnis* (Emsdetten i. Westf.: H. and J. Lechte, 1939).

18. John Paul II, "Creation Reveals God's Glory," par. 3.

19. B. L. Ramm, *Them He Glorified: A Systematic Study of the Doctrine of Glorification* (Grand Rapids, Mich.: Eerdmans, 1963).

20. John Paul II, "Creation Reveals God's Glory," par. 3.

mentary for us. Sometimes it is hidden by clouds (Ex 16:10, 24:16–18), it shines out like fire (Ex 24:15), it is present during a storm (Ps 97:1–6). And the reason is that glory does not belong natively to these created phenomena, but derives from God and refers always to him. "The stars shone in their watches, and were glad; he called them, and they said, 'Here we are!' They shone with gladness for him who made them" (Bar 3:34).

One place where God's glory and power is manifested in a special way is on Mount Sinai to Moses (Ex 24:16–17) and to the people of God in a myriad of ways. The glory of Sinai serves as a clear sign of divine benevolence at the heart of the covenant, and at the same time a reminder of the presence of God as creator and Lord. In later books of the Old Testament the glory of God is identified with his holiness, that is, with his transcendence and ineffability, given that he is the totally Other (Am 4:2; Is 40:25, 46:5; Ps 112:4). For this reason God cannot cede his glory to anybody: "I am the Lord, that is my name; my glory I give to no other, nor my praise to graven images" (Is 42:8). For God to give his glory to another would require him to contradict himself.

Several Old Testament texts indicate that the reason for the historical existence of Israel is that of proclaiming and declaring the glory of God before the whole world (Is 60:1–3, 66:18–19; Ps 96:6). In the words of John Paul II, "the whole created universe is a multiple, powerful and incessant appeal to proclaim the glory of the Creator."[21] The fundamental task of humans is to do just this. The chosen people of Israel however was not always up to the task of proclaiming God's glory to the world at large. And understandably so, as a clear eschatological element is present in Old Testament teaching on *kābôḏ Yahweh*: God's glory will not be proclaimed definitively until history comes to a close, at the *parousia* (Mt 16:27, 19:28, 21:31, 24:30).[22] It may be observed, in fact, as the time for the coming of the Messiah approached, that the topic becomes more and more important.[23]

21. Ibid., par. 5.

22. The term "glory" is used in Matthew and Mark almost always eschatologically, referring to the coming of Christ in glory at the end of time.

23. See Enoch 22:14; C. Rowland, *The Open Heaven: A Study of Apocalyptic in Judaism and Early Christianity* (New York: Crossroad, 1982), 95 and 280. See also *NIDNTTE* 1:764.

THE GLORY OF GOD IN THE NEW TESTAMENT

The motifs related to the glory of God in the Old Testament are to be found again in the New, in which the term *glory* is often accompanied by that of *power*.[24] The glory of God is present for example at the birth of the child Jesus (Lk 2:9, 14). The expression "to give glory to God" is frequently used (Lk 18:43; Jn 11:4; Acts 12:23; Rom 4:20). The difference introduced by the New Testament of course is that the glory of God is present in a singular, definitive, and insuperable way in Jesus Christ. The first thing the New Testament tells us is that Christ, the Word incarnate, carries the glory of God within himself in a way that is hidden to the world but is revealed to believers: "And the Word became flesh and dwelt among us, full of grace and truth; and we have beheld his glory, glory as of the only Son from the Father" (Jn 1:14). To his Father Christ appeals: "And now ... glorify me in your own presence with the glory which I had with you before the world was made" (Jn 17:5). And in the letter to the Hebrews Christ is said to "reflect the glory of God and bears the very stamp of his nature, upholding the universe by his word of power" (Heb 1:3, 2:7).

In spite of its hiddenness, it was possible for the disciples to perceive the glory of God at special moments of Jesus' life, for example at the transfiguration (Mt 17:2)[25] and the miracles. At the miraculous turning of water into wine at Cana, John tells us: "This, the first of his signs, Jesus did at Cana in Galilee, and manifested his glory; and his disciples believed in him" (Jn 2:11). Yet on the whole Jesus manifested his divine glory to the world reluctantly. This may be seen during his temptations in the desert (Mt 4:1–22; the devil said falsely: "I shall give to you all this power and their glory," Lk 4:6). Neither did he want to publicize his miracles (Mt 8:4, 9:30). His glory is hidden besides at the agony in the Garden (Mt 26:36–42).[26] Jesus openly admitted: "I do not seek my own glory; there is one who seeks it and he is the one who judges" (Jn 8:50). Yet in real terms, for

24. See Mt 24:30; Mk 13:26; Lk 4:6, 21:27; Eph 3:16; 2 Thes 1:9; 2 Pt 1:3; Jude 25; Rv 1:6, 4:11, 5:12, 7:12, 16:9. The same is to be found in the Old Testament: Ps 63:3; Sir 49:5; Dn 2:37.

25. See A. M. Ramsey, *The Glory of God and the Transfiguration of Christ* (London; New York: Longmans, Green, 1949).

26. See P. O'Callaghan, *The Christological Assimilation of the Apocalypse: An Essay on Fundamental Eschatology* (Dublin: Four Courts, 2004), 221–23.

those with eyes of faith, the incarnation of the Word is the definitive manifestation of the glory of God (Jn 1:14).

Paul speaks of the novelty of the presence of God's glory in the New Testament in comparison with that of the Old: "Now if the dispensation of death, carved in letters on stone, came with such splendor [*doxa*] that the Israelites could not look at Moses's face because of its brightness, fading as this was, will not the dispensation of the Spirit be attended with greater splendor [*doxa*]?" (2 Cor 3:7–8).[27] And it is not just that the glory of God in Christ is more intense than the glory revealed in the Old Testament, but it is actually foundational to the latter, as we read in the letter to the Hebrews: "He [Christ] was faithful to him who appointed him, just as Moses also was faithful in God's house. Yet Jesus has been counted worthy of as much more glory [*doxa*] than Moses as the builder of a house has more honor [*timē*] than the house" (Heb 3:2–3). What was present in the Old Testament was the glory of the Word which came to the fullest possible manifestation with the incarnation.

The glory of God is manifested in a singular way in the passion of Jesus by which he forfeited both life and human glory for the salvation of humanity (Mt 27:29–30, 40–42), and at his resurrection through which he became "the Lord of glory" (1 Cor 2:8). "Was it not necessary that the Christ should suffer these things and enter into his glory?," Jesus asked the disciples on the road to Emmaus (Lk 24:26). "Through him [Christ] you have confidence in God, who raised him from the dead and gave him glory, so that your faith and hope are in God" (1 Pt 1:21). Still, the high point of the manifestation of God's glory will take place at the *Parousia*, at the end of time, when Christ "will return in the glory of the Father,"[28] and the world will "behold my [Jesus'] glory which you [the Father] gave me in your love for me before the foundation of the world" (Jn 17:24). Besides, Jesus will communicate to believers the same glory he has received from the Father (Rom 3:23). By seeking out the glory of God, Christians are in a position to share in the glory of the cross and resurrection of Jesus. "For this slight momentary affliction is preparing for us an eternal weight of glory beyond all comparison, because we look not to the things that are seen

27. See L. L. Belleville, *Reflections of Glory: Paul's Polemical use of the Moses-Doxa Tradition in 2 Corinthians 3:1–18* (Sheffield: JSOT Press, 1991).

28. DH 150.

but to the things that are unseen; for the things that are seen are transient, but the things that are unseen are eternal" (2 Cor 4:17–18). The eternal weight of glory, the letter to the Corinthians says; this play on words between weight (the root of the Hebrew *kābôḏ*) and glory (*doxa*), should not be passed over lightly.[29] Elsewhere the New Testament speaks of the "unfading crown of glory" (1 Pt 5:4).

Living for the Glory of God

It should be clear from the above reflection that the created world, objectively speaking, is none other than the manifestation of God's power, of his holiness, of his glory. Creatures therefore are simply meant to recognize this fact, through faith and reason, and proclaim it in word and deed. Not to do so for creatures would constitute a falsehood, a refusal to recognize the living presence of the Word, the image, the Son through whom and for whom the world was created. All creatures, whether they like it or not, proclaim, cry out, the glory of God (Ps 18:2). "Worthy are you, Lord our God, to receive glory and honor and power, *for you created all things*; because of your will they came to be and were created" (Rv 4:11). Nonliving or nonintellectual creatures give glory to God necessarily though unconsciously; in technical terms they are said to give glory to God *materially*. But living, intelligent beings give glory to God *formally*, consciously, rationally, intelligently. Or at least they *should* do so. In any case, as C. S. Lewis says, "A man can no more diminish God's glory by refusing to worship Him than a lunatic can put out the sun by scribbling the word 'darkness' on the walls of his cell."[30]

Four aspects of the mystery of divine glory should be mentioned. First, those who behave in a proper manner are said to give glory to God, whereas those who do not, sin. "Eternal life to those who seek glory, honor, and immortality through perseverance in good works.... But there will be glory, honor, and peace for everyone who does good, Jew first and then Greek" (Rom 2:7, 10). The Book of Revelation speaks of those who "did not repent or give him glory" (Rv 16:9). In John's Gospel we read that un-

29. See R. P. Martin, *2 Corinthians* (Waco, Tex.: Word Books, 1986), 92.

30. C. S. Lewis, *The Problem of Pain* (New York: Macmillan, 1948), 41.

believers "preferred human praise [*doxa anthropōn*] to the glory of God [*doxa tou Theou*]" (Jn 12:43). In the letter to the Romans, we read that sinners "although they knew God they did not accord him glory as God or give him thanks. Instead, they became vain in their reasoning, and their senseless minds were darkened.... They exchanged the glory of the immortal God for the likeness of an image of mortal man or of birds or of four-legged animals or of snakes" (Rom 1:21, 23).

Second, humans are meant to glorify God not only on an individual basis, but also by ensuring that the whole of creation glorifies God in a cosmic and universal way. Creation glorifies God through humanity, who was given the singular privilege and task, at the moment of creation, of "having dominion over the fish of the sea and over the birds of the air, and over the cattle, and over all the earth, and over every creeping thing that creeps upon the earth" (Gn 1:26), a dominion of course that is exercised under God.[31] According to Maximus the Confessor, "humanity lies at the center of creation, as a 'workshop' that mediates between different elements and thereby brings together all the various divisions."[32] The seventh-century Cypriot theologian Leontios of Neapolis says that "creation does not venerate the Creator directly, on its own, but through us the heavens proclaim the glory of God; through us the moon offers God homage and the stars praise him; through us the waters, the rains and the dew, united with all other beings, adore and glorify God."[33] Karl Barth points out that "Man is the place within creation where the creature in its fullness is concentrated, and at the same time stretches beyond itself."[34] In the words of Romano Guardini, "by means of man all things must return to God as a kind of response."[35] Kathryn Tanner says: "The exceptional character of human beings would be as placeholders ... for creation generally, focal points for the worldwide imaging of the second person's relations with the other two."[36] And John Zizioulas says that "man is created to fulfill the destiny of the created world, and he does this both by giving his consent on

31. See O'Callaghan, *Children of God in the World*, 99–105.

32. McFarland, *From Nothing*, 79, paraphrasing Maximus.

33. Leontios of Neapolis, *Sermo contra Judaeos* III.

34. Barth, *Dogmatik im Grundriss*, 84.

35. R. Guardini, *Welt und Person: Versuche zur christlichen Lehre vom Menschen*, 2nd ed. (Würzburg: Werkbund, 1940), 145.

36. Tanner, *Christ the Key*, 142.

behalf of creation and by the authority he has to make use of creation."[37]

In the words of John Paul II, "This hymn of glory, inscribed in creation, awaits a being capable of giving it adequate conceptual and verbal expression, a being who will praise the holy name of God and narrate the greatness of his works (Sir 17:8). This being in the visible world is man. The appeal which goes up from the universe is addressed to him as the spokesman of creatures and their interpreter before God."[38] The task of exercising dominion over the world with which God equips humans and blesses them (Gn 1:27) is not only directed at improving and perfecting the earth—the created, material world—but also at ensuring that God is glorified.[39] It is as if humans are meant to gather up and identify with the joyful, *naif*, child-like, faithful, and unconscious response of the created elements of the world and direct them all in Christ to the Father. Man indeed becomes the mouthpiece and interpreter of creation.

In the third place, what does it mean for the creature to give glory to God? Fundamentally it means recognizing every created thing, every event, as creaturely in origin and destiny, in which we may perceive the goodness, power, truth, and beauty of God, in a word, his glory. In means to praise, to adore the Lord, for his own glory and for the glory he has generously placed in the created world. In the Liturgy of John Chrysostom we read:

> It is proper and just to sing to you, to bless you, to praise you, to thank you, to worship you in every place of your dominion. For you are God ineffable, inconceivable, invisible, incomprehensible, ever existing, yet ever the same, you, and your only-begotten Son, and your Holy Spirit. You brought us out of nonexistence into being, and again raised us up when we had fallen, and left nothing undone until you brought us to heaven and gave us your kingdom to come. For all this we thank you, and your only-begotten Son, and your Holy Spirit, for all that we know and that we do not know, for the manifest and hidden benefits bestowed on us.[40]

37. Zizioulas, "Creation and Salvation," 95.

38. John Paul II, "Creation Reveals the Glory of God," par. 6.

39. "For you laid the foundations of the world and have arranged for the changing of times and seasons; you have formed man in your own image and set humanity over the whole world in all its wonder, to rule in your name over all you have made, and for ever praise you in your mighty works, through Christ our Lord." *V Sunday Preface*, from *The Roman Missal*, ed. P. W. Carey and H. J. Nolan (Washington, D.C.: United States Conference of Catholic Bishops, 2011), 580.

40. Metropolitan Cantor Institute, Byzantine Catholic Archparcy of Pittsburg, *Anaphora of the*

The high point of giving glory to God of course is situated in the liturgy, the celebration of the Sabbath, which I considered in chapter 2. Charles Taylor notes that the coming of our present-day secular age in which God is no longer glorified is fundamentally due to "an eclipse of worship," a refusal to give thanks to God for all his gifts and graces.[41]

In a polytheistic or idolatrous context, giving glory and recognition to a variety of different, competing divinities is a complex business. In the Christian context, on the contrary, all the glory is given to God, because there is only one God, one creator, to be praised and glorified. Giving glory to God is simpler for Christians than it is for pagans, but it is also more radical and demanding. Besides, there is no part whatever of reality over which God is not Lord. God is not envious of anybody or anything, simply because he has nobody to be envious of. Plato in fact recognized that envy is absent from the divine because he is perfectly good.[42] Thus we can understand the words of Aquinas: "It is the same to say that God does all for himself [*propter seipsum*] as to say that he has made all creatures for their being."[43] Christians believe they have received all from God, and therefore there is only one port of call for their praise and gratitude: *Deo omnis gloria*,[44] all the glory should be given to God.

This attitude may be seen especially in the life of the Virgin Mary. In the hymn *The Magnificat* we read: "Mary said, 'My soul magnifies the Lord, and my spirit rejoices in God my Savior, for he has regarded the lowness of his servant. For behold, henceforth all generations will call me blessed; for he who is mighty has done great things for me, and holy is his name'" (Lk 1:46–49). Likewise the angels incessantly give glory to God, as we shall see in chapter 11. "The Old Testament especially emphasizes the special participation of the angels in the celebration of the glory which the creator receives as a tribute of praise on the part of the created world,"[45] says John Paul II.

Divine Liturgy of St. John Chrysostom, available at https://mci.archpitt.org/liturgy/Divine_Liturgy_Anaphora_Chrysostom.html.

41. See Taylor, *A Secular Age*. See my studies "The Eclipse of Worship: Theological Reflections on Charles Taylor's *A Secular Age*," *Euntes Docete* 62, no. 2 (2009): 89–123, and "Cultural Challenges to Faith: A Reflection on the Dynamics of Modernity."

42. See Plato, *Timaeus* 29a.

43. Thomas Aquinas, *De Pot.*, q. 5, a. 4.

44. See P. O'Callaghan, "Gloria de Dios," in *Diccionario de San Josemaría Escrivá de Balaguer*, ed. J. L. Illanes (Burgos: Monte Carmelo, 2013), 565–71.

45. John Paul II, "Creator of Things Unseen: The Angels," General Audience, July 30, 1986, par. 2.

And fourth, what can we say about the need for Christians to proclaim the glory of God and at the same time seek and achieve their own comfort and happiness and peace and prosperity? Does one have to be sacrificed for the sake of the other? Must humans renounce their own happiness in order to glorify God? Or may it be necessary to forego giving glory to God in order to live a fulfilled life? The response can only be as follows: human happiness and fulfillment consists *objectively* in recognizing and seeking the glory of God, though this may not always be the case *subjectively*. At certain stages in a person's life, giving glory to God may involve the renunciation of some moments of experienced happiness or immediate gratification, moments that are not compatible with doing the will of God.[46] Believers are invited to reach out for what Josemaría Escrivá called the "happiness of Glory."[47] In real terms the glory of God (the objective scope of the creation) and the good of the creature are one and the same thing.[48] "Blessed are you among women," said Elizabeth to Mary in Luke's Gospel, "and blessed is the fruit of your womb.... And blessed is she who believed that there would be a fulfillment of what was spoken to her from the Lord" (Lk 1:42, 45). And in Matthew we read: "Blessed are you Simon Bar-Jona! For flesh and blood has not revealed this to you, but my Father who is in heaven" (Mt 16:17). We see this especially in the Sermon on the Mount, where Jesus tells of the blessedness of the poor in spirit, those who mourn, the meek, those who hunger and thirst for righteousness, the merciful, the pure in heart, the peacemakers, and those who are persecuted (Mt 5:3–12).[49] Clearly, Christian happiness and fulfillment is compatible with sacrifice.

To be happy or blessed is an objective reality that may or may not always be experienced subjectively as such. In the context of a materialistic, hedonistic, monistic, individualistic ethical system, human happiness of course must be considered as a limited, competitive commodity, in such a way that the more one person has, the less others may have: my happi-

46. On the dynamics of immediate and deferred gratification, see P. O'Callaghan, "Wanting to be Loved. The Adventure of Loving," in *Loving and Teaching Others to Love: The Formation of Affectivity in Priestly Life*, ed. F. Insa and D. Parker (Rome: Edusc, 2021), 53–65.

47. Josemaría Escrivá, *The Way* (Cork: Mercier Press, 1953), no. 29.

48. See L. Scheffczyk, "Schöpfung als Vor-Ordnung der Gnade. Zur Schöpfungslehre M. J. Scheebens," *Divinitas* 32 (1988): 205–25.

49. On the term "blessed" and its objective quality, *NIDNTTE* 1:206–10, s.v. μακάριος.

ness therefore requires the sacrifice of that of others, and vice versa. This impression of course is a sign of the sinful human condition, an attempt to treat God as one like us. The Christian paradox, which finds its maximum expression in the life, death, and resurrection of Christ, lies in the fact that the fullest possible personal self-realization takes place by doing all things for the glory to God. "For whoever would save his life will lose it; and whoever loses his life for my sake and the gospel's will save it" (Mk 8:35; Phil 2:6–9).

Besides, it is quite clear that giving glory to God is not a one-way operation, directed from creatures to God. Jesus explains that humans share in the divine glory the Son gives the Father and the Father gives the Son (Jn 17:1, 5, 22, 24). Scripture speaks of the involvement of the Trinity in the giving and taking of glory (1 Pt 4:13). And Schwöbel observes: "glory is not a self-directed attitude, but the mutuality of glorifying the other and receiving glory from the other which constitutes the communion of the divine life. Trinitarian glory is communicating glory and communicated glory."[50]

50. Schwöbel, "God, Creation and the Christian Community," 169.

9

Creation, Conservation, *Concursus*, Providence, and Time

"WITH CREATION, God does not abandon his creatures to themselves. He not only gives them being and existence, but also, and at every moment, upholds and sustains them in being, enables them to act and brings them to their final end."[1] This point of the *Catechism of the Catholic Church* sums up Christian teaching in respect of creation and its immediate consequences. Not only did God create the world, but he conserves it in being (*conservatio,* conservation), he moves things to act according to their proper nature (*concursus,* which may be translated as concourse, enablement, running together, concurrence) and he leads them to their last end (*providentia,* providence, or *gubernatio,* governance). The four stages—creation, conservation, *concursus,* and providence—are conceptually distinguishable from one another, but in real terms there is a strong continuity between them as they all derive inseparably from God's powerful, simple, creative action; they "are simultaneously enacted dimensions of God's single work of provision."[2]

Athanasius describes the divine work in trinitarian terms:

> Seeing then all created nature, as far as its own laws were concerned, to be fleeting and subject to dissolution, lest it should come to this and lest the Universe should be broken up again into nothingness, for this cause He made all things by His own eternal Word, and gave substantive existence to Creation, and moreover did not leave it to be tossed in a tempest in the course of its own nature, lest it should run the risk of once more dropping out of existence; but, because He is good He guides and settles the whole Creation by His own Word, Who is

1. CCC, no. 301.
2. C. M. Wood, *The Question of Providence* (Louisville, Ky.: John Knox Press, 2008), 80.

Himself also God, that by the governance and providence and ordering action of the Word, Creation may have light, and be enabled to abide always securely. For it partakes of the Word who derives true existence from the Father, and is helped by Him so as to exist, lest that should come to it which would have come but for the maintenance of it by the Word; namely, dissolution.[3]

Thomas Aquinas has the following to say:

God is the cause of the actions of all things inasmuch as he gives them power to act and preserves them and applies them to action and inasmuch as by his power every other power acts. And when we add that God is his own power and that he is within each thing, not as part of its essence, but as holding the thing in being, it follows that he operates immediately in every operation, without excluding the operation of the will and nature.[4]

Let us consider the three elements one by one: conservation, *concursus*, providence.

Conservation

When something is fabricated, already existing matter is formed, figured, shaped. The object in question continues existing autonomously, and in principle no longer stands in need of further intervention on the part of the manufacturing agent in order to act and be itself. As we examine artificial objects we can discover the intelligibility they contain, and thus the mind of their maker, but we can also abandon them entirely, knowing that their existence and operation will continue unaltered whether we pay attention to them or not. This description however cannot be applied to the creative action of God, who not only gives things form or shape (essence or nature) but also existence, being. And this for the simple reason that "before" creation took place there was no matter to make things out of. Greek philosophy on the whole took it that prime matter of one kind or other existed before the world was made. And in that sense the conservation of things was of no particular interest to them. Things change and vary, indeed, but they basically lasted forever. For those who believed in a creating God, however, the conservation of the universe became a key issue.

3. Athanasius, *Contra Gentes* 41.

4. See Thomas Aquinas, *De Pot.*, q. 3, a. 7.

The doctrine of conservation is markedly different from the careless divine transcendence of the Stoics and from the suffocating immanence of the pantheists. The former disconnects God from the created world; the latter identifies the created world with God. The key point is that God keeps things in existence while maintaining his transcendence. In the Book of Job Elihu says: "If he should take back his spirit to himself, and gather to himself his breath, all flesh would perish together, and man would return to dust" (Jb 34:14–15). The Book of Psalms also speaks of the way God keeps things in existence. "O Lord, how manifold are your works! In wisdom you have made them all; the earth is full of your creatures.... These all look to you, to give them their food in due season.... When you hide your face, they are dismayed; when you take away their breath, they die and return to their dust" (Ps 104:24, 27, 29). The same teaching may be found in the Book of Wisdom: "For you love all things that exist, and loathe none of the things which you have made, for you would not have made anything if you had hated it. How would anything have endured if you had not willed it? Or how would anything not called forth by you have been preserved? You spare all things, for they are yours, o Lord who love the living" (Wis 11:24–26). And finally in the Acts of the Apostles we read that God "is not far from each one of us, for 'In him we live and move and have our being'; as even some of your poets have said, 'For we are indeed his offspring'" (Acts 17:27), words of Paul that reflect the teaching of the Stoics.[5] This conserving action is attributed to Christ by Paul in the very text that speaks most powerfully about creation: "He is before all things, and in him all things hold together" (Col 1:17). And also: "He reflects the glory of God and bears the very stamp of his nature, upholding the universe by his word of power" (Heb 1:3). The Church Fathers commonly allocate divine conservation to the seventh day of creation (the day of rest).[6]

Thomas Aquinas explains that the dependence of the universe on God is not only *in fieri*, "in becoming," in the very act of creation, but also *in esse*, in the existence of things.[7] "For the being of every creature depends

5. Respectively Aratus of Soli, *Phenomena* 5; Cleanthes, *Hymn to Zeus*. Both are of the third century B.C.

6. See Clement of Alexandria, *Stromata* VI, 16. He speaks of a double mode of creation.

7. See Thomas Aquinas, *ST* I, q. 104.

on God, so that not for a moment could it subsist, but would fall into nothingness, were it not kept in being by the operation of the divine power."[8] A being created *ex nihilo* can never become autonomously self-subsistent because God alone gives being to it, and no created being is in a position to acquire or maintain its existence autonomously.[9] Metaphysical necessity and autonomy simply do not belong to the created being. Thus conservation of all things is not a *new divine action* distinct from creation—something like the ongoing maintenance of a new building—but rather the *continuation* of the divine act by which things were created in the first place. It is possible to distinguish conceptually between creation and conservation, but in real terms they are totally bound up with one another. What has been created *ex nihilo* in fact cannot ever become self-perpetuating. Divine creation and conservation may be considered therefore a single divine act, outside time, without movement.[10] Sometimes the term *creatio continua,*[11] a continuous creation, is used, but in real terms it is not different from the original creative action.

This means of course that a kind of original nothingness is to be found at the heart of being. In the words of John Zizioulas, "if God had given creation the power to ensure its own survival, though it began in nothing, the world would be able to become eternal by nature. This would mean that God would have created another, eternal, god."[12] Later on he continues: "Since what is created has come out of nothing, nothingness will always be lurking behind it. If the created world could just as easily not exist, what prevents it from disappearing right now? It is only the good will of God that keeps it in existence.... Only an unbroken relationship of God sustains the world and prevents it from reverting back into nothing."[13] In effect, the created world always retains a real relationship with the creator.[14]

8. Ibid., a. 1, co.

9. See ibid.

10. Aquinas says: "conservatio rerum a Deo non est per aliquam novam actionem, sed per continuationem actionis qua dat esse, quae quidem actio est sine motu et tempore" (ibid., ad 3).

11. See Schönborn, "Catechesi," 42, although the literal term is not present in Aquinas. For a presentation and critique of the notion of *creatio continua,* see Sanz Sánchez, *Alfa e omega,* 104–6.

12. Zizioulas, "Creation and Salvation," 89.

13. Ibid., 92.

14. On the relationship between God and the world in Thomas Aquinas, see A. Krempel, *La doctrine de la Relation chez Saint Thomas: exposé historique et systématique* (Paris: J. Vrin, 1952); M. M. Rossi, *"Creatio in Creatura non est nisi relatio quaedam": Riflessioni su Summa Theologiae I, Q. 45, a. 3,"* in

The consequence of this position is clear, and even disconcerting: the possible annihilation of the world, hypothetically, would not involve a positive divine destructive action, but simply the ceasing of divine conserving action.[15] "The universe would pass away in the twinkling of an eye if God withdraws his ruling hand," says Augustine.[16] God of course is faithful to his plans and promises and this means the created world will continue existing. But at a metaphysical level such an annihilation would not be a contradiction, for the created world is completely contingent, as we saw at the end of chapter 1.

Concursus

God's action is not limited to maintaining things in being. Because the being of things is the very root of all they are and do, divine conservation involves the being *and* the action of creatures.[17] The divine action by which God moves each and every thing to act according to its nature is usually called *concursus divinum*, divine concourse, or "running together," and is inseparable from both creation and conservation.[18] The actions and movements of things belong intrinsically to their being; thus God acts so that each and every being acts according to the nature he has given it. The same metaphysical principle, what Thomas calls the *actus essendi*, the act of being, governs both being and action.[19] In an essentialist metaphysics, only the essence or nature would be attributable to the creator, and as such creaturely action would relate to God only indirectly. This may be found for example in the philosophy of Christian Wolff.[20]

Studi 1996, ed. D. Lorenz (Rome: Istituto san Tommaso, Pontificia Università S. Tommaso d'Aquino, 1997), 153–81; Sanz Sánchez, *Alfa e omega*, 64.

15. See *ST* I, q. 103, aa. 3–4.

16. Augustine, *De Gen. ad litt.* 4, 12:22.

17. A. Piolanti, *Dio nel mondo e nell'uomo* (Rome: Desclée, 1959), 114–33.

18. See P. Dumont, *Liberté humaine et concours divin d'après Suárez* (Paris: G. Beauchesne, 1936); C. Cardona, "El acto de ser y la acción creatural," *Scripta Theologica* 10 (1978): 1081–96; Aertsen, *Nature and Creature*, 315–19; D. J. Fitzgerald, "Without Me You Can Do Nothing: The Man and His Metaphysics," in *Jacques Maritain*, ed. J. F. X. Knasas (Notre Dame, Ind.: University of Notre Dame Press, 1988), 227–34; T. F. Tracy, "God and Creatures Acting: The Idea of Double Agency," in *Creation and the God of Abraham* (ed. Burrell et al.), 221–37.

19. See Thomas Aquinas, *De Pot.*, q. 3, a. 7.

20. See É. Gilson, *Being and Some Philosophers*, 2nd ed. (Toronto: Pontifical Institute of Mediaeval Studies, 1952), 112–21.

If that is the way things stand, if God moves all things to act according to their nature, it is not easy to explain the role and reality of things in themselves, in their independence and autonomy. God would seem to be the only actor, and thus the only one to take responsibility for what happens in the universe. Classical philosophy distinguishes, in the order of efficient causality, between the first cause (God alone) and second cause (that of the creature).[21] The fact that creaturely actions depend on two causes does not mean that each created action is the sum total of the two, as if each one contributed a certain percentage to the final product. That would be a case of different *created* agents collaborating in the same action, for example when a virus produces a cold when accompanied by bad weather, or a carriage is drawn along by two horses. First and second causes relate in a different way to one and the same action: both God and the creature are fully responsible for the action in question, but each one in its own order.

"The same effect is produced by God and by the inferior agent," says Thomas Aquinas, "by both in an immediate way, but diversely in each case."[22] God acts divinely, as creator, doing what no creature can ever do, and the creature acts in a creaturely way, as God gave it power. Thus creatures are truly the "second cause" of their actions, while God is the "first cause" of the same actions. Johann Quenstedt, a seventeenth-century Lutheran scholastic, wrote:

> God not only gives and preserves to second causes the power to act, but immediately influences the action and effect of the creature, so that the same effect is produced not by God alone, nor by the creature alone, nor partly by God and partly by the creature, but *at the same time by God and the creature,* as one and the same total efficiency, viz., by God as the universal and first cause, and by the creature as the particular and second cause.[23]

Some modern philosophers, such as Nicolas Malebranche, eliminate this double causality in the action of creatures and insist that God is the unique cause of all created actions, in that he does literally everything. This

21. See Thomas Aquinas, *ST* I, q. 105, a. 5, and *De Pot.*, q. 3, a. 7.

22. Thomas Aquinas, *SCG* III.70.

23. J. A. Quenstedt, *Theologia didactico-polemica* (Wittenberg, 1685), 1:531, cited by McFarland, *From Nothing*, 145.

position is usually called occasionalism, because creatures are taken to be the occasion on account of which God acts. For example, we commonly say that the sun heats and illuminates the earth. But in real terms, Malebranche says, only God does so. The sun is but the occasion for God's action. The sun's causality is but apparent. He says that "the efficacy of secondary causes is a fiction of the mind, that Aristotle's . . . *nature* is a chimera, that only God is strong and powerful enough not only to act in our soul but also to give the least motion to matter."[24] But this explanation takes away from the consistency and solidity of the created order, from the realism of created action and causality. In real terms divine omnipotence may be perceived precisely in the fact that God made creatures partake in his own causality.[25] The distinction between first and second causality thus confirms both the transcendence of God and the realism of the created order.[26]

Well before Malebranche, the twelfth-century medieval Jewish philosopher Moses Maimonides observed in respect of *kalam* philosophers (Muslim scholastics):

> They assert that when a man moves a pen, it is not the man who moves it; for the motion occurring in the pen is an accident created by God in the pen. Similarly the motion of the hand, which we think of as moving the pen, is an accident created by God in the moving hand. Only, God has instituted the habit that the motion of the hand is concomitant with the motion of the pen, without the hand exercising in any respect an influence on, or being causative in regard to, the motion of the pen.[27]

"Second" causality is sometimes confused with "instrumental" causality which also belongs to the order of efficient causality. But it should not be so. The instrumental cause with respect to the efficient cause is subordinate, and *facilitates* the work of the efficient cause, also when this is not divine but fully belonging to the creature (second causality). By way of example, the priest who administers baptism is the instrumental cause

24. N. Malebranche, *The Search after Truth: With Elucidations of The Search after Truth* (Cambridge: Cambridge University Press, 1997), 681.

25. See McFarland, *From Nothing*, 137–42.

26. McFarland says that "Deism fails to honor divine transcendence" (ibid., 139) because it assimilates divine and creaturely activity.

27. Maimonides, *Guide for the Perplexed* 1:71.73.

under God of the communication of divine grace, but is the second cause of the washing of the catechumen.

Providence

Providence is a central Christian doctrine with important theoretical and practical consequences.[28] According to the *Catechism of the Catholic Church,*

> we call "divine providence" the dispositions by which God guides his creation toward … perfection. By his providence God protects and governs all things which he has made, "reaching mightily from one end of the earth to the other, and ordering all things well" [Wis 8:1]. For "all are open and laid bare to his eyes" [Heb 4:13], even those things which are yet to come into existence through the free action of the creature.[29]

In the Lutheran *Heidelberg Catechism* we read that "God upholds, as it were by his own hand, heaven and earth together with all creatures, and rules in such a way that leaves and grass, rain and drought, fruitful and unfruitful years, food and drink, health and sickness, riches and poverty, and everything else, come to us not by chance but by his fatherly hand."[30] Likewise, the Anglican *Westminster Confession* says: "God, the great Creator of all things, upholds, directs, disposes, and governs all creatures, actions, and things, from the greatest even to the least, by his most wise and holy providence, according to his infallible foreknowledge, and the free and immutable counsel of his own will, to the praise of the glory of his wisdom, power, justice, goodness, and mercy."[31]

In this section, I shall first consider different aspects of the mystery of divine providence in scripture and church teaching, then in its relationship to Christ, to human freedom, and to Christian spirituality. In the coming sections within this chapter I shall look at two further issues as-

28. See G. de la Morena Barrio, *Providencia e historia: la acción de Dios en el mundo en las publicaciones actuales sobre la Providencia divina* (Rome: Edusc, 2019).

29. CCC, no. 302, citing Vatican Council I (DH 3003). On the notion of divine providence in scripture, see B. G. Boschi, "La Provvidenza nella Bibbia: alle origini del pensiero cristiano," *Sacra Doctrina* 68 (1972): 501–43; Galot, *Découvrir le Père,* 132–57.

30. *Heidelberg Catechism,* q. 27.

31. *Westminster Confession,* chap. 5.

sociated with providence: first, the place of modern science in the context of possible divine intervention in the created world, and the consequent consolidation of Deism; and second, the dynamics of temporality within providence.

SITUATING THE DOCTRINE OF PROVIDENCE

The notion of providence arises, Aquinas says, from a double conviction: the unity of the divine creating and conserving action, on the one hand, and the centrality in the Christian understanding of the ultimate end with the eschatological fulfillment of the universe, on the other. Thomas develops the notion however in a way that differs considerably from a deterministic understanding of creation, typical of the Stoics and Averroes, who sees the universe as brought along under the thrust of blind destiny.[32] This makes Aquinas's position relevant in the face of modern determinism as well.[33] In fact the reality of human freedom is essential to his explanation of providence. But neither may providence be considered as something accidental or external to creation, or the exclusive fruit of human action, for there is an indissoluble bond between providence on the one hand and the creative and conserving action of God on the other. "Providence is not extrinsic to things, but is merged intrinsically with them through the living immanence of God in things. God's plan is not imposed on creatures, but it constitutes them and founds them metaphysically."[34]

Aquinas made it possible to speak of providence and freedom by introducing the idea of second causality,[35] which we just examined. He says that

> God is at work in all creaturely activity, but not on his own without intermediaries, as if creatures were powerless to do anything by themselves: as if fire did not make things hot, but only God acting in the fire. That would deprive creation of all causal order and derogate the creator's power; for part of any agent's power is its ability to pass on power to act to its effects ... God acts in things in such a way that the things act themselves.[36]

32. See Thomas Aquinas, *I Sent.*, d. 39, q. 2; *De Ver.*, q. 5; *SCG* III.71–97; *ST* I, q. 22; *Comp. Theol.* 123–47. See J. M. Arroyo, *El tratado de la Providencia Divina en la obra de Santo Tomás De Aquino.*

33. See O'Callaghan, *Children of God in the World*, 452–54.

34. Piolanti, *Dio nel mondo e nell'uomo*, 100n3.

35. See M. J. Langford, *Providence* (London: SCM Press, 1981), 47–50.

36. Thomas Aquinas, *ST* I, q. 105, a. 3.

In this way Aquinas affirms the intrinsic value of the created world, its autonomy, its otherness, what we might call its authentic secularity.

The Calvinist theologian Karl Barth deals with the doctrine of providence at length,[37] rooting it in Christology and qualifying it eschatologically. However, the American Protestant theologian Langdon Gilkey and others[38] consider his explanation to be inadequate, because of "its reinforcement of a traditional tendency to regard the rest of creation as only a 'theatre' for the human drama, with no further meaning or purpose,"[39] a position likewise held by Calvin. What is particularly noticeable in Barth's doctrine of providence, Gilkey observes, "is the absence of any treatment of evil."[40] Evil, what Barth calls *das Nichtige,* or nothingness, is dealt with elsewhere in the latter's works, but not when he speaks of providence. However, this empties the notion of providence, "like some economic analysis in which self-interest has casually been omitted," in such a way that "nothing can be done by the creature except the will of God."[41]

Three elements go to make up Christian understanding of divine providence. First, the fact that God brings creatures to fulfillment and self-realization by means of the Word incarnate, Jesus Christ. As we saw earlier on, the presence of the Word within creation—made through him and for him—is so profound and thoroughgoing that an interventionist or extrinsic view of providence is unthinkable. Second, this does not mean that providence involves a kind of totalitarian determinism in the Stoic sense of the word. Christians are convinced that under God they are truly free, that the world can be changed and improved, that they have control over the future, at least to some extent. According to Origen, Celsus and Epicurus identified providence on the basis of "the unchangeable necessity of physical laws which regulate the phenomena of the cosmos. This necessity is called *physis* by Epicurus and in that way he divinizes nature."[42]

37. See Barth, *Church Dogmatics III/3,* and K. Tanner, "Creation and providence," in *The Cambridge Companion to Karl Barth,* ed. J. Webster (Cambridge: Cambridge University Press, 2000), 111–26.

38. See L. Gilkey, "The Concept of Providence in Contemporary Theology," *Journal of Religion* 43 (1963): 171–92; Wood, *The Question of Providence.*

39. Ibid., 231.

40. Gilkey, "The Concept of Providence," 189.

41. Ibid., 190.

42. Origen, *Contra Celsus* 136.

But the latter position is unacceptable for Christians. And third, providence from the standpoint of Christian faith relates not only to the created world as a whole, but to each and every being, especially to each and every human person, and therefore to Christian spirituality. Pagan doctrines for the most part hold that any justification of human dignity insisting on the greatness of the individual, or the transcendence or immortality of the latter's actions, is out of place, the fruit of vanity or narcissism.[43] But this is not the case with Christianity.

Before considering these three issues (Christology, freedom, spirituality), let us consider what scripture and official church teaching have to say on providence.

PROVIDENCE IN SCRIPTURE AND CHURCH TEACHING

The term "providence" (*pronoia* in Greek) is not frequent in scripture. It is found for the first time in Wisdom 14:3 and 17:2.[44] It is not used at all in New Testament. Nonetheless, the doctrine of providence may be found throughout the whole of scripture. It is expressed in different descriptions of what awaits us in the future, of what is foreseen, of what provides care for those in need (Rom 12:17; 2 Cor 8:21; 1 Tm 5:8). In the Book of Job we can observe the dilemma of the just man who asks what part his own life occupies in God's overall plan. "Oh, that I knew where I might find him, that I might come even to his seat! I would lay my case before him and fill my mouth with arguments" (Jb 23:3).

Besides, the Old Testament shows how God takes care of each and every one, with the affection of a mother and a father: "Out of the depths I cry to you, O Lord! Lord, hear my voice! Let your ears be attentive to the voice of my supplications!" (Ps 130:1). And elsewhere:

> Lord, you have been our dwelling place in all generations. Before the mountains were brought forth, or ever you formed the earth and the world, from everlasting to everlasting you are God.... For all our days pass away under your wrath, our years come to an end like a sigh.... Satisfy us in the morning with your steadfast love, that we may rejoice and be glad all our days. Make us glad as

43. See C. Schönborn, "L'homme créé par Dieu: le fondement de la dignité de l'homme," *Gregorianum* 65 (1984): 337–63.

44. See *NIDNTTE* 4:141–43, s.v. προνοέω.

many days as you have afflicted us, and as many years as we have seen evil (Ps 90:1–2, 9, 14–15).

God "with a gentle and strong hand" (Wis 8:1, *suaviter et fortiter* in its most well-known Latin translation) guides all things with firmness and sweetness, directing all events and beings toward their end. Yahweh is a provident and positive God, the God of the living, the God of persons, "the God of Abraham, of Isaac, of Jacob" (Mt 22:32). John Paul II says that God, "as a wise and omnipotent Father, is present and active in the world and in the history of every creature. He does this so that every creature, and specifically man, God's image, may be able to live life as a journey under the guidance of truth and love toward the goal of eternal life in God."[45]

The doctrine of providence in amply explained and justified in the New Testament, in the words of Jesus, particularly in the Gospels of Matthew and Luke, which contain three well-known passages:

Therefore do not be anxious, saying, "What shall we eat?" or "What shall we drink?" or "What shall we wear?" For the Gentiles seek all these things; and your heavenly Father knows that you need them all. But seek first his kingdom and his righteousness, and all these things shall be yours as well. Therefore do not be anxious about tomorrow, for tomorrow will be anxious for itself. Let the day's own trouble be sufficient for the day (Mt 6:31–34; see Lk 12:29–31).

And later on in the same Gospel:

Are not two sparrows sold for a penny? And not one of them will fall to the ground without your Father's will. But even the hairs of your head are all numbered. Fear not, therefore; you are of more value than many sparrows (Mt 10:29–31).

Again in Matthew, Jesus speaks of God's paternal care for all creatures:

Look at the birds of the air: they neither sow nor reap nor gather into barns, and yet your heavenly Father feeds them. Are you not of more value than they? And which of you by being anxious can add one cubit to his span of life? And why are you anxious about clothing? Consider the lilies of the field, how they grow; they neither toil nor spin; yet I tell you, even Solomon in all his glory was not arrayed

45. John Paul II, "Faith in Divine Providence Strengthens Our Reasons for Hope," General Audience, April 30, 1986, par. 1. The entire catechesis of John Paul II on providence occupies nine audiences from April 30 to June 25, 1986.

like one of these. But if God so clothes the grass of the field, which today is alive and tomorrow is thrown into the oven, will he not much more clothe you, o men of little faith (Mt 6:26–30; see Lk 12:24–28).

In these texts, John Paul II says, we can see how God looks after each and every creature: "the Lord Jesus not only confirmed the teaching on divine Providence contained in the Old Testament. He entered more deeply into the subject as regards humanity, every single person, treated by God with the exquisite delicacy of a father."[46] Athanasius said as much in a text already cited:

> The holy Word of the Father, almighty and all-perfect, uniting with the universe and having everywhere unfolded His own powers, and having illumined all, both things seen and things invisible, holds them together and binds them to Himself, having left nothing void of His own power, but on the contrary quickening and sustaining all things everywhere, each severally and all collectively.[47]

Romano Guardini puts this in an existential key: "God created me; he created me in the world, the world in which I live."[48] He speaks of an ordinary providence, the "providence which takes place continuously. In such a situation the whole becomes the manifestation here, now, as such, of the will of God for me, which subordinates everything to my salvation."[49]

In Vatican II's *Gaudium et Spes* we read: "God has fatherly concern for everyone.... For man would not exist were he not created by God's love and constantly preserved by it; and he cannot live fully according to truth unless he freely acknowledges that love and devotes himself to His Creator."[50] Another passage from *Gaudium et Spes,* often repeated by John Paul II, goes to the heart of the Christian doctrine of providence: "man ... is the only creature on earth which God willed for itself."[51] In other words God's love is directed not only toward the whole, but also to the part, to the individual, to the person. God is not concerned only with the "big picture," but also with the concrete person and their life, down to the last detail.

46. John Paul II, "Divine Providence Carries Out an Eternal Plan of Wisdom and Love," General Audience, May 14, 1986, par. 8.

47. Athanasius, *Contra Gentes* 42.

48. R. Guardini, *Die Existenz des Christen,* 2nd ed. (Munich: Schöningh, 1977), 88.

49. R. Guardini, *Das Gute, das Gewissen und die Sammlung* (Mainz: Matthias-Grünewald, 1931), 53.

50. *GS,* nos. 19 and 24.

51. *GS,* no. 24.

And in the declaration *Dignitatis Humanae*, we read that divine care for creatures is rooted in

> the divine law—eternal, objective and universal—whereby God orders, directs and governs the entire universe and all the ways of the human community by a plan conceived in wisdom and love. Man has been made by God to participate in this law, with the result that, under the gentle disposition of divine Providence, he can come to perceive ever more fully the truth that is unchanging.[52]

PROVIDENCE AND CHRISTOLOGY

But the heart of Christian doctrine on providence is not only to be found in the way Jesus' teaching reinforces and details that of the Old Testament. For Christ himself is the incarnation, manifestation, agent, presence, and concreteness of divine providence.[53] As the only Son, he exercises the Father's providence directly. In a text already cited, Athanasius speaks of "the Father of Christ, most holy and above all created existence, who like an excellent pilot, by his own Wisdom and his own Word, our Lord and Savior Christ, steers and preserves and orders all things."[54] This Christ-personalization of providence may be seen in three aspects of Jesus' words and ministry.

First, Christ as *shepherd*. In the Old Testament God is the shepherd of his people, the sheep of his flock. "The Lord is my shepherd; there is nothing I shall want" (Ps 23:1). But Jesus appropriates this title personally (Jn 10:1–21): "I am the good shepherd," Jesus says. "The good shepherd lays down his life for the sheep ... I know my own and my own know me, as the Father knows me and I know the Father; and I lay down my life for the sheep" (Jn 10:11, 14). Besides, this pastoral providence is directed to one and all, and intends to exclude no one: "What man of you, having a hundred sheep, if he has lost one of them, does not leave the ninety-nine in the wilderness, and go after the one which is lost, until he finds it?" (Lk 15:4).

Second, the Gospels speak extensively of the *solidarity* of Christ with human misery and misfortune. He personally attempts to resolve the

52. Vatican Council II, *Dignitatis Humanae*, no. 3.

53. Note has been made of Barth's neglect of "the contingent details of Jesus' historical life' in his earlier works." M. Higton, *Christ, Providence, and History: Hans W. Frei's Public Theology* (London: T and T Clark, 2004), 58. This was rectified somewhat in *Church Dogmatics IV*.

54. Athanasius, *Contra Gentes* 40.

problems and difficulties experienced by his disciples: suffering, pain, dismay, hunger, illness, diabolic possession. Among many other texts we may refer to this touching one: "O Jerusalem, Jerusalem, killing the prophets and stoning those who are sent to you! How often would I have gathered your children together as a hen gathers her brood under her wings, and you would not!" (Mt 23:27). The parable of the good Samaritan presents this particularly well (Lk 10:30–37). This fundamental attitude of Jesus throughout his ministry reaches its highpoint at his death on the cross in which he strove to alleviate the suffering of his disciples, although he himself would suffer to the full. To his captors he said: "if you seek me let these men [his disciples] go" (Jn 18:8). He wished to carry the load and alleviate his followers.

Third, Jesus himself takes charge of the *needs of his disciples*. Jesus encouraged his followers not to worry about what they would eat, or drink, or how they would rest, or dress, etc. In person he multiplied the loaves and fish (Mt 14:15–21), with his own power he converted the water into wine (Jn 2:1–12). In other words, the providential care Jesus promised on the part of the Father, he carried out himself in person, as the Son: "My Father is working still, and I am working" (Jn 5:17). After the death of John the Baptist, Jesus "withdrew from there in a boat to a lonely place apart. But when the crowds heard it, they followed him on foot from the towns. As he went ashore he saw a great throng; and he had compassion on them, and healed their sick" (Mt 14:13).

This direct connection between Christ's saving work and divine providence points at a deeper level to the action of the Word who exercises the Father's providence over every creature, and even more to what scripture calls the "predestination of Christ."[55] "Blessed be the God and Father of our Lord Jesus Christ . . . as he chose us in him before the foundation of the world, that we should be holy and blameless before him. He *predestined* us in love to be his sons through Jesus Christ, according to the purpose of his will" (Eph 1:3–5). This eternal predestination should not be confused either with blind destiny (as Stoics and other philosophers held) nor with an arbitrary decree of condemnation or salvation. Rather the predestination of Christ refers to "God's eternal choice, a paternal, intelligent

55. See O'Callaghan, *Children of God in the World*, 129–31 and 219–24.

and positive choice, a choice prompted by love."[56] This divine choice, John Paul II says,

> belongs to the intimate life of the most Holy Trinity. . . . It is a choice which . . . precedes the creation of the world . . . and of humanity in the world. Even before being created, man is "chosen" by God. This choice takes place in the eternal Son . . . that is, in the Word of the eternal Mind. Man is chosen in the Son to participate in the same sonship by divine adoption.[57]

However, two issues deeply challenge the Christian doctrine of providence: the role of human freedom in the light of God's providential action and the living out of Christian life or spirituality within providence.

DIVINE PROVIDENCE AND HUMAN FREEDOM

We have just seen that God guides each and every creature to its proper end. Yet we have also seen that creatures have their own consistency and proper operations. This is especially so when we speak of humans who are free and self-determined. How can these two elements be brought together? Is it meaningful to speak of divine providence and human freedom at one and the same time?[58] As Christians we hold to the Pauline axiom: "in everything God works for the good with those who love him, who are called according to his purpose" (Rom 8:27). We believe that God's saving and empowering action is present in the very midst of problems and pain and failure. And, "although God brings victory out of this concatenation of crises, it is evidently by working *against* the ways of the world rather than *through* them."[59] Thus providence "is neither a basis for optimism nor a denial of the tragic."[60] It does not provide a simplistic or saccharine explanation of *why* or *how* things happen. Thus it cannot be instrumentalized for historiographical or ideological purposes. Averil Cameron suggests that in earlier moments of history "the idea of Christian providence constituted a totalizing explanation, a kind of theory of everything."[61]

56. John Paul II, "The Mystery of Predestination in Christ," General Audience, May 28, 1986, par. 2.

57. Ibid., par. 3.

58. On the dynamics of human freedom, see O'Callaghan, *Children of God in the World*, 442–71.

59. McFarland, *From Nothing*, 154.

60. Ibid., 157.

61. A. Cameron, "Divine Providence in Late Antiquity," *Predicting the Future*, ed. L. Howe and A. Wain (Cambridge: Cambridge University Press, 1993), 118–43, at 121.

But experience shows it cannot be so, at least in the detail. H. Richard Niebuhr observed wryly that God "ministers indeed to all our good, but all our good is other than we thought."[62] Perhaps we may say that providence provides a hope-based conviction that God will bring things to their proper end in his own good time, to a "fullness of blessing for creatures beyond what is visible in the present."[63] Faith brings us to hold *that* God is provident, not *how* or *why* he is. In an eschatological context scripture in fact depicts God's providential work "as the radical reversal or overturning of worldly processes"[64] that cannot be compared to or predicted from the present situation or neatly fitted into our everyday experiences.

For the Stoics, the all-embracing quality of divine providence is looked upon as a motive for detachment and a quest for invulnerability. For Christians this is not the case, as the power of God, the energy of love (Gal 5:6), "poured into our hearts through the Holy Spirit" (Rom 5:5), enters deeply into the human heart, transforms and purifies it, moves it to act, but on no account eliminates human freedom, responsibility, or the consistency of the created world.[65] In better times, this spiritual conviction may well give rise to optimism and belief in progress. But throughout the twentieth century, with its particular emphasis on freedom, Gilkey observes that the notion of providence lost its central place in Christian life, becoming a kind of "rootless, disembodied ghost, flitting from footnote to footnote, but rarely finding secure lodgment in sustained theological discourse."[66] "The doctrine of the providence of God stands today as a particularly difficult, perhaps even impossible part of Christian dogmatics,"[67] clearly in

62. H. R. Niebuhr, *The Meaning of Revelation* (New York: Macmillan, 1941), 191.

63. McFarland, *From Nothing*, 158.

64. Ibid.

65. "Where for Stoicism the goal to be reached by *apatheia* is the realization of our true nature, a nature that is (in the words of Boethius) 'self-sufficient, strong, worthy of respect, glorious and joyful,' the Christian vision is not one of detachment and invulnerability, but rather one of being 'filled with the energy of love' (to use John Wesley's rendition of Gal. 5:6), to have 'God's love . . . poured into our hearts through the Holy Spirit' (Rm. 5:5), and thus to be subject to a transformation that probably awaits an application of the concept of *perichoresis* for anything like an adequate theological formulation." C. M. Wood, "Providence," in *The Oxford Handbook of Systematic Theology* (ed. Webster et al.), 91–104, at 92. On the Christian dynamics of freedom as a response to the divine gift, see O'Callaghan, *Children of God in the World*, 442–71.

66. Gilkey, "The Concept of Providence," 171.

67. H. Krötke, "Review of Reinhold Bernhardt, Was heisst 'Handeln Gottes'?," *Theologische Literaturzeitung* 125 (2000): 1190–93, at 1190.

need of renewal and revitalization.[68] George Lindbeck suggests: "Whether it will be possible to regain a specifically biblical understanding of providence depends in part on the possibility of theologically reading Scripture once again in literary rather than nonliterary ways."[69] And the philosopher Hans Frei has insisted on different occasions that the concreteness of divine providence may be found in the life and action of Jesus Christ among us. "The providential action of God over and in creation is not that of a mechanical fate to be read off of one occasion. God's work is mysteriously, abidingly mysteriously, coexistent with the contingency of events. The history of his providence is one that must be narrated."[70]

Reinhold Bernhardt in a major 1997 work on providence proposes three important moves with a view to properly situating and renewing the Christian doctrine of providence.[71] The first is to relocate it within the context of trinitarian reflection, in order to align it more closely not only with Christology but especially with pneumatology. The second, a sort of corollary to the first, is to eliminate the traditional separation between God's providential activity and his salvific activity, so that their deeper coinherence might be realized; perhaps the term *coinherence* suggests the trinitarian term *perichoresis*: providence, as we saw above, should be Christological. And the third move is to reconceive the notion of divine power in more radically Christian terms as the "power of weakness" (1 Cor 1:25), and to purge the doctrine of providence of understandings of power which do not befit its character as a Christian doctrine.

Speaking of providence, some scholars have discussed an "open theism," sometimes called "relational theism."[72] According to its propo-

68. See, e.g., E. Henderson and B. Hebblethwaite (eds.), *Divine Action: Studies Inspired by the Philosophical Theology of Austin Farrer* (Edinburgh: T and T Clark, 1990); T. F. Tracy, *The God Who Acts: Philosophical and Theological Explorations* (University Park: Pennsylvania State University Press, 1994). Of particular importance, see R. Bernhardt, *Was heißt "Handeln Gottes"? Eine Rekonstruktion der Lehre von der Vorsehung* (Gütersloh: Chr. Kaiser, 1997). See also T. P. Flint, "Divine Providence," in *The Oxford Handbook of Philosophical Theology*, ed. T. P. Flint and M. C. Rea (Oxford: Oxford University Press, 2009), 262–85.

69. G. A. Lindbeck, *The Nature of Doctrine: Religion and Theology in a Postliberal Age* (Louisville, Ky.: Westminster John Knox Press, 1984), 119.

70. H. W. Frei, *The Identity of Jesus Christ: The Hermeneutical Bases of Dogmatic Theology* (Philadelphia: Fortress Press, 1975), 163.

71. See Bernhardt, *Was heißt "Handeln Gottes"?*, and Wood, *The Question of Providence*, 209.

72. See Wood, *The Question of Providence*, 229.

nents,[73] "God does not control all events, but rather responds freely to the free actions of creatures—actions which may or may not be in accord with God's will."[74] The position may be seen in the work of John Sanders[75] and in Terrance Tiessen's book on the power of prayer.[76] Likewise Stone and Oord, in the wider context of process theology, contest what they call the classical "logic of sovereignty,"[77] by which God micromanages all events. It would seem of course that their position reflects a defective view of God's action, as if providence were to involve a "collaborative" relationship between God and creatures. Rather it reflects the realism of human freedom and the exquisitely paternal way in which God acts.

John Paul II in his catechesis offers the following reflection:

> Divine Providence is a sovereign affirmation of the whole of creation and, in particular, of man's pre-eminence among creatures. Providence constitutes the fundamental guarantee of the sovereignty of man himself in regard to the world. This does not imply the cancellation of the immanent determination of the laws of nature. But it excludes that materialistic determinism which reduces the whole of human existence to the "domain of necessity," practically annihilating the "domain of freedom" which the Creator on the contrary destined for man. God by his Providence never ceases to be the ultimate support of the "domain of freedom."[78]

The key to understanding human freedom in the context of providence is to be found, perhaps, in the paternity of God and the filial character of human life.[79]

73. See C. H. Pinnock, R. Rice, J. Sanders, W. Hasker, and D. Basinger, *The Openness of God: A Biblical Challenge to the Traditional Understanding of God* (Downers Grove, Ill.: InterVarsity Press, 1994).

74. Wood, *The Question of Providence,* 229.

75. See J. Sanders, *The God Who Risks: A Theology of Divine Providence,* 2nd ed. (Downers Grove, Ill.: IVP Academic, 2007).

76. See T. L. Tiessen, *Providence and Prayer: How does God Work in the World* (Downers Grove, Ill.: InterVarsity Press, 2000).

77. See B. P. Stone and T. J. Oord (eds.), *Thy Nature and Thy Name is Love: Wesleyan and Process Theologies in Dialogue* (Nashville, Tenn.: Kingswood, 2001).

78. John Paul II, "Divine Providence Continues to Care for Creation," General Audience, May 7, 1986, par. 7.

79. See O'Callaghan, *Children of God in the World,* 247–77.

PROVIDENCE AND CHRISTIAN SPIRITUALITY

Faith in divine providence of course goes to the heart of Christian spirituality. God intervenes in the lives of believers not only through revelation and doctrine, but in a direct, personal, and individual way. God, the almighty Father, is close to each one of his children. In the Book of Wisdom we read: "How would anything have endured had you not willed it? Or how would anything not called forth by you have been preserved? You spare all things, for they are yours, O Lord, who love the living. For your immortal spirit is in all things" (Wis 11:24–12:1). Christ the Son of God is *Emmanuel*, "God with us," and draws us into the life of the Trinity. He came to live "among his own people . . . he became flesh and dwelt among us" (Jn 1:11, 14).

Likewise the church, Christ's own body, in its life and ministry is involved in the dynamics of divine providence. John Paul II says:

> We can well say that the whole story of the Church in time consists in the constant and ardent search to find, to examine and to propose the signs of God's presence. The Church is guided in this by the example of Christ and by the power of the Spirit. For this reason the Church can, the Church wishes, the Church must proclaim and give to the world the grace and the meaning of divine Providence.[80]

But do we know what exactly God is doing and allowing in the lives of humans? What does our Christian "correspondence" to his provident action look like? Of particular importance here[81] is the need to strike the right balance between the now, the present moment, the exigencies of the immediate,[82] and the end, the eschatological future, our ultimate destiny.[83] Some would say we should hold on to the former, limiting ourselves to wholeheartedly accepting the situation we are now in as an unequivocal manifestation of God's will in which we experience and discern the "signs of the times" (Mt 16:3). Others would remind us of the predominance of the latter: that God's will has not yet been manifested fully, and will not

80. John Paul II, "Faith in Divine Providence," par. 3.

81. See McFarland, *From Nothing*, 155n34.

82. See R. Page, *God and the Web of Creation* (London: SCM, 1996), 63.

83. See O. O'Donovan, *Resurrection and Moral Order: An Outline for Evangelical Ethics* (Leicester: InterVarsity, 1986), 35.

be shown until the end of time, in such a way that the present is always provisional; in the meantime, we should do what we can to change and improve things.

The seventeenth-century Anglican divine William Sherlock offers an example of the former: "If we are poor, we must own this to be God's will and appointment that we should be poor; if we be rich, we must consider, that it is God's blessing which makes rich."[84] Speaking of centuries past there is something to be said for what Charles Wood called "the counsel of patient acceptance and endurance that has far outweighed the counsel of taking action to effect change."[85] Perhaps nowadays people would prefer to take more and more responsibility for their lives, not to accept things as they are, to act decisively: it would no longer be acceptable for Christian believers simply to avoid alleviating pain, one's own and that of others, or avoiding natural disasters, traditionally indeed called "acts of God."

At times God seems to treat his people in an arbitrary way. Is this a contradiction? No, because we believe *that* God is provident, and thus not arbitrary; but we do not know *how* he is provident, and so he may well *seem* to be arbitrary. It is undeniable that God allows suffering and evil. "Remember that you made me of clay," says Job to God, "and will you turn me to dust again? Did you not pour me out like milk and curdle me like cheese? You clothed me with skin and flesh, and knit me together with bones and sinews. You granted me life and steadfast love; and your care has preserved my spirit" (Jb 10:9–12). Summing up this teaching we may say with John Paul II that

> Divine Providence implies the recognition that in God's eternal plan, in his creative design, evil originally had no place. But once committed by man and permitted by God, evil is, in the last analysis, subordinated to the good: "Everything works for good" as the Apostle says (cf. Rom 8:28). But this is a problem to which we shall have to return. . . . It is necessary to reread this truth both in the texts where revelation speaks of it directly, and also where Sacred Scripture bears witness to it indirectly.[86]

And he continues:

84. W. Sherlock, A *Practical Discourse concerning Future Judgment* (London: W. Rogers, 1710), 288.
85. Wood, *The Question of Providence*, 222.
86. John Paul II, "Divine Providence Continues to Care for Creation," pars. 3–4.

Man can face up to his own existence in an essentially different way, when he has the certainty that he is not at the mercy of a blind destiny (fate), but depends on someone who is his Creator and Father. Therefore faith in divine Providence is inscribed in the first words of the Apostles' Creed: "I believe in God, the Father Almighty." This faith frees human existence from the different forms of fatalistic thought.[87]

An important point of reference for Christian spirituality, of course, may be found in the lives and experience of the saints. The *Catechism of the Catholic Church* refers to "the constant witness of the saints" to the doctrine of providence.[88] It goes on to mention

Catherine of Siena who said to "those who are scandalized and rebel against what happens to them," that "Everything comes from love, all is ordained for the salvation of man, God does nothing without this goal in mind." Thomas More, shortly before his martyrdom, consoled his daughter: "Nothing can come but that which God wills. And I make me very sure that whatsoever that be, seem it never so bad in sight, it shall indeed be the best." And Julian of Norwich wrote: "Here I was taught by the grace of God that I should steadfastly keep me in the faith ... and that at the same time I should take my stand on and earnestly believe in what our Lord showed in this time—that 'all manner [of] thing shall be well.'"[89]

St. Josemaría observes that "everything may collapse and fail. Events may turn out contrary to what was expected and great adversity may come. But nothing is to be gained by being perturbed. Furthermore, remember the confident prayer of the prophet: 'The Lord is our judge, the Lord gives us our laws, the Lord is our king; it is he who will save us.'"[90] And elsewhere: "We love this time of ours because it is in this time when we are called to achieve our personal sanctification. We will not admit naive longings that lead nowhere – the world has never been any better."[91] And finally he explains that faith in divine providence is fully compatible with the intelligent efforts believers should employ to solve life's problems.

87. Ibid., par. 8.

88. *CCC*, no. 313.

89. Ibid. The references are to Catherine of Siena, *Dialogue* IV, 138; *The Correspondence of Sir Thomas More*, ed. E. F. Rogers (Princeton, N.J.: Princeton University Press, 1947), letter 206, lines 661–63; and Julian of Norwich, "The Revelations of Divine Love," in *The Writings of Julian of Norwich* (University Park: Pennsylvania State University Press, 2006), 221–25.

90. Josemaría Escrivá, *Furrow* (New York: Scepter, 1987), 855, citing Is 33:22.

91. Josemaría Escrivá, *Christ Is Passing By* (Dublin: Four Courts, 1982), 123.

You can be sure that it is through the circumstances of ordinary life, ordained or permitted by the infinite wisdom of divine Providence, that we come close to God. But we shall not attain our goal if we do not strive to finish our work well; if we do not sustain the effort we put in when we began our work with human and supernatural zeal; if we do not carry out our work as well as the best do and, if possible, even better than the best. And I think that if you and I really want to, we will work better than the best, because we will use all the honest human means as well as the supernatural ones which are required in order to offer Our Lord a perfect job of work, finished like filigree and pleasing in every way.[92]

Providence, Science, and Deism

SCIENCE AND CREATION

The *findings* of empirical science, which attempt to describe the essence of reality, readily point back to the nature God gave the world when he created it. But scientists also take an interest in the act of creation itself, wishing to know that from which things and their complex intelligibility are ultimately derived. They attempt to go beyond *what* things are and *how* they work, and ask themselves *why* they are and what they are *for*, even though this leads them to consider issues that need to be treated in a philosophical and theological way.[93] Still, the Christian doctrine of creation is important in situating the task of scientists. The fact that God is metaphysically distinct from the created world is in fact what makes it possible for the latter to study the world without (directly) studying God, to understand the universe without interfering in divine life. Creation establishes a distinction between science and theology. That theology is theology, that is, the study of God, is what makes it possible for science to be science, the study of the created world. For Christians, theology is one thing; empirical science quite another. God is not mixed up with the world; the created world can be studied and understood autonomously, *etsi Deus non daretur*, "as if God did not exist," given that God's being does not coincide with that of the world. Einstein observed incisively that "the world of our sense experiences is comprehensible. The fact that it is comprehensible is a miracle."[94]

92. Josemaría Escrivá, *Friends of God* (New York: Scepter, 1981), 63.

93. See T. S. Kuhn, *The Structure of Scientific Revolutions,* 2nd ed. (Chicago: University of Chicago Press, 1996).

94. A. Einstein, *Out of My Later Years,* 2nd ed. (New York: Philosophical Library, 1950), 61.

Many theologians, philosophers, and scientists from the Middle Ages and the modern period, including Anselm, Albert the Great, Thomas Aquinas, Francis Bacon, and Isaac Newton, were convinced that science does not interfere with theology, and in most cases were completely at home with their Christian faith. But not only that: they were persuaded that good theology is what makes science possible. Trustful in the power of reason, in the accuracy of the senses, in the goodness of matter and in the intelligibility of the universe (all of which are creatures made through God's eternal Word), these thinkers gave life to a scientific movement, continuing right up to our own day, that has provided us with an extraordinary plethora of knowledge and information about the universe that we live in. Several authors refer openly to the fundamental role the doctrine of creation has played in the convictions that made the development of modern science possible.[95] Einstein observed that "science without religion is lame, but religion without science is blind."[96]

With the passage of time, however, this movement, deeply inspired by the transcendence of God and the autonomous realism of the created universe, weakened. Secularized science, divorced from its roots in divine creation and the theology of the *Logos*, attempted to go it alone. The autonomy that divine transcendence guaranteed became a pretense to isolate science. Perhaps Einstein was on to something when he said that "the man of science is a poor philosopher."[97] And it eventually transpired that Christianity from one day to the next seemed to be perceived as the prime antagonist of science.

But science in the strict sense is not in a position to give a satisfactory response to the question of existence. Scientists may deny this, and end up rejecting creation and a possible creator. Yet no matter how much science gets to know about things, about their essence or nature, about how they work and interact, it is simply unable to account for the fact of their existence. The biochemist Jacques Monod for example holds that existence

95. See S. L. Jaki, *The Savior of Science* (Washington, D.C.: Regnery Gateway, 1988); *Science and Creation: From Eternal Cycles to an Oscillating Universe* (Edinburgh: Scottish Academic Press, 1986); *God and the Cosmologists* (Edinburgh: Scottish Academic Press, 1989); J. J. Sanguineti, *Scienza aristotelica e scienza moderna* (Rome: A. Armando, 1992), 90. See also the works of A. N. Whitehead, P. Duhem, and C. Dawson.

96. Einstein, *Out of My Later Years*, 26.

97. Ibid., 59.

is the result of pure chance, that we live off probabilities, and are thrown into an immense universe which takes comfort in human irrelevance and fragility, a world in which a natural covenant has been broken, the "end to the ancient animist covenant between man and nature, leaving nothing in place of that precious bond but an anxious quest in a frozen universe of solitude."[98] Stephen Hawking claims that the so-called no-boundary proposal "predicts the spontaneous creation of an exponentially expanding universe."[99] "Because there is a law like gravity the universe can and will create itself from nothing. . . . Spontaneous creation is the reason there is something rather than nothing, why the universe exists, why we exist."[100]

Philosophers from time immemorial have contested this position that attempts to offer a "scientific" explanation for the existence of the universe, with Aristotle providing the first account. Besides, in the contemporary period "existentialist" philosophers, inspired by Kierkegaard, have reestablished the value of existence as a singular, mysterious, and elusive category that the mind can capture only indirectly. Martin Heidegger is particularly relevant, and speaks of the human being as *Dasein,* which literally means "being there." Being in its gratuitousness, impenetrability, otherness, and elusiveness challenges the human desire to dominate through knowledge and science. Humans may well experience *Angst,* a kind of contentless anguish in the face of existence (this is typified by Sartre and Heidegger among others), or they may experience the joy and amazement at the reality of the universe (Kierkegaard, Marcel), an experience that may well lead them to be convinced of the existence of the creator.

PROVIDENCE AND THE CONSOLIDATION OF DEISM

The historical divorce between Christian faith and science found expression in an important movement typical of the seventeenth and eighteenth centuries—Deism. In brief terms we may say that Deists accept that God created the universe, giving it its nature and rules, but since then has left it to its own devices: creation is accepted, but providence denied. God created the world, but its future is left to humans. This gave rise to an au-

98. Monod, *Chance and Necessity,* 170.

99. S. W. Hawking and R. Penrose, *The Nature of Space and Time* (Princeton, N.J.: Princeton University Press, 1996), 92.

100. Hawking and Mlodinow, *The Grand Design,* 180. I examined their position in chapter 1.

tonomous and anthropomorphic affirmation of the secular that finds deep roots in the late Middle Ages and the modern period.[101] The spiritual heart of Deism however involves a flight from God, from spiritual closeness to the creator; it is rooted in an indisposition to abandon oneself into the hands of a provident Father. God begins to be designated in a "scientific," technical, and impersonal way, as the great architect, the watchmaker God, the *deus ex machina*. Pagans desired divine closeness ardently and this brought them to vehemently seek out the divine with close and relevant gods, who did not actually exist. Christians perhaps got too used to a good thing, they became habituated to the closeness of a unique, all-powerful divinity incarnate called Emmanuel. To some degree, Deism arose because sinful human beings attempted to keep their distance from a loving, fatherly, though demanding God.

The first author to speak of Deism[102] was the sixteenth-century French Calvinist Pierre Viret when speaking of the followers of Faustus Socinus, saying of them that "they recognize God, but do not admit Christ, and they hold that the teachings of the Apostles and gospel writers are pure fable."[103] Among the English Deists, the philosopher Samuel Clarke[104] mentioned different schools of Deism: for some, that God had left everything in the hands of humans when he created the world; for others, that the sphere of divine providential action is limited to the cosmos; and lastly that divine providence is present also in the moral life of humans. Clarke assumed the latter position, in that way seriously conditioning public religious authority that gives expression to positive revelation or the church. Deism aspired to be the true religion: individualist, aesthetic, moralizing, centered on nature, closed in its rationalism, attentive to things in themselves. Grace and redemption are considered secondary.

The seventeenth-century English author Edward Herbert of Cherbury summed up his beliefs as follows: the existence of a supreme divinity with the right to receive our adoration, that is, religion and interior piety; pen-

101. See O'Callaghan, *Children of God in the World*, 50–63. The work of C. Taylor, *A Secular Age* (Cambridge, Mass.: Belknap Press of Harvard University Press, 2007), is of particular importance.

102. J. Forget, "Déisme," in *Dictionnaire de Théologie Catholique* (1920), 4:232–43; Scheffczyk, *Schöpfung und Vorlesung*, 121–35, traces Deism principally to Descartes.

103. See P. Viret, *Instruction chrétienne*, ed. A.-L. Hofer (Lausanne: L'Age d'Homme, 2004).

104. S. Clarke, *A Demonstration of the Being and Attributes of God, A Discourse concerning the Unchangeable Obligations of Natural Religion* (1706) (Stuttgart-Bad Cannstatt: F. Frommann, 1964).

ance as expiation of sin; and hope in reward or punishment after death.[105] No substantial role is played here by the church; no authoritative interpretation of scripture is allowed. In the seventeenth-century Charles Blount denies the existence of miracles; Anthony Ashley-Cooper (the third Lord of Shaftesbury) rejects the mysteries of the incarnation and the Trinity as irrelevant; John Toland in his 1696 work *Christianity not Mysterious* rejects all dogmas and revelation because he considers that God is accessible to us by the power of reason.[106]

The Deism of French and German authors was more ideological and openly anti-Christian than that of English writers. Of particular importance were the works of the French Encyclopedists (Diderot, Rousseau, and especially Voltaire). Rousseau sums up this view in "the three truths of religion," the existence of *God as a supreme being* who with his will moves the world; *matter* regulated by physical laws; and the *human soul* that is immaterial and free. With time French Deism became more radical, mechanistic, atheistic, with a tendency to deny creation and conservation.

In the eighteenth-century German context—Christian Wolff, Moses Mendelssohn, J. S. Semler, H. S. Reimarus, G. E. Lessing, and others—the key idea emerged that in the modern age humans have at last overcome an infantile need for revelation and are in a position to reach true religion by reason alone. The world is commonly considered in a purely rational way, as a huge, complex, programmed machine. According to Wolff God created the world but, once made, leaves it to its own devices.[107] Semler explains that the Jewish and Christian view of the world and of revelation marks a stage of immaturity in humanity; he strives to rationalize religion in order to make it definitively grownup.[108] Reimarus's proposal is even more explicit: historical revelation adds nothing to the eternal revelation made accessible to reason.[109] If God revealed later on it would mean that

105. See Herbert of Cherbury, *De veritate* (1645) (Bristol: University of Bristol, 1966), 9:289–307.

106. See J. Toland, *Christianity Not Mysterious*, ed. G. Gawlick (Stuttgart-Bad Cannstatt: F. Frommann, 1964).

107. See C. Wolff, *Vernünftige Gedanken von Gott, der Welt und der Seele des Menschen* (1733) (Hildesheim: G. Olms, 1965), c. 4, §557, 336.

108. See especially J. S. Semler, *Institutio ad doctrinam Christianam liberaliter discendam* (Halle, 1774).

109. See H. S. Reimarus, *Apologie oder Schutzschrift für die vernünftigen Verehrer Gottes* (Frankfurt a.M.: Insel, 1972), on the historical Jesus, later published by Lessing as *Fragments of an Anonymous Writer*.

his original work was imperfect. Besides, Reimarus excludes the concreteness of revelation from a single people (the Jews) or person (Jesus Christ) or institution (the Christian church) because revelation is destined for all. Lessing holds that the process of revelation constitutes simply a kind of divine pedagogy, for it contains nothing new. Its purpose is to stimulate the process of nature in such a way that we have to "substitute the written gospel with the eternal gospel." And just as there is an eternal revelation, there is also an "eternal providence."[110]

It is interesting to note that for Luther creation and providence more or less coincide; he explains them in a personal, existential, dynamic, and actualistic way: *creare est semper novum facere*, "to create is always to make anew."[111] Deist philosophers however went to the opposite extreme, separating creation from providence and eliminating the latter, thus affirming the value of human freedom, which is involved if not in creation, then certainly in providence.

Vatican Council I responded to these challenges and insisted on the need for revelation, faith, and providence, while strenuously insisting on the role of reason in the process.[112] Vatican Council II teaches of course the need for revelation, but also attempts to explain the true meaning of the *autonomy* of the created order.[113] In the constitution *Gaudium et Spes* we read: "Now many of our contemporaries seem to fear that a closer bond between human activity and religion will work against the independence of men, of societies, or of the sciences."[114]

> If by the autonomy of earthly affairs we mean that created things and societies themselves enjoy their own laws and values which must be gradually deciphered, put to use, and regulated by men, then it is entirely right to demand that autonomy. Such is not merely required by modern man, but harmonizes also with the will of the Creator. For by the very circumstance of their having been created, all things are endowed with their own stability, truth, goodness, proper laws and order.[115]

110. See G. E. Lessing, *Erziehung des Menschengeschlechtes* (Berlin, 1780), § 91.

111. Luther, *Resolutiones Disp. et indulgentiarum doctrina*, in *Dr. Martin Luthers Werke: Schriften*, 73 vols (Weimar: H. Böhlaus Nachfolger, 1883–2000) [hereafter WA], 1:563.

112. See DH 3027–33.

113. On revelation, see Vatican Council II, *Dei Verbum*, nos. 1–5; on the autonomy of the created order, see *GS*, no. 36.

114. *GS*, no. 36.

115. Ibid.

However, "if the expression, the autonomy of temporal affairs, is taken to mean that created things do not depend on God, and that man can use them without any reference to their Creator, anyone who acknowledges God will see how false such a meaning is. For without the Creator the creature would disappear."[116]

Providence and Temporality

This examination of creation, conservation, *concursus*, and providence leads us by the hand as it were to a necessary context and presupposition of creation, which is time, and by extension, temporality, narrative, history, and eschatological consummation. Fergusson states that "what God creates is not so much a 'thing' as a history or a narrative. The loss of this insight was 'the great historical calamity of the doctrine of creation.'"[117] Temporality is essential to the created world in a Christian context. Time qualifies the world substantially.

A CHRISTIAN UNDERSTANDING OF TIME AND TEMPORALITY

Of course God did not create the world within time, as if the latter was a kind of prime matter or vacuous, preexisting recipient. God created the world *ex nihilo*, so it would be more correct to say that time was created *along with* the world. This means that the created world is essentially temporal, although it is destined for eternal fullness. Time and eternity are bound up with one another in the mystery of God's creative act. But neither one nor the other is easy to fathom. Augustine in his deep and fleeting meditation on time[118] observes that while we all know what time is, we still find it exceptionally difficult to describe. The following reflection deals with the Christian understanding of time, based on the central reality of the incarnation of the Word, a vision which is clearly different from that of Greek philosophy.

116. Ibid.

117. Fergusson, "Creation," 78, citing Jenson, *Systematic Theology*, 2:14.

118. See Augustine, *Confessions* XI, 14. Jenson, "Aspects of a Doctrine of Creation," *The Doctrine of Creation* (ed. Gunton), 17–28, esp. 26, speaks of two possibilities in Augustine, time as an extension of the soul, or as a sheer metric of the world.

Greek thought is marked by a strong continuity between terms such as permanence, immortality, necessity, divinity. What does not change is immortal, necessary, real, true, divine, timeless. What does change is apparent or ephemeral. What we call "time" is thus the point of reference from which to observe movement and to measure it. In that sense time itself is considered a constant reality, fixed, necessary, inexorable, almost divine. The Greeks spoke of the divinity *chronos*, "time." Time is eternal, cyclical, and everything moves within it. "Time is the measure of movement according to the before and the after,"[119] said Aristotle. Humans experience time as separation, division, discontinuity between successive moments, situating each thing in its proper place. Time exercises dominion over the world in such a way that past, present, and future do not coincide. Besides, for the Greeks, the eternity of gods or heroes consists above all in the constant and uninterrupted passage of chronological time. Immortality is experienced as infinite duration. Humans have to adjust their lives to this dynamic and cannot change it. "For a Greek to admit the reality of change would mean to deny the rationality of the universe,"[120] said Christopher Dawson. "The Greek man experiences himself and the world primarily as nature, not as history,"[121] in the words of Michael Schmaus. Everything falls under the dominion of time, everything must yield to *chronos*.

It is not difficult to see that this physical and objective view of time, though valid as far as it goes, does not correspond fully to reality. From the *psychological* point of view, humans experience time more diversely than can be observed in the material cosmos: when there is pain, distraction, or incapacity to work, time seems to stretch out endlessly, boringly, giving us the impression that we are "wasting our time." When life is joyful and full, however, then time seems to "fly by," giving a sense of fullness and satisfaction. Besides, we have the capacity of bringing together at an intentional level what time seems to separate: past, present, and future. In the present moment the content of our memory, of our past experiences, meets up with the future that we expect or project. Both past and future pressurize the present, as it were, and they determine—or better, enrich

119. Aristotle, *Physics* IV, 11.

120. C. Dawson, *Progress and Religion* (London: Sheed and Ward, 1938), 154.

121. M. Schmaus, *Katholische Dogmatik, IV/2: Von den letzten Dingen* (Munich: M. Hueber, 1953), §293.

and humanize—the now, bringing us to live and act humanly and freely. We can experience a kind of coming together of past, present, and future, thus conquering the rigidity of time. This is sign of the workings of the spirit in the life of humans.[122]

Scripture offers a wider understanding of the dynamics of time and eternity than does Greek cosmology. The former is described using three Greek terms: *chronos,* duration or time that passes, more or less in the classical sense; *kairos,* or occasion, moment of grace, opportune moment; and *plērōma,* fullness or final completion.[123] On the one hand *chronos* unites and integrates the different *kairoi,* or occasions, giving them continuity and moving them toward the *plērōma,* or fullness; on the other hand it is not the *chronos* that gives meaning to life or history, but rather the *kairoi,* stages or events within the *chronos* on the path to the *plērōma* which provides the fullness of meaning. Without the *kairos,* there is time, but no history, no significant events, there is continuity but no novelty or progress. But without *plērōma* neither would there be any history, because history points toward something real and definitive and complete.

Scripture makes it clear that God changes the course of history and brings it to fullness,[124] seeking the cooperation of humans in this process, which is presided over principally by the divine Word, made flesh through the "yes" of the Virgin Mary. In Christ, time in all its richness falls entirely under the dominion of God. And this for the simple reason that time, like the rest of the created world, is a mere creature. But because time is inseparable from each and every creature, it would be more correct to say that God creates temporal beings, not time. Augustine says that time is created and so is distinct from divine eternity.[125] "Time is reckoned from the creation of the heavens and the earth,"[126] says Maximus the Confessor. "And how could creation take place in time, seeing time was born along with things which exist?," asks Clement of Alexandria.[127] Using the termi-

122. On the temporal and historical character of human life, see O'Callaghan, *Children of God in the World,* 472–94.

123. See *NIDNTTE* 4:701–7, s.v. χρόνος; 2:586–92, s.v. καιρός; 3:784–93, s.v. πλήρωμα.

124. See O'Callaghan, *Christ Our Hope,* 39–73.

125. See Augustine, *De Gen. contra Manich.* 1:2. See É. Gilson, "Creation and Time," in his *The Christian Philosophy of Saint Augustine* (New York: Random House, 1960), 189–96; J. Guitton, *Le temps et l'éternité chez Plotin* (Paris: Aubier, 1955), 175–222.

126. Maximus the Confessor, *De divinis nominibus schol.* V, 8.

127. Clement of Alexandria, *Strom.* VI, 16.

nology of Thomas Aquinas it would be more correct to say that time is a "con-creature," created inseparably with creatures.[128] "When there was no world there was no time,"[129] says Florovsky.

Hence we can say that "before" creation there was no time, but only God, perfect eternity, perfect presence, in which there is no distinction between past, present, and future. This is eternity, the *tota simul et perfecta possessio*[130] that Boethius speaks of: eternity is "the perfect and simultaneous total possession of unending life." Creatures "need" time in order to become what God wants them to be. We might say that time is that aspect of reality without which things would never become what they are meant to be, they would never realize their potentiality. Potentialities need time to develop. So we may look upon time is a kind of *space,* the space of acting, the possibility of self-realization, a mark of divine patience on the created world (2 Pt 3:9; Rom 2:4–6).

Although God is always the Lord of time and history, humans still cooperate under him in the realization of their possibilities. God seeks out human freedom and correspondence. So in an important way humans dominate time, controlling it, in accepting or rejecting divine gifts, acting within the *chronos* yet changing the course of history, sharing in the *kairos* under the ultimate dominion of God. The doctrine of the "communion of saints" (or the "communion of holy things," of supernatural realities) provides an illustration of this phenomenon, for human actions can extend in their efficacy, for good or for bad, over past, present, and future. As far as the life of grace is concerned, believers can perceive a mystical sharing in the divine presence and coincidence of past, present, and future. Such a coinciding is present fully only in God. But humans, divinized and recreated through the gift of the eternal, partake to a certain degree in this eternity.[131]

128. See Thomas Aquinas, *De Pot.,* q. 3, a. 1, ad 12.

129. Florovsky, "Creation and Creaturehood," 43.

130. Boethius, *De consol. phil.* V, pros. 6.

131. On the doctrine of divinization by grace, see O'Callaghan, *Children of God in the World,* 142–56.

ETERNAL GENERATION OF THE WORD AND THE ETERNITY OF CREATION

As we saw in chapter 5, Arius stated that there was a time when the Word was not. In this way he justified the subordination of the Word to the Father as a "second God" or "first creature." But the Council of Nicaea excluded that reading, saying that the Word was generated (not created) by the Father "before all ages."[132] A clear distinction was made between the eternal generation of the Word and the timebound creation of the cosmos. That the generation of the Word took place before all ages was not meant to indicate a chronological precedence of generation, but rather a cosmic and metaphysical precedence. The generation of the Word is above all ages, above all creatures. It is not something that happened once and for all a very long time ago, but is an eternal generation which happened, is happening, and will forever happen in the eternal, living present of God's trinitarian life, for in God and in the trinitarian processions there is no succession and development of the kind that may be found among creatures.

However, scripture seems to indicate that creation took place at a particular temporal moment (Gn 2:4; Jn 1:1). It speaks also of a divine activity "before" (in Greek, *pro,* which may also be translated as "above") the foundation of the world (Prv 8:22; Jn 17:5; Eph 1:4). With the persistent notion of an uncreated prime matter, authors inspired by neo-Platonism, such as Origen, argued that the world had existed always, "from-ever,"[133] as it were, and not only "forever" toward the future. Theologically speaking the idea is justified by saying that just as the Son is generated eternally, so also the world must exist eternally.

The idea was repeated during the Middle Ages, for example by Meister Eckhart who said that "in the very instant God existed, the world came into being.... The very moment God was, when he generated the Word, he also created the world," expressions which the church did not accept.[134]

132. See DH 125.

133. See H. A. Wolfson, "Patristic Arguments against the Eternity of the World," *Harvard Theological Review* 59 (1966): 351–67.

134. See DH 951 and 953. On Eckhart, see Scheffczyk, *Schöpfung und Vorlesung,* 102; J. Koch, "Meister Eckhart," in *Die Kirche in der Zeitenwende,* ed. E. Kleineidam and O. Kuss (Paderborn: Bonifatius, 1935), 277–309, esp. 295–98 on creation; M. H. Laurent, "Autour du procès de Maître Echkart," *Divus Thomas* 39 (1936): 436–44.

Eckhart does say that created beings come from God not of nature but on account of his free love.[135] But the eternal exemplars would seem to provoke in God the very act of creation, and Eckhart proclaims (provocatively): "I am the cause of God's existence."[136]

Obviously there is an important mystical side to Eckhart's teaching which should be taken into account. He attempts to express what the work of creation "looked like" from the standpoint of God's inner life. Still his teaching seems to suggest a similarity between generation and creation, which of course is illegitimate, for it would amount to the divinization of the material world.[137] Florovsky says that "the very notion of the beginning of time is this necessity of stopping, is the very impossibility of an infinite regression into the past."[138] And just as time began, it will, in a sense, come to an end, with the *plērōma*. Augustine has it that "the fullness of the times [*omne tempus*] does not always mean 'always' [*semper*]."[139] John Damascene says that "time, after the resurrection, will no longer be numbered by days and nights; rather, there will be one day without evening."[140]

Interestingly, Thomas Aquinas teaches that the notion that the world was created from all eternity is philosophically feasible,[141] and he takes it that the temporal finitude of the world may be looked upon as a truth of

135. See W. Bange, *Meister Eckeharts Lehre vom göttlichen und geschöpflichen Sein* (Limburg: Pallotiner, 1937), 247.

136. Koch, *Meister Eckhart*, 296.

137. See Augustine, *Confessions* XII, 15; *De Civ. Dei* VI. The same point is made by Basil, *Hom. 1 in Hex.*; Ambrose, *Lib. I in Hex.*; and Isidore, *De summo bono* I, 9.

138. Florovsky, "Creation and Creaturehood," 44.

139. Augustine, *De Civ. Dei* XII, 15.

140. John Damascene, *De fide orth.* I, 1.

141. See Thomas Aquinas, *ST* I, q. 46; *SCG* II.38; *De Pot.*, q. 3, a. 13; *De aeternitate mundi contra murmurantes.* On this question, see F. Hendrix, "Das Problem der Aeternitas mundi bei Thomas von Aquin," *Recherches de Théologie ancienne et médiévales* 39 (1967): 219–37; A. A. M. Ghisalberti, "La controversia scolastica sulla creazione 'ab aeterno,'" *Rivista di filosofia neo-scolastica* 60 (1968): 211–30; J. I. Saranyana, "La creación 'ab aeterno.' Controversia de Sto. Tomás y R. Marti con San Buenaventura," *Scripta Theologica* 5 (1973): 127–74; J. F. Wippel, "Did Thomas Aquinas Defend the Possibility of an Eternally Created World?," *Journal of the History of Philosophy* 19 (1981): 21–38; P. Mazzarella, "Creazione, partecipazione e tempo secondo san Tommaso d'Aquino," *Studia Patavina* 29 (1981): 309–35; B. S. Kogan, "The Problem of Creation in Late Medieval Jewish Philosophy," in R. Link-Salinger and J. Hackett (eds.), *A Straight Path: Studies in Medieval Philosophy and Culture: Essays in Honor of Arthur Hyman* (Washington, D.C.: The Catholic University of America Press, 1988), 159–73; J. B. M. Wissink (ed.), *The Eternity of the World in the Thought of Thomas Aquinas and His Contemporaries* (Leiden: E. J. Brill, 1990); R. C. Dales, *Medieval Discussions of the Eternity of the World* (Leiden: E. J. Brill, 1990).

faith,[142] though it cannot be proved by reason, as Bonaventure suggested it could.[143] In other words that the world could have existed from all eternity is not in conflict with reason. Indeed for us it is difficult to imagine a world existing "from-ever." But just as there is nothing philosophically contradictory in a world that will last forever, into the future, there is no reason why it could not have existed already for an infinite space of time, for it is simply a finite world. And this is so, for Aquinas, because this "eternity," this extension or infinitude in time, is totally different from the eternity of God—perfect, vital presence—and thus from the eternal generation of the Word.

142. See DH 800. Thomas says of the temporal finitude of the world: "sola fide tenetur, et demonstrative probari non potest" (*ST* I, q. 46, a. 2; see ibid., ad 6; *SCG* II.38).

143. See Bonaventure, *II Sent.*, d. 1, a. 1, arg 1, ad 2.

10

Creation and the Material World

THE CHALLENGE OF ECOLOGY

THE FOURTH LATERAN COUNCIL presents the universe created by God as threefold: the purely spiritual (angels), those beings composed by spirit and matter (humans), and the material (the physical cosmos). In the next chapter I shall consider some aspects of the theology of the angels, entirely spiritual beings. I have dealt with theological anthropology elsewhere,[1] and I shall look into the question of original sin in chapters 12 and 13, which has important implications in the area of anthropology. But in this chapter I shall consider some issues related to the material cosmos, the earth and the universe, God's gift to humanity that is meant to be received, understood, appreciated, respected, and used in gratitude. The topic connects well with the previous chapter on divine providence, in that our care for our common home shares in the task of "dominating" the world that God charged us with in creating us.

Situating the Challenge of Ecology in the Light of Faith

The challenge of ecology is, strictly speaking, a new one for Christian theology. Perhaps for the first time in history humans have found themselves in a situation where they may be in a position to destroy or seriously prejudice the future of the planet, the physical world they inhabit, their "common home," as Pope Francis calls it. The reality of global warming and pollution of the atmosphere, of the sea, of rivers, of the earth, of cities is well known

1. See O'Callaghan, *Children of God in the World.*

to one and all.[2] Obviously theology as such is not in a position to provide concrete economic and social solutions to a problem with a clearly empirical profile. Still, it should be in a position to reflect on the roots of the phenomenon and inspire lines of explanation and solution. Recent popes have spoken extensively about ecology, and especially so Pope Francis.[3]

Besides, theology may have something important to say on the matter given that in recent decades the contemporary ecological crisis has been ascribed by some to Christian faith and praxis. At the beginning of the twentieth century the sociologist Max Weber spoke of a progressive "disenchantment" of the natural world among Christians and post-Christians,[4] which led, he claimed, to an instrumentalized view of reality. This brought believers in some cases, it is said, to be less respectful of the world they lived in. In 1967 an American author, Lynn White, said that "since the roots of our trouble are so largely religious, the remedy must also be essentially religious, whether we call it that or not. We must rethink and re-feel our nature and destiny."[5] He suggested that Francis of Assisi be named patron of ecology, observing that "Francis tried to depose man from his monarchy over creation and set up a democracy of all God's creatures."[6] Whether this is true or not, John Paul II did name Francis patron of ecology in 1979.[7]

Another author, J. W. Forrester, warned in 1973 of the religious roots of the phenomenon of exponential growth.[8] The title of a work by a German author, Carl Amery, is sufficiently indicative of what is involved—*The End of Providence: The Disgraceful Consequences of Christianity*.[9] The catastrophe that is threatening, we are told, is the result of the misapplication of the Old Testament doctrine of dominion and subduing of creation that Genesis 1 speaks of. The practical outworking of this may be seen in a rampant ethics of consumerism, wastage, and overproduction. Amery refers to the superiority in this respect of Eastern and pantheistic religions,

2. Particularly influential was the work of R. Carson, *Silent Spring* (New York: Houghton Mifflin Harcourt, 2002).

3. See Francis, *Laudato Si'* (hereafter *LS*), Encyclical Letter, May 24, 2015.

4. R. Gerardi (ed.), *La Creazione: Dio, il cosmo, l'uomo* (Rome: Studium, 1990), 2.

5. L. White, "The Historical Roots of our Ecological Crisis," *Science* 155 (1967): 1203–7, at 1207.

6. Ibid., 1206.

7. See John Paul II, *Inter Sanctos*, Papal Bull, November 29, 1979.

8. J. W. Forrester, *World Dynamics*, 2nd ed. (Cambridge, Mass.: Wright-Allen, 1973), viii and 18–21.

9. Original: C. Amery, *Das Ende der Vorsehung: Die gnadenlosen Folgen des Christentums* (Rowohlt: Reinbek, 1972).

which encourage people to be more gentle with and respectful of nature and strive to act in communion with it.

But are these accusations justified? May Judeo-Christian revelation be blamed for the ecological crisis? At a substantial level it would seem not. More blame should be placed on philosophies openly opposed to Christianity: Marxism, radical economic liberalism, an understanding of nature as an amorphous and infinitely manipulable given (this may be seen for example in the works of Michel Foucault, which we shall see below). It is true that humans are placed at the summit of creation (Gn 1:26–28), and this could feasibly give rise to an anthropocentric vision of the world. However, as we saw in chapter 2, the high point of the creation narrative does not coincide with the creation of humans on the sixth day, but with the seventh day when God rested and man was invited to direct his love and attention and adoration to the creator. Besides, the vision typical of the Bible goes back for over three thousand years, whereas the roots of the present problem extend for no more than a tenth of that time.[10]

The seventeenth-century father of experimental science, Francis Bacon, said that "the nature of things betrays itself more readily under the vexations of art than in its natural freedom ... all the kernel being forced out and expelled with the torture and press of the method."[11] Bacon seems to be saying that science and technology are meant to force nature to speak, to reveal itself. Still, he did express the limits of human dominion over the universe in the following terms: "nature to be commanded must be obeyed."[12] In other words humans dominate over the universe by knowing and respecting and obeying its nature and inner workings.[13]

But others modern thinkers went further. René Descartes said that the purpose of science and the trades is "to make us lords and masters and possessors of nature."[14] Something of a kind may be found in Marx who set out clear-mindedly not to contemplate (and respect) but to transform the world. Then the twentieth-century humanist Marxist Ernst Bloch "in-

10. See Moltmann, *God in Creation*, 26.

11. F. Bacon, *Advancement of Learning* I, 1:6 and 17:9.

12. F. Bacon, *Novum Organum* (1620) I, 3.

13. Galileo, according to Ratzinger, says that "if nature did not voluntarily answer our questions but hid its secrets from us, then we would submit it to torture and in a wracking inquisition extract the answers from it that it would otherwise not give" *"In the beginning,"* 35.

14. Descartes, *Discourse on Method*, 51.

tensified this idea and gave it a truly terrifying mien. He said that truth is now what we take it to be and that the only truth is change."[15] The philosopher Michel Foucault considers humanity simply as an epistemological construct.[16] Human beings do not have an *a priori* constitution, or nature, on the basis of which they may act. Rather they realise and construct their own lives or identity, freely, individually, from beginning to end, convinced that nature, such as it is, is infinitely malleable, fully at the whim and disposal of humans. They look upon themselves as "self-made men" (or women) who, consequently, set about constructing for themselves a self-made world, with the aid of technology, as if they were autonomous divinities with no limits.[17]

Here lies the ideological root of the ecological problem. Ratzinger observes that in this modern understanding of human activity "there will no longer be any need for the sabbath, since human beings are their own creatures in every respect. . . . The humility of faith has disappeared, shattered on the arrogance of activity."[18] The Sabbath, in effect, marks the moment when believers stop to thank God for his gifts and recognize their nature and structure as divinely given. The position just described, of course, is light-years away from the Christian view of the world which contemplates the universe as a gift of the creator, who gave it a harmoniously integrated nature and purpose, a universe that is meant to exist for the glory of God.

The Nature of Human Dominion over Creation

Perhaps it is fair to say that Christian revelation has given (some) people the excuse to justify their (disorderly) desire to mistreat the universe. Faith in a loving, generous, magnanimous, forgiving Father God banished once and for all the time-immemorial fear humans experienced when faced with the power and unpredictability and capriciousness of the material cosmos. Doubtless, fear can be a teacher. But Ratzinger observes: "through faith in

15. Ratzinger, *"In the Beginning,"* 35. On Bloch, see P. O'Callaghan, "Hope and Freedom in Gabriel Marcel and Ernst Bloch," *Irish Theological Quarterly* 55 (1989): 215–39.

16. See M. Foucault, *The Order of Things* (New York: Vintage Books, 1994), 309.

17. See also Y. N. Harari, *Homo Deus: A Brief History of Tomorrow* (New York: Random House, 2017).

18. Ratzinger, *"In the Beginning,"* 37.

creation the world had been demythologized and made reasonable; that sun, moon, and stars are no longer strange and powerful divinities but merely lights."[19] Genesis presents man, created on the last of the six "days," as superior to the rest of the material cosmos, and alone destined to "have dominion over the fishes of the sea, and over the birds of the air" (Gn 1:26, 28). In words of the historian Paul Johnson, "Perhaps the most important single thing which the Judaeo-Christian tradition established was the principle of monotheism and the concomitant rejection of natural phenomena—sun, moon, trees, rivers, woods, and symbolic animals—as objects of worship."[20]

Christian faith teaches that there are no mysterious, semi-divine, evil forces, personified and jealous of their prerogatives, present within nature to restrain human enterprise by fear. God is eminently trustable, as is his great work, the created world which is "very good" (Gn 1:31). Humans are proud to exclaim: "The heavens are the Lord's heavens, but the earth he has given to the sons of men" (Ps 115:16). Man was created as God's supreme creature, capacitated and blessed to control and dominate the natural world.[21] By taking advantage of the patience and mercy of God (Rom 11:31) of course humans might well exercise this dominion sinfully, improperly, and instead of a dominion of service that is patient, attentive, prudent, persevering, and respectful, they may exercise one of destruction: impatient, careless, precipitated, fitful, and egoistic. Believers are meant to behave before the created world as competent managers, honest treasurers, faithful caretakers, good administrators, shepherds. The term used in the New Testament is "steward" (Lk 12:42–48, 16:1–13), deriving from the Greek *oikonomos*.[22]

Genesis 1:28 uses two terms to describe the actions of humans made in the image of God with respect to the created world: "to subdue" (*kāb-aš*), a term that is applied to the world in general, and "to dominate" (*rādāh*), referred to living beings, also in Genesis 1:26.[23] They are more or less equivalent.[24] Yet the first term refers to an absolute form of dominion, obtained by force (Jos 18:1), by war (Nm 32:22, 29), even to the point of

19. Ibid., 33.

20. P. Johnson, "Is Totalitarianism Dead?," *Crisis* (February 7, 1989): 16.

21. See O'Callaghan, *Children of God in the World*, 99–105.

22. See D. J. Ireland, *Stewardship and the Kingdom of God: An Historical, Exegetical, and Contextual Study of the Parable of the Unjust Steward in Luke 16:1–13* (Leiden: E. J. Brill, 1992), 5–47.

23. See especially H.-J. Zobel, "rāḏâ," *Theological Dictionary of the Old Testament*, ed. G. J. Botterweck, H. Ringgren, and H.-J. Fabry (Grand Rapids, Mich.: Eerdmans, 2004), 13:330–36.

24. Westermann teaches that the two terms are equivalent in *Genesis 1–11*, 147.

crushing other peoples (2 Sm 8:1) and enslaving them (Neh 5:5). The other one, *rādāh*, "to dominate," is applied in the Old Testament also to royal dominion (Ps 72:8, 110:2; Is 14:6; Ezek 34:4), as well to as the process of treading the grape (Jl 4:13); but it also evokes the idea of shepherding.

Besides, it is clear from scripture that the power of humans over the world is a limited one: the day is controlled by the sun, the night by the moon (Gn 1:14–18), murder of humans is illicit (Gn 9:6), and man is prohibited from eating of the tree of the knowledge of good and evil (Gn 2:16). There are many things we *can* do or can attempt to do, but which we *may not* do. All in all, we are reminded that "of the Lord is the earth and everything it contains" (Ps 24:1).[25] As we saw in the chapter on providence, God's power in Christ lies in the "power of weakness" (1 Cor 1:25), and believers should gladly and gently emulate this way of acting.

In effect, humans, in "dominating" the world, should by right act as its shepherd, for this is the way God acts and Christ reveals definitively. The issue here is not the *fact* of dominion, but the *way* in which it is carried out. So ecology, the care of our "common home," becomes an ethical issue that finds its deepest roots in the attitude the believer has toward the gift of creation.[26]

Ecology in Church Teaching

In its official teaching the church has given considerable importance to the question of ecology in recent decades, especially in the writings of Popes John Paul II,[27] Benedict XVI,[28] and Francis.[29] Many episcopal conferences have likewise paid special attention to the issue.[30] To start with, the *Catechism of the Catholic Church* says the following about ecology:

25. O'Callaghan, *Children of God in the World*, 102.

26. See ibid., 461–68.

27. On John Paul II, see S. Ewertowski, "Pope John Paul II and the Ecological Crisis," *Irish Theological Quarterly* 64, no. 4 (1994): 59–69; M. Lorbiecki and B. McKibben, *Following St. Francis: John Paul II's Call for Ecological Action* (Milan: Rizzoli, 2014).

28. See Benedict XVI, *The Garden of God: Toward a Human Ecology*, ed. M. M. Morciano (Washington, D.C.: The Catholic University of America Press, 2014).

29. See especially *LS*.

30. See the 1980 document of the German bishops' conference, in *HerderKorrespondenz* 34 (1980): 560–66; also the Filipino bishops, "Pastoral Letter on Ecology," *CBCP Monitor* 9 (January–February 1988). See also the statements of the United States Conference of Catholic Bishops, *Renewing*

The seventh commandment enjoins respect for the integrity of creation. Animals, like plants and inanimate beings, are by nature destined for the common good of past, present, and future humanity [Gn 1:28–31]. Use of the mineral, vegetable, and animal resources of the universe cannot be divorced from respect for moral imperatives. Man's dominion over inanimate and other living beings granted by the Creator is not absolute; it is limited by concern for the quality of life of his neighbor, including generations to come; it requires a religious respect for the integrity of creation.[31]

John Paul II has explained that the destruction of the material world is in real terms a reminder of the need to respect the natural law, the law inscribed in nature by God. In the 1991 Message for the World Day of Peace, entitled "Peace with God the Creator. Peace with all of Creation," he spoke of our first parents who

destroyed the existing harmony by deliberately going against the Creator's plan, that is, by choosing to sin. This resulted not only in man's alienation from himself, in death and fratricide, but also in the earth's "rebellion" against him (Gn 3:17–19; 4:12). All of creation became subject to futility, waiting in a mysterious way to be set free and to obtain a glorious liberty together with all the children of God (Rom 8:20–21).[32]

In effect, "when man turns his back on the Creator's plan, he provokes a disorder which has inevitable repercussions on the rest of the created order. If man is not at peace with God, then earth itself cannot be at peace."[33] This means that the ecological problem is not a purely technical one that requires technical solutions, but a moral problem that requires an ethical solution.[34] And John Paul suggests that "respect for life, and above

the Earth (1991), *Global Climate Change* (2001), and a wide variety of documents on particular issues. Also Patriarch Bartholomew of Constantinople has spoken on the need to repent of the harm we have inflicted on nature: "we all generate small ecological damage" and so must acknowledge "our contribution, smaller or greater, to the disfigurement and destruction of creation"; in his "Message for the Day of Prayer for the Protection of Creation," September 1, 2012, cited in *LS*, par. 8. He also states: "To commit a crime against the natural world is a sin against ourselves and a sin against God," "Address in Santa Barbara, California," November 8, 1997, in *On Earth as in Heaven: Ecological Vision and Initiatives of Ecumenical Patriarch Bartholomew*, ed. J. Chryssavgis (New York: Fordham University Press, 2012). See *LS*, pars. 8–9.

31. *CCC*, no. 2415, referring to John Paul II, *Centesimus Annus*, Encyclical Letter, May 1, 1991, par. 37.

32. John Paul II, "Message for the World Day of Peace," January 1, 1991, par. 3.

33. Ibid., par. 5.

34. See ibid., par. 15.

all for the dignity of the human person, is the ultimate guiding norm for any sound economic, industrial or scientific progress."[35]

In the 1991 encyclical *Centesimus Annus* he returns to the question, explaining in detail that man must consider himself a collaborator with God, treating the created world with the joy, respect, and astonishment that God placed in his heart. He observes:

> Equally worrying is the ecological question which accompanies the problem of consumerism and which is closely connected to it. In his desire to have and to enjoy rather than to be and to grow, man consumes the resources of the earth and his own life in an excessive and disordered way. At the root of the senseless destruction of the natural environment lies an anthropological error, which unfortunately is widespread in our day. Man, who discovers his capacity to transform and in a certain sense create the world through his own work, forgets that this is always based on God's prior and original gift of the things that are. Man thinks that he can make arbitrary use of the earth, subjecting it without restraint to his will, as though it did not have its own requisites and a prior God-given purpose, which man can indeed develop but must not betray. Instead of carrying out his role as a co-operator with God in the work of creation, man sets himself up in place of God and thus ends up provoking a rebellion on the part of nature, which is more tyrannized than governed by him.[36]

John Paul II's explanation of nature unconsciously rebelling against human tyranny is striking. It is reminiscent of the declaration of P. N. Destouches: "Hunt out the natural, it will return with a gallop."[37] And John Paul II goes on to insist that besides ecological problems in the strict sense of the word, relating to pollution, climate change, and sustainable development, we have to pay attention to "even more grave" issues, what he calls "human ecology," the ecology of life, of marriage, of family.[38]

Benedict XVI says the same thing:

> The importance of ecology is no longer disputed. We must listen to the language of nature and we must answer accordingly. Yet I would like to underline a point that seems to me to be neglected, today as in the past: there is also an ecology of man. Man too has a nature that he must respect and that he cannot manipulate

35. Ibid., par. 7.

36. John Paul II, *Centesimus Annus*, par. 37.

37. From Destouches, *La Belle orgueilleuse*.

38. See John Paul II, *Centesimus Annus*, par. 38.

at will. Man is not merely self-creating freedom. Man does not create himself. He is intellect and will, but he is also nature, and his will is rightly ordered if he respects his nature, listens to it and accepts himself for who he is, as one who did not create himself. In this way, and in no other, is true human freedom fulfilled.[39]

Benedict also made suggestions of a practical kind, for example that "technologically advanced societies must be prepared to encourage more sober lifestyles, while reducing their energy consumption and improving its efficiency."[40]

Pope Francis has spoken frequently on ecology and environmentalism and has taken many practical initiatives to reinforce awareness of the urgency of the issue. In his principal document on this topic, the 2015 encyclical *Laudato Si'*, chapter 1 attempts to describe the present ecological situation of the world, "which is in many ways unprecedented in the history of humanity."[41] Chapter 2 offers a reflection on ecology in the context of the doctrine of creation. Citing Benedict XVI he says that each of us is "conceived in the heart of God and for this reason 'each of us is the result of a thought of God. Each of us is willed, each of us is loved, each of us is necessary.'"[42] This lends special urgency to the task of caring for our common home, the earth. Francis finds the root of the problem in the fact that humans no longer see God as their creator:

A spirituality which forgets God as all-powerful and Creator is not acceptable. . . . It would also be mistaken to view other living beings as mere objects subjected to arbitrary human domination. When nature is viewed solely as a source of profit and gain, this has serious consequences for society. This vision of "might is right" has engendered immense inequality, injustice and acts of violence against the majority of humanity, since resources end up in the hands of the first comer or the most powerful: the winner takes all.[43]

39. Benedict XVI, Address to the Bundestag, Germany, September 22, 2011, "The Listening Heart. Reflections on the Foundations of Law."

40. Benedict XVI, "Message for the 2010 World Day of Peace," par. 9, cited in *LS*, par. 193.

41. *LS*, par. 17.

42. *LS*, par. 65, citing Benedict XVI, "Inaugural Homily of His Holiness Benedict XVI," April 24, 2005.

43. *LS*, pars. 75 and 82.

In fact "nature is usually seen as a system which can be studied, understood and controlled, whereas creation can only be understood as a gift from the outstretched hand of the Father of all, and as a reality illuminated by the love which calls us together into universal communion."[44] This fits into God's providential plan, as we saw in the previous chapter: "All creatures are moving forward with us and through us towards a common point of arrival, which is God, in that transcendent fullness where the risen Christ embraces and illumines all things."[45]

Francis recognizes that the world God created must develop and grow, and this may well involve pain and suffering, the pains of childbirth that Paul speaks of (Rom 8:22). "Creating a world in need of development, God in some way sought to limit himself in such a way that many of the things we think of as evils, dangers or sources of suffering, are in reality part of the pains of childbirth which he uses to draw us into the act of cooperation with the Creator."[46]

Chapter 3 of *Laudato Si'* deals with the anthropological roots of the ecological crisis and reflects on the ambivalent relationship between the exercise of human creativity and power. Francis admits that "an inadequate presentation of Christian anthropology gave rise to a wrong understanding of the relationship between human beings and the world.... Our 'dominion' over the universe should be understood more properly in the sense of responsible stewardship."[47] Chapter 4 goes on to speak of an "integral ecology" that takes into account the entirety of human reality and experience, in line with the teaching of John Paul II and Benedict XVI. It mentions some of the practical implications of an "ecology of daily life." Chapter 5 offers some lines of approach and action in the face of the ecological crisis. Chapter 6, the last one, presents a series of elements for an "ecological education" and spirituality, that involve among other things "an education in responsible simplicity of life, in grateful contemplation of God's world, and in concern for the needs of the poor and the protection of the environment."[48]

44. *LS*, par. 76.
45. *LS*, par. 83.
46. *LS*, par. 80.
47. *LS*, par. 116.
48. *LS*, par. 214.

In brief terms, we may say that for Francis the dominion we exercise over the planet is not divine in character: "the Bible has no place for a tyrannical anthropocentrism unconcerned for other creatures."[49] Besides, "disregard for the duty to cultivate and maintain a proper relationship with my neighbor, for whose care and custody I am responsible, ruins my relationship with my own self, with others, with God and with the earth."[50]

In the post-synodal exhortation *Querida Amazonia* (2020), Francis gives expression to his "dream" for an Amazon region "that can jealously preserve its overwhelming natural beauty and the superabundant life teeming in its rivers and forests."[51] He reminds us of the importance of contemplating and loving and belonging to the earth, and not just using and defending it. We need to "learn to contemplate the Amazon region and not simply analyze it, and thus appreciate this precious mystery that transcends us. We can love it, not simply use it, with the result that love can awaken a deep and sincere interest. Even more, we can feel intimately a part of it and not only defend it.... Let us awaken our God-given aesthetic and contemplative sense that so often we let languish."[52] Francis concludes by saying that

> an integral ecology cannot be content simply with fine-tuning technical questions or political, juridical, and social decisions. The best ecology always has an educational dimension that can encourage the development of new habits in individuals and groups.... A sound and sustainable ecology, one capable of bringing about change, will not develop unless people are changed, unless they are encouraged to opt for another style of life, one less greedy and more serene, more respectful and less anxious, more fraternal.[53]

Conclusion

Christian believers should not have a catastrophic attitude toward the situation of the world and its future, because they believe that God created the world intelligently and hope that he will lead it to its ultimate end by

49. *LS*, par. 68.
50. *LS*, par. 70.
51. See Pope Francis, *Querida Amazonia*, Apostolic Exhortation, February 2, 2020, par. 7.
52. Ibid., pars. 55–56.
53. Ibid., par. 58.

his providence. "We are not God," Pope Francis says. "The earth was here before us and it has been given to us."[54] Besides, Christians are convinced that salvation depends first of all on God's grace and moral rectitude, and not only on the materiality of the works we carry out. God made a world in which mistakes would be made, but could be subsequently rectified and redeemed. Yet Christians are meant to be creative in their quest for protecting the environment and for sustainable development, aware of the needs and rights of future generations. They are not surprised to learn that the sun shining on the earth for an hour and a half provides all the energy humanity presently consumes in one whole year.[55] Besides, they should be aware of the special dignity of human beings, who must be protected and loved, one by one, in a way that is clearly different from and superior to other creatures. Benedict said: "A supposedly egalitarian vision of the 'dignity' of all living creatures [may well] end up abolishing the distinctiveness and superior role of human beings. They also open the way to a new pantheism tinged with neo-paganism, which would see the source of man's salvation in nature alone, understood in purely naturalistic terms."[56] Likewise, Francis spoke of "an obsession with denying any pre-eminence to the human person."[57]

54. *LS*, par. 67.

55. See www.americanenergyindependence.com/solarenergy.aspx.

56. Benedict XVI, "Message for the 2010 World Day of Peace," par. 13. Paul Johnson observed that "there is among the more active environmentalists an element of pantheism, one might almost say of paganism.... The ideological scene ... may become more complicated by the next [twenty-first] century.... But whatever form this conflict of ideas takes, we can be confident that the radicals will continue to insist that human behavior can be transformed by [the] political process and that the state must play the leading role in this transformation. Hence those who remain skeptical of this contention ... must continue to focus on two fundamental points – the natural imperfection of human beings and the limits which must be imposed on state power." "Is Totalitarianism Dead?," 16.

57. *LS*, par. 90.

11

Creation and the Spiritual World

ANGELS AND DEMONS

IN THE PREVIOUS CHAPTER I considered the material side of the created universe and the ecological challenge it presents Christian believers with. In this chapter I shall look into the world of spiritual creatures, angels and demons, who have a relevant role to play, besides, in the divine providence with which God governs creation. As we saw in chapter 9, divine providence relates directly and principally to Christ's saving work: he is the good shepherd of humanity, the Lord of history, the *Logos* who creates all things and leads them to their proper end. With the Father he sends the Holy Spirit who guides us to the fullness of truth.

But scripture speaks frequently of other spiritual beings who are involved in this process of guiding the universe on its way: angels.[1] Angels belong purely and simply to the created realm, for they have been made

1. See A. Vonier, *The Angels* (London: Burns, Oates and Washbourne, 1934); P. Claudel, *Présence et prophétie* (Fribourg: Éditions de la librairie de l'Université Fribourg, 1942); J. Daniélou, *Les anges et leur mission d'après les pères de l'Eglise* (Paris: Desclée, 1951); P.-R. Régamey, *Les anges au ciel et parmi nous* (Paris: Fayard, 1961); M. P. Giudici, *Qui sont les anges* (Paris: Nouvelle Cité, 1985); V. Klee, *Les plus beaux textes sur les saints anges* (Paris: Nouvelles Editions Latines, 1984); R. Lavatori, *Gli angeli* (Turin: Marietti, 1991); B. Marconcini, A. Amato, C. Rocchetta, and M. Fiori, *Angeli e demoni: il dramma della storia tra il bene e il male* (Bologna: Dehoniane, 1991); P. Faure, *Gli angeli* (Cinisello Balsamo: Edizioni paoline, 1991); B. Mondin, *Gli abitanti del cielo: Trattato di ecclesiologia celeste e di escatologia* (Bologna: ESD, 1994); G. Gozzelino, *Angeli e demoni: l'invisibile creato e la vicenda umana* (Cinisello Balsamo: San Paolo, 2000); E. Muehlberger, *Angels in Late Ancient Christianity* (Oxford: Oxford University Press, 2013); P. O'Callaghan, "Angels," *Religions of the World: A Comprehensive Encyclopedia of Beliefs and Practices*, ed. J. G. Melton and M. Baumann, 2nd ed. (Santa Barbara, Calif.: ABC-CLIO, 2010), 1:114–18, and my "Il cielo e la terra (articolo 1 – paragrafo 5)," *Catechismo della Chiesa Cattolica. Testo integrale. Nuovo commento teologico-pastorale*, ed. R. Fisichella (Vatican City: Libreria Editrice Vaticana, 2017), 964–70; S.-T. Bonino, *Angels and Demons: A Catholic Introduction* (Washington, D.C.: The Catholic University of America Press, 2016).

by God *ex nihilo* like all other creatures. But at the same time, like humans (Gn 1:27), they are involved by divine will in the governance of the universe. The idea of angels as instruments of providence may be found in Church Fathers such as Justin,[2] Clement of Alexandria,[3] and Novatian.[4] Interestingly Athenagoras says that God "looks after the whole and the great in general terms," but leaves the details to the angels, who were created for this very purpose.[5] Thomas Aquinas likewise speaks of the guardianship of angels that "belongs to the execution of divine providence."[6]

The Angels in the Old Testament

Both the Old and the New Testaments speak frequently of the angels.[7] "Almost every page of the sacred script gives witness to the existence of the angels and archangels," says Gregory the Great.[8] In his catechesis Pope John Paul says:

> The name given to them by Sacred Scripture indicates that what counts most in revelation is the truth concerning the tasks of the angels in regard to humanity—angel (*angelus*) means "messenger." Used in the Old Testament, the Hebrew term *malak* signifies more precisely "delegate" or "ambassador," as does the Greek term, *aggelos*[9] and the Latin one, *angelus*. The angels, spiritual creatures, have a function of mediation and of ministry in the relationships between God and man.[10]

2. See Justin, *Apol.* II, 6.

3. See Clement of Alexandria, *Strom.* 1, 6.

4. See Novatian, *De Trinitate* 8.

5. Athenagoras, *Suppl.* 24:3.

6. Thomas Aquinas, *ST* I, q. 113, a. 2, co.

7. See M. Noth, "Separated Spiritual Substances in the Old Testament," *Catholic Biblical Quarterly* 29 (1966): 419–49; A. Caquot, *Handbuch der Dogmengeschichte*, ed. G. Tavard, A. Caquot, and J. Michl (Freiburg i.B.: Herder, 1968), 2:2b, 1–9; P.-E. Dion, "Les deux principales formes de l'angélologie de l'Ancien Testament," *Science et Esprit* 28 (1976): 65–82; J. Galot, "Existence personnelle et mission des anges," *Esprit et Vie* (May 4, 1989): 257–63; H. Cazelles, "Fondements bibliques de la théologie des anges," *Revue Thomiste* 90 (1990): 181–93; R. A. Stewart, "Angel," in *New Bible Dictionary* (ed. Wood), 36; *NIDNTTE* 1:120–24, s.v. ἄγγελος.

8. Gregory the Great, *Hom.* 34 *in Ev.*, 7.

9. See W. Grundmann, "Aggelos: Aggelos in the Greek and Hellenistic World," in *Theological Dictionary of the New Testament*, ed. G. Kittel, G. Friedrich, and G. W. Bromiley (Grand Rapids, Mich.: Eerdmans, 1964), 1:74–76.

10. John Paul II, "Creator of Things Unseen: The Angels," par. 1.

Old Testament texts not infrequently use the expression "the angel of the Lord,"[11] and this has been seen as a paraphrase for God himself who manifests himself to humanity and the world.[12] But this would seem to indicate that angels do not exist in their own right, but rather only God. This confusion is almost inevitable given the close relationship between the divine Spirit and the created spirit, between God and the angels who carry out his will faithfully and glorify him continually. Most Church Fathers however confirm that the texts speaking of "the angel of the Lord" refer truly to God's angels as finite personal created beings. Among them we may mention Augustine[13] and Gregory the Great, and later on Thomas Aquinas.[14] Even still, not everything said of the angels in the Old Testament can be referred to such finite created beings, because angels refer to and depend entirely upon God's life and action.[15]

In the Old Testament the angels are seen to exercise two special roles. The principal one is *to glorify God*, to praise the Lord. They exist for that very purpose. "In relation to the Blessed Trinity the purpose of the angels is principally that of praise. They are the glory of God and they give glory to God, they refer to him all the glory they possess. This angelic praise constitutes the heavenly liturgy, and is the great purpose of the angels."[16] "The Old Testament especially emphasizes the special participation of the angels in the celebration of the glory which the Creator receives as a tribute of praise on the part of the created world."[17] This may be seen especially in the Psalms. "Praise the Lord! Praise the Lord from the heavens, praise him in the heights! Praise him, all his angels, praise him, all his host!" (Ps 148:1–2). "Bless the Lord, O you his angels, you mighty ones who do his word, listening to the voice of his word!" (Ps 103:20).

11. See, e.g., Gn 16:10–13; 21:17–19; 22:11–17; Ex 3:2; etc. Gn 22:11–17 was directed to Jacob; Gn 31:13, "I am the god of Beth-el," to Moses at the burning bush; Ex 3:2 to Gideon (Jgs 6:11). Sometimes "the angel of the Lord" is openly distinguished from God, as in 2 Sm 24:16; Zec 1:12; but Zechariah does not consistently maintain the distinction (see Zec 3:1 and 12:8).

12. See Origen, *Hom. in Gen.* 8, 8; *Tom. 1 in Ioh.* 34. On this issue, see M. J. Lagrange, *Études sur les Religions Sémitiques* (Paris: V. Lecoffre, 1903).

13. See E. Klein, *Augustine's Theology of Angels* (Cambridge: Cambridge University Press, 2018). Augustine speaks especially of the worship role of angels.

14. See Thomas Aquinas, *De Pot.*, q. 6, a. 8, ad 3.

15. Galot, "Existence personnelle et mission des anges," 257.

16. J. Daniélou, *Le mystère de l'Avent* (Paris: Éditions du Seuil, 1948), 101.

17. John Paul II, "Creator of Things Unseen: The Angels," par. 2.

And the second role of the angels is that of *caring and solicitude for creatures*, especially humans. "A special care and solicitude for people is entrusted to the angels . . . whose requests and prayers they present to God, as mentioned, for example, in the Book of Tobit (cf. especially Tb 3:17 and 12:12)."[18] Psalm 91 proclaims: "For to his angels he has given command about you . . . upon their hands they shall bear you up, lest you dash your foot against a stone" (Ps 91:11–12). According to the Book of Daniel the tasks of angels as ambassadors of the living God extend not only to individual human beings and to those who have special duties, but also to entire nations (Dn 10:13–21).[19] They are especially involved in the work of salvation, as the following text from the *Catechism of the Catholic Church* explains.

Angels have been present since creation [Jb 38:7] and throughout the history of salvation, announcing this salvation from afar or near and serving the accomplishment of the divine plan: they closed the earthly paradise [Gn 3:24]; protected Lot [Gn 19]; saved Hagar and her child [Gn 21:17]; stayed Abraham's hand [Gn 22:11]; communicated the law by their ministry [Acts 7:63]; led the People of God [Ex 23:20–23]; announced births and callings [Jgs 13, 6:11–24; Is 6:6]; and assisted the prophets [1 Kgs 19:5], just to cite a few examples.[20]

The Angels in the New Testament

But the angels are present likewise in the New Testament. Their action and power may be seen clearly is in the way they accompany Christ on his mission.[21] "Let us look for a moment at this appearance of angels in Jesus' life, for it will help us to better understand their role—their angelic mission—in all human life,"[22] suggests Josemaría Escrivá. Thus the description of the role of the angels provided by the *Catechism of the Catholic Church*:

18. Ibid.

19. On the role of angels in protecting nations in apocalyptic literature, see D. S. Russell, "Guardian Angels of the Nations," in his *The Method and Message of Jewish Apocalyptic*, 3rd ed. (Philadelphia: Westminster, 1964), 244–49.

20. *CCC*, no. 332.

21. See H. Schlier, "Les anges dans le N.T.," in his *Essais sur le Nouveau Testament* (Paris: Cerf, 1968), 187–204; M. García Cordero, "Los ángeles según las creencias judías del tiempo de Jesús," *Ciencia Tomista* 115 (1988): 409–40; P. R. Carrell, *Jesus and the Angels: Angelology and the Christology of the Apocalypse of John* (Cambridge: Cambridge University Press, 1997); C. H. T. Fletcher-Louis, *Luke-Acts: Angels, Christology and Soteriology* (Tübingen: J. C. B. Mohr, 1997).

22. Josemaría Escrivá, *Christ Is Passing By*, 63.

Christ is the center of the angelic world. They are "his angels": "When the Son of man comes in his glory, and all the angels with him" [Mt 25:31]. They belong to him because they were created through and for him (Col 1:16).... They belong to him still more because he has made them messengers of his saving plan: "Are they not all ministering spirits sent forth to serve, for the sake of those who are to obtain salvation?" (Heb 1:14).[23]

In effect, frequently throughout the New Testament it is said that Christ is superior to the angels, "for in him all things were created, in heaven and on earth, visible and invisible, whether thrones or dominions or principalities or authorities—all things were created through him and for him" (Col 1:16).[24] "Good or bad, all are subject to him as Creator.... They derive their existence from him, and they owe their obedience to him through whom they have been conquered.... From the highest to the lowest, all alike are subject to Christ. They were created in him, through him and for him,"[25] for through him all things were made (Jn 1:3). In the letter to the Hebrews, Christ became "as much superior to angels as the name he has obtained is more excellent than theirs" (Heb 1:4).[26] This teaching is frequent and consistent throughout the New Testament (see Rom 8:38; Col 1:21; 1 Pt 3:22). Platonic and Gnostic teachers, on the other hand, held that angels were involved alongside the Word in the creation of the world (this was the position of Plato), which Paul did not accept, for all things were made through him and for him alone: only God creates.

Nonetheless, there is something paradoxical in the fact that, though Jesus surpasses the angels in being and glory, they accompany him always, facilitating his ministry, acting as it were as "mediators of the Mediator."[27]

23. *CCC*, no. 331.

24. See G. B. Caird, *Principalities and Powers: A Study in Pauline Theology* (Oxford: Clarendon Press, 1956); H. Schlier, *Principalities and Powers in the New Testament* (Freiburg: Herder, 1961); W. Carr, *Angels and Principalities* (Cambridge: Cambridge University Press, 1981).

25. O'Brien, *Colossians, Philemon*, 46.

26. "The comparison between Christ and the angels is not prompted by the problem of an angelomorphic christology (i.e., confusion over the nature of Jesus and that of the angels), or by the erroneous practice of venerating angels.... It provides a parallel to vv. 1–2a, where revelation through the prophets is contrasted with the ultimate word spoken through the Son. The angels in v. 4 are the counterpart to the prophets in v. 1 ... The assertion of Christ's exaltation over the angels prepares for the demonstration of that superiority (1:5–14). That demonstration is foundational to the thought that Christ's revelation is far superior to that mediated by the angels (2:1–4)." W. L. Lane, *Hebrews* (Waco, Tex.: Word Books, 1991), 16.

27. See F. V. Reiterer, K. Schöpflin, and T. Nicklas (eds.), *Angels. The Concept of Celestial Beings: Origins, Development and Reception* (Berlin: W. de Gruyter, 2007).

The presence and activity of the angels is constant throughout the life of Jesus on earth.[28] When God "introduces" his Son into the world, he says, "Let all God's angels worship him" (Heb 1:6). The angel Gabriel announces to Zechariah the birth of the Baptist (Lk 1:11), and to Mary the mystery of the incarnation (Lk 1:26); an angel tells Joseph that he should accept the child conceived by the Holy Spirit (Mt 1:20). At the birth of Jesus the angels announce the joyful news to the shepherds, singing the praise of God's only-begotten Son to the whole of creation: "Glory to God in the highest" (Lk 2:9–14). Throughout his public ministry, during the temptations in the desert, Jesus is comforted by the angels (Mt 4:11). At Gethsemane he was consoled by an angel (Lk 22:43) *in lieu* of the disciples who slept. In the glorious moment of the resurrection the angels were present: near the empty tomb they gave witness to Jesus' resurrection to the women (Mt 28:5–7; Mk 16:5–8; Lk 24:4–23; Jn 20:12). The apparition of the angels at the ascension of Jesus is particularly significant, for they explain to the apostles the true meaning of the "disappearance" of the Master, telling them that "this Jesus, who was taken up from you into heaven, will come in the same way as you saw him go into heaven" (Acts 1:10).

During the early stages of the life of the church, the angels are always present and particularly active, making sure that Christ's words and works penetrate every aspect of the life of the nascent Christian community. When the apostles were imprisoned, "at night an angel of the Lord opened the prison doors and brought them out and said, 'Go and stand in the temple and speak to the people all the words of this Life'" (Acts 5:19). An angel miraculously saved Peter from prison (Acts 12:7–11). When he returned home after his release his fellow Christians spontaneously exclaimed that "it was the angel of Peter" (Acts 12:15).[29] When Paul and his companions were about to be shipwrecked off Malta, an angel assured their salvation (Acts 27:23). Angels intervened in the conversion of the centurion Cornelius by inspiring Peter (Acts 10:3–12); the same thing happened with Philip on the road from Jerusalem to Gaza (Acts 8:26–29). According to the Book of Revelation, each church is presided over by an angel (Rv 2–3).[30]

28. See *CCC*, no. 333.

29. See J. H. Moulton, "It Is His Angel," *Journal of Theological Studies* 3 (1902): 514–27.

30. On the angels of the church in the Book of Revelation, see D. E. Aune, *Revelation 1–5* (Waco, Tex.: Word Books, 1997), 108–12.

Already in the Old Testament, angels were involved in the affairs of many nations (Dn 10:13, 10:20–11:10).

The Role of the Angels in the Life of Christians

Christian theologians and pastors have always been very aware of the presence and activity of the angels in the life of Christians.[31] According to Bernard of Clairvaux we owe the angels *reverentiam pro praesentia, devotionem pro benevolentia, fiducia pro custodia,*[32] "reverence for their presence, devotion for their benevolence, trust for their protection." "The Church confesses her faith in the guardian angels, venerating them in the liturgy with an appropriate feast [October 2] and recommending recourse to their protection by frequent prayer, as in the invocation 'Angel of God.'"[33] The angels protect the church and believers, but they also govern material things[34] and prepare the growth of Christianity among the pagans and in every nation and institution.[35] John Damascene says that the angels "are set over nations and places in accordance with their disposition by the Creator. They direct our affairs and help us. Moreover, they are ever around about God for the very reason that in accordance with the divine will and command they are above us."[36] Besides, many Church Fathers and theologians speak of the role of personal guardian angels.

THE GUARDIAN ANGELS

Origen says: "Each believer, though he be the humblest in the Church, is said to be attended by an angel, who is declared by the Savior always to

31. See G. Tavard, A. Caquot, and J. Michl, *Die Engel, Handbuch der Dogmengeschichte* (Freiburg i.B.: Herder, 1968), 2b; Daniélou, *Les anges et leur mission;* J. Turmel, "Histoire de l'angéologie des temps apostoliques jusqu'à la fin du IV siècle," *Revue d'histoire et de littérature religieuses* 3–4 (189–99): 289–308, 407–34, 533–52; Mondin, *Gli abitanti del cielo*, 37–76.

32. Bernard, *In Ps. 'Qui habitat,' sermo* 12:6.

33. John Paul II, "Angels Participate in the History of Salvation," General Audience, August 6, 1986, par. 7. The popular prayer to the guardian angels was composed by Alphonsus de Liguori: "O angel of God, my guardian dear, to whom God's love commits me here. Ever this day be at my side, to light and guard, to rule and guide. Amen."

34. See Athenagoras, *Suppl. pro christianis* 10; Origen, *Hom. X in Jer.* 6; Gregory of Nyssa, *Orat. Catech. Magna* 6:5.

35. See Mondin, *Gli abitanti del cielo*, 42.

36. John Damascene, *De fid. orth.* II, 3.

behold the face of God the Father."[37] And elsewhere he says: "The special angel of each one, even of the most insignificant members of the Church . . . unites his prayer to ours and collaborates, insofar as he can, in favor of what we ask of him."[38] Gregory of Nyssa says "there is a doctrine (which derives its trustworthiness from the tradition of the Fathers) which says that after our nature fell into sin, God did not . . . withhold his providence. No . . . he appointed an angel with an incorporeal nature to help in the life of each person."[39] Basil the Great says: "Every one of the faithful has beside him an angel as tutor and pastor, to lead him to life."[40] And Jerome: "Great is the dignity of souls that each one of them, from the very moment of birth, has an angel destined to protect it."[41] Hilary of Poitiers writes: "All the faithful are assisted by the help of these divine messengers according to what is written: 'the angel of the Lord is close to those who fear him.'"[42] For Gregory the Great the special attention and dedication of angels to humanity has deep Christological roots.

> Before the birth of our Redeemer, we had lost our friendship with the angels. Original guilt and our everyday sins had distanced us from their luminous purity. . . . But from the moment that the King of heaven took on our earthly flesh, the angels do not distance themselves any more from our wretchedness. They do not dare to esteem inferior to their nature the one whom they adore, seeing it exalted above them in the person of the King of heaven; and they do not disdain to recognize man as their companion.[43]

The same position may be found throughout the Middle Ages. Richard of St. Victor says that "the ministry of angels is not only temporal but also eternal, because with the help they give us now, we can obtain the inheritance of eternal life, and in that way share in the joy of their beatitude forever."[44] Thomas Aquinas explains the role of the guardian angel and adds that the role of the angels extends into the next life:

37. Origen, *De princ.* II, 10:7.
38. Origen, *De oratione* 11:1–5.
39. Gregory of Nyssa, *De vita Moysis* II, 45.
40. Basil, *Adv. Eun.* III, 1.
41. Jerome, *Comm. in Mt.* 18:20.
42. Hilary of Poitiers, *Tract. super Ps.* 124.
43. Gregory the Great, *In Ev. Hom.* 8:2.
44. Richard of St. Victor, *Comm. in Cant. Cant.*, 4.

Man while in this state of life, is, as it were, on a road by which he should journey towards heaven. On this road man is threatened by many dangers both from within and from without, according to Psalm 141:4: "In this way where I walked, they have hidden a snare for me." And therefore as guardians are appointed for men who have to pass by an unsafe road, so an angel guardian is assigned to each one as long as he is a wayfarer. When, however, he arrives at the end of life he no longer has a guardian angel; but in the kingdom he will have an angel to reign with him, in hell a demon to punish him.[45]

The sixteenth-century *Roman Catechism* confirms this long and constant tradition of the church:

In the journey we are making to our heavenly country our Father in heaven has placed over each of us an Angel under whose protection and vigilance we may be enabled to escape the snares secretly prepared by our enemy, repel the dreadful attacks he makes on us, and under his guiding hand keep the right road, and thus be secure against all false steps which the wiles of the evil one might cause us to make in order to draw us aside from the path that leads to heaven.[46]

And the *Catechism of the Catholic Church* has the following: "From its beginning until death, human life is surrounded by their [the angels'] watchful care and intercession. . . . Already here on earth the Christian life shares by faith in the blessed company of angels and men united in God."[47] The twentieth-century Orthodox author Sergei Bulgakov suggests that the activity of angels "towards us is never-ending and intense; still, it does not have an imperious and obliging character, but is, rather, a sweet and persuasive one."[48] The angels speak in silence, he adds, in that their action reflects the *kenosis* or self-emptying of Christ.[49]

The Role of the Angels in the Life of the Church

The same angels who praise God incessantly and assist us in our trials and travails are deeply involved in the church's life. "The Church is the place of

45. Thomas Aquinas, *ST* I, q. 113, a. 4, co.

46. *Roman Catechism* IV, 1, ed. J. McHugh and C. Callan (South Bend, Ind.: Marian Publications, 1972), 502.

47. CCC, no. 336.

48. S. Bulgakov, *Jacob's Ladder: On Angels* (Grand Rapids, Mich.: Eerdmans, 2010), 21.

49. See ibid., 25.

consolation and the assembly of the angels. The Church is where you will find the Cherubim and Seraphim," recites an ancient Coptic hymn.[50] According to Origen there are two churches, that of men and that of angels. Two churches, closely united, because the angels live with humans and carry their prayers to God. He says they carry out a more important role in the church than the apostles and their successors, the bishops.[51] Elsewhere in fact he says that every church is governed by two "bishops," one human, the other angelic.[52]

Their presence and activity is particularly effective and direct within sacramental and liturgical celebrations.[53] They are especially present throughout the celebration of the Eucharist.[54] For John Chrysostom during the Mass the angels surround the priest, the sanctuary, and especially the area around the altar, giving honor to the one who lies there.[55] Josemaría Escrivá says: "I adore and praise with the angels—it is not difficult, because I know that, as I celebrate the holy Mass, they surround me, adoring the Blessed Trinity."[56] And in the *Catechism of the Catholic Church* we read: "In her liturgy, the Church joins with the angels to adore the thrice-holy God. She invokes their assistance (in the funeral liturgy's *In Paradisum deducant te angeli*... 'May the angels lead you into Paradise...'). Moreover, in the 'Cherubic Hymn' of the Byzantine Liturgy, she celebrates the memory of certain angels more particularly (St. Michael, St. Gabriel, St. Raphael, and the guardian angels)."[57]

On the basis of different passages of the Old Testament and Paul, Church Fathers speak often of a complex hierarchy of angels, often in a liturgical context.[58] The best known classification is that of Dionysius the Areopagite (fifth or sixth century).[59] In his work *De coelesti hierarchia* he

50. W. H. Worrel (ed.), *The Coptic Manuscripts in the Freer Collection* (New York: Macmillan, 1923), 356.

51. See Mondin, *Gli abitanti del cielo*, 111.

52. See Origen, *Hom. in Luc.* 13.

53. As regards the baptism of catechumens, see Cyril of Jerusalem, *Protocatechesis* 5; Ambrose, *De sacramentis* 4:2.

54. See Tavard, *Die Engel*, §8.

55. See John Chrysostom, *Hom. in Eph.* 1, 3; *De Sacramentis* VI, 4; *Hom. in Asc. Domini* 1; *De Incomprehensibilitate Dei* 4.

56. Josemaría Escrivá, *Christ Is Passing By*, 89.

57. CCC, no. 335.

58. See Mondin, *Gli abitanti del cielo*, 28–30.

59. See Bonino, *Angels and Demons*, 57.

speaks of a hierarchy composed of three levels each with three orders of angels. In the top level are to be found the Thrones, the Cherubim (a term which means "to pray," "to bless") and the Seraphim (the "ardent" ones, the heavenly militia who protect the throne of God).[60] In the second are to be found the Powers, the Dominations, and the Virtues. On the third level we situate the angels, archangels, and the Principalities.[61] Certain archangels receive special attention in scripture, in particular the archangels Michael, Gabriel, and Raphael. Pope John Paul II sums up their role as follows.

It is appropriate to note that the Church honors the figures of three angels with a liturgical cult—those which Sacred Scripture calls by name. The first is Michael the Archangel (Dn 10:13–20; Rv 12:7; Jude 9). His name is a synthesis that expresses the essential attitude of the good spirits. *Mica-El* means "Who is like God?" This name expresses the salvific choice thanks to which the angels "see the face of the Father" who is in heaven. The second is Gabriel, a figure bound especially to the mystery of the incarnation of the Son of God (cf. Lk 1:19–26). His name means "my power is God" or "power of God," as if to say that at the culmination of creation, the incarnation is the supreme sign of the omnipotent Father. Finally, the third archangel is called Raphael. *Rafa-El* means "God heals." He is made known to us by the story of Tobias in the Old Testament (Tb 12:15–20), which is so significant for what it says about entrusting to the angels the little children of God, who are always in need of custody, care and protection.[62]

The Nature of Angels

Very little has been said in theology and church teaching on the nature of angels. Two fundamental affirmations however may be made. First in respect of the cult due to the angels, the Seventh Council of Nicaea in 787, against the iconoclasts, defended the legitimacy of images of the angels, and this for Christological reasons: because the Word became flesh, those who were created by him and serve him may be represented visibly.[63] And

60. On the cherubim, see E. Dhorme and L.-H. Vincent, "Les chérubins," *Revue biblique* 35 (1926): 328–56; R. De Vaux, *Bible et Orient* (Paris: Cerf, 1967), 231–50; R. Gilboa, "Cherubim: An Inquiry into an Enigma," *Biblische Notizen* 82 (1996): 59–75.

61. See Mondin, *Gli abitanti del cielo*, 6.

62. John Paul II, "Angels Participate in the History of Salvation," par. 8.

63. DH 601, confirmed at Trent (DH 1867).

second, in relation to Gnostic teachings, the church insisted on the fully created nature of angels. The Fourth Lateran Council speaks openly of angels and demons as creatures.[64] Recent church documents have spoken more extensively of the role of the angels: the *Creed of the People of God*, John Paul II's catechesis, and the *Catechism of the Catholic Church*.[65]

In effect, a lot is said in scripture about the mission of the angels, but very little about their *nature*. Jesus told us that the angels of children "contemplate the face of God" (Mt 18:10). Sometimes they take on a human appearance (Jn 20:12, Acts 1:10) even though it is clear that their nature excludes all corporeity. In effect, though the existence and role and service of angels is well known to us through scripture, we know little of their *nature*. Nonetheless Thomas Aquinas does speak openly and extensively on angelic nature in the wider context of a general theory of being and of anthropology. His presentation is quite singular in the history of theology[66] and valid for what it is worth.[67] Probably for that reason he was called the "Angelic Doctor."

Church Fathers had already established certain analogies between the human and angelic condition,[68] and not only in respect of their intellectual and volitive life, but also because on the whole they were convinced the

64. DH 800; see P. M. Quay, "Angels and Demons: The Teachings of IV Lateran," *Theological Studies* 42 (1981): 20–45; confirmed by Pius XII, *Humanae Generis*, Encyclical Letter, August 12, 1950 (DH 3891).

65. See Paul VI, *Creed of the People of God*, Motu proprio *Solemni hac liturgia*, June 30, 1968, pars. 8 and 29; John Paul II, General Audiences, July 9 to August 20, 1986; CCC, nos. 328–54.

66. Something of a kind may be found in Maximus the Confessor: see J. Gavin, *"They are like the angels in the heavens": Angelology and Anthropology in the Thought of Maximus the Confessor* (Rome: Institutum Patristicum Augustinianum, 2009).

67. See Thomas Aquinas, *De spiritualibus creaturis* and *ST* I, qq. 50–64 and 106–14. As regards the teaching of Aquinas on angels, see Mondin, *Gli abitanti del cielo*, 54–63; L. Zerbi, *Gli angeli* (Milan: Majocchi, 1870); J. Collins, *The Thomistic Philosophy of the Angels* (Washington, D.C.: The Catholic University of America Press, 1947); E. L. Rousseau, "Essence and *Supposit* in the Angels according to St Thomas," *Modern Schoolman* 33 (1956): 241–56; H. P. Kainz, *"Active and Passive Potency" in Thomistic Angelology* (The Hague: Nijhoff, 1972); J.-M. Vernier, *Les anges chez saint Thomas d'Aquin: Fondements historiques et principes philosophiques* (Paris: NEL, 1986); G. N. Casey, "Angelic Interiority," *Irish Philosophical Journal* 6, no. 1 (1989): 82–118, with a reply of H. P. Kainz, "Angelology, Metaphysics, and Intersubjectivity: A Reply to G. N. Casey," in ibid., 119–32; F. Sbaffoni, *San Tommaso d'Aquino e l'influsso degli angeli* (Bologna: ESD, 1993); T. Suarez-Nani, *Connaissance et langage des anges selon Thomas d'Aquin et Gilles de Rome* (Paris: J. Vrin, 2002); S.-T. Bonino, "L'ange e le prophète: la médiation angélique de la révélation prophétique selon Saint Thomas d'Aquin," *Revue Thomiste* 107 (2008): 531–71, and his *Angels and Demons*, 109–66.

68. See Mondin, *Gli abitanti dei cielo*, 37–54.

angels had a certain intrinsic corporeity besides their fundamental spiritual component.[69] They insisted on the bodily character of the angels with a view to explaining their finitude, created condition, individuality, and the distinction between them (for those who followed Aristotle), as well as allowing them to influence the material world (in keeping with the predominantly Platonic worldview of many Fathers). The first Father to insist on the complete spirituality of the angels was Gregory the Great. Even still, he added, "in comparison with our bodies, they are spirits; in comparison with the supreme and unlimited Spirit, they are bodily."[70]

Thomas Aquinas teaches that angels are creatures in the fullest sense of the word, and that they play no demiurgical role in respect of the creation of other creatures.[71] In other words they do not assist God in the creation of the world, though they do partake in the work of salvation and providence. Yet the main point he makes throughout his analysis refers to the full spirituality of the angels,[72] calling them "subsistent forms, independent of matter."[73] This doctrine has come to be accepted substantially by the church.[74] In that sense it is clear that while there is some analogy between angelic and human activity, man is simply not an angel and will never be one, insofar as he is destined to live forever with a risen corporeity.[75] Aquinas recognizes that in order to avoid Manichaean readings of creation Augustine spoke of a kind of materiality in angels with a view to ensuring their finitude and thus their created condition. But he holds that if there were no purely spiritual creatures, the created universe would not reflect in an adequate way the infinite, spiritual perfection of God.[76] From the pure spirituality of angels, Thomas draws the following significant conclusions.

69. On the history of the question (whether the angels are corporeal or exclusively spiritual), see Bonino, *Angels and Demons*, 111–21. On the question of material and angelic bodies in Augustine, see Klein, *Augustine's Theology of Angels*, 89.

70. Gregory the Great, *Moralia* 2:3.

71. See Thomas Aquinas, *ST* I, q. 45, a. 5, ad 1.

72. See ibid., q. 50, a. 2.

73. Ibid., a. 5, co.

74. See CCC, no. 328. Before Aquinas, see Lateran Council IV (DH 800). In CCC, no. 330 we read: "As purely spiritual creatures angels have intelligence and will: they are personal and immortal creatures, surpassing in perfection all visible creatures, as the splendor of their glory bears witness." A. Ara, "A proposito dell'immaterialità angelica," *Vivens Homo* 17 (2006): 95–108, disagrees with this position.

75. See O'Callaghan, *Christ Our Hope*, 100–102.

76. See Thomas Aquinas, *Comp. Theol.* 74; *ST* I, q. 50, a. 1.

First, because angels are completely spiritual, there is no reason why there should not be an enormous *number* of them in existence,[77] as scripture seems to indicate.[78] Second, the *finitude* of angels does not derive from matter (hylomorphism), but rather from the composition of act and potency present in every creature.[79] Unlike God who is pure act, the actions of angels are finite not because they are material, but because they do not exhaust their potency, and therefore their nature is finite. Third, the *individuation* of angels does not arise from matter as with other creatures—Aquinas attributes individuation of material creatures to the *materia quantitate signata,* "matter marked by quantity"—but because each angel belongs to a different *species.*[80] This surprising affirmation means that angels do not have a common angelic nature, as humans have a human one, a nature shared by their incarnate Savior. Thomas founds his explanation of the different species for each angel for each one on the doctrine of the hierarchy among angels.[81]

Fourth, from their spirituality Thomas deduces the *immortality* of angels.[82] As there is no composition between matter and form, they cannot corrupt. Jesus himself, speaking of the angels, said that in the future life the risen "cannot die any more, because they are equal to angels" (*isaggelos,* a New Testament *hapax legomenon,* or once-off term) (Lk 20:36). Of course the angels do not possess the essential immutability that only belongs to God (1 Tm 6:16). In fact, being creatures, they can make progress in knowledge and holiness, even though there is no material time as we know it, but rather what Aquinas calls *aevum.*[83] And because they are incorruptible they are therefore immortal.

Fifth, angels are not localized in *any particular place,* in the sense of a possible material and spatial circumscription.[84] For this reason empirical

77. See *ST* I, q. 50, a. 3.

78. See Dn 7:10; Lk 2:13, 8:30; Mt 26:53; Heb 12:22; Rv 5:11. According to Gregory the Great (*Moralia* 17:13), the phrase "thousands of thousands" used by the prophet Daniel (7:10) means that the number of angels, though finite for God, is, nonetheless, incalculable for us.

79. See Thomas Aquinas, *SCG* III.53. Rousseau, "Essence and *Supposit*"; Kainz, "'Active and Passive Potency' in Thomistic Angelology."

80. See Thomas Aquinas, *ST* I, q. 50, a. 4.

81. See ibid., q. 112, a. 4.

82. See ibid., q. 50, a. 5.

83. See ibid., q. 10, aa. 5–6.

84. See ibid., q. 52.

science is simply unable to deny or declare their existence. Angels can act on material things, in a way that is vaguely analogous to the way in which the soul acts on the body.[85] Their presence and location in the world is *not circumscribed* but *operative*. They do not enjoy divine omnipresence, of course, and therefore cannot act simultaneously in every place at the same time. Nonetheless, liturgical art has always depicted angels as winged creatures, in this way indicating their great agility or speed of movement.[86]

In the sixth place, Aquinas holds that angelic *intelligence* is clearly different from human intelligence on account of its perfect spirituality.[87] It is not like God's intelligence, which is identified with the divine substance, nor like the discursive or rational intelligence humans have. Their minds work in an intuitive way, immediately and without the support of organic memory or imagination. Because they have no senses they come to know things only by what Thomas calls infused intelligible species, received from God or from superior angels.[88] They do not know God in his essence but only indirectly either through known created things, or through direct divine illumination.[89] They can receive the gift of the beatific vision as humans do through the infusion of the *lumen gloriae*, the light of glory.

Seventh and finally, their *will* corresponds to their intelligence,[90] but without the obscure and unknown imperfections present in humans. Hence they act in a clear, lucid, instantaneous, and definitive way. They are unable to repent, and as scripture seems to indicate, they are amazed at the changeable quality of the human will (Lk 15:10) which is capable of repentance. *Tremunt videntes angeli versam vicem mortalium*: "the angels shudder and tremble seeing how the fate of mortal humans has changed."[91]

The French writer Paul Claudel put it in the following poetic way:

85. See ibid., q. 51, and q. 52, a. 3. Thomas says that "All corporal things are governed by the angels" (q. 110, a. 1).

86. See ibid., q. 53.

87. See ibid., qq. 54–55.

88. See ibid., qq. 56–58.

89. On communication between angels, see H. J. M. J. Goris, "The Angelic Doctor and Angelic Speech: The Development of Thomas Aquinas' Thought on How Angels Communicate," *Medieval Philosophy and Theology* 11 (2003): 1–19.

90. See Thomas Aquinas, *ST* I, qq. 59–61.

91. Divine Office of Readings, Easter season, hymn *Aeterne rex altissime*, in *Graduale Romanum* (Vatican City: Libreria Editrice Vaticana, 1974), 855.

The Angel ... has nothing to learn: he knows, he exists while looking. That is why the Prophet, who compares them to wheels, says that "the whole body of these wheels was covered with eyes" (Ezek 1:18).... There is no veil. Nothing in the Angel is opposed to the realization of the person, of that for which he is made, neither ignorance, nor weakness, nor obstacle of any kind. Consciousness occupies everything and immediately becomes a will like the circle in the circuit. The role is for him the same thing as existence. He breathes the Inspirer inexhaustibly. Vision in him provokes such a draw on the will, the Spirit tugs at the Spirit with such a stiffness that, in the coherence of all its infinitely complex rhythmic elements, there springs directly from the Nothingness the pronunciation of this admirable name, of this unquenchable being.[92]

The Role of the Angels in Spirituality and the Pastoral Life of the Church

Although the role of angels is central throughout scripture and in the life of the church, indeed in religions in general,[93] their place in Christian thought and devotion has diminished somewhat over recent centuries.[94] The existence and action of the angels was not an issue for Reformation theologians. Calvin said that faith in the angels is "supremely necessary in order to reject many errors."[95] But it has become decidedly secondary for Protestants in recent times.[96] Besides, several philosophers, among them Hobbes and Voltaire, were skeptical about their existence and activity, teaching that angels and demons are the product of human fantasy.[97] The liberal Protestant theologian Friedrich Schleiermacher, at the begin-

92. P. Claudel, "Notes sur les anges," in his *Présence et prophétie*, 225–301, at 243–44.

93. See *Geni, angeli e dèmoni: Egitto, Babilonia, Israël, Islam, Popoli altaici, India, Birmania, S. E. Asiatico, Tibet* (Rome: Ed. Mediterranea, 1994).

94. G. Bof, "Angeli," in *Nuovo Dizionario di Teología* (ed. Barbaglio and Dianich), 1933–45; R. Berzosa Martínez, *Ángeles y demonios: sentido de su retorno en nuestros días* (Madrid: BAC, 1996).

95. See John Calvin, *Institutions* I, 14:3.

96. Schleiermacher writes: "The Confessions of the Protestant Church have accepted these conceptions only incidentally, and the statements show clearly enough that they place no value on any teaching about angels. This does not in the least mean that the Reformers were unfamiliar with the subject or doubted the literal truth of the angelic appearances in the Biblical narratives: their Church hymns prove the contrary, but in the sphere of piety they attached no great value to the matter." F. D. E. Schleiermacher, *The Christian Faith* (Edinburgh: T. and T. Clark, 1948), §42, 158.

97. See T. Hobbes, *Leviathan* IV, 34; F. M. Voltaire, *The Philosophical Dictionary* (London: Wynn and Scholey, 1802), 6–9. Voltaire was skeptical about angels; see Bonino, *Angels and Demons*, 94–96.

ning of the nineteenth century, openly questioned their efficacy and spiritual relevance.[98] The principal difficulties in modern times have arisen in the context of the demythologizing projects of the biblical exegete Rudolf Bultmann and others. He has the following to say: "It is impossible to use electric light and the wireless and to avail ourselves of modern medical and surgical discoveries, and at the same time to believe in the New Testament world of spirits and miracles."[99] That is, there is no place for angels in the Christian *kerygma.*

Karl Barth does speak of the importance of angels in the history of salvation, but says that they are not persons, and are inferior to humans.[100] Paul Tillich says that angels are "concrete-poetic symbols of the structures or powers of being. They are not beings but participate in everything that is."[101] Karl Rahner defends the existence of angels but denies their pastoral relevance: "from the kerygmatic point of view there is no necessity at the present moment to place truths concerning the angels particularly in the foreground of preaching and instruction."[102]

It is true that Christians over the centuries have been somewhat hasty and injudicious in attributing exceptional atmospheric and pathological conditions in the world and in persons to the direct action of angels or demons. Nowadays certainly believers habitually seek out an empirical and scientific explanation for unexplained phenomena. Yet Christians do not believe in the existence and action of angels on account of empirical evidence; angels, being purely spiritual beings, do not enter the "radar" of human sensibility and intelligibility. We come to know of their existence only indirectly, principally through revelation and faith. Angelic action may be tangible or empirical but we are not in a position of knowing if it is truly angelic. Besides, whereas the existence of God can be demonstrated on a metaphysical basis,[103] that of the angels cannot, because as creatures

98. "The only tenet which can be established as a doctrine concerning angels is this: that the question whether the angels exist or not ought to have no influence upon our conduct, and that revelations of their existence are now no longer to be expected." Schleiermacher, *The Christian Faith*, §143, 159.

99. R. Bultmann, *Kerygma und Mythos* (Hamburg: Herbert Reich, 1954), 1:17 (author's translation). On the demythologizing of scripture in respect of the angels, see Bonino, *Angels and Demons*, 97–101.

100. See Barth, *Church Dogmatics III/3*. See also M. Lindsay, "The Heavenly Witness to God: Karl Barth's Doctrine of Angels," *Scottish Journal of Theology* 70, no. 1 (2017): 1–18.

101. P. Tillich, *Systematic Theology I* (Chicago: University of Chicago Press, 1953), 260.

102. K. Rahner, "Angels," in *Encyclopedia of Theology: The Concise Sacramentum mundi*, ed. K. Rahner (New York: Crossroad, 1982), 4–13, at 13.

103. See Thomas Aquinas, *ST* I, q. 2, a. 3.

they are completely contingent, not necessary. There is no necessary reason why they should exist. Empirically we could only say they exist should we encounter them as subsistent beings, and of course we only encounter their action. Historically however it is interesting to note that whenever faith in the angels diminishes, faith in God also declines.[104] Still, in the words of Johann Auer, "in attempting to get rid of the angels, we would need to make a complete revision of Sacred Scripture, and with it the entire history of salvation."[105]

One might ask why angels do not show their power, make more noise, make themselves seen. It should be kept in mind of course that they live in order to give praise to God, and so serve other creatures in obedience to the will of God. "God made angels for love, because he wished there to be beings who would rejoice in the richness of his glory and draw their happiness from that.... The first and supreme creatures live out their existence not only in a sense of wonderment which overwhelms them, but even more as an adoration that overflows, in a love that gives itself entirely, in a service that spends itself."[106] "The Old Testament especially emphasizes the special participation of the angels in the celebration of the glory which the creator receives as a tribute of praise on the part of the created world."[107] Divine praise, giving glory to God, is the "noise" that the angels make, "the rumor of angels" as Peter Berger called it.[108] For the angels the task of praising God completely supersedes the rest, in that way manifesting the glory of God in the clearest way possible. Pagan divinities, often compared with angels, live in a completely different way, because they strive to draw the attention of humans to themselves, not to God. But the angels strive to direct our attention to God. Perhaps to them could be applied the words of the Sermon on the Mount: "Let your light so shine before men, that they may see your good works and give glory to your Father who is in heaven" (Mt 5:16). Acting in this way they probably achieve much more in our lives than we imagine they are doing.

John Paul II in his catechesis says the following:

104. Auer, *Die Welt – Gottes Schöpfung*, 387.

105. Ibid., 388 (author's translation).

106. Ibid., 411–12 (author's translation).

107. John Paul II, "Creator of Things Unseen: The Angels," par. 2.

108. See P. L. Berger, *A Rumour of Angels: Modern Society and the Rediscovery of the Supernatural* (London: Penguin, 1969).

Providence, as the loving Wisdom of God, was manifested precisely in the creation of purely spiritual beings, so as to express better the likeness of God in them. They are superior to all that is created in the visible world, including man, who is also the indelible image of God. God who is absolutely perfect Spirit, is reflected especially in spiritual beings which by nature, that is, by reason of their spirituality, are nearer to him than material creatures.... Sacred Scripture ... has inspired the poetry and art of the Christian centuries which present the angels to us as the "court of God."[109]

A decline of devotion to the angels among Christian faithful may also derive from the perception of an excess of mediations between the world and God. As believers we are convinced that we have a "direct line" to God, who is our Father and with whom we can converse continually (Lk 18:1). Protestant theology, though historically it did not doubt the existence nor deny the action of angels, put that teaching under strain by relativizing the role of created mediations.[110] Of course at an absolute level, God stands in no need of mediators, not only for creation, but also for salvation. Charles Taylor speaks of the passage in modern times from a *porous or embedded identity,* in which other beings—both spiritual and material—are constantly present and intervene, to a *buffered self* which seals us off from the interventions and power of other beings.[111]

Still, we should remember how mediations make creation more harmonious and beautiful, and express the fact that God is a communion of persons.[112] In that sense John Paul II said that

the truth about the angels is in a certain sense "collateral," though inseparable from the central revelation, which is the existence, the majesty and the glory of the Creator which shines forth in all creation ... and in God's salvific action in the history of the world. The angels are not creatures of the first order, in the reality of revelation. However, they fully belong to it, so much so that sometimes we see them carrying out fundamental tasks in the name of God himself.[113]

When the role of objective mediations is marginalized, humans may come to consider themselves capable of establishing a relationship with God

109. John Paul II, "Creator of All Things, Seen and Unseen," General Audience, July 9, 1986, par. 4.
110. See Tavard, *Die Engel,* §24.
111. See Taylor, *A Secular Age.*
112. See O'Callaghan, *Children of God in the World,* 369–74.
113. John Paul II, "Creator of All Things, Seen and Unseen," par. 3.

with their own powers. For mediations share in the gift-quality of grace itself. In real terms Christians are always deeply in need of the help and accompaniment of their fellow-creatures, both spiritual and material. Historically, observes Johann Auer, "whenever little or nothing has been said about the angels, the consideration of the relationship between Creator and creature has occasioned views close to *pantheism or deism,* two doctrines that disfigure the image divine revelation has of God."[114]

Church Teaching on the Devil and Demons

From the witness of scripture, the church has always held to the existence of evil spirits, fallen angels, called the devil, or demons, or Satan, who, though created by God as angels, "good in nature, they have become wicked by themselves. But man sinned at the suggestion of the devil,"[115] as the Fourth Lateran Council says. The latter doctrine was taught to counter the Gnostic position of the Cathars who held that the devil is *natively* evil and perverse. This of course would contradict the original goodness of all creation.[116] The fact is that idolatry and polytheism in pagan religions induced people to consistently accept the existence of intermediate divinities, some of which were a source of comfort and assistance, and others of evil and corruption. Christian teaching however holds that all creatures, without exception, depend completely for their existence on an all-powerful, good God, and in themselves are good at an ontological level. Some have fallen due to the perversion of the will. Athanasius says: "the demons have not been created in a way indicated by the name we give them; for God made nothing evil, and even they have been made good. From the time they have fallen, however, from the heavenly wisdom, they have been groveling on the earth."[117]

This teaching[118] has been confirmed by recent church documents

114. Auer, *Die Welt – Gottes Schöpfung,* 430.

115. DH 800. Other official church texts include DH 1347, 1521, 1541, 1668, 1694, 1696.

116. See Quay, "Angels and Demons."

117. Athanasius, *De vita Antoni* 22.

118. See J. Daniélou, *Théologie du Judéo-Christianisme* (Paris: Desclée, 1958), 167–96; G. Biffi, *La bella, la bestia e il cavaliere: Saggio di teologia inattuale* (Milan: Jaca Book, 1984), 84–91; W. Kasper and K. Lehmann (eds.), *Diavolo – Demoni – Possessione* (Brescia: Queriniana, 1985); G. Salvini, "La fede cristiana e il diavolo," *Civiltà Cattolica* 3270 (1986): 90–100; G. H. Tavard, *Satan* (Paris: Desclée, 1988);

and popes: Vatican II documents,[119] Paul VI,[120] John Paul II,[121] Benedict XVI,[122] and Francis.[123] A detailed study entitled *Christian Faith and Demonology* was prepared in 1975 under the auspices of the Congregation for the Doctrine of the Faith.[124] It should be noted, however, that the church has never really wanted to give excessive importance to the devil and his angels. As C. S. Lewis said, "There are two equal and opposite errors into which our race can fall about the devils. One is to disbelieve in their existence. The other is to believe, and to feel an excessive and unhealthy interest in them. They themselves are equally pleased by both errors and hail a materialist or a magician with the same delight."[125] And in the document *Christian Faith and Demonology,* just mentioned, we read: "It would . . . be incorrect to hold that Christianity, forgetful of the universal Lordship of Christ, had at any time made Satan the privileged subject of its preaching, transforming the Good News of the Risen Lord into a message of terror."[126]

The Devil and Demons in Sacred Scripture

Scripture gives ample witness to the existence and activity of the devil and demons.[127]

SATAN AND DEMONS IN THE OLD TESTAMENT

The Old Testament speaks of a malevolent spirit, the enemy of God and of man, in a wide variety of ways. Nonetheless, teaching about the devil is

---

J. Galot, "Satan," *Esprit et Vie* (April 13, 1989): 209–16; Mondin, *Gli abitanti del cielo*, 200–315; Marconcini et al., *Angeli e demoni.*

119. See Vatican Council II, *Ad Gentes,* December 7, 1965, nos. 3 and 14; *GS,* no. 37b; Vatican Council II, *Lumen Gentium,* November 21, 1964, nos. 35a and 48d.

120. See especially Paul VI's General Audiences of June 29 and November 15, 1972.

121. John Paul II, "The Fall of the Rebellious Angels" and "Christ's Victory Conquers Evil," General Audiences, August 13 and 20, 1986.

122. See Benedict XVI, "Homily at the Conclusion of the Year for Priests, Solemnity of the Sacred Heart," June 11, 2010.

123. See Pope Francis, "Morning Meditation," October 30, 2014.

124. Congregation for the Doctrine of the Faith, *Christian Faith and Demonology,* June 26, 1975. The document was prepared by a group of theologians.

125. C. S. Lewis, *The Screwtape Letters* (San Francisco, Calif.: HarperSanFrancisco, 2001), preface.

126. *Christian Faith and Demonology,* preface.

127. S. Lyonnet, "Le Démon dans l'Ecriture," *Dictionnaire de Spiritualité,* vol. 3 (1957), 141–52. See also BDAG 226, s.v. διάβολος; *NIDNTTE* 1:691, s.v. διάβολος.

not a central aspect of scripture. This is so first because the devil is not considered a principal protagonist of the history of salvation, but a decidedly secondary one. God, in Christ, is the prime protagonist, as is God's people, and humans in general. Second, the Old Testament drastically disapproves of any kind of idolatry. Of course a particular emphasis on the existence and activity of demons could easily move in that direction.

Of particular interest from the literary and theological point of view is the following poem in the Book of Isaiah which provides interesting material to understand the situation, the fall, and punishment of the devil.

> How you are fallen from heaven, O Day Star [literally, the "shining one," rendered as *Lucifer*], son of Dawn! How you are cut down to the ground, you who laid the nations low! You said in your heart, "I will ascend to heaven; above the stars of God I will set my throne on high; I will sit on the mount of assembly in the far north; I will ascend above the heights of the clouds, I will make myself like the Most High." But you are brought down to Sheol, to the depths of the Pit (Is 14:12–15).

The text clearly refers to the tyrants who were responsible for the exile in Babylon.[128] Still, given the use of different parts of the text in the New Testament (especially Luke, John, and the Book of Revelation, as well as the prophet Daniel)[129] and in the Church Fathers, it provides useful elements to understand the nature and *modus operandi* of the devil. Besides, it would seem that there was a keen awareness of demons and diabolic possession among the Jews at the time of Jesus.[130]

CHRIST AND THE DEVIL IN THE NEW TESTAMENT

In the New Testament a variety of images portrays the existence and activity of the devil and the fallen angels. Between diabolic activity and the establishment and development of the kingdom of God by Jesus there is open opposition. The latter says: "If it is by the Spirit of God that I cast out demons, then the kingdom of God has come upon you" (Mt 12:28). Frequently found are terms such as "evil spirits" (Acts 19:15) and "impure spir-

128. See J. D. W. Watts, *Isaiah 1–33* (Waco, Tex.: Word Books, 1985), 264.

129. See Dn 10:13; 11:36; Lk 10:15, 18; Jn 12:31; Rv 2:28; 8:10; 9:1; 12:9.

130. See M. García Cordero, "Los espíritus malignos según las creencias judías del tiempo de Jesús," *Ciencia Tomista* 116 (1989): 417–56.

its."[131] The term *daimōn* (from which comes the English word "demon") is the Septuagint translation of these terms (1 Sm 16:14, 23).[132] *Daimōn* is also used in the New Testament, especially in Matthew's Gospel (8:31, 9:34, 12:24).[133] Derived from the term *daiones*, "divine beings," the demons nonetheless are not considered as truly divine, but created.

The Old Testament on several occasions uses the Hebrew term *Satanas*, especially in the Book of Job, in which the devil is presented as an inspector of humanity, his tempter and the one who tests his fidelity (Jb 1:6–9, 12; 2:1–4, 6–7). In Zechariah 3, Satan is said to accuse the priest Joshua before God, but he is defended by an angel. The term means adversary, calumniator, accuser, and therefore enemy of God and man. It is usually translated as *diabolos*,[134] a Greek term which means divide, to break into two (*dia / ballo*), from which comes "devil." Satan is the great calumniator, the source of all division, the one who breaks up unity.

But *Satanas* is also used in the New Testament as a proper name. Satan is considered "the prince of demons" (Mk 3:22). During Jesus' temptations in the desert, the term *diabolos* is used habitually, but to the tempter Jesus uses the proper Hebrew name: "Get behind me, Satan! For it is written, 'You shall worship the Lord your God and him only shall you serve'" (Mt 4:10). In fact Peter himself was called Satan by Jesus when he attempted to readjust the teaching and mission of the Master: "Get behind me, Satan!" (Mt 16:23). Satan is described in the Book of Revelation as the one "who accuses them [our brethren] day and night before our God" (Rv 12:10). It also speaks of the dragon or the ancient serpent (Rv 12:3, 9; 13:2), confirming in this way the diabolic identity of the tempter of Eve (Gn 3:1). It is interesting to note that in the Book of Job the accusing action is determined by Satan's *envy* of humans (Jb 1), although he is ultimately incapable of following through on his threats, for which he always requires divine permission. Jesus spoke of the power exercised in his name by the apostles: "The seventy returned with joy, saying, 'Lord, even the demons are subject to us in your name!' And he said to them, 'I saw Satan fall like lightning from heaven'" (Lk 10:17).

131. Mt 10:1; Lk 4:36; 6:18; Acts 8:7.

132. See *NIDNTTE* 1:631–33, s.v. δαίμων.

133. To be precise, "the noun δαίμων occurs only once (Matt 8:31 [in the plural]; also in a few other passages), whereas δαιμόνιον is used more than 60x (all but 10 in the Gospels)" (ibid., 632).

134. *NIDNTTE* 4:267–68, s.v. Σατάν.

Our knowledge of the existence and activity of the devil "and his angels" (Mt 25:41) derives not only nor even principally from the biblical texts and from our reflection on the mystery of evil, but above all from the words and works of Christ, who presented himself as the tireless and unconditional adversary of the devil, his mission being that of defeating him once and for all. In effect, the life of Jesus constitutes a continuous battle against the devil. The fact that the devil is thrown out is a sign that the kingdom of God is active (Lk 11:20). On many occasions Jesus casts out demons (Mt 7:22; 8:16, 31; 9:34; 10:8; 12:24, 27). Even though Satan is designated by Jesus as "ruler of this world" (Jn 16:11), the power of Christ is by far superior and of another order. By means of the cross that is the obedience of Jesus to the Father, the devil "will be cast out" (Jn 12:31). As regards diabolic activity, Jesus speaks of him as the one who sows the weeds amidst the wheat (Mt 13:25, 28, 39), who robs the word of God from the hearts of humans (Mt 13:19) and, above all, strives to draw humans away from their faith in him. He calls the unbelieving Jews "sons of the devil," and says:

> Why do you not understand what I say? It is because you cannot bear to hear my word. You are of your father the devil [*diabolos*], and your will is to do your father's desires. He was a murderer from the beginning, and has nothing to do with the truth, because there is no truth in him. When he lies, he speaks according to his own nature, for he is a liar and the father of lies (Jn 8:43).

The same message is to be found in 1 John 3:8: "He who commits sin is of the devil; for the devil has sinned from the beginning."

According to these Johannine texts, two specific marks may be attributed to the work of the devil.[135] First, that he is "a liar and the father of lies."[136] As John Paul says:

> These texts help us to understand the nature and the dimension of the sin of Satan. It consists in the denial of the truth about God, as he is known by the light of the intellect and revelation as infinite Good, subsistent Love and Holiness. The sin was all the greater, in that the spiritual perfection and the episte-

135. See J. Giblet, "La puissance satanique selon l'Evangile de Jean," in H. Limet and J. Ries (eds.), *Anges et démons: actes du colloque de Liège et de Louvain-la-Neuve* (Louvain-la-Neuve: Centre d'histoire des religions, 1989), 291–300.

136. On the demonology of John, see A. González, "La demonología del cuarto evangelio," *Miscelánea Comillas* 48 (1967): 21–40.

mological acuteness of the angelic intellect, with its freedom and closeness to God, were greater. When, by an act of his own free will, he rejected the truth that he knew about God, Satan became the cosmic "liar and the father of lies" (Jn 8:44). For this reason he lives in radical and irreversible denial of God, and seeks to impose on creation—on the other beings created in the image of God, and in particular on people—his own tragic "lie about the good" that is God. In the Book of Genesis, we find a precise description of this lie, a falsification of the truth about God, which Satan (under the form of a serpent) tried to transmit to the first representatives of the human race—God is jealous of his own prerogatives and therefore wants to impose limitations on man (cf. Gn 3:5). Satan invites the man to free himself from the impositions of this yoke, by making himself, "like God."[137]

In tempting humans the devil attempts to twist and manipulate the truth, especially about God. His activity is the ultimate "fake news." Nonetheless, there is nothing automatic in the devil's activity, for humans are still responsible for their own transgressions. "It is not the devil but men's own carelessness which causes all their falls and all the ills of which they complain,"[138] Chrysostom says.

And second, Jesus presents the devil as the "murderer from the beginning," the one who destroys life. John Paul comments:

In this condition of existential falsehood, Satan—according to St. John—also becomes a "murderer." That is, he is one who destroys the supernatural life which God had made to dwell from the beginning in him and in the creatures made "in the likeness of God"—the other pure spirits and men. Satan wishes to destroy life lived in accordance with the truth, life in the fullness of good, the supernatural life of grace and love. The author of the Book of Wisdom wrote: "Death has entered the world through the envy of the devil, and those who belong to him experience it" (Wis 2:24).[139]

The devil not only attempts to separate humans from God and from one another, but he strives, besides, to introduce the power of death and corruption into the world.

137. John Paul II, "The Fall of the Rebellious Angels," par. 5.
138. John Chrysostom, *De Diab. Temptatore, hom.* 2.
139. John Paul II, "The Fall of the Rebellious Angels," par. 6.

The Existence of the Devil and the Fallen Angels

Throughout history there have been obvious exaggerations in respect of the extension and power of diabolic activity and possession. The notion of "the rights of the devil" was proposed to explain the enslavement humans suffer on account of sin. It was said that Jesus, dying on the cross, ceded his life to the devil so as to redeem us from his power. These theories, suggested by Origen and others,[140] never entered the theological mainstream.[141] Still, the malefic power of the devil over humans was generally affirmed by Church Fathers and theologians.[142]

But in modern times the existence and activity of the devil have frequently been contested, relativized, or even denied. The biblical texts cited above are interpreted in a mythical, poetic, or exhortative way.[143] Evil is commonly accounted for in terms of the limited ontological structure of reality, in spite of the fact that this easily leads to dualism or to a denial of evil. It is suggested that the discourse on the devil is simply a cipher for the ills that afflict humans; the devil therefore would not be at the origin of evil in man but the other way around: evil in man would be at the source of the invented "existence" of the devil, whom we project outside ourselves as a kind of scapegoat.[144]

The church and especially the popes have spoken with remarkable in-

140. See Origen, *In Rm.* 2:13 and 3:7; *In Io.* 1, 39; *In Exodo* 6:9. On the question in general, see J. Rivière, *Le dogme de la Rédemption: Essai d'étude historique* (Paris: V. Lecoffre, 1905), 373–486, and *Le dogme de la Rédemption: études critiques & documents* (Louvain: Bureaux de la Revue, 1931), 165–214, esp. 200–203.

141. Gregory Nazianzen, *Oratio* 45:22, opposed the theory.

142. John Chrysostom rejected the position of those who said that "it is not the devil but personal carelessness of humans that causes all their falls and all the misfortunes they complain about" (*De Diab. Temptatore, hom.* 2).

143. See for example H. Haag, *Abschied vom Teufel: Vom christlichen Umgang mit de Bösen* (Düsseldorf: Patmos, 2000). See the critique by J. Ratzinger, "Farewell to the Devil," in his *Dogma and Preaching* (San Francisco, Calif.: Ignatius Press, 2011), 197–205. "Haag bids the devil farewell, not in his capacity as exegete or interpreter of Scripture, but rather as a contemporary, who considers the existence of the devil untenable.... [He] judges *contrary* to the biblical text, on the basis of *his* notions, what is supposed to be 'compatible' with modern thinking. But things are not quite that simple, for in the Bible there are in fact statements that cannot be included in its faith testimony but must be described as the framing world view within which the actual thought is expressed" (198). See also the negative review of Haag by L. Scheffczyk in *Münchener Theologische Zeitschrift* 26 (1975): 387–96.

144. The Book of Leviticus speaks of the devil who inhabits the desert (*háza'zel*), to which is sent the scapegoat who carries the sins of the people (16:8, 10, 26).

sistence on the devil's existence and activity, noticeably so in recent decades. In 1972 Paul VI spoke memorably of the "smoke of Satan filtering through the cracks and the crevices of the Church."[145] Commenting on the expression "deliver us from evil" in the *Our Father* he offered the following graphic description of diabolic temptation:

> The refusal to recognize it [the devil] moves out of the framework of Biblical and ecclesiastical teaching; that is, whoever makes it [the devil] a principle in its own right, not having, like every creature, its origin in God; or explaining it as a pseudo-reality, a conceptual and fantastic personification of the unknown causes of our ailments.... We can suppose its sinister action where the denial of God becomes radical, subtle and absurd, where lying becomes hypocritical and powerful, against the obvious truth, where love is extinguished by a cold and cruel egoism, where the name Christ is challenged by a conscious and rebellious hatred [1 Cor 16:22; 12:3], where the spirit of the Gospel is mystified and disproved, where despair is affirmed as the last word, etc.[146]

Likewise John Paul II spoke of the devil in audiences we have already cited. So also has Benedict XVI referred to the activity of the devil,[147] as has Pope Francis on many occasions with notable insistence.[148] This doctrine may be found also in the 1998 *Ritual of Exorcisms.*

The Fall of the Devil and the Temptation of Humanity

Scripture tells us that the devil was created as a good angel, but that he fell and sinned.[149] And throughout history he attempts to infect humans with his own disgrace.

145. Paul VI, "Essere forti nella fede," Homily, September 29, 1972, in *Insegnamenti Paolo VI* 10 (1972): 707.

146. Paul VI, "Free Us from Evil," General Audience, November 15, 1972.

147. See Benedict XVI, General Audiences of February 17 and March 13, 2011. See also the review of the book of H. Haag mentioned above.

148. Pope Francis refers to the devil with notable frequency and clarity. In a morning meditation on November 30, 2014, he said: "To think that some people have attempted to make us think 'that the devil is a myth, an image, an idea, the idea of evil.' Whereas 'the devil exists and we should struggle against him.' St. Paul reminds us of this, 'the word of God tells us so,' but even still, it would seem 'that we are not quite convinced' of this reality."

149. Among the texts indicating the fall of the angels may be included Jb 4:18; Is 14:12–15; Ezek 28:12–19; Mt 25:41; 2 Pt 2:4; Rv 12:9.

THE FALL OF SATAN

What kind of sin did the devil commit that turned him into a liar and a murderer, into what Irenaeus called "an apostate angel"?[150] A few suggestions may cast light on this mysterious fall in a highly intelligent spiritual being, superior in the natural sphere to all humans."

First, scripture speaks of a clear opposition between the role of the archangel Michael (which means "who is like God?") and the *non serviam* ("I will not serve," Jer 2:20) attributed to Satan (Dn 10:13–14, 12:1), a disobedience to God that is rooted in pride. The Book of Revelation describes this mysterious battle between Michael and the devil, the latter under the guise of the "dragon," as follows:

> Now war arose in heaven, Michael and his angels fighting against the dragon; and the dragon and his angels fought, but they were defeated and there was no longer any place for them in heaven. And the great dragon was thrown down, that ancient serpent, who is called the Devil and Satan, the deceiver of the whole world—he was thrown down to the earth, and his angels were thrown down with him (Rv 12:7–9).

Second, the temptations Jesus undergoes in the desert (Mt 4:1–11) indicate something of the nature of the devil's own fall. Benedict XVI asks:

> What is the essence of the three temptations to which Jesus is subjected? It is the proposal to exploit God, to use him for one's own interests, for one's own glory and for one's own success. And therefore, essentially to put oneself in God's place, removing him from one's own existence and making him seem superfluous. Each one of us must therefore ask him- or herself: what place does God have in my life? Is he the Lord or am I?[151]

The devil essentially renounced the Lordship of God and sought to be worshipped in his place (Mt 4:9).

Third, the devil was the one to instigate the death of Jesus; speaking to the chief priest, officers, and elders, Jesus called the moment of own his arrest "your hour and the power of darkness" (Lk 22:53), an expression that refers to the action of the devil (Mt 22:3; Acts 26:18). In tempting

150. Irenaeus, *Adv. Haer.* V, 24, 3.
151. Benedict XVI, "General Audience," February 13, 2013.

humans the devil attempts to murder, to eliminate the life of grace, the life of Christ in the believer, to kill Christ himself. The devil in inspiring the death of Christ sought to destroy the Word incarnate, he attempted to wreck the mediation through which salvation comes to us in human flesh, in that way actively seeking out the perpetual separation of God and humans. With some Church Fathers it may be said that the sin of the angels, like that of humans, was one of rejecting the Christ, of not believing in the Word who would be made incarnate.[152] Perhaps the devil wished to retain a kind of angelic monopoly of mediation over creation. Irenaeus speaks of the sin of devil saying it was rooted in his envy for the creation of humans.[153] That naturally inferior human beings could be supernaturally superior to the devil and his angels would be intolerable. This may be applied to the devil's attempts to destroy the priesthood. Benedict XVI said during the year of priests (2010): "It was to be expected that this new radiance of the priesthood would not be pleasing to the 'enemy'. . . . He would have rather preferred to see it disappear, so that God would ultimately be driven out of the world."[154]

Fourth and lastly, scripture emphasizes the total opposition between the Virgin Mary and the devil, already indicated in the Book of Genesis: "I will put enmity between you and the woman, and between your seed and her seed; he shall bruise your head, and you shall bruise his heel" (Gn 3:15).[155] The same idea is proposed in the Book of Revelation (12:1–6), a text that refers directly to church and people of Israel, and on that basis to Mary. With her unconditional acceptance of God's will and call, and in spite of a keen awareness of her own limited human nature (Lk 1:48), inferior to that of the angels, Mary was the one who made the incarnation possible, and so the salvation of humanity. She gave humanity to the Word, a humanity the devil wished to destroy and eliminate. And in fidelity to God's Word she became queen of heaven, not only of humans, but also of the angels. Dante Alighieri says that the angels surround Mary, calling her "the face that best resembles Christ."[156]

152. See John Chrysostom, *De Diab. Temptatore, hom.* 3:2.

153. See Irenaeus, *Adv. Haer.* VI, 11:3 and 40:3.

154. Benedict XVI, "Homily at the Conclusion of the Year for Priests, Solemnity of the Sacred Heart," June 11, 2010.

155. On this text, see C. Pozo, *María en la obra de la salvación,* 2nd ed. (Madrid: BAC, 1990), 147–75.

156. Dante Alighieri, *Paradiso* 32:85: "la facia che a Cristo più si somiglia."

As a result of his fall, the devil was condemned forever with his angels, to "everlasting fire" prepared for them (Mt 25:41).[157] The church opposed the proposal of Origen to the effect that the devil would be reconciled with God at the end of time, what is called the *apokatasasis*, or universal reconciliation. "It is the irrevocable character of their choice, and not a defect in the infinite divine mercy, that makes the angels' sin unforgivable. 'There is no repentance for the angels after their fall, just as there is no repentance for men after death.'"[158] With the angelic fall, the devil's intelligence becomes definitively obscured, while remaining angelic, intuitive, and lucid. No longer is he capable of understanding the divine logic that joins evangelical simplicity with joyful humility, unquestioning service, and the wisdom of the cross (1 Cor 1:18–25). In the deepest sense of the word he becomes a liar and murderer, for his whole identity is marked in a twisted way. He lives off hate and sterility and frustration, maliciously and pointlessly attempting to destroy life. The devil becomes obstinate in evil and attempts to communicate his own lying and murderous identity to humans. Georges Bernanos, in his *Diary of a Country Priest*, says: "I sometimes think of Satan as trying to get hold of the mind of God, and not merely hating it without understanding, but understanding it the wrong way round; thus unknowingly struggling against the current of life, instead of swimming with it: wearing himself out in absurd terrifying attempts to reconstruct in the opposite direction, the whole work of the Creator."[159]

THE TEMPTATION OF HUMANS

Peter's first letter warns Christians to be aware of temptation and the tempter: "Be sober, be watchful. Your adversary the devil prowls around like a roaring lion, seeking some one to devour" (1 Pt 5:8). Thomas Aquinas is of the opinion that the devil tempts humans not by controlling their will or intellect, but by influencing their imagination.[160] Spiritual authors commonly hold that temptation may be overcome without particular difficulty as long as believers live in the grace of God and humbly count on his help. The *Shepherd of Hermas* says: "Fearing the Lord, you will do all things

157. See O'Callaghan, *Christ Our Hope*, 192–95.

158. CCC, no. 393, citing John Damascene, *De fide orth.* 2:4.

159. G. Bernanos, *The Diary of a Country Priest* (London: Fount, 1977), 55.

160. See Thomas Aquinas, *ST* I-II, q. 80, aa. 2–3.

well. This is the fear which you ought to have, that you may be saved. But fear not the devil; for, fearing the Lord, you will have dominion over the devil, for there is no power in him. He has no power over the servants of God who place in him all their trust; do not be afraid, he [the devil] will flee from you."[161] And Ambrose says: "The Lord who cancelled your sin and forgave your guilt can protect and guard you from the snares of the devil who is your adversary, in such a way that your enemy, who attempts to bring about guilt, does not surprise you. But whoever trusts God does not fear the devil: 'If God is for us, who is against us?' (Rom 8:31)."[162]

The *Catechism of the Catholic Church* sums up this teaching as follows:

> The power of Satan is . . . not infinite. He is only a creature, powerful from the fact that he is pure spirit, but still a creature. He cannot prevent the building up of God's kingdom. Although Satan may act in the world out of hatred for God and his kingdom in Christ Jesus, and although his action may cause grave injuries—of a spiritual nature and, indirectly, even of a physical nature—to each man and to society, the action is permitted by divine providence which with strength and gentleness guides human and cosmic history. It is a great mystery that providence should permit diabolical activity, but "we know that in everything God works for good with those who love him" (Rom 8:28).[163]

The Phenomenon of Diabolic Cult and Possession

Given that the devil does tempt people and can truly influence their lives, the church has never neglected the ministry of exorcism and the phenomenon of demon-possession.[164] Just as Jesus cast out demons, the church through God's grace acts to overcome this malefic presence. The *Catechism of the Catholic Church* puts it as follows:

> When the Church asks publicly and authoritatively in the name of Jesus Christ that a person or object be protected against the power of the Evil One and withdrawn from his dominion, it is called exorcism. Jesus performed exorcisms and from him the Church has received the power and office of exorcizing [Mk 1:25–26; 3:15; 6:7, 13; 16:17]. In a simple form, exorcism is performed

161. Shepherd of Hermas, *Mandata* 7.
162. Ambrose, *De sacramentis* VI, 4:30.
163. *CCC*, no. 395.
164. See C. Balducci, *Gli indemoniati* (Rome: Coletti, 1959).

at the celebration of Baptism. The solemn exorcism, called "a major exorcism," can be performed only by a priest and with the permission of the bishop. The priest must proceed with prudence, strictly observing the rules established by the Church. Exorcism is directed at the expulsion of demons or to the liberation from demonic possession through the spiritual authority which Jesus entrusted to his Church. Illness, especially psychological illness, is a very different matter; treating this is the concern of medical science. Therefore, before an exorcism is performed, it is important to ascertain that one is dealing with the presence of the Evil One, and not an illness.[165]

Christ distinguished between ordinary illnesses and those involving demonic possession. The former were healed by the laying on of hands or by anointing, the latter by commanding the demon to depart (see, e.g., Mt 10:8; Mk 6:13; Lk 13:32; Acts 8:7, 19:12). Possession was not continuous, but when it was verified it often produced effects that were violent (Mk 9:18). Blindness and dumbness, when caused by possession, would presumably have been persistent (see Mt 9:32, 12:22).[166]

It was not infrequent in the past to attribute unrecognized medical symptoms to the malignant action of the devil: depression, schizophrenia, epilepsy, etc. Some believers perhaps were drawn by superstitious practices to attribute to the devil an excessive influence over the life of humans.[167] The saints have generally been more circumspect about doing so. Theresa of Avila asked the opinion of John of the Cross in respect of one Sister Elizabeth, apparently possessed by the devil, and was told "she has no demon, but rather an excess of melancholy."[168] Many if not most psychologists nowadays dismiss the idea of demonic possession, for example the German author T. K. Oesterreich, even at the beginning of the twentieth century.[169] He maintains that the equivalents of possession today are "a particularly extensive complex of compulsive phenomena." On the other hand, there is the classic work by J. L. Nevius, a missionary doctor in

165. *CCC*, no. 1673.

166. See J. S. Wright, "Demon Possession," in *New Bible Dictionary* (ed. Wood), 271.

167. Congregation for the Doctrine of the Faith, *Christian Faith and Demonology*, no. 1.

168. See John of the Cross, *Obras* (Burgos: El Monte Carmelo, 1922), 7:102.

169. Oesterreich's 1921 German work was published in English as *Possession, Demoniacal and Other: Among Primitive Races in Antiquity, the Middle Ages, and Modern Times* (London: Thompson Press, 2010). So also W. Sargant, *Battle for the Mind: A Physiology of Conversion and Brainwashing* (Garden City, N.Y.: Doubleday and Co., 1957) and *The Mind Possessed: A Physiology of Possession, Mysticism and Faith Healing* (Garden City, N.Y.: Doubleday and Co., 1973).

China, who looks upon demonic possession as a genuine phenomenon.[170]

It could also happen that a demon could seize on a repressed facet of someone's personality, and from this center influence a person's actions. The demon may induce hysterical blindness or dumbness, or symptoms of other illnesses, such as epilepsy. Among many peoples, epileptic fits have been traditionally regarded as a sign of possession by a spirit or a god, and indeed epileptics are often psychically sensitive. But the Bible does not link epilepsy with demonic possession, and even the description of the fits of the possessed boy (Mt 17:14; Mk 9:14; Lk 9:37), seems to indicate something more than mere epilepsy. The nature of epilepsy is still not fully understood, but it can be artificially induced in apparently normal people.[171] Students of personality disorders know that it is often impossible to say just how these are triggered in the first place. Some of these cases may be due to demonic possession.

Modern scientific discoveries have shown that the corporeal and human roots of such conditions can be successfully treated with normal medical procedures. However, the presence of diabolic cult seems to be more and more extended in the times we live in, and this indicates the need to facilitate the ministry of exorcism, in keeping with the Lord's instruction: "Heal the sick, raise the dead, cleanse those who have leprosy, drive out demons. Freely you have received, freely give" (Mt 10:8). In the words of Benedict XVI, "For this reason God sent his Son into the world: to set men and women free from the domination of Satan, 'the origin and cause of every sin.' God sent him in our mortal flesh so that he might become a victim of expiation, dying for us on the Cross."[172]

170. See J. L. Nevius, *Demon Possession and Allied Themes: Being an Inductive Study of Phenomena of Our Own Times*, 5th ed. (Chicago: Fleming H. Revell Co., 1900).

171. See for example W. G. Walter, *The Living Brain* (Harmondsworth: Penguin Books, 1961), 60.

172. Benedict XVI, "Angelus," March 13, 2011, citing the text of the renewal of baptismal promises of the Easter liturgy.

PART 3

The Mystery of Evil and Original Sin

12

A Brief History of the Doctrine of Original Sin

AT THE BEGINNING OF CHAPTER 7, I reflected on the mystery of pain and evil, how it affects our understanding of the created world, and how it can be interpreted in the light of revelation. More specifically, I noted that evil and pain are both *suffered* and *caused* by humans. *Suffered,* because evil presents itself as an unwanted, mysterious power or force that pressures and limits and often destroys human life, thus opening the mind to a wide variety of questions with no obvious solution. Likewise evil is *caused* by humans who often inflict evil on others (and on the material world as a whole, as we saw in chapter 10) through their free, responsible actions deriving from the human will. Evil is thus both unwilled (by the one who suffers it) and willed (by the one who inflicts it).

In the next two chapters I shall consider the mystery of *the origins of evil* in the wider context of what has been clearly established in the early chapters: that God is all-powerful and good, and therefore cannot and will not be the ultimate source of evil (though mysteriously he may permit it). God sent his Son, Jesus Christ, to redeem us (or save us) from evil at the deepest possible level. The ultimate fruit of the work of redemption is eternal life, perpetual union with God. Yet Christ by saving and bringing us eternal life also revealed what *the mystery of evil he was saving us from* consisted of. This has come to be known in the history of dogma as *original sin.* For sin, the transgression of the divine command, is not just personally committed, but also handed on, not just inflicted, but also suffered.

This chapter will concentrate on the historical development of the doctrine of original sin, from the time of the Church Fathers, through the Middle Ages and the Council of Trent, and up to the modern period. And this with a view to ascertaining what the church actually teaches on the matter, the minimum Christian believers should hold. The next chapter will attempt to offer a systematic reflection on the reality of original sin, taking into account the original situation humanity was constituted in, the Fall of our first parents and its effects, and the handing on of original sin to the rest of humanity. It should become clear that the theology of original sin is very much a "work in progress," for many issues of a theological kind still have to be clarified.

The doctrine of original sin has a long history, of course, finding its roots in the Gospels and especially in the Pauline letters. I shall consider the latter in the coming chapter. Interestingly, the notion of original sin is to be found well developed in Qumran literature.[1] At a systematic level it was developed by several Church Fathers, among them Irenaeus, Origen, the Cappadocians, and especially Augustine. Several local synods in the fifth and sixth centuries, inspired by Augustine's writings, provide a succinct explanation of church teaching on the matter. The doctrine on original sin developed also throughout the Middle Ages, even though it did not occupy center-stage. But it became the center of attention again in the sixteenth century on account of the teaching of Martin Luther who came to identify original sin with *concupiscence,* human inclination to sin, to which the Council of Trent responded in detail, thus providing the principal official church text on original sin.

In the modern period, original sin as a theory and explanation of reality was developed by theologians, both Protestant and Catholic, but challenged by philosophers. Throughout the last century or so, besides a wider knowledge of biblical and theological questions associated with our understanding of original sin, important scientific issues have forced us to refocus our understanding of the origins of humanity, especially in the areas of ethnology, evolution, and anthropology. In this chapter I shall present principally the respective positions of Augustine, Luther, the Council of Trent, and recent church teachings. In the next I shall inquire systematically into the teaching.

1. F. Manzi, "Il peccato, la sua universalità e le sue origini negli scritti qumranici," *Scuola Cattolica* 126 (1998): 371–406.

Elements of the History of Original Sin in Church Fathers

SIN AND SALVATION IN EARLY CHURCH FATHERS

Although the doctrine which later came to be called "original sin" is passed over in silence by several of the earliest Church Fathers,[2] it was developed by later ones, among them Irenaeus, Tertullian, Origen, the Cappadocians, John Chrysostom, and Ambrose.[3] Irenaeus centers his attention on the power of Christ's work of redemption. Clearly opposed to the Gnostics who insisted forcefully on the Fall of the human race, Irenaeus insisted mainly on the mercy of God, in the incarnation and on human freedom.[4]

Since it was impossible for man, once he had been conquered and broken, to overcome sin, he was modeled again and obtained the prize of victory, and since it was impossible for man who had been crushed by the power of sin to take part in salvation, the Son worked one and the other: being the Word of God, he descended from the Father, he became incarnate, he descended right down into death, and he brought about the "economy" of our salvation.[5]

On several occasions Irenaeus suggests that our first parents lived and acted as infants from the point of view of moral responsibility.[6]

On the whole, however, many of the early Church Fathers had quite a negative view of human nature. For Tertullian, according to Refoulé, "man, after the fall of Adam, is above all a sinner in which evil has become a kind of second nature. He is the first one to teach the doctrine of original sin, even though he did not perceive all the consequences it would have....

2. J.-M. Maldamé, *Le péché originel: foi chrétienne, mythe et métaphysique* (Paris: Cerf, 2008), 48.

3. M.-M. Labourdette, "Le péché originel dans la Tradition vivante de l'Église," *Revue Thomiste* 84 (1984): 357–98, esp. 369–78; M. Hauke, *Heilsverlust in Adam: Stationen griechischer Erbsündenlehre: Irenäus – Origenes – Kappadozier* (Paderborn: Bonifatius, 1993); Maldamé, *Le péché originel*, 47–60. In the Roman liturgy, G. Lukken, *Original Sin in the Roman Liturgy: Research into the Theology of Original Sin in the Roman Sacramentaria and the Early Baptismal Liturgy* (Leiden: E. J. Brill, 1973). See also an older history: N. P. Williams, *The Ideas of the Fall and of Original Sin: A Historical and Critical Study* (London: Longmans Green, 1927).

4. Maldamé, *Le péché originel*, 51.

5. Irenaeus, *Adv. Haer.* III, 18:2; Maldamé, *Le péché originel*, 48–52.

6. See Irenaeus, *Adv. Haer.* III, 38:1–3; *Demostr.* 14.

For him, as for the Fathers of the first centuries, death, sin and Satan are synonymous."[7] The depth of sin however may be seen in the liberating light of salvation brought by Christ. And just as redemption by Christ is real and true, so also is the sin of Adam.

Origen offers a somewhat spiritualist view of the early Fall, within an allegorical interpretation of the text of Genesis. Philo of Alexandria had already said that paradise is not a geographical place, but refers rather the human soul. Origen took it that man is in the image of God in respect of his soul, but not as regards the body, which he clearly underrates.[8] Besides, he holds to the preexistence of souls, all made together at the beginning of creation. By their sin they "fall" into the flesh. Death, understood as the temporary enclosure of the soul within the body, was introduced into the world by sin. Sin itself involved infidelity of the soul and separation from the spirit, by which it lost its likeness to God. Our continuity with Adam has been broken, and thus the likeness to God is diminished in later human generations.

The Cappadocians also offer a somewhat spiritualist view of original sin. Gregory of Nyssa wrote extensively about the creation of humanity[9] in the wider context of the Old Testament teaching on the image of God and human sexuality.[10] But he insists that humans are authors of evil through a mistaken use of their free will, not God. Still, God does retain some kind of responsibility. The dilemma is worked out according to Gregory in the context of the historical maturation of humanity. God allows a certain proliferation of evil with a view to intervening at the opportune moment.

Basil the Great on the other hand develops a view of Adam's fall based on a literal and not allegorical exegesis of Genesis, in his work on the six days of creation, the *Hexameron*. Among other things he holds that death does not derive principally from sin, but from the natural constitution of humans.

7. F. Refoulé, introduction to Tertullian, *Le baptême, le premier traité chrétien* (Paris: Cerf, 1976), 15 and 18.

8. See especially Origen's work *De principiis*.

9. Gregory of Nyssa, *Sermones de creatione hominis*, which are possibly spurious, as well as his *Orat. Catech. Magna*.

10. On the sense of human sexuality in Gregory, see O'Callaghan, *Children of God in the World*, 525–26.

John Chrysostom also speaks in his *Homilies on Genesis* of the sin of Adam, insisting on the freedom and power God gives to humans, as well as the power of divine grace. He considers paradise as a real place where man sinned and was enfeebled and passed on this situation to Cain, Noah, and others. He pays special attention to the moral and psychological sense of original sin. He observes that Genesis allows us to understand the beauty of human life but also the complexity of human action. He contrasts the two Adams: Adam was the prophetic figure of Christ, and just as we are all in Adam on account of death, so also we are justified in Christ. He finds difficulty in explaining the solidarity of humans in sin, because he is aware that personal sin cannot be transmitted. Thus he would say that humans are born sinners only in a derived sense, but they certainly experience a strong inclination to sin.

Ambrose of Milan played an important role in developing the doctrine of original sin within Latin theology. He also applied the allegoric method to the Book of Genesis to understand its moral and spiritual meaning in his *Hexameron*. Paradise for him is the garden of the soul, and the source of its life is Christ. Still, he has a realistic rather than a metaphorical view of original sin and insists on the true responsibility of our first parents, avoiding the notion that they were like infants. Besides, Adam is not simply the first man, but humanity as a whole.

All in all, we may say that the Greek Fathers were well aware of "the absolute need for salvation brought by Christ and the presence of sin as structural to the human condition, a sin that is handed on from one generation to the next."[11] They provide a thoroughly Christological reading of Genesis, and understand Adam from Christ. They speak of the sin of Adam rather than original sin, a term used for the first time by Augustine. On the whole, besides, there is continuity between Latin and Greek authors.

ORIGINAL SIN IN AUGUSTINE

Augustine reflects on the mystery of evil in a true theological light.[12] McFarland speaks of his "non-empirical and soteriological orientation." His

11. Maldamé, *Le péché originel*, 59.

12. On Augustine, the bibliography on original sin is vast. For example, E. Buonaiuti, "The Genesis of St. Augustine's Idea of Original Sin," *Harvard Theological Review* 10, no. 2 (1917): 159–75; J. Clémence, "Saint Augustin et le péché originel," *Nouvelle Revue Théologique* 80 (1948): 727–54; A.-M. La

understanding of sin is not the result of a mere phenomenological reflection. He locates "sin theologically as that which is truly known only as it is forgiven—as a corollary of the doctrine of grace and not as an explanation for the experience of evil."[13] Though fully aware of the outworkings of evil in the life of humans at a phenomenological level,[14] Augustine is convinced that since the world has been created good by God, evil cannot but be a *privatio boni*, the privation of the good. In other words, the darkness of evil, such as it is, can only be fully known in the light of the good, or more specifically, the evil of sin is known indirectly, though with certainty, in the light of divine grace which Christ obtained for humanity by dying on the cross. After breaking away from his earlier Manichaean view of evil as partially constitutive of reality, Augustine's concern for evil and sin becomes entirely Christological in character because it is considered as the counterpart of the life of grace.[15]

As regards original sin, his reading of scripture is as follows: Adam, the head of the human race, sinfully forfeited for himself and for the whole of humanity the gifts of original justice, falling into a wretched state of death, suffering, ignorance, incapacity to overcome evil, and above all, enmity with God. Humanity becomes as the result of Adam's sin a *massa damnata*, a fallen mass.[16] Only by means of the grace of salvation won for us by Christ and received in faith can humans overcome this disgrace.

Bonnardière, "Le verset paulinien Rm., v. 5 dans l'œuvre de saint Augustin," *Augustinus Magister* (Paris: Études augustiniennes, 1954), 2:657–65; A.-M. Dubarle, "La pluralité des péchés héréditaires dans la tradition augustinienne," *Revue des études augustiniennes* 3 (1957): 113–36; V. Grossi, "Il peccato originale nella catechesi di S. Agostino prima della polemica pelagiana," *Augustinianum* 10 (1970): 325–59 and 458–92; P. F. Beatrice, *The Transmission of Sin: Augustine and the Pre-Augustinian Sources* (Oxford: Oxford University Press, 2013 [1978]); P. J. Weithman, "Augustine and Aquinas on Original Sin and the Function of Political Authority," *Journal of the History of Philosophy* 30, no. 3 (1992): 353–76; G. Bendinelli, "Agostino e il peccato originale," *Il peccato originale tra teologia e scienza*, ed. A. Olmi (Bologna: Edizioni Studio Domenicano, 2008), 53–85; A. Jacobs, *Original Sin: A Cultural History* (New York: HarperOne, 2008); Maldamé, *Le péché originel*, 81–95; J. Lopes Pereira, *Augustine of Hippo and Martin Luther on Original Sin and Justification of the Sinner* (Göttingen: Vandenhoeck and Ruprecht, 2013); L. Cova, *Peccato originale: Agostino e il Medioevo* (Bologna: Il mulino, 2014); G. Malavasi and A. Dupont, "Imitazione o trasmissione dei peccati dei padri nei figli? Dibattiti teologici sul concetto veterotestamentario di *peccata patrum* nella controversia pelagiana," *Gregorianum* 100, no. 3 (2019): 487–519.

13. I. A. McFarland, "Original Sin," *T&T Clark Companion to the Doctrine of Sin*, ed. K. L. Johnson and D. Lauber, 306–18 (London: T and T Clark, 2016), 310 and 315.

14. For example, on the bad inclinations of infants, see Augustine, *Confessions* I, 7.

15. On the theology of grace in Augustine, see A. Trapè, *S. Agostino: Introduzione alla dottrina della grazia*, 2 vols. (Rome: Città Nuova, 1987–90); O'Callaghan, *Children of God in the World*, 157–73.

16. Augustine, *De 83 Quaestionibus* 9, 68:3; *De Divinis Quaestionibus ad Simplicianum* I, 16. On these texts, Buonaiuti, "The Genesis of St. Augustine's Idea of Original Sin."

When studying Augustine's teaching on original sin it should be kept in mind that his was the first great synthesis of this theme, although he was aware it belonged to Christian tradition.[17] Besides, his theology was controversial and polemical in nature, starting with an effort to overcome an early Manichaeism, which later on extended in a drawn-out struggle with Pelagianism and Donatism. But above all Augustine's explanation was Christological: as believers we understand every aspect of original sin in the light of Christ's work of salvation and redemption. I shall return to this principle in greater detail at the beginning of the next chapter.

Pelagius, a British monk who lived at the same time as Augustine, had emptied the doctrine of original sin by holding, in the words of the *Catechism of the Catholic Church,* "that man could, by the natural power of free will and without the necessary help of God's grace, lead a morally good life; he thus reduced the influence of Adam's fault to bad example."[18] Pelagius said that "when I must promote the reform of customs and holiness of life, I begin by demonstrating the strength and value of human nature and clearly define its faculties, with a view to moving the spirit of my listeners to carry out many acts of virtue."[19] Augustine realized right away that this teaching would have made the incarnation of the Word and the entire economy of salvation superfluous. For Pelagius Christ was simply a great teacher, who exhorted us to a holy life through his words and actions and good example.[20] It is not as if he denied redemption or the grace of Christ, but he regarded the latter simply as a kind of supplementary help. Understandably Augustine reacted with energy and insisted on the corruption present in human nature, both body and soul, on account of original sin, which required God's justifying and recreating activity in the soul of each person in order to live a truly Christian life.

Augustine's position was substantially accepted at the Fifteenth Council of Carthage in the year 418, in the presence of Augustine himself, and was subsequently approved by Pope Zosimus.[21] The corresponding canons were taken up by the Council of Trent in 1546. In the decades after the

17. Augustine, *Contra Julianum Pelagianum* 6, 12, 39.

18. CCC, no. 406. For a more detailed explanation of the position of Pelagius, see O'Callaghan, *Children of God in the World,* 158–60.

19. Pelagius, *Epist. Pelagii ad Demetiadem* 2.

20. See Pelagius, *Expositiones XIII epist. Pauli* 45–48.

21. DH 222–24 and 231.

death of Augustine there developed a position which later on came to be known as semi-Pelagianism, which holds that human effort is sufficient to live a Christian life once sanctifying grace has been received. The Second Council of Orange, in 529, before delving into the question of grace and clarifying the question of semi-Pelagianism, explained church teaching in two canons, the first presenting original sin in Adam, the second the transmission of that sin. Again both canons may be found in the decree of the Council of Trent.

Original Sin during the Reformation and the Council of Trent

The theology of the Middle Ages substantially accepted Augustine's understanding of original sin. However, sin is not generally placed at the center of theological reflection, but rather nature and virtues, rooted of course in the doctrine of creation and grace. Of particular importance were the texts of Anselm[22] and Thomas Aquinas,[23] both of whom described the Fall as a loss of original justice, in such a way that original sin may be described essentially as a privation of original justice. I shall take up this notion in greater detail in the next chapter. Eastern Orthodox authors spoke of ancestral sin in general terms, whereas Latin theologians spoke on the whole of original sin in terms of the transmission of guilt.[24]

But things changed notably with the teachings of the Protestant reformers, Calvin and especially Luther. Of course, sixteenth-century Protestant theologians did not deny original sin. Quite the contrary. For the most part they "taught that original sin has radically perverted man and

22. See Anselm, *On the Virginal Conception and Original Sin,* which prepared the way for Thomas. On Anselm, see R. Martin, "La question du péché originel dans saint Anselme," *Revue des sciences philosophiques et théologiques* 5 (1911): 735–49; K. A. McMahon, "Anselm and the Guilt of Adam," *The Saint Anselm Journal* 2, no. 1 (2004): 81–89; and S. Visser and T. Williams, "Original Sin, Grace and Salvation," in their *Anselm* (Oxford: Oxford University Press, 2009), 241–51.

23. O. Lottin, "Les théories du péché originel au XIIème siècle II & III," *Recherches de théologie ancienne et médiévales* 12 (1940): 78–103 and 13 (1941): 236–71; J.-M. Dubois, "Transmission et rémission du péché originel. Genèse de la réflexion théologique de saint Thomas d'Aquin," *Revue des études anciennes* 19 (1983): 283–311; M.-M. Labourdette, "Aux origines du péché de l'homme d'après saint Thomas d'Aquin," *Revue Thomiste* 85 (1985): 357–98; M. Leblanc, "Aspects du péché originel dans la pensée de saint Thomas d'Aquin," *Revue Thomiste* 93 (1993): 567–600.

24. See McFarland, "Original Sin," 313.

destroyed his freedom; they identified the sin inherited by each man with an insurmountable inclination to evil (*concupiscentia*)."[25] It was commonly held that, in their present condition, humans sin in every action they perform with their own will. This corruption is profound and incurable. Luther would say that man is *simul iustus et peccator*, at once both just and sinner.[26] The classical Lutheran position is that redemption does not affect the depths of our being but just provides an external or forensic justification: God simply forgives our sin, but grace does not as such recreate humans or penetrate the human heart.[27] "What is original sin, then?," Luther asked. "According to the subtleties of the scholastic theologians, it is the privation or lack of original justice.... But according to the Apostle [Paul] and the simplicity of Christian understanding, it is the total, complete and universal privation of the rectitude and power of good in all the energies of body and soul, in the whole person, interior and exterior."[28]

In effect, Luther identifies original sin with human concupiscence. And because he considers concupiscence to be powerful and invincible, original sin remains perpetually. "As the ancient Fathers said," Luther continued, "original sin is the very stimulus [*fomes*] of nature, the law of the flesh, the battle of the members, the despondency [*languor*] of nature, the tyrant, the original illness,"[29] a position later assumed and developed by the Lutheran philosophers Immanuel Kant and Søren Kierkegaard.[30] Sin is not so much an act of the will but rather a deeply rooted state of enmity with and alienation from God—Luther says that the free will of humans is just a "mere word"[31]—an innate downward tendency in humans, incapable of overcoming their bad inclinations. For this reason, according to the classical Lutheran doctrine, the grace of baptism does not truly heal hu-

25. *CCC*, no. 406.

26. See P. O'Callaghan, *Fides Christi: The Justification Debate* (Dublin: Four Courts Press, 1997), 35.

27. See ibid., 46–54.

28. Luther, *Disp. On Psalms* (WA 56:312).

29. Ibid., 313.

30. See I. Kant, *Religion within the Boundaries of Mere Reason* (Cambridge: Cambridge University Press, 1996), and other works; S. A. Kierkegaard, *The Concept of Anxiety: A Simple Psychologically Orienting Deliberation on the Dogmatic Issue of Hereditary Sin* (Princeton, N.J.: Princeton University Press, 1980). See also D. Cornati, "La filosofia del peccato originale da Kant a Kierkegaard," *Scuola Cattolica* 126 (1998): 407–32, and G. Riconda, *Il peccato originale nel pensiero moderno* (Brescia: Morcelliana, 2009).

31. Luther, WA 1:359.

mans; rather God saves them exteriorly in virtue of the merits of Christ in spite of human efforts and sin. The doctrine of Calvin is of a kind, though less pessimistic as regards the powers of human nature.[32]

The church reacted to the challenge of the Reformers mainly at the Council of Trent, which went on for nearly twenty years (1545–63). Fathers present at the Council were aware of the importance of the question of original sin, as it set the scene for many other issues regarding salvation, grace, sacraments, ecclesiology, etc. The fifth session, Trent's first of a dogmatic kind, considered the doctrine of original sin in five canons. It was promulgated in 1546, the year Luther died. Apart from Luther's own teaching, several other theological positions were to be found among Council fathers. First that of Augustine, which, though somewhat pessimistic, was shared in general lines by all the participants; second, the typical theologies of the Middle Ages, those of Anselm and Aquinas, which understood original sin in terms of the privation of original justice; third, the teaching of the Renaissance humanists, such as Erasmus and Zwingli, who, more or less like Pelagius, considered Christ principally as a moral master; fourth and last, the teaching of the Manichaean Anabaptists who taught that sin was an exclusively a personal matter, not inherited, and therefore that baptism could only be received with personal consent, as adults and not as children.[33]

In effect, five canons go to make up the teaching of Trent's fifth session on original sin.[34] First, on the fact and effects of original sin, which reads as follows:

Canon 1. If anyone does not confess that the first man, Adam, when he transgressed the commandment of God in paradise, immediately lost the holiness and justice in which he had been constituted, and through the offense of that

32. See O'Callaghan, *Fides Christi*, 54.

33. On the different theological positions, see *Concilium Tridentinum: Diariorum, Actorum, Epistularum Tractatuum nova collectio* (Fribourg: Ed. Soc. Goerresiana, 1901), 5:212.

34. See DH 1511–15. There was a sixth canon in the fifth session (DH 1516) explaining that the decree did not intend to get involved in the issue of the Immaculate Conception of Mary. Translations of these texts are taken from J. Neuner and J. Dupuis (eds.), *The Christian Faith in the Doctrinal Documents of the Catholic Church*, 2nd ed. (New York: Alba House, 1982). On the decree, A. Vanneste, "La préhistoire du décret du Concile de Trent sur le péché originel," *Nouvelle Revue Théologique* 86 (1964): 355–68 and 490–510; Z. Alszeghy and M. Flick, "The Tridentine Decree on Original Sin," *Gregorianum* 52, no. 4 (1971): 595–637; L. Scheffczyk, "Die Erbsündenlehre des Tridentinums im Gegenwartsaspeckt," *Forum Katholische Theologie* 6 (1990): 1–21.

prevarication incurred the wrath and indignation of God, and thus death with which God had previously threatened him [Gn 2:17] and, together with death, captivity under his power "who had the power of death, that is, the devil" [Heb 2:14], and that the entire Adam through that offense of prevarication was changed in body and soul for the worse, let him be anathema.

This canon, which is very similar to one found in the Second Council of Orange (529),[35] speaks of the fact of original sin, in a clearly historical context, as a Fall from the original state of holiness and justice. The text does not attempt to provide an explanation of the *essence of the state* resulting from original sin, but is limited to describing its *effects,* which are five: the loss of holiness and justice, and as a result, the anger of God, death, enslavement to the devil, and damage done to human nature. Little was said of the state of sin in all probability in order to avoid entering into a discussion of the different theological schools present at the Council. I shall consider the question in the next chapter however. It is interesting to note besides that the text does not speak of the state in which man was "created" but rather that in which he was "constituted," in order, probably, not to identify the creation of the world with the elevation of humans to grace.

Canon 2. If anyone asserts that the transgression of Adam injured him alone and not his posterity [1 Cor 1:15, 21], and that the holiness and justice which he received from God, which he lost for himself alone and not for us also; or that he, being defiled by the sin of disobedience, has transmitted only death and the pains of the body into the whole human race, but not sin also, which is the death of the soul, let him be anathema, since he contradicts the Apostle who says: "By one man sin entered into the world and by sin death; and so death passed upon all men, in whom all have sinned" [Rom 5:12].

The second canon, similar to the second canon of the Second Council of Orange,[36] claims that the sin committed personally by Adam (this is usually termed *peccatum originale originans*) is passed on to the rest of humanity (technically called *peccatum originale originatum*). It would not be enough to say that Adam handed on some of the effects of sin, such as death and bodily suffering. In fact, the text describes original sin as the death of the soul, which is similar in some respects to that of the body. On

35. See DH 371.
36. See DH 372.

the basis of Romans 5:12 the Council teaches that all humans are in some way involved in the sin of Adam; I shall deal with the exegetical difficulties of this text in the next chapter.

Canon 3. If anyone asserts that this sin of Adam, which in its origin is one, and by propagation, not by imitation, transfused into all, which is in each one as something that is his own, is taken away either by the forces of human nature or by a remedy other than the merit of the one mediator, our Lord Jesus Christ [1 Tm 2:5], who has reconciled us to God in his own blood [Rom 5:9], "made our justice, sanctification and redemption" [1 Cor 1:30]; or if he denies that that merit of Jesus Christ is applied both to adults and to infants by the sacrament of baptism rightly administered in the form of the Church, let him be anathema. "For there is no other name under heaven given among men by which we must be saved" [Acts 4:12]. Hence that declaration: "Behold the Lamb of God, behold him who takes away the sins of the world" [Jn 1:29] and that other: "As many of you as have been baptized, have put on Christ" [Gal 3:27].

This third canon is perhaps the most complex of the five. It is similar to the second canon of Fifteenth Council of Carthage (418).[37] The question of the *transmission* of original sin from head to members is broached. The canon teaches that the original sin transmitted is a true sin in each person, who therefore stands in need of being redeemed by Christ. The key phrase is the following: "this sin of Adam, which in its origin is one, and by propagation, not by imitation, transfused into all which is in each one as something that is his own" (*propagatione, non imitatione ... et inest unicuique proprium*). Shortly before the Council one Figgius had argued that the sin of Adam was numerically one, but that it is simply imputed (or assigned) to each one of us.[38] If this were the case, there would be no need to speak of the transmission of sin to the rest of humanity, nor that sin could be considered as proper to each one. At best, both sin and forgiveness would be imputed to humans. However, Trent clearly teaches that a true sin, an alienation from God, is handed on to each and every one and is present in them, in such a way that we can say that all humans are born sinners. Again the Pelagian position, which reduced original sin to the bad example of Adam, is sidelined, for sin is transmitted "by propagation, not by imitation." It would seem that the term "propagation" is equivalent to

37. See DH 223.

38. See *Concilium Tridentinum*, vol. 5, no. 4.

that of "generation."[39] Interestingly, the Council of Carthage had used the Latin term *generatio* here instead of *propagatio*.[40] But more on this later on.

Canon 4. If anyone denies that infants, newly born from their mothers' wombs, are to be baptized, even though they be born of baptized parents, or says that they are indeed baptized for the remission of sins [Acts 3:28], but that they derive nothing of original sin from Adam which must be expiated by the washing bowl of regeneration for the attainment of eternal life, from which it follows that in them the form of baptism for the remission of sins is to be understood not as true but as false, let him be anathema, for what the Apostle has said, "by one man sin entered into the world, and by sin death, and so death passed upon all men, in whom all have sinned" [Rom 5:12], is not to be understood otherwise than as the Catholic Church has everywhere and always understood it. For in virtue of this rule of faith handed down from the apostles, even infants who could not as yet commit any sin of themselves, are for this reason truly baptized for the remission of sins, in order that in them what they contracted by generation may be washed away by regeneration [DH 223]. "For, unless a man be born again of water and the Holy Ghost, he cannot enter into the kingdom of heaven" [Jn 3:5].

This canon, directly taken from the Fifteenth Council of Carthage,[41] confirms against the Anabaptists the validity of the universal ecclesial practice of *baptizing infants*. It is interesting to note that this Council of Carthage, the oldest in the church to teach about original sin, draws its authority from the ecclesial praxis of baptizing infants rather than adults. The baptism of infants of course would be meaningless if there was only such a thing as personally committed sin. As we saw above, sin/evil is not only something we *do* or inflict, but also something we *suffer*, we receive. Interestingly, Luther was also opposed to the Anabaptists, affirmed the universality of original sin in which each one is born, and insisted on the need for infant baptism.[42]

The final canon is exclusive to Trent, and clarifies church teaching with respect to Luther.

39. See R. Gibellini, *La generazione come mezzo di trasmissione del peccato originale* (Brescia: Queriniana, 1965).

40. DH 223 reads: "In eis regeneratione mundetur, quod generatione traxerunt."

41. See ibid.

42. See Luther, *Large Catechism XIIIa*, 4.

Canon 5. If anyone denies that by the grace of our Lord Jesus Christ which is conferred in baptism, the guilt of original sin is remitted, or says that the whole of that which belongs to the essence of sin is not taken away, but says that it is only canceled or not imputed, let him be anathema. For in those who are born again God hates nothing, because "there is no condemnation" [Rom 8:1] to those who "are truly buried together with Christ by baptism unto death" [Rom 6:4], who walk not according to the flesh [Rom 8:1], but, putting off the old man and putting on the new one who is created according to God [Eph 4:22–24, Col 3:9–10], are made innocent, immaculate, pure, guiltless and beloved of God, "heirs indeed of God, joint heirs with Christ" [Rom 8:17], so that there is nothing whatever to hinder their entrance into heaven.... But this holy council perceives and confesses that in the one baptized there remains concupiscence or an inclination to sin [*concupiscentiam vel fomitem*] which, since it is left for us to wrestle with, cannot injure those who do not acquiesce but resist manfully by the grace of Jesus Christ; indeed, "an athlete is not crowned unless he competes according to the rules" [2 Tm 2:5]. This concupiscence, which the Apostle sometimes calls "sin" [Rom 6:12–15; 7:7, 14–20] the holy council declares the Catholic Church has never understood to be called sin in the sense that it is truly and properly sin in those born again, but in the sense that it is of sin and inclines to sin.

This final canon is of particular interest in the context of the church's rejection of certain tenets of Luther's teaching, specifically whether original sin may be identified with the concupiscence that remains in humans even after baptism (likewise called *fomes peccati*, or the "stimulus of sin"). During the years of the Counter-Reformation Cardinal Robert Bellarmine wrote that "the entire controversy between Catholics and Lutherans lies just on this point: whether the *corruption of nature* and especially *concupiscence in itself*, as it remains in the baptized, is, truly, original sin."[43]

The fact is that Luther intended to take this position directly from Augustine who appears to hold, in certain polemical anti-Pelagian texts, the true sinfulness of concupiscence.[44] Some Augustinians at Trent, Seripandus for example, wished to include this doctrine in the final text. But his proposal was not accepted. Baptism takes away "the whole of that which belongs to the essence of sin," the canon says, in such a way that *in renatis*

43. R. Bellarmine, *De amissione gratiae et statu peccati*, in his *Opera* (Paris: Vivès, 1871), 5:401.

44. See Augustine, *In Tr. ad Io.* 5:1, on Jn 8:44, says that "those things which proceed from man are false, as our Lord Jesus Christ Himself has said, 'He that speaks a lie speaks of his own' (Jn 8:44). No one has anything of his own except falsehood and sin." This phrase is cited in the Second Council of Orange, canon 22 (DH 392).

enim nihil odit Deus, "in those who are born again God hates nothing." God loves the person who has been justified with an efficacious and transforming love, even though a certain habitual *inclination* to sin may remain in their lives. The text makes it clear that concupiscence is not an imputable sin in itself, but *ex peccato est et ad peccatum inclinat,* "is of sin and inclines to sin," a phrase inspired in Augustine.[45]

Trent's fifth canon is of exceptional importance for Christian spirituality and morality. Sin and concupiscence are not the same thing, even though the latter derives from former and leads to it. Sin can only take place where there is *consent* to temptation, be it internal (concupiscence) or external. The church confirmed its teaching on this issue by condemning the teachings of Baius, Jansen, and Pasquier Quesnel in the following centuries.[46]

Recent Church Teachings

Neither Vatican council dealt with the issue of original sin in a systematic way. Still, Vatican II's constitution *Gaudium et Spes* provides the following general description of the reality of original sin:

> Although he was made by God in a state of holiness, from the very onset of his history man abused his liberty, at the urging of the Evil One. Man set himself against God and sought to attain his goal apart from God. Although they knew God, they did not glorify Him as God, but their senseless minds were darkened and they served the creature rather than the Creator. What divine revelation makes known to us agrees with experience. Examining his heart, man finds that he has inclinations toward evil too, and is engulfed by manifold ills which cannot come from his good Creator.... Therefore man is split within himself. As a result, all of human life, whether individual or collective, shows itself to be a dramatic struggle between good and evil, between light and darkness. Indeed, man finds that by himself he is incapable of battling the assaults of evil successfully, so that everyone feels as though he is bound by chains. But the Lord Himself came to free and strengthen man, renewing him inwardly and casting out that

45. See J. A. Sayés, *Antropología del hombre caído: El pecado original* (Madrid: BAC, 1991), 203.

46. The doctrine of Baius was rejected by Pope Pius V in the Bull *Ex Omnibus Afflictionibus* (1567), in DH 1901–80, esp. 1925–27; that of Jansen by Pope Innocent X, in the Constitution *Cum Occasione* (1653), in DH 2001–7; and by Pope Alexander VIII in the decree of the Holy Office of 1690, in DH 2301–32, esp. 2307 and 2311; finally the doctrine of Quesnel was condemned by Pope Clement XI in the Constitution *Unigenitus Dei Filius* (1713), in DH 2400–2502, esp. 2439–40. On the doctrine of grace in these authors, see O'Callaghan, *Children of God in the World,* 205–9.

"prince of this world" (Jn 12:31) who held him in the bondage of sin. For sin has diminished man, blocking his path to fulfillment.[47]

The church's teaching on original sin may also be found in a summarized form in *The Creed of the People of God*, promulgated by Pope Paul VI in 1968 and clearly based on the teaching of Trent. The dense text goes under five headings: (1) the fact of original sin; (2) the universality of the fallen state, common to all humans; (3) the "state of original justice" at the beginning of human history; (4) the effects of original sin; and (5) the way it is transmitted.

We believe [1] that in Adam all have sinned, which means that [2] the original offense committed by him caused human nature, common to all humans, to fall to a state in which it bears the consequences of that offense, [3] and which is not the state in which it was at first in our first parents—established as they were in holiness and justice, and in which man knew neither evil nor death. [4] It is human nature so fallen, stripped of the grace that clothed it, injured in its own natural powers and subjected to the dominion of death, that is transmitted to all men, and it is in this sense that every man is born in sin. [5] We therefore hold, with the Council of Trent, that original sin is transmitted with human nature, "not by imitation, but by propagation" and that it is thus "proper to each one."[48]

The doctrine of original sin is also developed amply in the 1986 catechesis of John Paul II and in the *Catechism of the Catholic Church*, published in 1992, as well as in several pronouncements of Popes Benedict XVI and Francis.[49]

47. *GS*, no. 13. In *GS*, no. 22, we find a Christological reading of original sin: "For by His incarnation the Son of God has united Himself in some fashion with every man. He worked with human hands, He thought with a human mind, acted by human choice, and loved with a human heart. Born of the Virgin Mary, He has truly been made one of us, like us in all things except sin. As an innocent lamb He merited for us life by the free shedding of His own blood. In Him God reconciled us to Himself and among ourselves; from bondage to the devil and sin He delivered us." See also *GS*, nos. 2 and 18, and *Apostolicam Actuositatem*, no. 7. On original sin in Vatican II, see G.-H. Baudry, "Le péché originel à Vatican II," *Esprit et vie* 101 (1991): 657–68; C. Boureux and C. Théobald (eds.), *Le péché originel: Heures et malheurs d'une dogme*, 5th ed. (Paris: Concilium, 2005).

48. Paul VI, *The Creed of the People of God*, no. 16, from the Apostolic Letter *Solemni Hac Liturgia*, June 30, 1968. See C. Pozo, *El credo del pueblo de Dios: comentario teológico* (Madrid: BAC, 1968).

49. John Paul II, General Audiences of August 27 to December 17, 1986; *CCC*, nos. 385–421. We shall consider the position of Ratzinger/Benedict XVI in the next chapter. Francis referred to original sin in morning meditations (November 11, 2013) on the subject of corruption; in the "Homily on the Solemnity of the Immaculate Conception" (December 8, 2015); and at the catechesis on baptism (April 25, 2018).

13

A Systematic Consideration of the Doctrine of Original Sin

IN THE PREVIOUS CHAPTER I attempted to present what the church has taught on the topic of original sin. In this chapter, which is more systematic, three issues will be considered that are present in a variety of church documents.[1] First, the state of "justice and holiness" in which our first parents lived before the Fall, the original state of humanity. Second, the trial and Fall of our first parents, what is usually called the *peccatum originale originans*, "originating original sin," the act of original sin. Third and last, the question of the transmission of original sin to the whole of humanity, what is termed *peccatum originale originatum*, "originated original sin," or the state of sin handed on to humans at large.

I have already pointed out that the theology of original sin is in many ways a "work in progress." This means that a good number of the proposals made in the coming pages will be necessarily provisional in nature. Many issues need still be clarified, and the fundamental teaching of the church, presented in the previous chapter, needs to dialogue deeply with the find-

1. The bibliography on original sin is vast. Some of the material in this chapter previously appeared in P. O'Callaghan, "Una lectura cristológica de la doctrina del pecado original," *Scripta Theologica* 46, no. 1 (2014): 161–80. Among other works, see C. Baumgartner, *Le péché originel* (Paris: Desclée, 1969); D. Bonhoeffer, *Creation and Fall* (Grand Rapids, Mich.: Fortress Press, 1997); G. Colombo, "Tesi sul peccato originale," *Teologia* 15 (1990): 264–76; P. De Letter, "Original Sin, Privation of Original Justice," *The Thomist* 17 (1954): 469–509; M.-M. Labourdette, "Le péché originel dans la Tradition vivante de l'Église," *Revue Thomiste* 84 (1984): 357–98; L. Scheffczyk, *Schöpfung als Heilseröffnung: Schöpfungslehre* (Aachen: M. M. Verlag, 1997); I. A. McFarland, "The Fall and Sin," in *The Oxford Handbook of Systematic Theology*, ed. J. Webster, K. Tanner, and I. R. Torrance (Oxford: Oxford University Press, 2007), 140–59; O. Crisp, "Original Sin and Atonement," *The Oxford Handbook of Philosophical Theology*, ed. T. P. Flint and M. C. Rea (Oxford: Oxford University Press, 2009), 430–51; I. A. McFarland, "Original Sin," in *T&T Clark Companion to the Doctrine of Sin*, ed. K. L. Johnson and D. Lauber (London: T and T Clark, 2016), 303–18.

ings of biblical exegesis and science, especially as regards the beginning of the universe, the identity of our first parents, evolution, anthropology, etc. But before examining these issues, let us consider original sin from a methodological stance, concretely from a Christological and trinitarian point of view.

Situating Original Sin in the Light of the Revelation of the Trinity

Strange to say, original sin may justly be considered more visible and tangible than many other revealed Christian mysteries. G. K. Chesterton wrote, ironically, that "certain new theologians dispute original sin, which is the only part of Christian theology which can really be proved."[2] Likewise the American theologian Reinhold Niebuhr, in an extensive study of original sin, insisted some sixty years ago on its tangible realism.[3] And according to the philosopher Max Horkheimer, following through on an intuition of Schopenhauer:

> The greatest doctrine of both religions, Jewish and Christian, is that of original sin. This doctrine has determined history up till our present age, and it still determines it for those who think. This doctrine is possible only on the presupposition that man has been created by God and given free will. The first thing man did was to commit this great sin in paradise, and it is on that basis that the history of humanity needs a theological explanation.[4]

McFarland puts it theologically: "if all human beings stand in need of salvation that they cannot secure themselves, then it follows that they are marked by a congenital resistance to God and God's work. This is original sin.... Human sinfulness must be viewed as a congenital state and not just as a condition we acquire through our own individual actions subsequent to birth."[5]

Pope Benedict XVI offered the following reflection on the occasion of the solemnity of the Immaculate Conception in 2008:

2. G. K. Chesterton, *Orthodoxy* (London: Bodley Head, 1908), 78.

3. See R. Niebuhr, *The Nature and Destiny of Man* (New York: C. Scribner's and Son, 1964), 1:150–300; G. Rees, "The Anxiety of Inheritance: Reinhold Niebuhr and the Literal Truth of Original Sin," *Journal of Religious Ethics* 31, no. 1 (2003): 75–99.

4. M. Horkheimer, *Die Sehnsucht nach dem ganz Anderen* (Hamburg: Fursche-Verlag, 1970), 55.

5. McFarland, "Original Sin," 306.

The existence of what the Church calls "original sin" is unfortunately glaringly obvious, if we merely look around us and first of all within ourselves. The experience of evil is in fact so consistent that it imposes itself and raises in us the question: where does it come from? Especially for a believer, this question is even more profound: if God, who is absolute Goodness, created all things, where does evil come from? The first pages of the Bible (Gn 1–3) respond precisely to this fundamental question which challenges every human generation with the narrative of Creation and of the fall of our first parents: God created all things so that they might exist and in particular he created the human being in his own image; he did not make death but death entered the world through the envy of the devil (cf. Wis 1:13–14; 2:23–24) who, rebelling against God, deceived men and women and induced them to rebel as well. This is the drama of the freedom which God accepts to the very end for love, but promises that a woman's son will crush the head of the ancient serpent (Gn 3:15).[6]

It is usually taken for granted that the biblical source of original sin is to be found in the early chapters of Genesis, which describe in detail the creation and Fall of humans and their subsequent disgrace. However, in keeping with Paul, Augustine, and many other authors, it is more correct to say that the doctrine of original sin does not derive from empirical or phenomenological data, or from Genesis 2–3, but from an in-depth consideration of Christology and Christian soteriology. "Christ manifests man to man," Vatican II says;[7] specifically, Christ by saving the whole of humanity shows us that all humans are born sinners, and are thus needful of salvation. Of course we all have some experience of evil and sin and alienation; all religions attempt to provide a solution to them. Still, to understand original sin in its radical quality, we may say that Christ, in saving the world, shows us not only what salvation consists of (eternal life, final resurrection, communion with God in heaven), but also what we are being saved *from*. That is, he manifests to us not only the *terminus ad quem* of salvation, but also its *terminus a quo*, the state of sin—original and personal—that humans are immersed in, yet saved from. Our personal experience of sin and suffering can give us some idea of the mystery of evil, but the full truth of our fallen nature and glorious destiny is shown to us principally through the life and words and deeds of Jesus Christ.[8]

6. Benedict XVI, "Angelus," December 8, 2008.

7. *GS*, no. 22; on this text, O'Callaghan, *Children of God in the World*, 64–85.

8. On the Christological side of original sin, see I. Sanna (ed.), *Questioni sul peccato originale* (Padova: Edizioni Messaggero, 1996).

Thus we may consider the mystery of sin, and especially original sin, in the light of revelation and salvation, in the context of the action of God, the Father, who is revealed by the Son in the power of the Holy Spirit. First, sin is presented in the Old Testament in terms of an *offense* to Yahweh, who is the only God, good and omnipotent. There is no secondary godhead, a Demiurge for example, to whom certain sins or aspects of sin might be directed or by whom certain ways of behavior be justified. There is only one God, one creation, one single, simple human life, lived *coram Deo,* whether one likes it or not. Moral action pleases or displeases the creator. Judeo-Christian monotheism makes the distinction between moral intention and moral object unthinkable: what a person intends to do and what they actually do is present equally before the one God; God sees our hearts and our hands. To designate the notion of sin, the Greeks used the term *hamartia,*[9] which refers to serious offenses, though perhaps involuntary in kind, against a deity. But *hamartia* is normally understood as a mistake (the term literally refers to the archer "missing the target"), that usually takes place on account of ignorance or negligence. In other words, humans sin because they do not know any better. A properly educated and instructed person, on the contrary, is less likely to sin. And "repentance" from sin simply involves recognition of one's mistake and a corresponding process of reeducation.

From the Christian (and Jewish) standpoint, however, sin is more than that. It is the fruit of rebellion against God, and is considered as something quite different from simply making a mistake as a result of ignorance or weakness. Rather it is a conscious, knowing rejection of God and his gifts, perpetrated by humans, who have been made in his image and likeness. In contrast with the Greek understanding, for Christians knowledge is the *cause* of sin, whereas ignorance may well offer an excuse. There is something coldly conscious, savage, despairing, and tragic in the rebellion of the creature against its creator. It is not a simple error, an unintended, careless mistake, but a true, willing, conscious, intentional destruction of the powerful, covenantal, filial, perpetual communion God himself has wanted to establish with humans. Sin, in other words, though committed by humans, is determined in its inner nature by the One who is offended, the creator.

9. BDAG 50–51, s.v. ἁμαρτία; *NIDNTTE* 1:255–64, s.v. ἁμαρτάνω.

John Paul II suggests in fact that the primary effect of original sin is that of abolishing the paternity of God in the mind of believers, replacing it with the universal master-slave paradigm Hegel speaks of.[10] He observes that "original sin attempts to abolish [divine] paternity, destroying its rays which permeate the created world, placing the truth that is Love in doubt and leaving humanity alone and lost with the sensation of a master-slave relationship."[11] This brings us to consider the question of our knowledge of original sin through Christ's revelation of the eternal Father.

Second, the Old Testament teaching on sin, and especially on original sin, is revealed definitively in the New, through the words, works, life, death, and resurrection of Jesus Christ, the new Adam. "What is important is to show that at the center of this historical plan there is only one Figure: Christ . . . the only one who gives meaning to the whole," says Camille Dupont in his study of original sin.[12]

Benedict XVI reflected on several occasions on the biblical figures of Christ as the new Adam, the source of saving grace, and that of Adam, the source of sin, as Paul explains in the letter to the Romans (5:12–21). He shows that though many elements of the doctrine of original sin may be found in Genesis 3, which is notoriously difficult to interpret, the real locus is in to be found in Romans 5. Benedict says:

> Paul traces the history of salvation from Adam to the Law and from the latter to Christ. At the center of the scene it is not so much Adam, with the consequences of his sin for humanity, as much as it is Jesus Christ and the grace which was poured out on humanity in abundance through him. The repetition of the "all the more" with regard to Christ [in Rom 5] stresses that the gift received in him far surpasses Adam's sin and its consequent effects on humanity, so that Paul could reach his conclusion: "but where sin increased, grace abounded all the more" (Rom 5:20). The comparison that Paul draws between Adam and Christ therefore sheds light on the inferiority of the first man compared to the prevalence of the second.[13]

10. See O'Callaghan, *Children of God in the World*, 268–70.

11. John Paul II, interviewed by V. Messori, in the former's *Crossing the Threshold of Hope* (London: J. Cape, 1994), 227–29, at 228.

12. C. Dumont, "La prédication du péché originel," *Nouvelle Revue Théologique* 83, no. 2 (1961): 113–34, at 134; see also G. Martelet, *Libre réponse à un scandale: La faute originelle, la souffrance et la mort*, 2nd ed. (Paris: Cerf, 1986).

13. Benedict XVI, "Adam and Christ: From Original Sin to Freedom," General Audience, December 3, 2008.

In effect, in order to understand the sin of Adam we need to consider Christ's work of salvation, for Christ is light and Adam darkness, Christ is life and Adam death, Christ is holiness and Adam sin.[14] Benedict continues:

> It is precisely in order to highlight the immeasurable gift of grace in Christ that Paul mentions Adam's sin. One could say that if it were not to demonstrate the centrality of grace, he would not have dwelt on the treatment of sin which "came into the world through one man and death through sin" (Rom 5:12). For this reason, if, in the faith of the Church, an awareness of the dogma of original sin developed, it is because it is inseparably linked to another dogma, that of salvation and freedom in Christ. The consequence of this is that we must never treat the sin of Adam and of humanity separately from the salvific context, in other words, without understanding them within the horizon of justification in Christ.[15]

The *Catechism of the Catholic Church* puts this principle succinctly, referring besides to the pneumatological complement to Christ's saving work: "We must know Christ as the source of grace in order to know Adam as the source of sin. The Spirit-Paraclete, sent by the risen Christ, came to 'convince/convict the world concerning sin' (Jn 16:8), by revealing him who is its Redeemer."[16]

The same position may be found in the teaching of Augustine with respect to Pelagius. It is easily taken for granted that for him the doctrine of original sin stands on its own merits, *a se stante*, given the exceptional attention he pays to it. But Augustine's position is clearly and deeply Christocentric. He explains that Pelagius's emphasis on good works, on human capacity to overcome sin, on the centrality of good example is important and relevant, but simply not enough, because it renders Christ's work of salvation, indeed the incarnation itself, superfluous. Original sin must be understood in the light of salvation. The New Testament is hidden in the Old, indeed, but the latter is illuminated and clarified only in the light of the New, that is with the full revelation that comes to us in Jesus Christ.[17] The Augustinian scholar Agostino Trapè had the following to say:

14. See M. Gagliardi, *La cristologia adamitica: tentativo di recupero del suo significato originario* (Rome: Pontificia Università Gregoriana, 2002).

15. Benedict XVI, "Adam and Christ: From Original Sin to Freedom."

16. CCC, no. 388.

17. Augustine, *Quaest. in Hept.* 2:73.

It is from the theology of redemption that Augustine deduces the theology of original sin, and not vice versa as is often thought. Original sin constitutes a separation from God because Christ has reconciled us with God; all are subject to original sin because Christ has redeemed all. It is not merely the imitation of the bad example of Adam because redemption is not merely the imitation of the good example of Christ. There are thus two solidarities, opposite in character but necessarily joined together, with Adam and Christ.[18]

Augustine does use the surprising expression *massa damnata* to refer to fallen humanity, but also, alongside it, the term *massa redempta,* redeemed humanity.[19] And again the latter sheds light on the former, not the other way around. Trapè continues: "On the level of theological argumentation the sequence moves from the *massa redempta* to the *massa damnata*.... There is in Augustine a basic optimism rooted in his Christological doctrine, which illuminates the mystery of grace summarized in the dual solidarity with Adam and with Christ."[20] In the words of Marcel Neusch, "original sin would be meaningless were it not to be re-read in the dialectic unity of salvation history. Of this history, Christ was the corner stone. And original sin is on the shadow-side. Now, the shadow can only be seen in the light. Thus it should be said that there is only one economy of salvation, and this precludes original sin from being considered as an isolated reality."[21] Morna Hooker speaks of original sin as the "flip side" of salvation by Christ.[22]

Likewise Walter Kasper offers the following description of original sin in the context of the salvation offered by Christ:

18. A. Trapè, "St Augustine," in J. Quasten (ed.), *Patrology* (Westminster, Md.: Christian Classics, 1986), 4:434. Trapè continues with important citations of Augustine: "'The entire Christian faith consists in the cause of these two men' (*De pecc. orig.* 24:28), 'One man and one man: one who leads to death, one who gives life' (*Sermo* 151:4). 'Each man is Adam, just as in those who believe each man is Christ' (*In Ps.* 70, 2:1)."

19. "Through this Mediator there is reconciled to God the mass of the entire human race which is alienated from Him through Adam." Augustine, *Sermo* 293:8.

20. Trapè, "St Augustine," 434. This position was proposed in the first place by another student of Augustine's, K. Adam, *Die geistige Entwicklung des hl. Augustinus* (Augsburg: Haas und Grabherr, 1931), 38. On the parallel between Christ and Adam, see also Augustine, *De pecc. orig.* 2, and also G. Philips, *L'union personnelle avec le Dieu vivant* (Leuven: Leuven University Press, 1989), 45.

21. See M. Neusch, "Le péché originel. Son irréductible vérité," *Nouvelle Revue Théologique* 118 (1996): 237–57, at 255 (author's translation).

22. See M. Hooker, "Adam in Romans 1," in her *From Adam to Christ: Essays on Paul* (Cambridge: Cambridge University Press, 1990), 23–84.

> Original sin means that the universal situation determining everyone inwardly is in fact opposed to the original saving will of God, who created everything in view of Christ and wills to fulfill all in him. It means that the salvation which God had intended for man as man is not actually mediated through his origin, so that there is in fact an opposition between his orientation to Christ and his determination through the universal shared sinfulness.[23]

Jaroslav Pelikan makes the acute observation that the doctrine of original sin has by and large "developed *a posteriori*, by a process which, proceeding from the salvation in Christ and from infant baptism, made the diagnosis fit the cure."[24] Simone Weil explained this epistemology as follows: "we experience good only by doing it.... When we do evil we do not know it, because evil flies from the light."[25] Only the light of grace can illumine the obscurity of sin. We know the good better or worse, but directly, yet we know evil only indirectly, only in the light of the good.

In effect, the one who reveals what sin "does" to God is the Son, the Word made flesh, Jesus Christ. "For with you is the fountain of life, and in your light we see light" (Ps 36:10). Christ is the life of the world, the life that is light (Jn 1:4). He is the light who shows up the darkness of sin, just as turning on a light in a room shows up the stains and defects that darkness attempts to hide. And this revelation finds its high point on Calvary, when Jesus, the innocent victim, dies for the sins of the guilty perpetrator, humankind, thus showing his unbreakable communion with the Father, and the Father's faithful love, through him, for humanity. But his death, though accepted in full willingness, was not Jesus' spontaneous desire: "My Father, if it is possible, let this cup pass from me; nevertheless, not as I will, but as you will" (Mt 26:39). The object of his desire was the salvation of humanity and in that he identified fully with the will of his Father. But saving humanity involved him being judged, rejected, pummeled, tortured, and killed by sin. Indeed, his death was the fruit of sin, objectively speaking the gravest sin ever committed. And just as the cross on which he died proclaimed his unchangeable love for the Father and for humanity in

23. W. Kasper, *Jesus the Christ,* 2nd ed. (London; New York: T and T Clark, 2011), 191.

24. J. J. Pelikan, *The Christian Tradition: A History of the Development of Doctrine,* vol. 1: *The Emergence of the Catholic Tradition* (Chicago: University of Chicago Press, 1971), 204. Ratzinger, *"In the Beginning,"* 62.

25. S. Weil, *Gravity and Grace* (London: Routledge, 2003), 71.

the face of that injustice, so also the resurrection proclaimed the Father's immutable love for him and for humanity. The cross revealed humans' rejection of the love of God made flesh: it was and is the ultimate revelation of what sin "does" to God. Yet the resurrection shows up how God reacts to that sin, giving us his Son back again, glorious and everlasting, and, inseparably, the gift of the Spirit and the grace of justification.

Third, the whole life of Jesus Christ, especially his passion, death, and resurrection, *reveals and expresses* the unity, power, love, and mercy of the Father. But the sending of the Holy Spirit applies to each person and situation this living, regenerative light and grace.[26] John Paul II, in his 1986 Encyclical Letter *Dominum et Vivificantem,* undertakes a profound reflection of the inner reality of sin, especially of original sin.[27] The entire document provides a gloss on John's Gospel: "I tell you the truth: it is to your advantage that I go away, for if I do not go away, the Counselor [the Holy Spirit] will not come to you; but if I go, I will send him to you. And when he comes, he will convince the world concerning sin and righteousness and judgment: concerning sin, because they do not believe in me" (Jn 16:7–9). In effect, the role of the Holy Spirit is that of convincing the world as a whole—and each one personally—concerning sin because, being the divine Gift in person, he shows humans in the depth of their heart that creation is a gift of God that should be accepted in faith, and that sin constitutes precisely a rejection of that gift or an attempt to manipulate it. "God remains the first and sovereign source for deciding about good and evil, through the intimate truth of being, which is the reflection of the Word, the eternal Son, consubstantial with the Father."[28] And the Holy Spirit is the one who gently and insistently convinces the sinner that the gift of creation should be accepted and received and used with gratitude and joy, not maltreated and abused. In doing so he uncovers and overcomes the reality of sin in the human heart.

Having considered sin in the light of creation, revelation, salvation, and

26. See O'Callaghan, *Children of God in the World,* 273–77.

27. See John Paul II, *Dominum et Vivificantem,* Encyclical Letter, May 18, 1986, par. 27. See G. Colombo, "'Dominum et vivificantem.' L'enciclica di Giovanni Paolo II," *Teologia* 11 (1986): 109–34; J. Morales, "El Espíritu Santo 'Creador' en la Encíclica 'Dominum et vivificantem,'" *Scripta Theologica* 20 (1988): 627–42.

28. John Paul II, *Dominum et Vivificantem,* par. 36.

glorification, I shall now examine the different moments that go to make up the mystery of the narrative of original sin.

The State of Original Holiness and Justice

As we saw in the previous chapter, the church has spoken of a state of holiness and justice in which our first parents were "constituted" (to use Trent's expression) before the Fall.[29] Created "in the image and likeness of God" (Gn 1:27), humans were placed by God in the Garden of Eden: "the Lord God planted a garden in Eden, in the east; and there he put the man whom he had formed. And out of the ground the Lord God made to grow every tree that is pleasant to the sight and good for food, the tree of life also in the midst of the garden, and the tree of the knowledge of good and evil" (Gn 2:8–9). Thomas Aquinas describes the situation of humans in paradise by means of the following triad: given that the soul was subject to God, the inferior powers of the soul were subject to the superior ones, and the body was subject to the soul.[30] And John Paul II in his catechesis puts it as follows:

> In the light of the Bible, the state of man before sin appears as a condition of original perfection. Genesis expresses this in a certain way by the image of "paradise" that it offers us. We may ask what the source of this perfection was. The answer is that it was found above all in friendship with God by means of sanctifying grace, and in the other gifts that in theological language are called *preternatural*, which were lost through sin. Thanks to such divine gifts, man, who was joined in friendship and harmony with his principle of being, had and maintained in himself an interior equilibrium. He was not worried about the prospect of decay and death. The "dominion" over the world, which God had given man from the beginning, was realized first of all in man himself, as dominion over himself. In this self-dominion and equilibrium he had the "integrity" (*integritas*) of existence, in the sense that man was intact and well-ordered in all his being. He was free from the triple concupiscence that inclines him to the pleasures of the senses, to coveting earthly goods, and to asserting himself against the dictates of reason.[31]

29. On the topic of paradise in contemporary theology, M. Hauke, "Das Paradies in der Theologie der Gegenwart," *Annales Theologici* 11, no. 2 (1997): 429–58.

30. See Thomas Aquinas, *ST* I, q. 95, a. 1. See J.-B. Kors, *La justice primitive et le péché originel d'après s. Thomas: les sources – la doctrine* (Paris: J. Vrin, 1930).

31. John Paul II, "Sin Involves the Misuse of God's Gifts," General Audience, September 3, 1986, par. 5.

In this state, to all appearances, humans lived in friendship with God, they did not suffer unduly, they were physically integral; they dominated over created things with ease and were not hurt or threatened or damaged by them. In this state Augustine said that man was immortal, but he specified: *posse non mori*, "he was capable of not dying," which did not mean he could not die. In fact he did die upon sinning. Only in heaven, Augustine says, can we say of humans, *non posse mori*, that they become "incapable of dying."[32]

DID PARADISE REALLY EXIST?

But do we know that such a state of justice and holiness really existed? There are important indications in scripture that that would seem to say so. However there is little in the line of conclusive archeological or historical evidence to prove the existence of a primitive paradise inhabited by humans. Yet from the theological point of view, our knowledge about the state of original justice, though indirect and lacking in specifics, is real. It is possible to say *that* there was such a state, although we can say very little about *what* it consisted of. This conviction is based on the certainty that Christ restored to us the justice we had lost, forgiving our sins, offering us the friendship of the Father, making us children of God, allowing us to reach heaven and definitive immortality. In other words, he gave back to us what we lost through sin. If there had not been a state of original justice it would make little sense to say that Jesus is the Savior of a world created good by God. As we saw above, we know of the fact of original justice through that of salvation: "where sin increased, grace abounded all the more" (Rom 5:20). God gave back to us *more* than we had lost by sin.

The common acceptance of evolution, as we saw in chapter 1, convinces us that the world as we now know it is the fruit of a long and complex process of growth and development: from original chaos and disorder, through the birth and development of different life forms, to the order and richness of the present world. Within this process it would seem that *homo sapiens* appeared on earth some hundred thousand years ago, and modern man about sixty thousand years after that. This view of things would seem to contrast with the image of the original world and of humanity depict-

32. Augustine, *De Gen. ad litt.* 6:36.

ed by the Book of Genesis—elevated, harmonious, just. The biblical view speaks in fact of a direct, immediate creation of humans by God, in a highly developed state from a spiritual and even intellectual standpoint. And this would seem to be difficult to justify scientifically.

Of course, the findings of science in respect of the origins of humanity are still at an early stage. But understandably some authors have suggested in the light of its findings that it might be better to avoid the notion of original justice altogether. This has been done in three different ways.

First, some hold that the term "original sin" may be used to describe the psychological, sociological, and cultural situation humans found themselves in as part of incipient human society.[33] "Sin" would designate as it were a lack of integration within humanity, a faulty solidarity, and would find expression in the present moment as a "sin of the world," a collective situation of poverty, imperfection, and underdevelopment. The subject of this sin, a sin of the world, would simply be primitive humanity itself at the early stages of its development. Although it is perfectly acceptable of course to speak of such a primitive situation, a pessimistic or even Manichaean impression may be given in the sense that sin was an original and permanent condition of humans that cannot ultimately be overcome.[34]

A second position, inspired by Teilhard de Chardin and an evolutionist philosophy, looks upon original sin as the discrepancy between the real situation of man at the beginning and the eschatological perfection which has not yet been achieved and to which he is destined.[35] Original sin in other words would simply designate imperfection, deficiency with respect to the ideal. This provides a more optimistic view of things, for it presents the world being saved gradually. Paradoxically however it presents evil as something physical and therefore more or less part of the structure of things, and thus inevitable. It does not fit entirely with Jesus' words: "What comes out of the mouth proceeds from the heart, and this defiles a man" (Mt 15:18).

A third position speaks of what has been called "virtual original jus-

33. See P. Schoonenberg, *Man and Sin: A Theological View* (London: Sheed and Ward, 1965); C. Tresmontant, *Introduction à la théologie chrétienne* (Paris: Éditions du Seuil, 1974), 556–84; A. Manaranche, *Je crois en Jésus-Christ aujourd'hui* (Paris: Seuil, 1968), 150–57.

34. See John Paul II, *Reconciliatio et Penitentia*, Apostolic Exhortation, December 2, 1984, par. 16.

35. A. Hulsbosch, *God in Creation and Evolution* (New York: Sheed and Ward, 1965), 14–23.

tice."[36] According to church teaching there is an evil component present in the heart of each person born into the world. Man in himself is born inclined downward. This state is overcome substantially by baptism but is not simply equivalent to a physical illness, psychological weakness, or social unease. It is a state of sin, of alienation from God, truly present in the person, a sin overcome by baptism. Original sin is present in us, one author says, as "an incapacity to love God over all things and therefore to avoid grave personal sins."[37] So far, so good, at least as regards the effects of original sin.

But we may ask: where does this "incapacity" to love God, this "egoistic option," come from in the first place? How did originating original sin arise? Maurizio Flick, following other authors,[38] does not deny the existence of a real state of original justice, preceding sin, in which humans lived in conscious intimacy with God. According to him when man commits his primitive sin, he loses a virtuality that would have led him gradually and surely toward an ever fuller development of his capacities. Original justice would not be "a more perfect actualization of humanity, lost by subsequent sin," he says, but rather "a virtuality—a seed, a power—really possessed but phenomenologically not manifested, and later on lost."[39]

The weak point of the argument however lies in the fact that this virtuality would not be manifested phenomenologically, and therefore humans could not be considered as truly *responsible* for the loss of something they knew little or nothing about. As we saw earlier on humans can sin in a meaningful way only because they *know* they are the privileged depository of God's gifts and grace. Otherwise what we call sin would become synonymous with what is humanly speaking meaningless and irresponsible. This would mark a return to the Aristotelian view of sin (*harmartia*) as the fruit of ignorance, and redemption as the result of knowledge.[40]

36. The principal author who defends this is M. Flick, "Peccato originale," in *Nuovo Dizionario di Teologia* (ed. Barbaglio and Dianich), 1131–50, esp. 1140.

37. Ibid., 1143.

38. See K. Rahner, "Erbsünde und Monogenismus," *Theologie der Erbsünde*, ed. K.-H. Weger (Freiburg i.B.: Herder, 1970), 176–223; M. Flick and Z. Alszeghy, *Il peccato originale* (Brescia: Queriniana, 1972).

39. Flick, "Peccato originale," 1147.

40. So the tendency would be to dehistoricize the Fall. This may be found in R. Niebuhr, *The Nature and Destiny of Man*, inspired by Kierkegaard: "The inevitable outcome of the tension between the human capacity for self-transcendence on the one hand, and the contingency of spatio-temporal

At an intuitive level it is difficult for us to imagine what the state of original justice might have looked like. Yet in real terms there is no special need to do so; in fact, any attempt to describe this state in detail might well involve a useless and unfounded curiosity. Besides, the objections arising from the theory of evolution constitute no significant obstacle to the acceptance of the state of original justice. If we understand Christian holiness in terms of an ever-growing communion with God, lived in evangelical simplicity, as Jesus revealed it to us, it might have happened that humans lived within a very elementary culture, with little of what we nowadays call civilization, while being superior to the civilized on account of their relationship to God. Jesus asks: "'Who is the greatest in the kingdom of heaven?' And calling to him a child, he put him in the midst of them, and said, 'Truly, I say to you, unless you turn and become like children, you will never enter the kingdom of heaven. Whoever humbles himself like this child, he is the greatest in the kingdom of heaven'" (Mt 18:1–4). Such a state might have endured for a short period of time and left little tangible mark on culture or society. Irenaeus considered this possibility.[41]

Other authors have pointed out the need to insist on the realism of the state of original justice, whatever it may have consisted of. The Italian theologian Giuseppe Colombo[42] opines that such a state may not be excluded

---

existence on the other: sin follows when human beings try and (inevitably) fail to reconcile their condition of freedom and the constraints of finitude" (1:194). This position seems to derive sin from ontology, making the former inevitable. So it would be better to see sin as socially mediated, following F. Schleiermacher, *The Christian Faith*, 3rd ed. (London: T and T Clark, 2016), 282–304. Different explanations combine the effects of genetic constitution and social transmission: P. Hefner, *The Human Factor: Evolution, Culture, Religion* (Minneapolis, Minn.: Fortress Press, 1993), chap. 8, and M. H. Suchocki, *The Fall to Violence: Original Sin in Relational Theology* (New York: Continuum, 1994), chaps. 5–7. As a result some hold on to the notion of a historical Fall: H. Blocher, *Original Sin: Illuminating the Riddle* (Grand Rapids, Mich.: Eerdmans, 1997), 58–62; I. A. McFarland, *In Adam's Fall: A Meditation on the Christian Doctrine of Original Sin* (Malden, Mass.: Wiley-Blackwell, 2010).

41. See Irenaeus, *Adv. Haer.* IV, 38:1; *Epideixis* I, 1:14 and II, 1:46.

42. Colombo, "Creazione," in *Nuovo Dizionario di Teologia* (ed. Barbaglio and Dianich), 184–210, at 206: "A nostro giudizio, [la giustizia originale] è una tesi irrinunciabile, non solo sotto il profilo dogmatico ... ma anche sotto quello teoretico. Infatti sotto il profilo teoretico, l'abbandono della teologia dello stato originario spingerebbe la teologia in un'aporia a nostro giudizio intollerabile, cioè all'affermazione di una condizione umana nella quale l'uomo esiste, ma senza trovarsi 'situato' rispetto a Dio: è infatti evidente che l'abbandono della teologia dello stato originario riduce l'uomo in uno stato di 'neutralità' rispetto a Dio, dal quale esce grazie alla propria opzione personale. Ora, di fronte a questa ipotesi, noi abbiamo due difficoltà gravi: ci sembra contraddittoria l'affermazione di un'esistenza umana antecedente alla determinazione del rapporto etico-spirituale con Dio; inoltre ci sembra che la visione conseguente a questo principio vada nel senso opposto a quella insegnata dalla rivelazione,

either for dogmatic or theoretical reasons.[43] In the absence of original justice humans would have lived, he says, without being situated before God, occupying a state of neutrality before their creator. But such a neutrality would be unthinkable, he says, especially when at a later stage humans would have to establish their relationship with God "on their own," for this would give rise to a Pelagian anthropology.

Perhaps we might say that the knowledge we do have of original justice and holiness is indirect: we have some knowledge of our redeemed state; behind that comes the sinful state of humans; and further back again, the state of original justice. So the *fact* of original justice is acceptable, whereas the *details* are inevitably obscure. It would be unwise for Christians to attempt imagining the state our first parents lived in with excessive precision and exactness. Still, certain elements may be mentioned as so many positive counterpoints to the negative effects of original sin which we shall consider later on.

ELEMENTS OF THE STATE OF ORIGINAL HOLINESS AND JUSTICE

Four aspects of the state of original holiness and justice may be considered on the basis of biblical texts. First, the core of original justice is one of friendship and intimacy with God. Made in the image and likeness of the creator, scripture speaks of Adam being placed in paradise, the holy forest. This provides a way of saying that God exercised a special care over him, seeking a suitable companion for him (Gn 2:18), "walking in the garden in the cool of the day" (Gn 3:8). Perhaps we may say that our first parents were constituted in a state of grace, and lived in paradise as sons and daughters of God, especially if we take into account that God constituted fallen humans as his children through baptism in virtue of Christ's work of redemption.

---

cioè assegni fatalmente una priorità all'uomo nella determinazione del rapporto con Dio; cioè sia in sostanza una visione pelagiana. Sotto questo profilo, la teologia dello stato originario, naturalmente 'aggiornata' secondo le esigenze critiche ma eventualmente integrate dalla riflessione teologica, ci sembra la condizione necessaria e irrinunciabile per salvaguardare il senso della rivelazione cristiana e con essa il senso stesso dell'uomo."

43. Moschetti explains that a Christocentric approach to original sin requires the affirmation of the *state of original justice*, easily eliminated by an evolutionist perspective, without the dead weight of the mythological superstructures of a golden age: S. Moschetti, "La teologia del peccato originale: passato, presente, prospettive," *Civiltà Cattolica* 1 (1989): 245–58.

Second, we may consider the question of what is usually called the preternatural gifts of our first parents. Besides the gift of grace, our first parents received other gifts from God, not belonging to supernatural life as such, but rather to the perfection of human nature.[44] John Paul II, in his catechesis on original justice, describes the state of humans as they "came from the hands of God and lived in full intimacy with him (cf. Gn 2:8–25). The Book of Ecclesiastes also says that 'God made man righteous' (Eccl 7:29).... Before sin, man possessed sanctifying grace with all the supernatural gifts that make him righteous before God. We may sum all this up by saying that man was in friendship with God at the beginning."[45] The following text of the Book of Sirach, which provides a gloss on Genesis 1:26–28, gives credence to these affirmations:

> The Lord ... endowed [humans] with strength like his own, and made them in his own image. He placed the fear of them in all living beings, and granted them dominion over beasts and birds.... He made for them tongue and eyes; he gave them ears and a mind for thinking. He filled them with knowledge and understanding, and showed them good and evil. He set his eye upon their hearts to show them the majesty of his works.... And they will praise his holy name, to proclaim the grandeur of his works. He bestowed knowledge upon them, and allotted to them the law of life (Sir 17:1–11).

Third, among the gifts mentioned in scripture are those of impassibility and knowledge. It would seem that our first parents in the state of original justice *did not suffer*, certainly not in the same way as we do. Being physically integral and lords and not (yet) slaves of the created world (Gn 1:27), they dominated whatever could inflict damage, suffering, or oppression, both interior and exterior. This immunity may be inferred from the fact that they were severely and painfully chastised on account of the sin they committed. In the words of Trent, "the entire Adam through that offense of prevarication was changed in body and soul for the worse."[46] To the

44. On the notion of preternatural gifts, J. H. Murphy, *The Preternatural Gifts of Our First Parents in the Fathers of the First Four Centuries* (Maynooth: St. Patrick's College, 1947); W. H. Principe, "Preternatural," in *New Catholic Encyclopedia*, 2nd ed. (Detroit: Thomson/Gale, 2003), 11:686–87; E. A. Asogwa, *The Preternatural Question in the Theology of Original Justice* (Rome: Pontificia Università della Santa Croce, 2019).

45. John Paul II, "Sin Involves the Misuse of God's Gifts," par. 4. John Paul II speaks in this audience of the preternatural gifts in par. 5.

46. DH 1511.

woman God said: "I will greatly multiply your pain in childbearing; in pain you shall bring forth children, yet your desire shall be for your husband, and he shall rule over you." And to Adam he said, "Because you have listened to the voice of your wife, and have eaten of the tree of which I commanded you, 'You shall not eat of it,' cursed is the ground because of you; in toil you shall eat of it all the days of your life; thorns and thistles it shall bring forth to you; and you shall eat the plants of the field" (Gn 3:16–18). So it is not just a question of the physical pain they might have experienced, but also of spiritual and moral suffering, often connected with sin itself. Of particular importance was the sense of shame they experienced on account of their sin (Gn 3:7, 10). From the fact of suffering we can infer that before sinning they lived in a state of harmony, comfort, and impassibility, whatever that consisted of.

This does not mean of course that our first parents were exempt from sensation, for unlike the angels, they were composed of matter and spirit, flesh and bones. In that sense they could experience pain as a disturbance of the nervous system, indicator of their created, material nature. Neither were the passions absent, for the latter constitute an essential part of human nature. Certainly at the outset of creation the passions were balanced, and inclined humans only to the good. As there was no moral perturbation in the heart of our first parents, the passions had nothing of concupiscence, no sinful, disordered, egoistic inclination. The abundance of the divine excluded sinful inclinations (temptations) of an interior kind.[47]

In connection with exemption from suffering it may also be possible to infer the presence of *the gift of knowledge* through the illumination of the intellect (Sir 17:5–6, 9). Only by means of knowledge could humans understand and carry out the mandate received to dominate the created world (Gn 1:28), to cultivate the Garden of Eden (Gn 2:15), to name the animals and birds (Gn 2:20). Obviously this did not involve a perfect knowledge of existing reality. In fact the imperfection of their knowledge was a contributing factor to their sin (Gn 3:2–5). This aspect of original justice is confirmed Christologically by the fact that becoming a believing Christian involves receiving divine revelation, being illumined with the light of faith, a light that had been lost through sin.

47. Thomas Aquinas explains that Christ, though he possessed a fully human nature, did not experience concupiscence on account of the fullness of grace (*ST* III, q. 15, a. 2).

In the fourth place we may consider the preternatural gift of *immortality*. Making humans in his own image and likeness (Gn 1:27), God destined them for immortality (Wis 2:23). Scripture teaches insistently that death entered the world through sin.[48] But Christ came to save us and give us immortality anew, so that "every one who sees the Son and believes in him should have eternal life; and I will raise him up at the last day" (Jn 6:40). According to Augustine, man in paradise *posse non mori*, was capable of not dying.[49] The *Creed of the People of God* confirms this by saying that with original sin human nature was "subjected to the dominion of death." Presently I will consider the way in which original immortality was lost through sin. But an important question arises: if humans had been faithful to God and not sinned, what kind of profile would their subsequent immortality have assumed? Would they have lived on forever on earth in the same bodily circumstances they were created and born in? Or would their earthly existence have come to an end? What kind of immortal existence would have ensued? I will return to the issue later on in this chapter.

The Trial and the Fall of Adam

Scripture speaks openly of the *trial and Fall* of humans in paradise, especially in Genesis 2–3. To understand these texts fully, however, we need to consider them, as always, from the point of view of the saving work of Jesus Christ, the new Adam, the Savior of the world, as represented in Romans 5 and elsewhere.

Of course the starting point for the trial and Fall of humans depends on the fact of their being truly human and *free*. That our first parents were created in the image and likeness of God is commonly taken to mean that humans are created free.[50] Florovsky says that "the reality and substantiality of created nature is manifested *in creaturely freedom*.... Without [human] autonomy nothing happens in creation.... There is no irresistible grace, creatures can and may lose themselves, are capable, as it were, of

48. See O'Callaghan, *Christ Our Hope*, 260–73.

49. See Augustine, *De Gen. ad litt.* 6:36.

50. See O'Callaghan, *Children of God in the World*, 442–44, referring to Tertullian, Gregory of Nyssa, Augustine, John Damascene, Thomas Aquinas, Bernard of Clairvaux, and also Descartes. Gregory Nazianzen says that "God legislates human self-determination," *Or. 45 in S. Pascha* 28.

'metaphysical suicide.' The possibility of metaphysical suicide is open to creation. But the power of self-annihilation is not given."[51] It is also true that in the light of the trial and Fall of humanity that the dynamics of human freedom come to light.

First of all, the *trial*. The Book of Genesis presents the trial of humans not as a test of physical strength, of psychological endurance, or of spiritual intelligence. Rather humans are offered the opportunity of confirming their recognition of, gratitude to, and love of God for the gift of creation, of freely being able to live in filial communion with and obedience to him. "The Lord God took the man and put him in the Garden of Eden to till it and keep it. And the Lord God commanded the man, saying, 'You may freely eat of every tree of the garden; but of the tree of the knowledge of good and evil you shall not eat, for in the day that you eat of it you shall die'" (Gn 2:15–17).

Eating the fruit of the trees in Eden refers primarily of course to human nutrition, the maintenance of the life that God, the God of the living, communicated freely to humans. But what of the tree of the knowledge of good and evil? What was special about this particular tree? From a literary standpoint, it would seem to evoke the Babylonian myth *Gilgamesh*. In it we read: "when the gods created humans, they established death for them, but held on to life for themselves."[52] The gift of life, represented by the tree, according to the Babylonian myth, belongs to the gods, and they hold on to it jealously.

But the God of the Old Testament is a different God. According to Genesis 2–3 he fully intends to magnanimously communicate life and power and immortality to humans, giving them the means to exercise their freedom truly, significantly. "Whereas the Gilgamesh reference to the tree of life is pointless (it is an empty hope, because the gods do not want humans to have this gift), in Scripture the first man had at his disposal the tree of life; that is to say, God was not jealous of the gift of immortality, and gave humans the possibility of living forever."[53] The tree of the knowl-

51. Florovsky, "Creation and Creaturehood," 48.

52. *Gilgamesh*, table 9, col. 4, in G. Furlani, *Miti babilonesi e assiri* (Florence: Sansoni, 1958), 224 (author's translation).

53. E. Galbiati and A. Piazza, *Pagine difficili della Bibbia: Antico Testamento*, 2nd ed. (Milan: Massimo, 1985), 197 (author's translation).

edge of good and evil speaks therefore of the gift of life and immortality which creatures should not attribute to themselves but only to their creator, to the Lord of the universe who gives it to them freely. Nonetheless they are invited to use their gifts and talents in accordance with the will of God, for the glory of God. And their sin in "eating the forbidden fruit" was at heart one of rejecting God's gift of creation, the gift of being, the gift of life, the gift of truth, which they attempted to enjoy as if they were not the fruit of God's love.

In the catechesis of John Paul II we read:

> The tree of the knowledge of good and evil recalls symbolically the absolute limit which man, as a creature, must recognize and respect. Man depends on the Creator and is subject to the laws by which the Creator has established the order of the created world, the essential order of existence (*ordo rerum*). Man is also subject to the moral norms which regulate the use of freedom. The primordial test is therefore aimed at the person's free will, at his freedom. Will man confirm the fundamental order of creation in his conduct, and recognize the truth that he himself is created, the truth of the dignity that belongs to him as the image of God, but also the truth of his creaturely limitation?[54]

Ratzinger comments as follows on the sin of Adam:

> The order of the covenant—the nearness of the God of the covenant, the limitations imposed by good and evil, the inner standard of the human person, creatureliness: all of this is placed in doubt.... Human beings who consider dependence on the highest love as slavery and who try to deny the truth about themselves, which is their creatureliness, do not free themselves; they destroy truth and love.... Sin is, in its essence, a renunciation of truth.[55]

Rejecting the dependency on God that derives from the gift of creation: this is what the first sin consisted of.[56]

The trial of Adam may be understood and clarified further in the light of the trial (or temptation) of Christ, the new Adam. It is clear that Jesus was severely tested or tempted throughout his life. He was tempted in the

54. John Paul II, "Sin Involves the Misuse of God's Gifts," par. 7.

55. Ratzinger, *"In the Beginning,"* 70.

56. See G. R. Castellino, "Il peccato di Adamo: Note a Romani V, 12–14," *Bibbia e oriente* 16 (1974): 152–61; H. C. Askani, "Quand Adam et Eve ont-ils péché?," *Études théologiques et religieuses* 71 (1996): 361–77.

desert for forty days by Satan who strove to distract him from the mission his Father had given him (Mt 4:1–11), trying to get him to act in a more efficacious, easy, or spectacular way, by drawing attention to himself. He was tempted by humans who were "seeking a sign" (Mt 12:38–42).[57] He was tempted and tested by the incomprehension and ignorance of those who listened to him, and especially by their "hardness of heart" (Mk 3:5; 16:14) and lack of faith (Mt 6:30; Mk 8:12). But above all he was tested during the passion and death on the cross before which he exclaimed: "My Father, if it is possible, let this cup pass from me" (Mt 26:39).

Yet Christ remained steadfast throughout all these trials and temptations, which he endured with pained and faithful perseverance, filially united to his Father, with an obedience which literally cost him his life (Phil 2:7). If he had come down from the cross, as was proposed to him (Mt 27:39), he would have undercut the taunts of his enemies who had put him there in the first place, he would have avoided death and, if we can trust the words of the chief priests (Mt 27:42), he might even have obtained the conversion of those present, all of which would have been beneficial. But he did not do so; he obeyed the Father for love of humanity, he drank the chalice to the last drop.

Yet the sin of Adam was one of disobedience to the divine command, for he loved himself at the expense of God and of others; and this is what was undone by the obedience of the new Adam to the Father for love of humanity. "For as by one man's disobedience [Adam's] many were made sinners, so by one man's obedience [Christ's] many will be made righteous" (Rom 5:19). Adam's rejection of God's creative work was undone by Christ's full acceptance of the world created through him and for him (see chapter 6). In this way the floodgates of divine mercy and magnanimity were opened anew. Jesus, the new Adam, not only annulled the disobedience of Adam but revealed the latter's transgression precisely as disobedience, specifically as a lack of willing, filial submission to the God who had created him.

Then the Fall. Scripture clearly presents us with the image of our first parents, fully human and free, failing the test, truly sinning. Whatever the details, it was fundamentally an event that really took place, an event that

57. See O'Callaghan, *The Christological Assimilation*, 206–9.

changed history once and for all.[58] John Paul II says: "it cannot be denied that one sure element emerges from the detailed account of the sin. It describes a *primordial event*, that is, a fact, which according to revelation took place at the beginning of human history."[59] Ratzinger puts it as follows: "Sin is not spoken of in general as an abstract possibility but as a deed, as the sin of a particular person, Adam, who stands at the origin of humankind and with whom the history of sin begins."[60]

Nonetheless, the trial and Fall of humans is expressed in scripture in clearly symbolic and mythical language. This might seem to indicate that original sin was not an event but rather a permanent and timeless situation of humans, inclined perennially toward evil, an integral part of human ontology, and not so much an event that changed the course of history. We have already seen that some authors consider original sin to be a mere *paradigmatic situation* describing the fallen nature of humanity as a whole, instead of being considered as a sinful event followed by a sinful state. If this were the case, the trial and Fall of Adam would not be historical events, but just mythical or historicized descriptions of the common, original, and permanent situation of each person. Original sin would thus be just a typical sin.[61]

Some contemporary Protestant authors stress in a pessimistic key that original sin speaks of the primitive existential poverty of humans and the universe, of their natural and cosmic immaturity.[62] In fact Irenaeus of Lyons said that our first parents were like children at the beginning of histo-

58. See O'Callaghan, *Children of God in the World*, 472–94, especially as regards the two meanings of the term "historical."

59. John Paul II, "Original Sin Causes a Fundamental Change in Mankind," September 10, 1986, par. 1.

60. Ratzinger, *"In the Beginning,"* 71.

61. See *Catholic Faith for Adults: A New Catechism* (New York: Herder and Herder, 1967), no. 252, the so-called *Dutch Catechism*. "The fundamental aspect of Gn 3 is to present human wretchedness: death, struggle between humans, oppression, the harshness of work and birth, the silence of God, who says nothing as if he had abandoned his creature." Z. Alszeghy, "La riflessione sistematica nei racconti protozoici," in *Problemi e prospettive di teologia dogmatica*, ed. K. H. Neufeld (Brescia: Queriniana, 1983), 153–69, at 164 (author's translation).

62. See P. Althaus, *Die christliche Wahrheit: Lehrbuch der Dogmatik*, 2nd ed. (Gütersloh: C. Bertelsmann, 1949), 383; K. Barth, *Church Dogmatics IV/1* (Edinburgh: T and T Clark, 2004), 478–513; E. Brunner, *Der Mensch im Widerspruch: die christliche Lehre vom wahren und vom wirklichen Menschen*, 3rd ed. (Zürich: Zwingli, 1941), 105–43, and *Die christliche Lehre von Schöpfung und Erlösung* (Zürich: Zwingli, 1950), 101–31; P. Tillich, *Systematic Theology* (Chicago: University of Chicago Press, 1956), 2:29–44; and Pannenberg, *Systematic Theology*, 2:231–65.

ry.[63] Something of a kind is presented in an optimistic light by Teilhard de Chardin.[64] Among the idealists, Kant and Lessing defended a similar theory.[65] Original sin would thus take place within the gradual, evolving passage of humans from an instinctive and animal-like existence to a thinking and conscious state. The exegete D. F. Strauss, with a certain dose of liberal optimism, interpreted the original Fall and consequent salvation in terms of a passage of humans from the limitations of childhood to the adult age of freedom and maturity.[66] According to these descriptions, whether taken in pessimistic or optimistic terms, humans are not said to have sinned, but to be sinners. That is the meaning attributed to Genesis 3.

That original sin involved a historical Fall, however, may be appreciated in the light of the concrete historicity of Christ's act of redemptive obedience on the cross (Rom 5:19). Jesus' obedience to the Father and love for humanity were not simply an attitude, a virtue, a spirit, but rather manifested time and again as a series of conscious, punctual, faithful, obedient actions taking place throughout his lifetime, culminating in his death on the cross. On the basis of Christ's life we may say that the sin of Adam did not refer to an anonymous impersonal power or attitude which mysteriously pressurized and oppressed humans, but to a truly free act or series of actions that that changed the course of history.

The Effects of Original Sin on Humanity

Before dealing with the issue of the *transmission* of original sin I shall consider the question of the effects of original sin on Adam in the first place, and on account of him, on the rest of humans. The *Catechism of the Catholic Church* says:

> In that sin man *preferred* himself to God and by that very act scorned him. He chose himself over and against God, against the requirements of his creaturely status and therefore against his own good. Constituted in a state of holiness, man was destined to be fully "divinized" by God in glory. Seduced by the devil,

63. See Irenaeus, *Adv. Haer.* IV, 38:1; *Epideixis* I, 1:14, and II, 1:46.

64. See Glässer, *Konvergenz.*

65. See C. Morerod, "La sécularisation de la providence et du péché originel chez Kant," *Nova et Vetera* 73, no. 1 (1998): 27–49.

66. See Auer, *Die Welt – Gottes Schöpfung*, 526.

he wanted to "be like God," but "without God, before God, and not in accordance with God."[67]

Seven effects of original sin may be noted in our first parents.

First, the first and fundamental effect of original sin is *the loss of divine friendship*, that is the life of grace, of communion with God, and the filial inheritance. Trent says that humans "immediately lost the holiness and justice in which they had been constituted, and through the offense of that prevarication incurred the wrath and indignation of God."[68] This situation involves not simply a *lack* of grace, but truly the *loss* of grace, a privation. John Paul II in his catechesis considers sin above all as a breaking of the covenant with God and a personal act of injustice.[69] "Sin is also a stain and an impurity. Therefore Ezekiel speaks of 'defilement' with sin (Ezek 14:11), especially with the sin of idolatry which the prophets frequently compare to 'adultery' (Hos 2:4.6–7). Hence even the Psalmist asks: 'Purge me with hyssop, and I shall be clean; wash me, and I shall be whiter than snow' (Ps 51:7)."[70]

Thomas Aquinas compares the state of justice with that of the Fall, and teaches that man, in falling, lost the light and beauty of the soul, as well as the life of the soul which is charity, and fell into a kind of *turpitudo animae*, "a deformity of the soul," which produces the death of the soul, the inevitable fruit of separation from God, who is the source of all life.[71] This is not a simple passage from a state of goodness to a neutral state, but actually involves humans moving away from God, to the point of being spurned as it were by God, just as our first parents were ejected from paradise by the angels (Gn 3:23–24), and sinners will be condemned at the last judgment (Mt 25:41).

In fact, scripture speaks of the hate that God has for sinners (Wis 11:25, 14:9; Ps 5:7; Sir 12:3). Those rejected by God live under the threat of extermination (Gn 6–11). The prophet Isaiah says:

67. *CCC*, no. 398, citing Maximus the Confessor, "Contemplatio modi quo Adami transgressio facta sit," *Ambiguorum liber* (Gn 3:5). Augustine says that the mistake of humans was that of "not wanting to be like him for himself, but rather trying to be like God by his own powers" (*De Trin.* X, 5:7).

68. DH 1511 and *CCC*, no. 399.

69. See John Paul II, "Sin Breaks Man's Covenant with God," General Audience, October 29, 1986.

70. John Paul II, "The Sin of Man and the 'Sin of the World,'" General Audience, November 5, 1986, par. 4.

71. See P. O'Callaghan, "The Effects of the Passion and Death of Christ in the Doctrine of St Thomas Aquinas," *Excerpta ex Dissertationibus* (Pamplona: Eunsa, 1987), 11:377–417.

Hear, O heavens, and give ear, O earth; for the Lord has spoken: "Sons have I reared and brought up, but they have rebelled against me. The ox knows its owner, and the ass its master's crib; but Israel does not know, my people does not understand." Ah, sinful nation, a people laden with iniquity, offspring of evildoers, sons who deal corruptly! They have forsaken the Lord, they have despised the Holy One of Israel, they are utterly estranged (Is 1:2–4).

Paul, speaking in the context of the abundance of divine mercy says: "Among these we all once lived in the passions of our flesh, following the desires of body and mind, and so we were by nature children of wrath, like the rest of mankind. But God, who is rich in mercy, out of the great love with which he loved us, even when we were dead through our trespasses, made us alive together with Christ" (Eph 2:3–5).

But what does the anger, hate, and wrath of God toward sinners consist of? How could a God who is love hate sinners? The first thing to be said of course is that God's rejection of the sinner may not be considered his last word, for God is rich in mercy, as the text just cited clearly teaches (Eph 2); in fact the Genesis account of the Fall ends with what has been called the protogospel, the promise of future salvation: "I will put enmity between you and the woman, and between your seed and her seed; he shall bruise your head, and you shall bruise his heel" (Gn 3:15). Still, according to the witness of scripture, God is presented as spurning those who have permanently rejected his love.[72]

The fact that Christ redeemed us through his death and resurrection means that he established anew our friendship and communion with God. Mysteriously he identified himself with death, the fruit of sin, thus *reconciling* humanity with God: "All this [the love of Christ, his death on the Cross, salvation] is from God, who through Christ reconciled us to himself and gave us the ministry of reconciliation; that is, in Christ God was reconciling the world to himself, not counting their trespasses against them, and entrusting to us the message of reconciliation" (2 Cor 5:18–19). When man sinned he separated himself from God (thus becoming his enemy), from others (living in conflict), and from himself (death). And Christ not only restored what Adam had destroyed (communion with God, with others and with self) but also *revealed* what had been destroyed within the very process of restoration or reconciliation.

72. See O'Callaghan, *Christ Our Hope*, 213–15.

In the words of Ratzinger, "Human beings have their selves not only in themselves but also outside of themselves: they live in those whom they love and in those who love them and to whom they are 'present.' Human beings are relational.... But sin means the damaging or the destruction of relationality.... The Son, who is by nature relationship and relatedness, reestablishes relationships."[73]

Specifically, in his unbreakable union with the Father Christ showed the destiny of humans as one of communion with God, and sinfulness as a profound separation from him. In Romans 8:19–21 we read the following description of the Fall and redemption, already considered in chapter 3, in terms of a powerful opposition between bondage, decay, futility on the one hand, and the glorious freedom of God's children on the other: "For the creation waits with eager longing for the revealing of the sons of God; for the creation was subjected to futility, not of its own will but by the will of him who subjected it in hope; because the creation itself will be set free from its bondage to decay and obtain the glorious liberty of the children of God."

Second, another effect of original sin that Genesis 3 and the following chapters is different manifestations of *human conflict.* Genesis 3 presents Adam and Eve mutually accusing one another of the sin committed. Later on Cain killed Abel, and an ample spiral of violence between humans began, well documented throughout the Old Testament. Yet this was healed by Christ who came into the world with the double commandment of love of God and love of neighbor. Christ loved humans and gave himself over for them to the point of losing his own life, allowing them to go free (Jn 18:4–9) and constituting them as his friends (Jn 15:14) and members of his very body (Eph 5:30). In this way he overcame the perverse logic of enmity between brothers and sisters, or at least he introduced into the world a current of love and forgiveness which would eventually make the full communion of humanity possible. Christ's healing of bonds within human society revealed the breakup of human solidarity occasioned by original sin. Again, "Christ manifests man to man."

In the third place, a significant effect of original sin is the introduction of *death and suffering* into human life, the loss of the gift of immortality. We read in the *Catechism of the Catholic Church*:

73. Ratzinger, *"In the Beginning,"* 72 and 76.

The harmony in which they had found themselves, thanks to original justice, is now destroyed: the control of the soul's spiritual faculties over the body is shattered; the union of man and woman becomes subject to tensions, their relations henceforth marked by lust and domination (Gn 3:7–16). Harmony with creation is broken: visible creation has become alien and hostile to man (Gn 3:17, 19). Because of man, creation is now subject "to its bondage to decay" (Rom 8:21). Finally, the consequence explicitly foretold for this disobedience will come true: man will "return to the ground" (Gn 3:19), for out of it he was taken. Death makes its entrance into human history (Rom 5:12).[74]

Many passages of scripture confirm the close bond between sin and death, beginning with the expulsion of our first parents from paradise (Gn 3:19, 23). The Book of Wisdom explains it as follows: "because God did not make death, and he does not delight in the death of the living. For he created all things that they might exist, and the generative forces of the world are wholesome, and there is no destructive poison in them; and the dominion of Hades is not on earth" (Wis 1:13). "For God created man for incorruption [Greek, *aphtarsia,* which means incorruption or immortality],[75] and made him in the image of his own eternity, but through the devil's envy death entered the world, and those who belong to his party experience it" (Wis 2:23).[76] The letter to the Romans makes this especially clear.[77] "Therefore as sin came into the world through one man and death through sin, and so death spread to all men because all men sinned" (Rom 5:12). "For the wages of sin is death, but the free gift of God is eternal life in Christ Jesus our Lord" (Rom 6:23).[78] Lastly, the letter of James

74. *CCC,* no. 400. And elsewhere: "Even though man's nature is mortal, God had destined him not to die. Death was therefore contrary to the plans of God the Creator and entered the world as a consequence of sin (Wis 2:23–24)" (*CCC,* no. 1008). The *Catechism* adds that "the Church's Magisterium, as authentic interpreter of the affirmations of Scripture and Tradition, teaches that death entered the world on account of man's sin." See also *GS,* no. 18.

75. See BDAG 155, s.v. ἀφθαρσία.

76. See L. Mazzinghi, "'Dio non ha creato la morte' (Sap 1,13). Il tema della morte nel libro della Sapienza," *Parola, Spirito e Vita* 32 (1995): 63–75.

77. In the words of Dubarle: "Considering the general intention of the narrative, we may deduce here the earliest origin of the teaching of St. Paul has formulated with complete clarity, when he attributes to Adam the introduction of sin into the world, and not only of death. This is not a new revelation but rather an abstract of the real content of the old narrative." A.-M. Dubarle, *Le péché originel dans l'Écriture* (Paris: Du Cerf, 1967), 62.

78. On notion of "wages" as applied to death, C. C. Caragounis, "'Οψώνιον: A Reconsideration of Its Meaning," *Novum Testamentum* 16 (1974): 35–57; *NIDNTTE* 3:583, s.v. ὀψώνιον: "The point of the verse is that sin pays out wages, set over against God's gift (χάρισμα) of eternal life."

puts it as follows: "Then desire when it has conceived gives birth to sin; and sin when it is full-grown brings forth death" (Jas 1:15).

But would it not be more correct to say that death is simply a characteristic of creation itself, of the finitude of created beings, of the perishable quality that marks all multicellular life?[79] Perhaps humans should realistically accept it as such, rather than fighting against it or trying to explain it away in ethical or mythical terms. For one who believes in God as creator, however, acceptance of the naturalness of death would mean that it should be seen as a manifestation of the will of God, an integral part of the eternal divine project, that would need to be considered in a positive light.[80]

Thomas Aquinas sums up Christian teaching on the origin of death in the following formula: *necessitas moriendi partim ex natura, partim ex peccato*:[81] the need for humans to die derives in part from nature, from the physical, biological condition of humans, in part from sin. This is not to say of course that sin and nature are equal parts in the process, for the simple reason that they are not commensurate categories that might be quantitatively compared. For what is original in God's plan is immortality; sin, which stalls human life and potentially destroys it, is an accident, albeit an important one.[82]

Clement of Alexandria,[83] on the basis of a Platonic dualistic anthropology and in continuity with Origen, suggested that death is natural for humans in that it involves only the destruction of the body, whereas sin—which is fruit of our ignorance of the Father[84]—would involve only the death of the soul. This is based however on a dualistic anthropology which would not hold in the light of the resurrection of the dead. Athanasius ar-

79. In the coming pages I have followed O'Callaghan, *Christ Our Hope,* 261–65.

80. Karl Barth suggests that "death belongs to the life of the creature and is thus necessary to it" (*Church Dogmatics III/2*, 639). Likewise, Karl Rahner says: "The end of the human being as a spiritual person is an active immanent consummation, an act of self-completion, a life-synthesizing self-affirmation, an achievement of a person's total self-possession, a creation of himself, the fulfillment of his personal reality." *On the Theology of Death* (New York: Herder and Herder, 1965), 40.

81. Thomas Aquinas, *III Sent.*, d. 16, a. 1, arg. 1, co. Elsewhere, he says: "mors est et naturalis . . . et est poenalis" (*ST* II-II, q. 164, a. 1, ad 1); "mors quodammodo est secundum naturam et quodammodo contra naturam" (*De malo*, q. 5, a. 5, ad 17). On this issue, see J. Pieper, *Death and Immortality* (South Bend, Ind.: St. Augustine's Press, 2000), 128.

82. According to Aquinas, immortality in man is originally due to God's action: *ST* I-II, q. 85, a. 6, co., and *Comp. Theol.*, 152.

83. See Clement of Alexandria, *Strom.* IV, 12:5; see also Origen, *De princip.* I, 2:4.

84. See Clement of Alexandria, *Strom.* II, 34:3.

gued that death is natural insofar as the *possibility* of death is written into nature, whereas the concrete *fact* of death is due to sin: neither nature nor sin suffices for death to take place, for they act concomitantly.[85] This position became quite common among the Church Fathers and may be considered the received position in Catholic theology: that the *possibility* of death is of nature, but the *fact* is a punishment for sin.

In recent times, some theologians attempted to explain mortality simply in terms of the finitude of human nature.[86] They held that only the subjective experience of death experienced by sinners (fear, anguish, etc.) may be understood as the result of sin.[87] The position was assumed by the Encyclopedist philosophers (Diderot, D'Alembert, Voltaire),[88] who taught that death was totally natural, and that the proper thing for a mature person to do was to overcome the fear of death, accepting it through the cultivation of philosophy. Throughout the twentieth century, however, some Protestant theologians recovered the realism of the bond linking sin and death that scripture clearly speaks of. They look upon death in terms of divine judgment on sinners, not just as the human sense of guilt but as an expression of God's wrath.[89] Insofar as sin involves separation from God as well as alienation from other people and from the cosmos itself, it makes sense to consider death as the "triumph of total non-relationship,"[90] as the inner and most logical consequence of sin.[91]

And what would have happened if our first parents had never sinned? Would they have died? If the "death as finitude" argument is correct, they would have had to die sooner or later. Yet if death is, strictly speaking, a

85. See Athanasius, *De inc.* 4.

86. See Pannenberg, *Systematic Theology,* 2:265–75. In Catholic theology, H. Köster, *Urstand, Fall und Erbsünde in der katholischen Theologie unseres Jahrhunderts* (Regensburg: F. Pustet, 1983), 71.

87. See, for example, Schleiermacher, *The Christian Faith,* §76:2, 319.

88. See D. Hattrup, *Eschatologie* (Paderborn: Bonifatius, 1992), 120–24.

89. They include Althaus, Brunner, Barth, and Jüngel. On these authors, see W. Pannenberg, *Systematic Theology,* 2:269n324. On the theology of death, see ibid., 3:556–63. Authors such as Oscar Cullmann insist that death derives directly from sin: *Immortalité de l'âme ou Résurrection des morts? Le témoignage du Nouveau Testament* (Neuchâtel: Delachaux et Niestlé, 1956), 33–46. Pannenberg admits that death is a consequence of finitude. But he adds: "The distinction between finitude and death may be seen here in the fact that it is precisely the sinners' non-acceptance of their finitude [Gn 3:5] that delivers them up to death," *Systematic Theology,* 3:561. See also Barth, *Church Dogmatics III/2,* 628–33.

90. E. Jungel, *Tod* (Stuttgart: Kreuz, 1971), 150.

91. See G. Gozzelino, *Nell'attesa della beata speranza: Saggio di escatologia cristiana* (Turin: Elle di Ci, 1993), 440–43; J. Ratzinger, *Eschatology: Death and Eternal Life* (San Francisco, Calif.: Ignatius Press, 1988), 80–101.

punishment for sin, then we would have to conclude that in its absence humans would have lived on forever. But this does not seem to fit in with biblical witness to the fact that Adam's life on earth, even in the absence of sin, was considered as a trial, a test of faith, finite in time, that was meant to come to a close at some stage. A trial that never ends is no longer a trial; in fact it may well be a misery. All we can conclude is that if humans had not in fact sinned, the end of life would probably have been different than it is now. Instead of the prospect of a dramatic end, or a drawn-out, painful destruction and decay of humans, we might surmise that they would have acquired immortality, body and soul, and eternal life, at the conclusion of their earthly lives, in a way not unrelated to the *dormitio Mariae*, Mary's Assumption.[92] In effect, Mary was conceived immaculately, without any trace of original sin, she lived a life without sin, and at the end of her earthly pilgrimage, once the path of faith was over, she was assumed, body and soul, into heaven,[93] entering into the fullness of her heavenly prize.[94] Perhaps we can say that if our first parents had been faithful to God's word and gifts they might also have been assumed into heaven at the end of their earthly sojourn. In fact the idea of faithful prophets being assumed into heaven is not uncommon in the Old Testament (1 Mc 2:58; Ps 48:9; Sir 48:9, 49:14).

This argument finds a support in the saving work of Christ who, dying on the cross in obedience to the Father, proclaimed that life is entirely a gift of the Father, and is not at the arbitrary disposal of humans. The fact that he accepted death, however, is an indication that it is not a pure and simple equivalent of sin. With the resurrection God in Christ gave humans back the gift of immortality, the grace of eternal life and the promise of final resurrection at the end of time. Again we see how Christ manifests man to man, as a light projected onto the primitive darkness of sin, revealing the latter as estrangement from God, as the breakup of human relationships, as the destruction of human life itself.[95]

92. See Jüngel, *Tod*, 128.

93. See DH 3900–3904.

94. See Pozo, *María en la obra de la salvación*, 314–24. Germanus of Constantinople said that Mary was assumed into heaven *ut ex hoc etiam a resolutione in pulverem deinceps sit alienum*, "so that she would be spared from being dissolved into dust." *Oratio in dormitionem SS. Deiparae*, in J.-P. Migne (ed.), *Patrologiae cursus completus, series graeca* (Paris: 1857–86), 98:345.

95. L. Scheffczyk suggests that human immortality before the Fall would consist of "the promise,

Fourth, the Council of Trent speaks besides of *submission or enslavement to the devil* as the result of original sin.[96] By our first parents' sin, the devil has acquired a certain dominion over man, even though man remains free. Original sin, the *Catechism of the Catholic Church* says, entails "captivity under the power of him who thenceforth had the power of death, that is, the devil."[97] Paul insists frequently on the fact that sin results above all in the loss of freedom, enslavement: to disordered passions, to acquired habits, to previous decisions, and also to the devil. To those who did not wish to listen to his words, Jesus said: "You are of your father the devil, and your will is to do your father's desires" (Jn 8:44). It may be noted besides that enslavement to the devil, who instigated sin in the first place, is linked with the destructive power of death, for "through the devil's envy death entered the world" (Wis 2:24).

We have already seen how the words and works of Christ show up the slavery induced by sin and the war Satan wages on humanity. Jesus was the implacable and definitive foe of Satan and came to the world to defeat him once and for all. The whole of Jesus' life, and especially the final moments of his passion and death, constituted a battle to the end with the devil and a definitive victory over him. Even though Satan is described as the prince of this world (Jn 16:11), he is cast out by the power of Christ (Jn 12:31), and the kingdom of God is established (Mt 12:28). Christ, we are told in the letter to the Hebrews, "partook of the same [human] nature, that through death he might destroy him who has the power of death, that is, the devil, and deliver all those who through fear of death were subject to lifelong bondage" (Heb 2:14–15). He liberates us from the power of the devil and at

excluding all fear of death, of an entirely gratuitous transformation, at the end of our earthly existence" in his "Die Erbschuld zwischen Naturalismus und Existentialismus. Zur Frage nach der Anpassung des Erbsündendogmas an das moderne Denken," *Münchener Theologische Zeitschrift* 15 (1964): 17–57, at 53. And in his "Sin Involves the Misuse of God's Gifts," John Paul II taught: "Thanks to the divine gifts, man, who was joined in friendship and harmony with his principle of being, had and maintained in himself an interior equilibrium. He was not worried about the prospect of decay and death. The 'dominion' over the world, which God had given man from the beginning, was realized first of all in man himself, as dominion over himself. In this self-dominion and equilibrium he had the 'integrity' (*integritas*) of existence, in the sense that man was intact and well-ordered in all his being" (par. 5). On the contrary, "Man was created by God for immortality. Death appears as a tragic leap in the dark, and is the consequence of sin, as if by an immanent logic, but especially as the punishment of God." "The State of Man in Fallen Nature," General Audience, October 8, 1986, par. 5.

96. See John Paul II, "The Fall of the Rebellious Angels," General Audience, August 13, 1986.

97. CCC, no. 407, citing Heb 2:14 and DH 1511.

the same time reveals to us something of what that enslavement involved.

Fifth, original sin *damaged the whole human being.* Trent says that man "was changed in body and soul for the worse."[98] For Paul VI fallen human nature is "injured in its own natural powers."[99] And John Paul II teaches: "Here we are dealing not only with immortality and exemption from many sufferings, gifts lost because of sin, but also with interior dispositions of the reason and will, that is, with habitual energies of the reason and will. As a consequence of original sin the whole man, body and soul, has been thrown into confusion."[100] The *Catechism of the Catholic Church* says that "the harmony in which they [our first parents] had found themselves, thanks to original justice, is now destroyed: the control of the soul's spiritual faculties over the body is shattered; the union of man and woman becomes subject to tensions, their relations henceforth marked by lust and domination. Harmony with creation is broken: visible creation has become alien and hostile to man."[101]

As regards the spiritual faculties of humans, this deterioration "consists in a darkening of the intellect's capacity to know the truth, and in a weakening of free will. The will is weakened in the presence of the attractions of the goods perceived by the senses and is more exposed to the false images of good elaborated by reason under the influence of the passions."[102] Theologians have always insisted that this deterioration is a relative and not an absolute one,[103] for man is not interiorly corrupt, as Luther had suggested.

> Even after original sin, man can know by his intellect the fundamental natural and religious truths, and the moral principles. He can also perform good works. One should therefore speak rather of a darkening of the intellect and of a weakening of the will, of "wounds" of the spiritual and sensitive faculties, and not of a loss of their essential capacities even in relation to the knowledge and love of God.[104]

98. DH 1511.
99. Paul VI, *Creed of the People of God*, par. 16.
100. John Paul II, "The State of Man in Fallen Nature," par. 6.
101. *CCC*, no. 400.
102. John Paul II, "The State of Man in Fallen Nature," par. 7.
103. Ibid.
104. Ibid.

Sixth, an important effect of original sin is *the inclination to sin,* or *concupiscence* that remains in humans even after baptism. It is often called *fomes peccati* (the Latin term *fomes* literally means a kindling or inflaming, a stimulus). As we saw above, Trent taught that this inclination or stimulus is not itself sin, but is "of sin and inclines to sin."[105] In other words, concupiscence produces sin only when willingly consented to. John Paul II explains: "As a consequence of original sin, concupiscence is the source of the inclination to various personal sins committed by people through the evil use of their faculties (these sins are called actual, to distinguish them from original sin). This inclination remains in man even after holy Baptism. In this sense everyone bears in himself the 'stimulus' of sin."[106]

From the Christological point of view we can say that Christ, in saving humans, gradually heals the damage done by sin and overcomes concupiscence by grace, with his word and with the promise of future resurrection. But whereas Christ assumed death, as we saw above, he did not assume concupiscence. The fullness of grace that marked his entire existence eliminated all inclination to sin.[107] Concupiscence would have had no meaning in his life, for he was "tempted ... in every respect, yet without sin" (Heb 4:15). Besides, the life, works, and preaching of Jesus show up humans as damaged beings, who stand in need of grace, patience, repeated explanations and above all, abundant charity, affection, understanding, and forgiveness. Jesus did not force conversion on people because he knew the human heart was wounded and needed time and space to overcome concupiscence and difficulties. In contemplating the life and words of Christ we can better appreciate the complex nature and dynamic of the wounds inflicted on humans by original sin, at the same time as he heals them.

Seventh and lastly, original sin had the effect not only of damaging humans in intellect, will, and spirit, but also of *inverting the proper relationship between humanity and nature,* undoing the task and blessing of dominating over the earth that Genesis 1:26–28 speaks of. By sinning humans in a sense attempted to divinize nature by putting it in the place of God, thus disobeying the divine mandate. In the words of Zizioulas,

105. DH 1515.

106. John Paul II, "The State of Man in Fallen Nature," par. 8.

107. See Thomas Aquinas, *ST* III, q. 15, a. 2.

Adam succumbed to temptation to declare himself "God" and set out to redirect creation from the uncreated God to his own, created self. In deciding that everything should refer to him, his fall was also the fall of creation. . . . Man attributed nature with characteristics that belong to God. Since conflict with nature made man realize how much weaker he is, he began to believe himself to be inferior to nature. Overawed by creatures, he began to divinize the forces of nature and then to placate them, so that idolatry became another consequence of man's fall. . . . The deification of creation is a tragedy for mankind and for nature too.[108]

Human Responsibility for Original Sin

Grace is not our own. It comes from God as a pure gift in Christ. But neither is sin.[109] In fact sin is not just an act, but a condition we are born into;[110] we may inflict evil on others but we are also afflicted by evil. McFarland observes: "The will does whatever it wants, but it cannot want whatever it wants. . . . Just as grace and salvation are not at bottom matters of personal virtue, neither are sin and damnation fundamentally matters of personal vice." And he concludes: "Original sin is an ontological rather than a moral category,"[111] although it has moral consequences. One of the problems of Pelagian theology was that sin was seen as both unavoidable and culpable.[112] The fact that sin can afflict us obliges us to distinguish between constitutive factors of human existence and nature on the one hand and personal sinful actions on the other, that is, between the state and the act of sin. Pannenberg looks upon sin as a *state* of alienation from God that precedes all human acts, although "sin does not come about without our own cooperation and . . . consent."[113] Karl Barth tries to avoid distinguishing between what we are and what we do, but still he says: "Man sins, but more than that, he is a sinner."[114]

108. Zizioulas, "Creation and Salvation," 98. I have already considered this issue in chapter 10.

109. See McFarland, "The Fall and Sin," 146.

110. See E. Farley, *Good and Evil: Interpreting a Human Condition* (Minneapolis, Minn.: Fortress Press, 1990).

111. McFarland, "The Fall and Sin," 148 and 153.

112. Ibid., 144. The classical critique of F. R. Tennant in his three-volume series, *The Origin and Propagation of Sin; The Sources of the Doctrine of the Fall and Original Sin; The Concept of Sin* (Cambridge: Cambridge University Press, 1902–1912).

113. Pannenberg, *Systematic Theology*, 2:262.

114. Barth, *Church Dogmatics IV/1*, 495.

Some accounts of original sin considered above explain it in terms that give little or no responsibility to the concrete human being who acts freely within history. To some degree this was the position of Irenaeus and Theophilus of Antioch, who took it that Adam and Eve were like children when they sinned.[115] Others look on the first transgression as an act of perfect, lucid, and individual freedom, almost diabolic in its clarity, and therefore undertaken with full responsibility. This for example is the position of Origen,[116] who identifies man primarily with his soul, his spiritual (angelic) essence. Sin precedes the creation of matter, he says, and consists of a purely spiritual, angelic, fully responsible act, that brings about the creation of the material world and occasions our fall into bodily matter. But it should be noted that for Origen original sin, such as it is, is universal because *all* humans sinned as spirits, one by one. Those who did not sin, in fact, were the angels. Thus original sin is not transmitted as such from one person to another,[117] for all became sinners one by one. In other words there is no original sin, but just personal sin.

In respect of Origen's explanation two observations may be made. First, he associates the notion of full responsibility directly with the non-transmitted nature of original sin. This seems to indicate that moral responsibility and transmission are somewhat antithetical. And second, his explanation of original sin involves a negative view of the material world which was created by God for the purpose of purifying fallen humans. In other words, matter and the world exists on account of sin. The final reconciliation of the world (*apokatastasis*), according to Origen, will involve the resurrection of the dead in the context of a merely ethereal materiality.

As we saw earlier on, however, the effects of original sin for our first parents and for humanity were devastating; the very world we live in shows its marks clearly. Adam lost divine friendship for himself and for humanity and set in motion a deeply destructive process. The very fact of the incarnation of the Word shows how seriously God has taken this transgression. But the question arises: how was it possible for our first parents to sin so grievously? They were constituted in perfect harmony of body

115. See Irenaeus, *Adv. Haer.* IV, 18:1; Theophilus of Antioch, *Ad Autolyc.* II, 25.

116. See Origen, *Contra Celsus* VII, 50; *De princip.* 2, 8:3, and 2, 9:6; *In Gen.* III, 21.

117. On the ambivalence of question of the transmission of original sin in Origen, see Sayés, *Antropología del hombre caído,* 99–102.

and soul. Their sin was not one of weakness or bad habit. They did not enjoy the beatific vision of course, but lived in grace and enjoyed the infused virtues in abundance. In this situation of spiritual fortitude and serenity, how could they have committed so grave a sin? Where did its malice derive from?

THE SOCIAL ASPECT OF ORIGINAL SIN

For the most part, Christian tradition, based on scripture, has held that the Fall did not involve the sins of the flesh, even though certain elements of the temptation narrative might suggest this (e.g., the role of the serpent).[118] Rather it was considered a sin of mistrust, disobedience, and pride.[119] The *Catechism of the Catholic Church* finds the root of this temptation in a loss of faith and trust in God: "Man, tempted by the devil, let his trust in his Creator die in his heart and, abusing his freedom, disobeyed God's command. This is what man's first sin consisted of. All subsequent sin would be disobedience toward God and lack of trust in his goodness."[120] Thomas Aquinas says that the *only* sin our first parents were capable of committing, given the virtuous rectitude of their lives, was one of pride,[121] and that they were induced to do so by the devil. "The first man sinned chiefly by coveting God's likeness as regards 'knowledge of good and evil,' following the serpent's instigation, namely that by his own natural power he might decide what was good, and what was evil for him to do; or again that he should of himself foreknow what good and what evil would befall him."[122] And the *Catechism* observes: "Behind the disobedient choice of our first parents lurks a seductive voice, opposed

118. Mythology often represents serpents in relation to sexual transgressions. Among the Canaanites, serpents figured among the fertility divinities. This is why a possible sexual explanation was given by some Church Fathers; for example, Clement of Alexandria, *Strom.* III, 17. On the issue, see J. Coppens, "L'interprétation sexuelle du péché du paradis dans la littérature patristique," *Ephemerides Theologicae Lovanienses* 24 (1948): 402–8; F. Asensio, "¿Tradición sobre un pecado sexual en el Paraíso?," *Gregorianum* 30 (1949): 490–520; 31 (1950): 35–62, 163–91, 362–90. Ratzinger, "In the Beginning," 66, says that in an Eastern religious setting, "the serpent was a symbol of that wisdom which rules the world and of the fertility through which human beings plunge into the divine current of life and for a few moments experience themselves fused with its divine power."

119. Thus Augustine, *Enn. in Ps.* 70.

120. CCC, no. 397.

121. See Thomas Aquinas, *ST* II-II, q. 163, a. 1.

122. Ibid., a. 2, co.

to God, which makes them fall into death out of envy."[123] Mark Robson says that the poet "Milton, in *Paradise Lost*, tells us that Sin was born out of Satan's head as he hatched thoughts of his own pride. God has given us creative indeterminate capacities. We discovered that we could conceive of thoughts, plans and ideals that warp the values that God embodies."[124]

Denying the existence and activity of the devil and the fallen angels makes it particularly difficult for us to understand the gravity, malice, and destructive power of original sin. It is clear that the sin of our first parents, committed with full freedom and responsibility, was human and not angelic, and involved the acceptance of temptation without which such a sin would have been unthinkable.

We correctly think of sin in personal, individual terms: individuals *act* sinfully and fall into a personal *state* of sin for which they are responsible. But as we have just seen, sin has a social side to it insofar as humans may be *induced* into sin by others, experiencing the pressure of evil; besides, sin can become collective. In fact, scripture tells us that the sin of our first parents was social, in that it became contagious and common very quickly. "No one sins entirely alone and no one sins without adding to the collective burden of mankind."[125] It was committed individually, but it did not begin in a solitary fashion; neither did it remain that way. The woman was tempted by the serpent, representative of the devil. She in turn tempted the man to follow suit and eat of the tree of knowledge of good and evil: "she took of its fruit and ate; and she also gave some to her husband, and he ate" (Gn 3:6). A double temptation produced a double shame and mutual recrimination: "then the eyes of both were opened, and they knew that they were naked" (Gn 3:7). Both began to justify themselves, seeking a scapegoat for their transgression in the other. "God said, 'Who told you that you were naked? Have you eaten of the tree of which I commanded you not to eat?' The man said, 'The woman whom you gave to be with me, she gave me fruit of the tree, and I ate'" (Gn 3:11–12).

123. CCC, no. 391.

124. Robson, *Ontology and Providence*, 176.

125. B. Byrne, *Reckoning with Romans: A Contemporary Reading of Paul's Gospel* (Wilmington, Del.: M. Glazier, 1986), 116.

OUR FIRST PARENTS

In the sense that I have just considered, original sin was not merely *individual*—responsible therefore, the fruit of personal freedom—but also *social*, in that it involved the action of and cooperation with other people, and in the first place with the devil. This brings us to consider the difficult question of the precise identity of what I have called until now our first parents, "Adam" and "Eve."[126] Traditionally it has been taken for granted that original sin was committed literally by the first two individuals of the human species created by God, Adam and Eve, who were, besides, united conjugally, and from whom we all descend. In this way it was possible to offer a straightforward explanation of the universality of sin and therefore of universal salvation: the whole of humanity fell in the first couple who transmitted the fallen human condition to all the rest through generation; and Christ, the new Adam, redeemed it. This position is usually called *monogenism.*[127]

Findings in biblical exegesis and science over the last century and a half, however, have put this position under considerable strain. New hypotheses have arisen in respect of the beginnings and transmission of original sin, described in terms of *polygenism.*[128] This would involve the existence of several more or less developed and independent groups of humans existent at the beginning of the human race from which humanity as a whole is descended. Clearly this explanation cannot account for the universality of sin by way of human generation as simply as does monogenism. Four questions are involved here, the first exegetical, the second scientific, the third Magisterial, the fourth theological. Perhaps at this stage, we may say that whereas monogenism fits well with the doctrine of faith (the universality of sin and of salvation) but is more difficult to justify scientifically, with polygenism things are the other way around: the hypothesis is more in keeping with

126. See A. Chapelle, "Méditation sur 'nos premiers parents'," *Nouvelle Revue Théologique* 112 (1990): 702–17.

127. See R. Garrigou-Lagrange, "Le monogénisme n'est-il nullement révélé, pas même implicitement?," *Doctor communis* 2 (1948): 191–202; K. Rahner, "Erbsünde und Monogenismus," *Theologie der Erbsünde*, ed. K.-H. Weger (Freiburg i.B.: Herder, 1970), 176–223.

128. See the study of A. Suarez, "Can We Give Up the Origin of Humanity from a Primal Couple Without Giving Up the Teaching of Original Sin and Atonement?," *Science & Christian Belief* 27, no. 1 (2015): 59–83.

the findings of science, yet harder to marry with the doctrine of the faith. Whatever solution is given to the dilemma, a clear or definitive conclusion is not possible at the present moment. This issue very definitely is a work in progress. Thus the suggestions and explanations offered in the coming pages are plainly provisional in character.

First, the biblical question, given, of course, that Genesis is an exceptionally difficult text to interpret. The name Adam, traditionally taken as a personal name, derives in fact from the Aramaic *'adamah,* literally meaning "what is drawn from the earth," and may well have a collective rather than personal meaning. Thus it could easily be translated as "humanity," or "humans." This collectivity would constitute the subject of the primitive transgression. Besides, the primordial serpent spoken of in Genesis 3:1 could well refer to an idolatrous symbol before whom humans might have committed a common, shared crime of idolatry. These observations of course refer principally to the linguistic interpretation of Genesis and not necessarily to its theology, which must be understood in terms of the entirety of scripture, both Old and New Testaments, and especially in the light of Romans 5.[129]

The second question is scientific in character. The idea of a collective subject for original sin is proposed on the basis of the evolution of the human race: "The best available evidence suggests that modern humans emerged as a splinter population from pre-existing hominid groups within the last quarter of a million years."[130] This would make it difficult to hold that all humans descend from a single couple, thus calling monogenism into question. What does seem possible however is the theory of *monophyletic identity,* according to which the whole of humanity has a single biological origin situated in a female individual who lived anywhere from fifty thousand to a hundred thousand years ago, probably in southern Africa.[131] McFarland makes the following valid observation on this proposal. "While it is true that all modern human beings do share a common male

129. In the words of Ratzinger, "it would be wrong to understand Adam—word and history—only as a collective name for humanity." Quoted in S. Sanz Sánchez, "Joseph Ratzinger y la doctrina de la creación: los apuntes de Münster de 1964 (y III). Algunos temas debatidos," *Revista Española de Teología* 74, no. 3 (2014): 453–96, at 484n94.

130. McFarland, "The Fall and Sin," 143. See also P. Enns, *The Evolution of Adam: What the Bible Does and Doesn't Say about Human Origins* (Grand Rapids, Mich.: Brazos Press, 2012).

131. See R. L. Cann, M. Stoneking, and A. C. Wilson, "Mitochondrial DNA and Human Evolution," *Nature* 325, no. 1 (1987): 31–36.

and female ancestor (the so-called 'Y-chromosomal Adam' and 'mitochondrial Eve'), these two individuals were not contemporaries and neither was the first modern human."[132]

Clearly therefore the monophyletic explanation is not equivalent to monogenism. Still, in the context of Christian anthropology, which is based on the profound union between body and soul,[133] there need not be a substantial opposition between the two. After all, wherever there is a living human body, there is a human person.

It has been proposed that the beginning of the human race involved God infusing a spiritual soul into a first couple of hominoids.[134] They went on to sin—we are told—and passed on their fallen condition to the rest of humanity. This is a problematic explanation, however, firstly because it involves a process of hominization that could easily be contrived as dualistic and Platonic,[135] and secondly because it fails to explain satisfactorily how original guilt is handed on to the rest of humans who do not descend from the original fully human couple into whom God infused a soul. McFarland observes:

> Attempts . . . to place "Adam and Eve" in Mesopotamia in the Neolithic period simply give up on the logic of Augustine's position, since by that time human beings had already spread over the globe and thus cannot all have descended from this putative pair. Robert Jenson's proposal . . . that "Adam and Eve" were "the first community of our biological ancestors who disobeyed God's command" is more consistent with the Augustinian position (so long as it is understood that all modern humans descended from this first group of disobedient hominids), but it would seem to require at least some transmission of original sin "by imitation" within this population group.[136]

In any case perhaps it is fair to say with Ratzinger that "biological polygenism and theological monogenism may not form an exclusive alternative."[137] Perhaps they can go together.

132. McFarland, "The Fall and Sin," 143n3.

133. See O'Callaghan, *Children of God in the World*, 406–41.

134. Thus Suarez, "Can We Give Up the Origin of Humanity?"

135. This is explained in O'Callaghan, *Children of God in the World*, 430–35.

136. McFarland, "Original Sin," 309n8. He refers to D. R. Alexander, *Creation and Evolution: Do We Have to Choose?* (Oxford: Monarch Books, 2008), and R. W. Jenson, *Systematic Theology, vol. 2: The Works of God* (New York: Oxford University Press, 1999), 150. Specifically on Adam and Eve, see Alexander, "Creation and Evolution," 242–43.

137. J. Ratzinger, quoted in Sanz Sánchez, "Joseph Ratzinger y la doctrina de la creación," 482n82.

The third question: the principal church documents dealing with original sin—the Councils of Carthage, Orange, and Trent, the *Creed of the People of God,* John Paul II's *Catechesis,* the *Catechism of the Catholic Church*—refer generally to our first parents in apparently monogenistic terms. In 1950 Pope Pius XII in the encyclical *Humani Generis,* after accepting in general terms the theory of evolution said:

> When, however, there is question of another conjectural opinion, namely polygenism, the children of the Church by no means enjoy such liberty. For the faithful cannot embrace that opinion which maintains that either after Adam there existed on this earth true men who did not take their origin through natural generation from him as from the first parent of all, or that Adam represents a certain number of first parents. Now it is in no way apparent how such an opinion can be reconciled with that which the sources of revealed truth and the documents of the Teaching Authority of the Church propose with regard to original sin, which proceeds from a sin actually committed by an individual Adam and which, through generation, is passed on to all and is in everyone as his own.[138]

In 1966 Pope Paul VI insisted that polygenism is still a nondemonstrated hypothesis and that original sin refers above all to the obedience of Adam, the "first man."[139] John Paul II considers that the words of Pope Paul "are valid and a stimulus for further research."[140] It would seem that recent popes have left the question of monogenism and polygenism as an open one.

In the fourth place, what can we say theologically of Adam and Eve? What has scripture to say on the matter at a wider level? How does the question of our first parents appear in the light of the saving work of

---

Likewise, see K. W. Kemp, "Science, Theology, and Monogenesis," *American Catholic Philosophical Quarterly* 85 (2011): 217–36. Ratzinger extends this explanation as follows in a 1964 text: "The event of humanization in its inner depths goes beyond biological categories. That is to say, even though it is very likely that hominization began within a population in a polygenic way, it is still possible that the genial *blitz* of thinking out transcendence took place for the first time in one or two individuals. Biological polygenism and theological monogenism are not necessarily exclusively antithetical, because the level of the questions they respond to do not coincide completely." Quoted in S. Sanz Sánchez, "Joseph Ratzinger e il peccato originale: riflessioni a proposito di un libro mancato," *Revista Española de Teología* 78 (2019): 439–57, at 451 (author's translation).

138. Pius XII, *Humani Generis,* Encyclical Letter, August 12, 1950, par. 37.

139. Paul VI, "Discourse to Participants in a Symposium on Original Sin," July 11, 1966.

140. John Paul II, "Consequences of Original Sin for All Humanity," General Audience, October 1, 1986, par. 4.

Christ? The first thing to note is the parallelism Paul establishes between Adam and Christ, within which the individuality of Christ seems to pair off with that of Adam. And just as Christ is not an abstract representative of humanity, but a real man who lived in a concrete culture and history, so one might think that Adam and Eve were not simply typical representatives of primitive humanity, generic names representing the male and the female, but real persons with a personal history of grace and disgrace. In the light of the life of Jesus, Paul in Romans 5 clarifies the identity of Adam as follows:

> Therefore as sin came into the world *through one man* [*heis anthrōpos*] and death through sin, and so death spread to all men because all men sinned.... But the free gift is not like the trespass. For if many died through one man's trespass, much more have the grace of God and the free gift in the grace of that one man Jesus Christ abounded for many.... If, because of one man's trespass, death reigned through that one man, much more will those who receive the abundance of grace and the free gift of righteousness reign in life through the one man Jesus Christ. Then as one man's trespass led to condemnation for all men, so one man's act of righteousness leads to acquittal and life for all men. For as by one man's disobedience many were made sinners, so by one man's obedience many will be made righteous (Rom 5:12, 15, 17–19).

The message of the text would seem to be the following: Christ in person saved humanity, because Adam in person had sinned. However, most authors do not consider that the text justifies a necessary parallelism between two individuals, Christ and Adam. The biblical scholar Pierre Grelot writes: "In the case of Christ, the term 'only one' clearly designates his person. However in the case of Adam, it would be abusive to establish the thesis of biological monogenism on the basis of this term in Rom 5:12abc, 17a, 18ac etc. *The unity of origin* of the human race is dogmatic, but the way in which this takes place does not belong to theological reflection."[141] This position is shared substantially by many other modern authors.[142]

141. P. Grelot, "Pour une lecture de Romains 5, 12–21," *Nouvelle Revue Théologique* 116, no. 4 (1994): 495–512, at 508 (author's translation). A detailed exegetical study by F. Gómez Velasco, "Por un solo hombre. Estudio exegético de Rm 5,12–21," *Mayéutica* 22 (1996): 67–128, shows the text does not speak of Adam in person.

142. See A. Léonard, *Les raisons de croire* (Paris: Fayard, 1987), 177–231. See the summary and critique of Leónard's work in G.-H. Baudry, *Le péché dit originel* (Paris: Beauchesne, 2000), 387–411. See also P. Masset, "Réflexion philosophique sur le péché original," *Nouvelle Revue Théologique* 110 (1988):

It may be observed that the parallelism between Christ and Adam could be claimed regarding the creation of Eve from the side of Adam and the creation of the church from that of Christ, and yet the symbolic nature of the Eve narrative does not undermine the origin of the church in Christ's redemptive death. We may note besides that a solidly based scientific polygenist explanation of Adam and Eve has yet to be provided.

Still, it may be added that the monogenist understanding, for what it is worth, does not exclude the social origin of sin. Sin as *temptation* (and not as *sin*) does not take place with man in pure solitude (Gn 2:18). Rather, human relationships instead of being lived out as expressions of humans made in the image and likeness of God, became an occasion of them moving away from God. We still have to discover what it meant for Adam to have been the head of the human race in such a way that his sin passed on to all the rest. For this purpose let us now consider this question of the transmission of original sin.

The Transmission and Diffusion of Original Sin

The church teaches that original sin is transmitted by our first parents to other humans not by imitation but by propagation, and that the sin resides in each one as their own. However, it is not clear what exactly the term "propagation" actually means, though it would seem to be equivalent to generation.[143] This position is represented principally in the works of Augustine. Some of his earlier writings suggest that sin is transmitted on the basis of the sinful nature of the acts of human procreation,[144] a position definitely absent in later works. After all, generation could not be the *efficient cause* of original sin but rather the *instrument* or perhaps *occasion* by which it is transmitted. The difference is important. The *Catechism of the Catholic Church* offers the following helpful explanation:

879–902; H. Rondet, *Le péché originel dans la tradition patristique et théologique* (Paris: Fayard, 1967), 292 and 321; and on G. Fessard, B. Pottier, "Interpréter le péché originel sur les traces de G. Fessard," *Nouvelle Revue Théologique* 111 (1989): 801–23; L. Bouyer, *Cosmos* (Paris: Du Cerf, 1982), 89–97, and *Le Fils éternel* (Paris: Du Cerf, 1974), 496.

143. DH 1513 and Gibellini, *La generazione come mezzo di trasmissione del peccato originale.*

144. See Sayés, *Antropología del hombre caído*, 116–23.

By this "unity of the human race" all men are implicated in Adam's sin, as all are implicated in Christ's justice. Still, the transmission of original sin is a mystery that we cannot fully understand. But we do know by Revelation that Adam had received original holiness and justice not for himself alone, but for all human nature. By yielding to the tempter, Adam and Eve committed *a personal sin*, but this sin affected *the human nature* that they would then transmit *in a fallen state*. It is a sin which will be transmitted by propagation to all mankind, that is, by the transmission of a human nature deprived of original holiness and justice. And that is why original sin is called "sin" only in an analogical sense: it is a sin "contracted" and not "committed"—a state and not an act.[145]

And John Paul II in his catechesis says that "the Bible describes in the subsequent chapters of Genesis, and also in other books, how sin 'invaded' the whole world as a result of Adam's sin, by a kind of universal infection of all humanity."[146]

He is aware that

it is especially in regard to original sin in this meaning [as handed on to humans] that modern culture raises strong reservations. It cannot admit the idea of a hereditary sin, connected with the decision of a progenitor and not with that of the person concerned. It holds that such a view runs counter to the personalistic vision of man and to the demands which derive from full respect for his subjectivity.[147]

At the same time John Paul II observes that

original sin in Adam's descendants does not have the character of personal guilt. It is *the privation of sanctifying grace* in a nature which has been diverted from its supernatural end through the fault of the first parents. It is a "sin of nature," only analogically comparable to "personal sin." In the state of original justice, before sin, sanctifying grace was like a supernatural "endowment" of human nature. The loss of grace is contained in the inner "logic" of sin, which is a rejection of the will of God, who bestows this gift. Sanctifying grace has ceased to constitute the supernatural enrichment of that nature which the first parents passed on to all their descendants in the state in which it existed when human

145. CCC, no. 404.

146. John Paul II, "The Universality of Sin in Human History," General Audience, September 17, 1986, par. 1, and CCC, no. 401.

147. John Paul II, "The Church's Teaching on Original Sin," General Audience, September 24, 1986, par. 5.

generation began. Therefore man is conceived and born without sanctifying grace.[148]

TRANSMISSION OF ORIGINAL SIN IN SCRIPTURE

Several scriptural texts indicate that the sin of our first parents was in some way handed on to the rest of humanity. Of particular importance are the indirect ones which speak of the universality of sin among humans,[149] which is a direct complement of the universality of salvation in Christ.[150] "Surely there is not a righteous man on earth who does good and never sins" (Eccl 7:20).[151] In the Book of Sirach we read: "From a woman sin had its beginning, and because of her we all die" (Sir 25:24). And the Psalmist experiences the infection of evil that invades human life, as follows: "Behold, I was brought forth in iniquity, and in sin did my mother conceive me" (Ps 51:5).[152]

In the New Testament we read: "We have all sinned and fallen short of the glory of God" (Rom 3:23). And in Ephesians: "Among these we all once lived in the passions of our flesh, following the desires of body and mind, and so we were by nature children of wrath, like the rest of mankind. But God, who is rich in mercy, out of the great love with which he loved us ... made us alive together with Christ" (Eph 2:3–5). "Children of wrath," that is, of divine wrath, is "that which comes through birth rather than that which is acquired later.... So, in their natural condition, through birth, men and women are 'children of wrath.'"[153] That is, all humans are born in the state of alienation from God, what we call original sin.

Of particular importance is Romans 5:12, already cited: "Therefore as sin came into the world through one man and death through sin, and so

148. John Paul II, "The Consequences of Original Sin for Humanity," General Audience, October 1, 1986, par. 5.

149. See P. Heinisch, *Theology of the Old Testament* (Collegeville, Minn.: Liturgical Press, 1955), 245–48.

150. *CCC*, no. 402.

151. See also Lv 12:2; Jb 14:4; Sir 19:16; Jas 3:2; etc.

152. See A. Feuillet, "Le verset 7 du Miserere et le péché originel," *Recherches de science religieuse* 31 (1944): 5–26, holds that this text does not demonstrate the transmission of original sin, but only certain aspects of the contagion of sin in humanity.

153. Lincoln, *Ephesians*, 99. See also A. Bonhöffer, *Epiktet und das Neue Testament* (Giesen: Alfred Töpelmann, 1911), 146–54.

death spread to all men because all men sinned."[154] The Vulgate translates the text "because all men sinned" as follows: *in quo omnes peccaverunt.* This clearly indicates the inclusion of the sin of all humans in that of Adam, in whom all men sinned. Augustine followed this translation,[155] and the Council of Trent cited Romans in this way.[156]

However in the period before the Protestant Reformation some authors, such as Erasmus of Rotterdam, rejected the above translation for linguistic reasons.[157] Erasmus pointed out that the original Greek *eph'hō,* translated as *in quo* in the Vulgate, should by right be translated into Latin as *propter quod,* or *eo quod,* that is, "on account of which." The neo-Vulgate translation of Romans 5:12 in fact renders it as *eo quod.* "On account of which" has also become the common translation of the expression in other languages. John Paul II recognizes the validity of the new translation in his catechesis, but observes that it

> does not change the basic truth in St. Paul's text, namely, that Adam's sin . . . had consequences for all humanity. Moreover, in the same chapter of the Letter to the Romans the Apostle wrote: "By one man's disobedience all became sinners" (Rom 5:19), and in the preceding verse: "One man's trespass led to condemnation for all men" (Rom 5:18). St. Paul connects the sinful situation of all humanity with the fault of Adam.[158]

154. J. L. Caballero, "Rm 5,12 y el pecado original en la exégesis católica reciente," *Scripta Theologica* 46, no. 1 (2014): 121–40.

155. See Augustine, *Contra duas epist. Pelag.* 4, 7:7. See G. Di Palma, "Ancora sull'interpretazione agostiniana di *Rom* 5,12: *'et ita in omnes hominem pertransiit, in quo omnes peccaverunt',*" *Augustinianum* 41, no. 1 (2004): 113–34; A. Lozano, *Romanos 5: La vida de los justificados por la fe y su fundamento, la reconciliación por nuestro Señor Jesucristo* (Estella: Verbo Divino, 2012), 182–226, which considers the position of Ambrosiaster and Augustine.

156. See DH 1512.

157. See Erasmus, *In Ep. ad Rom. V.*, in *Erasmus' Annotations on the New Testament: Acts, Romans, I and II Corinthians,* ed. A. Reeve and M. A. Screech (Leiden: E. J. Brill, 1990), 363–76. "Erasmus objects that Augustine was mistaken. The apostle did not say *eph' hē* ('in whom,' feminine), referring to *hamartia* ('sin') or Eve. *Eph'hō* ('in whom,' masculine) is to be taken as an absolute act, neither the lapse of Eve nor the sin of Adam. One cannot escape the figure of speech (*tropus*) used by the apostle." M. Anderson, "Erasmus the Exegete," *Concordia Theological Monthly* 40, no. 11 (1969): 722–46, at 730. Besides, according to Faustus Socinus, *Praelectiones theologicae* (Racov, 1609), chap. 4 (10), we must interpret Ps 51:5 figuratively (ibid., 12) and take *eph'hō* in Rom 5:12 in sense of *eo quod* or *quatenus* (ibid., 14). Still, we should keep in mind the Pelagian overtones of Erasmus's doctrine.

158. John Paul II, "The Consequences of Original Sin for Humanity," par. 3.

DIFFERENT EXPLANATIONS OF THE TRANSMISSION OF ORIGINAL SIN

But what does this transmission involve? How can *sin* be transmitted from one generation to the next? It is interesting to note that the Old Testament notion of corporate personality makes it easier to understand how the sin of one, especially that of a parent, could be passed on to another, the son or daughter.[159] The notion of moral solidarity arises frequently in the Old Testament, within the covenant God has established with his people, although with Ezekiel and other prophets things begin to change, and sin is looked upon more and more in an individual way, insofar as each one is meant to fully assume their own responsibility. It is true that neither Jews[160] nor Muslims[161] accept the doctrine of original sin as Christians understand it, but the notion of corporate personality and human solidarity, for good or for ill, is to be found in both.

In any case, several ways have been suggested to explain the mechanism, as it were, of the transmission of original sin. One is the Pelagian position of *transmission by example*. Successive generations scandalize their descendants and successors with their disordered lifestyle and lead them to sin, which gradually becomes contagious throughout the earth. The

159. See H. W. Robinson, "The Hebrew Conception of the Corporate Personality," in *Werden und Wesen des Alten Testaments*, ed. P. Volz, F. Stummer and J. Hempel (Berlin: Töpelmann, 1936), 49; J. W. Rogerson, "The Hebrew Conception of Corporate Personality: A Reexamination," *Journal of Theological Studies* 21 (1970): 1–16; O'Callaghan, *The Christological Assimilation*, 72.

160. "Original sin does not appear in the Bible as an innate depravity common to all human beings in consequence of the fall of the first parents. Rather, the biblical tradition knows that 'there is no man who does not sin' (I Kgs 8:46; Eccl 7:20). The hyperbolic language in which the psalmist describes his own sinfulness, 'I was even born in iniquity, my mother conceived me in sin' (Ps 51:7; Gen. 8:21), only stresses the ineluctable character of sin. Nobody can escape from it, as the sin can also be involuntary (Lv 4–5) or proceed from ignorance (Gen 20:6; Nm 22:34). A man is responsible for all his actions." E. Lipinski, "Sin," *Encyclopaedia Judaica*, ed. F. Skolnik (New York: Keter, 2007), 18:621–24, at 622.

161. "Islam rejects any notion of original sin and correlatively any notion of salvation brought about by Jesus. In Islam each person is responsible for his or her own actions, and each person must seek forgiveness directly from Allah for sins committed. While there are holy persons and teachers in Islam, there is no priesthood, no sense of mediation of the divine, for each believer can directly approach Allah. Muslims tend to read the Christian position on original sin as implying that human beings are basically evil, which is more the Reformed position than the Catholic one. For Muslims, all human beings are essentially good and only need forgiveness for sins they actually commit." N. J. Ormerod, *Creation, Grace, and Redemption, Theology in Global Perspective* (Maryknoll, N.Y.: Orbis Books, 2007), 88.

problem with this explanation of course is that it does not really explain the universality of original sin. The only way Adam's bad example could end up affecting *all* humans is because in the heart of each one some kind of perversion is already present that is triggered more or less negatively by the lives of others. And we still have to find the roots of this perversion.[162] Pelagius's example-based account just puts off the question of the universality of human sinfulness.

Second, Peter Abelard and others, in the twelfth century, suggested that what was transmitted was the *chastisement due to sin*.[163] All would be equally afflicted by it. This position however was rejected by the Council of Sens in 1140.[164] And the reason is clear: man suffers punishment only if he is alienated from God, only if he is truly a sinner. It would be unjust for him to be chastised should there be no sinful condition. Besides, the explanation provides a somewhat extrinsic or forensic view of original sin.

Another way of accounting for the transmission of original sin is by seeing it in terms of the *transmission of concupiscence*, or weakness of the soul. This position was held by Luther.[165] But according to Trent concupiscence is not sin, although it derives from and inclines toward sin. Again this would not provide a complete and satisfactory explanation.

A fourth possibility is that humans, insofar as they belong to human society, would be infected by the *sin of the world*, or in the structures of sin, in perverse laws and customs, in consolidated forms of misbehavior, present in society at large. In this way original sin would become a common inheritance of all. But again this sin of the world needs to be an expression of a sinful perversion present in the heart of each one. For it is in this perversion that the reality of original sin lies.

Fifth and last, we may suggest the following view of the transmission of original sin. Thomas Aquinas, in an attempt to explain the communication of Christ's saving grace to sinners, puts it as follows in this important text:

> Original sin in Adam, which is a sin of nature, is derived from his actual sin, which is a personal sin, because in him the person corrupted the nature; and

162. Of course imitation and generation are not entirely separable in that both involve interpersonal encounter between humans: Maldamé, *Le péché originel*, 195–96.

163. See Peter Abelard, *Ethica* 3.

164. See DH 728.

165. O'Callaghan, *Christ and Mediation*, 124–25.

by means of this corruption the sin of the first man is transmitted to posterity, inasmuch as the corrupt nature corrupts the person. However, grace is not given by Christ to us by means of human nature, but solely by the personal action of Christ Himself.[166]

So Aquinas distinguishes in Adam between *personal sin*, the fruit of his sinful action, and the *sin of nature*, committed by Adam and communicated as a kind of corruption of the nature of other humans, that is, as a sinful state. By contrast, Christ transmits saving grace to each one personally through faith. In other words, grace is not transmitted automatically to all humans, but requires Christ's personal action in each case, for each person, and their personal correspondence. But sin *as guilt* is transmitted to all, and not just the *effects* of sin, such as bad example, concupiscence, chastisement, structural sin, etc. But how can a "state of guilt" be transmitted to all humans, from one to all the rest? How can the action of one person corrupt the nature as a whole? What kind of human solidarity is involved in making this possible?

In the above text of Aquinas it is interesting to note the contrast between the passive, impersonal way in which corrupt nature is communicated to all humans, from Adam as the fallen head of the human race, and the active way in which Christ communicates justifying grace personally to each and every believer. A similar position may be found in Augustine.[167] Once Adam's sin has been committed it is transmitted to humanity necessarily, in spite of Adam's intentions or whatever regrets he may have had, because by his sin he has forfeited many of the gifts God had given him, in particular that of being head of the human species, charged with the communication of God's grace to humanity. From that moment onward only the new head of the human race, the new Adam, our Savior Jesus Christ, is in a position to undo the damage and reconstitute the lost unity and communion by redemption and grace.

In the light of Christ who redeems humanity perhaps we can explain

166. Thomas Aquinas, *ST* III, q. 8, a. 5, ad 1. The text continues: "Hence we must not distinguish a twofold grace in Christ, one corresponding to the nature, the other to the person, as in Adam we distinguish the sin of the nature and of the person." See also ibid., q. 69, a. 3, ad 3.

167. Augustine writes: "Omnis autem homo Adam; sicut in his qui crediderunt, omnis homo Christus, quia membra sunt Christi" (*Enn. in Ps.* 70, 2, 1). He makes it clear that all humans become sinners through Adam, but are justified only by personal faith in Christ.

the mystery of the transmission of original sin in the following way. Adam was designated by God as the head of humanity. In him, and from him, and through him, God wished to communicate his good gifts to humanity . . . gifts not only of nature but also of grace. Had they not sinned, our first parents would have been instrumental in handing on God's grace to their descendants.[168] This position is carefully explained by M.-J. Scheeben.[169] Adam had not been constituted as an isolated human being, an individual closed in on himself, but rather as the depository of divine goods destined for humanity as a whole, the first man, the head of humanity, the father of all, living in communion not only with God but also—virtually—with all his descendants who would inhabit the earth. With his personal sin he lost the divine gifts—of grace certainly, of nature to a lesser extent—for himself and for humanity. And specifically he was no longer the head of the human race. No longer would he be the point of reference for the unity of humanity. In fact, according to the Old Testament Abraham, not Adam, is presented as our "father in the faith" (Heb 11:8). Adam's sin broke up the solidarity and communion of humans with God and with one another. Thus it is not so much that sin is transmitted, but rather that grace is *not* transmitted. The project of reestablishing communion began with Abraham and reached its culmination and realization in Christ.

How can we justify this explanation? Indirectly, as always, on the basis of the saving work of Christ. In effect, the work of redemption—primordially a divine work that involves Christ's humanity and ours—was one of *reconstituting* the unity of the human race, of humans with God and under God, of humans with one another, and of the individual human being with

168. On the instrumentality of humans in respect of the transmission of grace, see O'Callaghan, *Children of God in the World*, 507–11.

169. According to Scheeben, original justice would have been passed on from parents to children, instrumentally of course. "Since the generative faculty of human nature depends on the material component of that nature, and is exercised by a material act that is perceptible to the senses, grace also was bound up with the same act; grace was to come to Adam's descendants through the placing of this act, and hence in a sacramental manner." M.-J. Scheeben, *The Mysteries of Christianity* (St. Louis, Mo.: Herder, 1946), 564. Marriage "had a special relationship with grace in that, free from the effects of original sin, Adam and Eve were destined to transmit human life to their offspring in such a way that divine life would be simultaneously conferred." W. Newton, "The Contribution of Matthias Joseph Scheeben to the Theology of Marriage," *INTAMS Review* 16, no. 2 (2012): 184–93, at 189. E. P. Okafor, *Marriage as Sacrament in Creation according to Bonaventure, Scheeben and John Paul II* (Rome: Pontificia Università della Santa Croce, 2019), 143–49.

himself or herself, as we saw earlier on. This was and is fundamentally a work of *reconciliation*, of piecing together, of reestablishing relationships. And this work is carried out by Christ—"the personal action of Christ himself," Aquinas says—in the Holy Spirit, as an artisanal work, one by one, piece by piece, person by person. Of course only God is capable of doing this—the incarnate God through the divine Spirit who is closer to creatures than they are to themselves.

Hence we can say that original sin (the *peccatum originale originatum*) is not transmitted to humanity as a positive evil reality, a malignant virus as it were, but rather as the *lack* of a reality (communion with God, with others, with oneself) which *should* have been transmitted to humanity through the agency of our first parents. What is "transmitted" is a rupture of relationships or, as the medieval masters put it, *the privation of original justice*.[170] Where the old Adam breaks up and destroys, Christ, the new and eternal Adam, unites us to God and to one another, as he reveals us to ourselves. We might even say that the *essence* of the transmission of original sin lies in a *lack* of transmission ... or better, in the interruption of the transmission of the gifts of grace that God wanted to communicate abundantly to humanity through other humans from all eternity.[171] And we perceive and appreciate this dynamic as we contemplate the saving, reconciling, reuniting work of Christ.

There is a paradox here, however. An individualistic anthropology—based on an exaggerated and legalistic view of human responsibility—makes it difficult for us to appreciate the value and realism of human solidarity. At best, biological solidarity may be admitted, beyond which there would be a vast unconnected multiplicity of monadic "I"s, all of them incommunicable, imprisoned, separated, atomic, autonomous egos that establish whatever relationships they decide upon with other people, without limits of any kind. Here is the paradox: the very absence of solidarity, which in principle would seem to exclude all possibility of the transmission of a common guilt, is itself a sign and proof that original sin has been "transmitted" to each one. We should not be surprised then that the deep *real solidarity* between humans which makes the transmission of original

170. See Lottin, "Les théories du péché originel au XIIème siècle, II & III."

171. See O'Callaghan, *Children of God in the World*, 509–11.

sin possible is reflected in a lack of *sense of solidarity* among humans. In other words, original sin blocks the sense of solidarity that makes its transmission possible.

The Value of the Doctrine of Original Sin

Doubtless, the doctrine of original sin is difficult to explain satisfactorily. The theology involved is certainly a work in progress. Nevertheless it provides an important contribution to understanding the role of evil in a world made good by God. It is both realistic and optimistic. Realistic because it takes into account the true situation of people's lives, and optimistic because through God's power it can be overcome. The Calvinist author Jonathan Edwards says that the doctrine of original sin "teaches us to think no worse of others than of ourselves: it teaches us that we are *all*, as we are by nature, *companions* in a miserable helpless condition; which, under a revelation of the divine mercy, tends to promote mutual *compassion*."[172]

John Paul II concludes: "The Church's teaching on original sin can be extremely valuable for modern people. Having rejected the data of faith in this matter, they can no longer understand the mysterious and distressing aspects of evil which they daily experience. They end up by wavering between a hasty and unjustified optimism and a radical pessimism bereft of hope."[173] Likewise in the *Catechism of the Catholic Church* we read: "The doctrine of original sin, closely connected with that of redemption by Christ, provides lucid discernment of man's situation and activity in the world.... Ignorance of the fact that man has a wounded nature inclined to evil gives rise to serious errors in the areas of education, politics, social action, and morals."[174]

Besides, the doctrine of original sin plays an important role in theology, spirituality, and moral life.[175] First of all, it does so by magnifying the role of divine grace and explicating the central place it occupies in Christian life. Second, it serves "to circumscribe the will as the locus, but not

172. J. Edwards, *Original Sin* (New Haven, Conn.: Yale University Press, 1970), 424; originally titled *The Great Christian Doctrine of Original Sin Defended* (1758).

173. John Paul II, "The Church's Teaching on Original Sin," par. 5.

174. CCC, no. 407, citing John Paul II, *Centesimus Annus*, par. 25.

175. See McFarland, "The Fall and Sin," 155–57.

the source, of personal identity. . . . While we can do what we want, we cannot want what we want."[176] In the third place, original sin helps us "establish a fundamental human solidarity before God," a solidarity that is deeply seated and profoundly relevant to our lives. And lastly, the doctrine of original sin "provides a framework for enlarging the category of actual sin to include practices that may previously have been viewed as morally neutral (e.g. slavery) or even virtuous (e.g. the systematic subordination of women)."[177] For sin is not just a personal issue, but a deeply communitarian one.

176. Ibid., 156; see also his "Original Sin," 307.
177. McFarland, "The Fall and Sin," 156.

Conclusion

A SUMMARY OF THE CHRISTIAN DOCTRINE OF CREATION

CHRISTIANS BELIEVE THAT GOD made the world *ex nihilo,* which literally means "out of nothing," that is, without material, spiritual, temporal, or ideal presuppositions of any kind.[1] "To create means to give being to the creature," says Thomas Aquinas.[2] Thus creation may be described, in the words of John Paul II, simply as God's "gift of existence to each and every being."[3] Neither did creation take place within a preexisting timeframe, for time itself is a creature, or better, God created the world as a temporal reality, in such a way that time "began" with creation.[4] The joyful conviction that the universe was created entirely by God was solidly established in Christian preaching and teaching by the second century, in the face of Platonic and Gnostic worldviews that held, in a variety of ways, that God gave shape to the world by impressing forms on eternally preexisting matter by means of a *Logos* or Demiurge.[5] The conviction that the world was created *ex nihilo* is to be found throughout the whole of the Old and New Testaments, although it develops gradually over an extended period.[6] It has been taught consistently by the church[7] and is accepted on the whole by both Jewish and Muslim theologians.[8] Besides, to an important degree the knowledge of God as creator is accessible to human reason, itself a creature, although certain aspects of the mystery of creation (for example, its ultimate purpose) may only be understood in the light

1. See 1–3, 28–35.
2. Thomas Aquinas, *In Io. lect* V, no. 133.
3. John Paul II, General Audience, "Creation Reveals God's Glory," March 12, 1986, par. 2.
4. See 241–442.
5. See 108–20, 127–39.
6. See 35–95.
7. See 118–26.
8. See 4–5, 39–74, 357.

of divine revelation. This means that creation *ex nihilo* is not purely a faith conviction; and as a result, humans experience a natural conscientious imperative to recognize and take special care of God's great gift.[9]

That the universe has been created by God *ex nihilo* has important consequences for the way we understand both the God who creates and the created world itself. The following sections will attempt to respond to three basic issues regarding God's work of creation, which may be described as the *fact* of creation, the *why* of creation, and the *what* of creation.

The Fact of Creation

First, the *fact* that God created the universe. If we accept that God created the world *ex nihilo*, without external presuppositions of any kind, then we can say that creation came to exist exclusively as the result of a willing divine decision: God created the world freely, without interior or exterior constrictions or conditions of any kind. On the one hand this means God is completely *transcendent* to the world.[10] And on the other hand, it means that creation exists and acts entirely under divine initiative, guidance, beckoning, and power. No aspect or facet of the created world can act independently of the divinity, on the margin of the divine will. For this reason, we can say not only that God *created* the world, but also that he keeps it in existence (this is called *conservatio*, conservation),[11] he moves creatures to act in accordance with the nature he has given them (this is usually called *concursus*, divine concourse),[12] and finally he leads/guides them to perfection and completion (this is *providentia*, or divine providence).[13]

This means of course that the world not only "depends" on God in general terms, in the sense that God retains influence over it to a greater or lesser degree. The entire existence of creatures depends on God, to the point that creatures perpetually "hang off" God's creating and conserving action as it were, in such a way that for the world to disappear it would be

9. See 34–35.
10. See 157–62.
11. See 214–17.
12. See 214–20.
13. See 220–31.

enough for God to stop paying attention to it. As a result, the deepest reality of all created beings, both material and spiritual, lies in the *relationship* they have with the creator: they have no existence or relevance outside this founding relationship. The created universe is inherently relational not only in the sense that the parts relate to one another, but principally because each creature exists in virtue of a relationship totally rooted in the creative action of God:[14] thus we may say that each creature stands in a *radical* relationship with God.

In spite of the fact that God is in complete "control" of the created world, creation is not a part of God's being; God and creatures do not amalgamate or mix at an ontological level.[15] As a result, Christian faith completely excludes *pantheism* (which means "everything is God")[16] and even partial pantheisms, present for example in views which see the spiritual world as sharing in God's being (Platonism and Gnosticism).[17] For this reason therefore we may say that the created world is "autonomous" with respect to the creator in two ways: in its being which, though received from God, is real and exercises a true causality; and in its laws and nature which again, though received from God, are truly present in, proper to, and active within it.[18] This double autonomy is what makes it possible for us to consider and understand the world from a *scientific* standpoint in relative independence from the study of God, what is called theology,[19] and in a *secular* mode reflecting its otherness from God.[20] Still, the affirmation of the world's "autonomy" provides an important challenge to the theology of providence and miracles, both of which speak of God's ongoing interventions in the universe.[21]

We may conclude therefore that God's ontological transcendence with respect to creation is fully compatible with his immanence to it.[22] God is above creation and independent of it, but acts at the deepest possible level

14. See 216–17.
15. See 108–18.
16. See ibid.
17. See 102–8.
18. See 161, 240–41.
19. See 9–11, 27–35.
20. See 221–23.
21. See 237–41.
22. See 157–62.

within it. The created world depends on God but God does not depend on it. Divine ontology or metaphysics—the consideration of God's being—is simply distinct from created ontology; they are two different metaphysical systems, obeying two different sets of rules. That the world was created by God gives rise to a typically Christian vision of metaphysics according to which the *existence* of creatures, *that* they are, cannot be explained on the basis of their *essence* or nature, of *what* they are; put differently, the fact that things exist cannot be explained by or deduced from the knowledge we have, however perfect, of their nature. In other words, science, which studies the nature of reality, will never be in a position to discover fully how or why things exist in the first place.[23] Although there is a strict distinction between the divine and the created sphere, a double ontology if you wish, a certain "duality" and flexibility and an intrinsic temporality is present within the single, unitary project that is the created world. For God created the universe as a temporal, living, growing, developing reality, capable of evolution.[24]

The fact that all things derive from God and depend on him (they depart from him, as it were, this is called the *exitus*, or "leaving" of all things from God) means that they all must refer and point back to him as their ultimate end (or returning: *reditus*). Thus all creatures by the simple fact of existing manifest God's glory and must refer back to God in all things. In effect, humans are meant to recognize the divine origin of creation and God's ongoing sovereignty over it in a conscious manner, consciously giving glory to God in all their actions.[25] The same may be said of the spiritual creatures called angels.[26] Both humans and angels are meant to give God conscious, formal glory. Other creatures are said to give God material glory. The formal glorification of God takes place principally in the Church's liturgy,[27] but also in the everyday life of Christians.

But this does not mean that creatures are actually giving something back to the creator, for the simple reason that everything they have is received from God in the first place. In that sense creatures do not give glory

23. See ix, xi, 9–11.
24. See 14–23.
25. See 208–9.
26. See 260–94.
27. See 207–12.

to God in the strict sense of the word.[28] Rather they recognize through adoration and praise that all glory and power and richness and worth comes from God in the first place. For creatures to do everything for the glory of God means simply that they strive to reflect and express the power and splendor of God in their own lives, recognizing that the created world, as well as their own lives and actions and ways of behavior, find their origin entirely in God and must point back to him. After all, "the heavens tell of the glory of God; and the firmament proclaims his handiwork" (Ps 19:2).

Thus Christian faith excludes the position of Deists,[29] who, while affirming the world as created, deny divine providence: God would create the world and set it in motion, but then—deists would say—allows it act of its own accord, independently, in such a way that humans do not recognize any finality or ultimate purpose present *a priori* within the created world, but rather attempt to establish or construct it as if God did not exist. The contemporary ecological crisis and challenge has brought believers and nonbelievers alike to recognize not only the fragility of our planet, and the serious damage we may well be inflicting on it, but also the need to respect the created, natural world, with all its laws and interactions, as a gift of God, and treat it accordingly.[30] In that sense the purpose or scope of the created world may on no account be determined entirely or decided autonomously upon by spiritual creatures—humans or angels—or appended to the world by them. The fact is that the purpose and end of each and every creature is written into creation itself, implanted in it by God, even though angels and humans are meant to recognize and actualize this consciously, intelligently, and freely.[31] This is what is meant by the idea that the created world not only derives from God as the principle or origin of everything, but is, besides, destined to return to God and share his life to the fullest possible extent. The created world in other words seeks out eschatological fulfillment under the power of God and the free will of creatures.

It may be added that the high point of the biblical account of creation is not the creation of humans in the image and likeness of God on the sixth

28. See 207–8.
29. See 237–41.
30. See 248–59.
31. See 164–97.

day (Gn 1:26–28) but rather the fact that God rested from his work of creation and sanctified it on the seventh day: "And on the seventh day God finished his work which he had done, and he rested on the seventh day from all his work which he had done. So God blessed the seventh day and sanctified it, because on it God rested from all his work which he had done in creation" (Gn 2:2–3). What gives meaning to the created world is not just that it derives from God, not only that through work and effort in collaboration with others the human family builds up the world as we know it, but above all that it points back to God, in thanksgiving and adoration and praise and awe. Thus the high point of creation, its ultimate purpose, is situated beyond humans themselves, in liturgical celebration, especially in the Eucharist.[32] Pope Benedict XVI writes: "Creation is projected towards divinization, towards the holy wedding feast, towards unification with the Creator himself."[33]

Now that we have considered the *fact* of creation (*that* the universe is created by God), we can reflect on *who* God the Creator is, and *why* he created the universe in the first place.

The God Who Creates and Why He Created

Who then is the *God who creates*? If creation takes place *ex nihilo*, without presuppositions of any kind, then creation must be an entirely free act on God's part. God is placed under no external constraint to create the universe. He does so with infinite, divine freedom. Thus at the deepest possible level the created world must be considered as metaphysically *contingent*: it might have existed, or it might not; it exists as it does but it might have existed very differently. Strictly speaking the created world is unnecessary, "is not called for."[34] The world as it is adds nothing to God. It is dependent on God, entirely dependent, but in no way complementary to him; it does not contribute to enriching his inner life.[35] Besides, given that God created the world, he made it just as he wished it to be. As a result, Christian believers can confidently say two things: that nothing or

32. See 41–42, 209–10.

33. Benedict XVI, *Ecclesia de Eucharistia*, Encyclical Letter, April 17, 2003, par. 8.

34. Schmitz, *The Gift: Creation*, 32.

35. See O'Callaghan, "Can God Be Enriched?"

nobody in the universe is ultimately necessary, and that the created universe is as God designed it to be.[36]

Should the world have been made or shaped by God from a previously existing reality external to him, whether material or spiritual, then the act of creation would not be entirely free, but rather more or less conditioned, just as the freedom of human decisions is limited or guided or affected by external circumstances. Had God been pressurized as it were by external factors in creating the world, then the "why" he created would have been modified by the "what" that already existed; the ultimate constitution of the world would be conditioned by the previous one. Besides, the world in both its existence and essence would reflect divine life only partially, but not fully.

This brings to consider a further question, perhaps the most essential one: *why* did God actually create the universe in the first place? And if he did, why did he create it as it is? Both questions, which involve the existence and the essence (or nature) of the world respectively, point back entirely to the inner life of God who made the world.

An important issue arises when we attempt to understand the freedom that marks God's creative action.[37] Aristotle and his commentators during the Middle Ages, as well as other Greek philosophers, took it that the world is as necessary as its maker; in other words, the universe existed always just as God had. Nominalist philosophers during the Middle Ages, working in a Christian context, took it on the contrary that the creation of the world was an arbitrary act; it was simply willed into existence by God without any good reason for doing so, or better, by divine will alone, independently of reason; as the popular phrase has it, the world would be "good for nothing."[38] We may ask: is the God who creates purely a God of reason, the *Logos*, who implants his "logic" on a world whose actual existence is of little importance? Or is he a God of will, who blindly or enthusiastically gives rise to a world without ultimate meaning?

Scripture teaches that God is both: that he knows and implants his own logic and wisdom in creatures, and that he wills the world into existence in an act of unpredictable power and love, as an act of art and risk.

36. See 155, 175.
37. See 164–97.
38. See Williams, "'Good for Nothing'?"

So we can say that God freely willed to bring the world into existence, but that he did so for a reason, a purpose, an end, a scope. This is what the question "why did God create the world?" responds to: God acted freely, but for a reason. Understanding the motivation God had in creating the world can help us resolve the classical tension between creation as rational but necessary and creation as free but arbitrary.[39]

The question regarding why God created refers inevitably, of course, to God's own trinitarian life. God—Father, Son, and Holy Spirit—who is pure act, is completely happy and satisfied with his own tri-Personal life and existence. He is *in se et ex se beatissimus,* as Vatican Council I says, "most happy in himself and of himself." And the Council adds that God created "not for the increase of his own happiness, nor for the acquirement of his perfection, but in order to manifest his perfection through the benefits which he bestows on creatures."[40] God created the world not as a self-seeking hobby or personal therapy, but as an act of pure self-giving and love.[41]

The Old Testament speaks of God creating the world through "wisdom" and "the word."[42] The New Testament continues in this direction and amplifies it; it teaches that God has created the world *through* the eternal Word (in Greek, *Logos*) who became incarnate in Jesus Christ (according to the prologue of John's Gospel),[43] *through* Christ and *for* Christ—in Paul's teaching mainly present in 1 Corinthians and Colossians—in such a way that Christ "upholds the universe by his word of power" (Heb 1:3).[44] For he "created heaven and what is in it, the earth and what is in it, and the sea and what is in it" (Rv 10:6), and may thus be called "the Alpha and the Omega, the beginning and the end" (Rv 21:6).[45] Church Fathers in the following centuries developed the theology of God creating the world through and for Jesus Christ in critical dialogue with Platonic and neo-Platonic philosophers and in a trinitarian context.[46]

39. See 171–76.

40. DH 3002.

41. See 180–82.

42. See 67–74, 87–89.

43. See 87–95.

44. See 78–87.

45. See S. M. McDonough, "Being and Nothingness in the Book of Revelation," in *Creation ex nihilo* (ed. Anderson and Bockmuehl), 77–98.

46. See 128–44.

Platonists, such as Arius of Alexandria in the early fourth century, considered the making of the world in terms of a mediating process between the supreme divinity on the one hand, and prime matter on the other, through the agency of the divine *Logos* or Demiurge (the artisan of the created world), the "first creature" who was made by God for the express purpose of giving shape to the rest of the world, putting order on unruly matter. For Arius this meant of course that the Word is subordinate to God.[47]

Church Fathers from the fourth century, such as Athanasius and Hilary of Poitiers, on the contrary, taught that the divine Word is fully divine, "consubstantial" with God (as the Council of Nicaea taught in 325 A.D.), equal to the Father to such a degree that he is called the only-begotten Son, made incarnate in Jesus Christ.[48] Thus, though the Word/Son mediates the world into existence, he does not exist for the sake of the created world, for he is eternally generated by the Father as Son in complete independence of the world's actual or eventual existence, and lives only for the Father. For this reason we may conclude that the Word/Son does not exist *for* the world, but just the other way round: the world exists in function of the Word, *for* the Word/Son. Thus the created world, in its origin and historical development, is meant to *conform* entirely (though eschatologically) to God's Word, made incarnate in Jesus of Nazareth. For this reason the New Testament presents Jesus Christ as the Lord of the universe, and therefore as the One who will judge the universe and everything in it at the end of time, to manifest its conformity (or otherwise) to God's original design (or Word).

And just as the Holy Spirit gives personal expression to the love of the Father for the Son and of the Son for the Father, so also the Holy Spirit acts continuously within creation to establish the greatest possible conformity of each element of the created world with the Word/Son, which will reach its culmination in the *eschaton*, at the end of time.[49] Understandably, many Church Fathers and theologians speak of the mystery of the Father who creates the world through and for the Son in the power of the Holy Spirit.[50]

47. See 135–39.

48. Nicaea "stressed above all else the heterogeneity of the created and the Creator in contradistinction to the 'consubstantiality' of generation." Florovsky, "Creation and Creaturehood," 47.

49. See 180–82.

50. See 188–96.

This teaching may be summed up in the following terms: the Father loves the Son in the Spirit and the fruit *ad extra* of this love is the created universe which is (1) entirely under the paternal dominion of God, (2) pierced perpetually by the love of God, by the Holy Spirit, and (3) with the calling, throughout history, of becoming more and more like the Son. God seeks his Son (the Word) with love (in the Holy Spirit) in the whole of creation. For God has created the world out of love, as a gift of existence.[51]

The "What" of Creation

After having reflected on the *fact* and the *why* of creation, let us now consider the *what* of creation, the nature and functioning of the world as it comes from God's hands, as it reflects the divine Word/Son under the power of the Holy Spirit. Scripture makes it clear that the creation of the real world sets a process in motion, a temporal narrative.[52] It marks the beginning of history, of salvation, a long and arduous path toward eschatological perfection. The created world is essentially *temporal*.[53] This has implications for three important issues.

The first is that the development and growth of the created world is real, not imagined or apparent. The world is a reflection of God's design, of the Word/Son, not as a dead replica, but a living, growing reality. Christian authors have generally avoided the idea that the whole created world is already present, whole and entire, in the mind and intentionality of God (this is usually called *panentheism*, which literally means that "all is in God").[54] But neither is the intelligibility of the world simply the result of the autonomous action of creatures. God created a world that was structured and destined to develop, to grow, to progress, not one that would simply continue to be what it was at the very first moment of its existence, as creationists usually claim.[55] In that sense to say that the created univer-

51. See J. M. G. Barclay, *Paul and the Gift* (Grand Rapids, Mich.: Eerdmans, 2015). On this work, see P. O'Callaghan, "New Perspectives on Paul: A Reflection on Luther's Permanent Contribution to the Doctrine of Christian Grace on the Occasion of the Fifth Centenary of the Reformation," *Nova et Vetera* (English edition) 16, no. 3 (2018): 797–833.

52. See 52–55.

53. See 241–47..

54. See 175–76.

55. See 14, #22.

seevolves, especially the living universe, is fully compatible with Christian faith. Evolution may be described as "the process by which different kinds of living organisms . . . have developed and diversified from earlier forms during the history of the earth." The fact that God can create a living universe with its own internal laws and dynamics that is in a position to develop and grow and improve, is a sign of far greater divine power, goodness, fantasy, and "creativity" than if God just created a universe with fixed unchangeable essences and species, that endure endlessly in time.[56]

This does not mean of course that God carelessly abandons the universe to its own devices or to the exclusive governance of humans. God is faithful to his eternal design and when he creates things and (especially) spiritual beings such as angels and humans, he accompanies them one by one in their existence and development until they achieve their plenitude of life. This is usually called divine providence.[57] Within this process a special role is played for the whole universe by an abundance of purely spiritual beings called angels,[58] to whose existence and activity scripture, spirituality, theology, and the liturgical life of the church give ample expression. Likewise humans, made in God's image and likeness (Gn 1:27–28), cooperate with God to achieve ultimate dominion over the world.

To believe in divine providence by which God guides the universe to its proper end does not mean that God directly intervenes in the created world as if he had not given things their own nature and autonomy. Ontological confusion between the divine and the created would compromise his transcendence and eliminate his being creator. Efforts to close the gap between the divine and the created order—different kinds of pantheism,[59] "process theology,"[60] and so forth—constitute in real terms a return to the pagan categories which scripture, the Church Fathers, and official church teaching decisively eschewed. Still, God does guide the universe and all creatures as first cause, without eliminating the proper causality of creatures as second causes.

The second issue that arises within a developing, temporal world, is

56. See 14–23.
57. See 220–47.
58. See 260–94.
59. See 109–15.
60. See 115–18.

that of evil, the *mysterium iniquitatis*, "the mystery of wickedness," the problem and experience of badness in the world. One of the principal problems that arises when dealing with the *why* and the *what* of the created universe is the experience of evil. Evil—all kinds of pain, suffering, impropriety, ugliness, sorrow, desolation, and death—makes its appearance abundantly felt throughout the process of the real-life development of the world. Things do not turn out as they are meant to; they do not achieve their ultimate end; the world is full of distressing and unnerving discrepancies between what things are and what they should be or might be. And this discrepancy produces pain, suffering, hurt, questioning, especially in humans. On the one hand, the causes that bring about suffering and pain seem to be structurally present in the world, as part of its original makeup; this is usually referred to as "physical evil." But on the other hand, at a deeper level, evil is often experienced as a reality inflicted willingly by some beings on others; this is usually called "moral evil." In other words, evil may not be reduced to a purely physical, impersonal experience of imperfection, hardship, privation, and limitation. It is not simply the price to pay for a finite created universe in development. It refers ultimately to the will of one who inflicts evil or allows it to take place.[61]

Christian believers accept wholeheartedly that God created the world out of love for creatures. And so they proclaim that God is *good*. But in saying that God created the world without presuppositions of any kind, *ex nihilo*, they say that God is *almighty* and that the world is as God wants it to be, warts and all. But this means that God is in some ways responsible for evil in the world. Now is it possible to hold on to the two attributes at the same time, and proclaim that God is both good and almighty? If God is good then the created world should be full of goodness, joy, happiness, and plenitude. But the presence of evil in the world seems to belie this. So we can only conclude that God is either good or almighty but not both at the same time. Either he is a fond grandfather who dotes on the universe but is incapable of overcoming evil and pain; or he is a cruel, all-powerful tyrant and is not prepared to do so. Throughout history Jewish and Christian believers have held tenaciously to divine omnipotence, but have been tempted to blaspheme the creator on account of their experience of evil

61. See 375–76.

and injustice, coming to doubt the goodness of God.[62] But blasphemy, like anger, is a passion and cannot endure endlessly, and so believers are gradually drawn to deny God's omnipotence and accept his generic, ineffectual goodness, falling into idolatry: God would benevolently oversee a complex world in which many "gods" assume control of a wide variety of jurisdictions and domains.[63]

Summing up: the fact that God created the world without presuppositions of any kind obliges us to accept that God has real responsibility for suffering in the world and to some degree for evil. Ultimate blame could be spread around had the world been made out of preexisting matter or if God acted in collaboration with other divinities. But God alone made the world. This is why believers direct their prayers to God not only for supplementary assistance and consolation, but also for their very life and spirit and survival.

This brings us, in the third place, to the doctrine of original sin. God created man "in his image and likeness," the Book of Genesis tells us (1:27).[64] This means, among other things, that he freely created beings who are free and responsible. Citing John Damascene, Thomas Aquinas says that "man is made to God's image, insofar as the image implies an intelligent being endowed with free-will and self-movement.... Inasmuch as man too is the principle of his actions, he has free-will and control of his actions."[65] God, who created humans through and for his eternal Son, constituted them from the beginning as his beloved children,[66] expecting from them a free, joyful recognition of his gifts and love, as they give all the glory to him. According to scripture our first parents, tempted by Satan, the fallen angel, in the guise of a serpent, abused the created world God had offered them as a gift and failed to respond to his call, through pride, disobedience, and mistrust. As a result they lost their filial intimacy and friendship with God (called "original justice"), came under the power of death and suffering and the devil, were damaged in their natural faculties of intellect and will, as well as their relationships with other people, and

62. See 119–21.

63. See 210.

64. See O'Callaghan, *Children of God in the World*, 89–117.

65. *ST* I-II, prol., citing John Damascene, *De fide orth.* II, 12.

66. See O'Callaghan, *Children of God in the World*, 247–77.

came to experience a powerful inclination toward sin, called concupiscence. The fallen state of Adam, the head of the human race, is propagated universally throughout humanity in such a way that all humans are born "children of wrath" (Eph 2:3); this is commonly called original sin. A significant proportion of the evil, suffering and pain that occurs in the created world, both then and now, must be attributed, however indirectly, to this original Fall.[67]

To redeem fallen humanity from sin, God sent his only Son, Jesus Christ, the Word through whom and for whom the world was created in the first place. He is the new Adam who would reestablish a filial friendship of humans with God, overcoming the power of death, suffering, and the devil, purifying our faculties, reestablishing relationships, and overcoming sin to its very roots. Salvation does not involve a denial or rejection of the created world, but rather an overcoming of the fruits of sin and the reconciliation of a fallen world unable to renew itself. Thus Christians speak of salvation *of* the world, but not of salvation *from* the world.

The doctrine of original sin and salvation may be read in a relational key if we understand that just as sin separated humans from God, from other people, from themselves, and from the created world, so also the saving power of Christ reconciles us with God, with others, with ourselves, and with creation: the One through and for whom the world was made creates us anew, recreates us, reorients us to our proper end, reestablishes communion within creation, reconciles us with our brothers and above all with the eternal Father. And whereas humans are capable of seriously damaging, though not destroying, God's work by sin, they are not in a position to put it back together again. The redemption of mankind in other words is strictly a divine work, a work of grace.[68]

The doctrine of original sin was developed by Church Fathers, especially Augustine, and by official church teaching, in particular at the Council of Trent in 1546.[69] But it is rooted in scripture, in the early chapters of the Book of Genesis which describe the creation and fall of humans (Gn 2–3) of course, but principally in Paul's letter to the Romans (Rom 5–7).[70]

67. See 165–71.
68. See 297–320.
69. See 299–309.
70. See 315–16.

Christ's saving words and works—and especially his cross—teach us what sin "does" to the Father, who brings us back into filial union with him in the power of the Spirit. We deduce the theology of original sin from that of redemption, and not the other way around. We perceive the reality of original sin as we contemplate the saving work of Christ the redeemer. Original sin constitutes a separation from God because Christ has reconciled us with God; sin is universal because Christ redeemed one and all; sin is not merely an imitation of the good example of Adam insofar as redemption is not simply an imitation of the upright moral behavior of Christ.[71] As the *Catechism of the Catholic Church* puts it, "We must know Christ as the source of grace in order to know Adam as the source of sin."[72]

The doctrine of original sin and consequent redemption provide a highly realistic and optimistic understanding of the situation of humanity, for it contains a reminder that sin, which is the fundamental root of evil, suffering, and pain, can and will eventually be overcome by the power of God's grace, received in faith, with a power that springs from the incarnation, life, death, and resurrection of Jesus Christ, through whom and for whom the world was made in the first place.

71. See 306–10, 357–58.

72. *CCC*, no. 388.

SELECTED BIBLIOGRAPHY

Anderson, G. A., and M. Bockmuehl, eds. *Creation ex nihilo: Origins, Development, Contemporary Challenges.* Notre Dame, Ind.: University of Notre Dame Press, 2018.

Auer, J. *Die Welt – Gottes Schöpfung.* Second edition. Regensburg: F. Pustet, 1983.

Barth, K. *Church Dogmatics III/1–4.* Edinburgh: T and T Clark, 1958–61.

Bauer, W., F. W. Danker, W. F. Arndt, and F. W. Gingrich, eds. *A Greek-English Lexicon of the New Testament and Other Early Christian Literature.* Third edition. Chicago: University of Chicago Press, 2000.

Bouyer, L. *Cosmos: The World and the Glory of God.* Petersham, Mass.: St. Bede's Publications, 1988.

Burrell, D. B., C. Cogliati, J. M. Soskice, and W. R. Stoeger, eds. *Creation and the God of Abraham.* Second edition. Cambridge: Cambridge University Press, 2013.

Catechism of the Catholic Church. Second edition. Washington, D.C.: United States Catholic Conference, 2000.

Denzinger, H., P. Hünermann, and A. E. Nash, eds. *Enchiridion symbolorum, definitionum et declarationum de rebus fidei et morum.* Forty-third edition. San Francisco, Calif.: Ignatius Press, 2012.

Fabbri, M. V., and M. Á. Tábet, eds. *Creazione e salvezza nella Bibbia.* Rome: Edusc, 2009.

Fergusson, D. "Creation." In *The Oxford Handbook of Systematic Theology*, edited by J. Webster, K. Tanner, and I. R. Torrance, 72–90. Oxford: Oxford University Press, 2007.

Florovsky, G. "Creation and Creaturehood." In his *Creation and Redemption*, 3:43–78. Belmont, Mass.: Nordland, 1976.

Francis. *Laudato Si'.* Encyclical Letter. May 24, 2015.

Grillmeier, A. *Christ in the Christian Tradition, vol. 1: From the Apostolic Age to Chalcedon.* Atlanta, Ga.: John Knox Press, 1975.

Gunton, C. E., ed. *The Doctrine of Creation: Essay in Dogmatics, History and Philosophy.* Edinburgh: T and T Clark, 1997.

———. *The Triune Creator: A Historical and Systematic Study.* Grand Rapids, Mich.: Eerdmans, 1998.

John Paul II. *Catechesis on Creation.* January 8 to December 17, 1986.

Kehl, M., H.-D. Mutschler, and M. Sievernich. *Und Gott sah, das es gut war: Eine Theologie der Schöpfung.* Munich: Herder, 2006.

Luther, Martin. *Dr. Martin Luthers Werke: Schriften.* 73 vols. Weimar: H. Böhlaus Nachfolger, 1883–2000.

Maspero, G., and P. O'Callaghan. *Creatore perché Padre: Introduzione all'ontologia del dono.* Siena: Cantagalli, 2012.

May, G. *Creatio ex nihilo: The Doctrine of "Creation Out of Nothing" in Early Christian Thought.* Edinburgh: T and T Clark, 1994.

McFarland, I. A. *From Nothing: A Theology of Creation.* Louisville, Ky.: Westminster John Knox Press, 2014.

Migne, J.-P., ed. *Patrologiae cursus completus,* series latina. Paris: 1844–64.

O'Callaghan, P. *Children of God in the World: An Introduction to Theological Anthropology.* Washington, D.C.: The Catholic University of America Press, 2016.

———. "Can God Be Enriched? On the Metaphysical Underpinnings of von Balthasar's Theology." *Irish Theological Quarterly* 84, no. 2 (2019): 175–94.

Pannenberg, W. *Systematic Theology,* vol. 2. Edinburgh: T and T Clark, 1994.

Ratzinger, J. *"In the Beginning." A Catholic Understanding of Creation and the Fall.* Grand Rapids, Mich.: Eerdmans, 1990.

Robson, M. I. T. *Ontology and Providence in Creation: Taking* ex nihilo *Seriously.* London: Continuum, 2008.

Sanz Sánchez, S. *Alfa e Omega: Breve manuale di protologia ed escatologia.* Rome: Fede e cultura, 2020.

Scheffczyk, L. *Schöpfung und Vorsehung.* In M. Schmaus, A. Grillmeier, L. Scheffczyk, M. Seybold, E. Naab (eds.), *Handbuch der Dogmengeschichte, 2,2,1.* Freiburg im Breisgau: Herder, 1963.

Schwöbel, C. "God, Creation and the Christian Community: The Dogmatic Basis of a Christian Ethic of Createdness." In *The Doctrine of Creation,* edited by Gunton, 149–76.

Silva, M., ed. *New International Dictionary of New Testament Theology and Exegesis.* Second Edition. 5 vols. Grand Rapids, Mich.: Zondervan, 2014.

Sokolowski, R. S. *The God of Faith and Reason: Foundations of Christian Theology.* Washington, D.C.: The Catholic University of America Press, 1995.

Vatican Council II. *Gaudium et Spes.* December 7, 1965.

Wenham, G. J. *Genesis 1–15.* Dallas, Tex.: Word Books, 1987.

Westermann, C. *Genesis 1–11.* Minneapolis, Minn.: Fortress, 1984.

Wood, C. M. *The Question of Providence.* Louisville, Ky.: John Knox Press, 2008.

Zizioulas, J. D. "Creation and Salvation." In *Lectures in Christian Dogmatics,* edited by D. H. Knight, 83–119. London: T and T Clark, 2008.

INDEX OF NAMES

GENERAL INDEX

God's Gift of the Universe: An Introduction to Creation Theology
was designed in Arno with Quadraat Sans and composed by
Kachergis Book Design of Pittsboro, North Carolina. It was
printed on 55-pound Natural Offset and bound by
Maple Press of York, Pennsylvania.